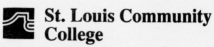

St. Louis Community College

Forest Park
Florissant Valley
Meramec

Instructional Resources
St. Louis, Missouri

Sir Thomas Malory and the Cultural Crisis
of the Late Middle Ages

American University Studies

Series IV
English Language and Literature

Vol. 39

PETER LANG
New York · Bern · Frankfurt am Main · Paris

Robert Merrill

Sir Thomas Malory
and the Cultural Crisis
of the Late Middle Ages

PETER LANG
New York · Bern · Frankfurt am Main · Paris

Library of Congress Cataloging-in-Publication Data

Merrill, Robert
Sir Thomas Malory and the cultural crisis of the late Middle
Ages.

(American university studies. Series IV, English
language and literature; vol. 39)
  Bibliography: p.
  Includes index.
  1. Malory, Thomas, Sir, 15th cent. Morte d'Arthur.
2. Arthurian romances—History and criticism.
3. Quests in literature. 4. Literature and society—
England. 5. Civilization, Medieval. 6. Fifteenth
century. I. Title. II. Series.
PR2047.M47 1987   823'.2   86-27318
ISBN 0-8204-0303-2
ISSN 0741-0700

CIP-Kurztitelaufnahme der Deutschen Bibliothek

Merrill, Robert:
Sir Thomas Malory and the cultural crisis of the
late Middle Ages / Robert Merrill. – New York;
Bern; Frankfurt am Main; Paris: Lang, 1987.
  (American University Studies: Ser. 4, English
  Language and Literature; Vol. 39)
  ISBN 0-8204-0303-2

NE: American University Studies / 04

Printed by Weihert-Druck GmbH, Darmstadt, West Germany

For Maria Hall

Le moi est toujours haissable.

--Blaise Pascal, **Pensees**

Let us therefore not look for certainty and stability. Our reason is always deceived by fickle shadows; nothing can fix the finite between two Infinites, which both enclose and fly from it.

--Blaise Pascal, **Pensees**

The riddle of history is not in Reason but in Desire; not in labor, but in love . . . repressed Eros is the energy of history.

--Norman O. Brown, **Life Against Death**

Cultural history is a very perilous field, but it does not seem to be accidental that Western culture, which exploited the incoherence of its ultimate explanatory systems by creating modern science, is also the geographical area in which there is to be found the greatest incidence or at least a modest exploitation of ideological incoherence and instability, nor that in the culture area of the West is to be found the greatest proportion of the population which experiences the life enhancement of the negative inversions of the ultimate sanctions: economic ease, the privileges of freedom, pleasures and the enhancement of the individual's own value (i.e. human dignity).

--Morse Peckham, **Explanation and Power**

Contents

Preface and Acknowledgements

The question this study attempts to answer is one that has bothered me for about ten years. It is, what makes an artist tell his story, paint a picture, or compose a melody? The answers frequently given about a sense of beauty or form, a wish for fame, a desire to please or entertain, a love of language, color, sound, shape, or a moral sensibility just simply do not satisfy because so much of art is frankly not beautiful, ill-formed, boring, frustrating, and immoral. When art succeeds in all of these categories, it can be quite trivial. Great desires for qualities such as beauty, morality, or form reveal only an inability to find them in the present life or an inordinate craving for order. Artists seem driven by something much deeper and more socially pervasive, something which the critic who is the author of these theories about art has perhaps never himself felt and therefore would never see in a work of art.

It seems to me that art is primarily an attempt to exemplify cultural crises. The best art arises in cultural groups undergoing profound changes in their own structures and in the way people conceive of human nature and social relations. Cultural crises suggest a profound loss of faith in the most fundamental assumptions of one's civilization. These are the assumptions which should guide behavior and ideals, and when belief in these propositions fails behavior often becomes compulsive, excessively predictable or unpredictable, violent, deviant, and unexplainable. What we see most often in great art is the troubled behavior of an Oedipus, a Hamlet, an Ancient Mariner, a Stavrogin or, most especially, a Lancelot or Tristram. Our task is to understand these lives, for in so doing we conduct an analysis of culture itself and possibly come to some comprehension of the way in which the culture was modified. We understand such behavior if we look at it closely enough, as Sigmund Freud has written, "He that has eyes to see and ears to hear may convince himself that no mortal can keep a secret. If his lips are silent, he chatters with his finger tips; betrayal oozes out of him at every pore. And thus the task of making conscious the most hidden recesses of the mind is one which is quite possible to accomplish" (Collected Papers, III, 94).

As critics, therefore, our job needs to be a psychological and sociological one; we follow Wolfram's Parzival who sets out in search of the symbolically sick King Amfortas and symbolically dead land. At first Parzival fails because he does not yet know that in order to restore the king and land to health he must ask a question. When he finally understands enough, he approaches Amfortas and asks, "Oeheim, waz wirret dir?"--"Uncle, what is troubling you?" Amfortas gives no answer, for the answer has preceded the question. To search or to ask is to be healed. The question is the solution, for one only begins to search and question after he has begun to doubt and disbelieve. Amfortas had been for years lying in his castle wishing to die and believing his life to be lost. Life itself was troubling him, but it troubled Parzival just as much. What Parzival and Amfortas knew as life itself can be termed their culture. Culture is the sum of knowledge by which the world is known; culture thus enables one to see continuities in the actions of various individuals, to make predictions, and to regard life as ordered and stable. But Parzival and Amfortas find health only when they recognize that it is the life they know or culture which oppresses them.

So much of what has been written about **Le Morte Darthur** attempts to articulate the various tenets of the culture which Malory depicts: knighthood, love, kingship, worship, and many more of the abstractions through which the diversity of individual lives are organized and reduced into coherent and philosophically elegant structures. Such critical approaches assume that the history of culture is the history of humankind, much in the same manner that historians often confuse the history of governments or nations and the history of people. Without adequate analysis, a tradition of Arthurian criticism has assumed a natural and necessary relationship between persons such as Lancelot or Tristram and the cultural ideals of chivalry. This study proposes to turn that analysis on its head, and regard all abstractions such as knighthood as socially constructed behavioral paradigms to which individuals are more or less openly compelled to adhere. Because the explanatory processes of the dominant culture serve only the needs of institutional legitimation, not pluralistic personal needs, a knight cannot articulate the problems of compliance he experiences in any socially valid vocabulary. Instead, he and many others engage in excessively violent fights, adulterous love affairs, and puzzling self-destructive acts. In the discussions that follow, I propose to turn to Malory's Tristram, Lancelot, Palomides and others to ask the crucial question, "What is troubling you."

Traditional approaches conceal the terrible personal problems a knight like Tristram has in being the ideal knight his culture demands him to be. It is just as likely to read the initiation quest of any knight as a part of the process of the dominant culture to subsume another pre-social individual under its control as it is to read it as a quest for self-fulfillment. But only in the former analysis are the tensions and psychoses of a cultural crisis recognized. The attainment of the status of perfect knighthood, as so many studies call Malory's central theme, is also the loss of personhood and the production of over-determined individuals who no longer can respond to a diversity of stimuli that the world inevitably presents. The process of perfection is also a narrowing process. I regard the characters of Malory's fiction as persons because, quite simply, their existence for us as twentieth century readers is no different than that of a Henry V or a Geoffrey Chaucer whom we have not personally met and whose existence is entirely fixed in documentary and artifactual leavings. History is as much an intellectual construction as fiction, differing only in the instruction I give myself for thought when I begin examining the records. This emphasis is important if we are to resist the impulse to convert Lancelot or Tristram themselves into abstractions.

No project of this size can be the work of a single person. To all of those who aided me in the writing of this book, I owe far more gratitude than any comment here could repay. I can only offer this book as a tribute to Jeffrey Helterman, Morse Peckham, Peter Sederberg, and William Matalene for being teachers and friends; to Thomas Wilkinson for his many insightful comments and stimulating conversations; to Joan Diana, Marcia Henderson, and Janice Lopasky, librarians at Penn State University whose infinite patience and kind assistance made this project a lot easier. I wish also to thank my parents for years of encouragement; the College of Liberal Arts at Pennsylvania State University and the Office of Research at the University of South Carolina for financial support. And finally, thanks to Maria Hall who helped prepare the final manuscript.

Throughout this study, I have followed the new MLA style of parenthetical documentation. Readers will find within the discussions a brief citation following each reference to source material. Complete bibliographic information can be found in the "References" section following the text. For page references to Malory's **Le Morte Darthur,** I have departed somewhat from scholarly practice by citing page numbers from Vinaver's second, single volume edition (1971) rather than from the three-volume edition. This is the edition most likely to be owned and read by the greatest number of people, and it incorporates corrections made to the earlier three-volume editions so that, as Vinaver himself claims, "the text now offered [1971] approximates more than any I have so far published to a definitive edition."

R. M.
Harveys Lake, PA
November 1986

Wherto they answerd, and one in specyal sayd, that in hym that shold say or thynke that there was never suche a kyng callyd Arthur myght well be aretted grete folye and blyndenesse, for he sayd that there were many evydences of the contrarye. Fyrst, ye may see his sepulture in the monasterye of Glastyngburye; and also in Polychronycon, in the fifth book, the syxth chappytre, and in the seventh book, the twenty-thyrd chappytre, where his body was buryed, and after founden and translated into the sayd monasterye. Ye shal see also in th'ystorye of Bochas, in his book **De Casu Principum,** parte of his noble actes, and also of his falle . . . in the castel of Dover ye may see Gauwayns skulle and Cradoks mantel; at Wynchester, the Rounde Table; in other places Lancelottes swerde and many other thynges. . . .

And I, accordyng to my copye, have doon sette it in enprynte to the entente that noble men see and learne the noble actes of chyvalrye, the jentyl and vertuous dedes that somme kynghtes used in tho dayes, by whyche they came to honour, and how they that were vycious were punysshed and ofte put to shame and rebuke; humbly bysechyng al noble lordes and ladyes wyth al other estates, of what estate or degree they been of, that shall see and rede in this sayd book and werke, that they take the good and honest actes in their remembraunce, and to folowe the same; wherin they shalle fynde many joyous and playsaunt hystoryes and noble and renomed actes of humanyte, gentylnesse, and chyvalryes. For herein may be seen noble chyvalrye, curtosye, humanyte, frendlynesse, hardynesse, love frendshyp, cowardyse, murdre, hate, vertue, and synne. Doo after the good and leve the evyl, and it shal brynge you to good fame and renommee.

--William Caxton, 1485

1.

Sir Thomas Malory:

His Milieu and His Critics

1.1 Malory, Myth and History

By all accounts, Thomas Malory's life in the declining stages of the medieval world was difficult. The conclusion is the same whether the Thomas Malory who wrote the Le Morte Darthur was the Sir Thomas Malory of Newbold Revel in Warwickshire who was appealed year after year before the King's Bench for such crimes as robbery, kidnapping, insurrection, rape, extortion, destruction of property and who lived in and out of prison always under bond; or whether he was the Thomas Malory of Studley Royal and Hutton Conyers in Yorkshire who seems to have been a more sophisticated outlaw and followed the adventures of Sir Humphrey Neville in opposing Edward IV, thereby earning for himself either imprisonment or exile and enough of Edward's wrath to be specifically excluded from a general pardon of rebels in 1468 and again in 1470. None of these charges, it is true, exists without a great deal of uncertainty, but as William Matthews, in his study of the troubled career of Sir Thomas Malory, The Ill-Framed Knight, points out, the middle years of the fifteenth century were uncommonly unruly and allegations about the involvement of the author of a famous romance of chivalry are very likely true (43-47). Johann Huizinga refers simply to "The Violent Tenor of Life," and he sees the period as one of those peculiarly unsettled stages in which the world shifts radically its understanding of itself. Malory's lifetime is not only the period

3

of great civil upheaval but of theological and philosophical revolutions also. One is reminded of the late eighteenth and early nineteenth centuries which began with the American and French Revolutions and grew up with the Napoleonic wars and the national revolutions of the next half-century. At such periods, certain sensitive individuals become aware that the scheme of ideas which had explained their world and their lives no longer applies to current situations and is inadequate for solving their problems. Morse Peckham, in discussions of the Romantics, calls this psychological phenomena "explanatory collapse." The lives of such individuals suggest a refusal to live under an ideology which simply will not satisfy their deepest and sincerest perceptions about the world, and they will not, therefore, accept the authority of the inherited verbal explanatory world to control their behavior.

An orthodoxy, any regnant scheme of ideas, maintains the validity of its principles by defining virtue and individual value in terms of its own doctrines. For example, D. W. Robertson in explaining away the rebelliousness of courtly love writes that "All things are beautiful, St. Augustine says, 'in their order' but if of our own free choice we descend from a higher beauty, proper to reason, to a lower beauty, proper to the senses, we deserve the penalty by virtue of Divine Law" (Preface, 73). But to certain individuals, such insistence on an order of beauty which can no longer be perceived in present situations is mere repression, coercion in favor of abstractions and not men in real-life situations. The explanatory system deprives those who deviate of value in their lives, and it is with no little irony that the writers of courtly love advocated the hierarchy with a vengeance by substituting the beauty of a woman, proper to the passions, for the beauty of God, proper to the reason, and asserting the value of the womanly beauty with all the power of art and poetry they could muster. The advocates of a new order, because they are refocusing man's understanding of himself from precepts to individuals, choose what appears by comparison with the orthodoxy to be anarchy and chaos. It may well be that Sir Thomas Malory was just such a new man.

If there is a lack of evidence about Malory's life and his personal beliefs, his work Le Morte Darthur provides all the material necessary to show that he belongs to the analytic or deconstructive tradition of the later Middle Ages, beginning with the great innovators of courtly love and Arthurian Romance--Chrétien de Troyes, Gottfried von Strassburg, Wolfram von Eschenbach, and Guillaume de Lorris--and culminating in the theologians of the Protestant Reformation, particularly Martin Luther, the substance of whose ninety-five theses nailed to the church door at Wittenberg in 1517, a scant forty-six years after Malory's death, is the core of the new order of the individual and self-valuation: justificatio per solam fidem. The analytic tradition in medieval literature marks a cultural transcendence parallel to the process occurring at the same time in theology and the sciences, a shift from an a priori and institutionally controlled system of moral and metaphysical principles to a somewhat chaotic notion of individualism. The orientation of western culture, as a result of these innovators, shifted from the transcendental to the here and now. For science it was simply the decision not to interpret phenomena of the natural world from a theological point of view but rather from, as Francis Bacon repeatedly asserts, human and individual needs. Malory's principal knights--Lancelot, Tristram, Lamerok, and Palomides--eventually, as we shall see in the course of this book, make themselves larger than the institution they should have lived to serve. In the course of the romance, the moral code of the institution loses the ability to make the knights' lives seem meaningful, and yet the orthodox position holds that only through the institution may a knight maintain his identity and value. Such forced meaninglessness makes the code of the destroyer of all knights. In order to replace the meaning in their lives, the knights resort to reckless and violent self-assertion, the destructiveness of which eventually places them in a life and death confrontation with the very institution which they are pledged to support. Dynadan, who comes finally to represent the reasonable and responsible--that is, non-rebellious--knight recognizes immediately the Byronic character of Lancelot and Tristram:

> 'But ye fare,' seyde sir Dynadan, 'as a man that
> were oute of hys mynde that wold caste hymselff
> away. And I may curse the tyme that ever I sye
> you, for in all the worlde ar nat such two knyghtes
> that ar so wood as ys sir Launcelot and ye, sir
> Trystram! For onys I felle in the felyshyp of sir

Launcelot as I have done now with you, and he
sette me so a worke that a quarter of a yere I
kepte my bedde.   Jesus deffende me,´ seyde sir
Dynadan, `frome such two knyghtys, and specially
frome youre felyshyp.´   (313)

In advocating reason and moderation, Dynadan offers the
only possible means of salvaging the Round Table. But we must
never forget that Dynadan survives within the institution by
becoming its fool; he is throughout the "japer." Even Dynadan
is finally murdered by other knights of the Round Table while
on the quest for the Holy Grail.   The ideological shift to the
self would mean nothing less than the beginning of the process
which would deconstruct what C. S. Lewis in The Discarded
Image has called the "Medieval Synthesis." The term synthesis
is important since it implies that the world is ordered as a
coherent, comprehensive, and rational whole and that the goals
of political endeavors such as the Round Table are simply to
make society conform in all its parts to the vast harmony of the
whole.   To delineate this whole was, of course, the purpose of
the greatest of medieval philosophers and theologians of the
synthetic tradition.   As Gerald Phelan writes,

The philosophy of St. Thomas purports to provide
the rational explanation (complete in principle and
capable of indefinite development in demonstrative
detail and application) of the universe as a whole
and of its relation to God, as the Creator and Ruler
of the world, insofar as such explanation can be
afforded by the light of reason unaided by Faith.
The world of things and the world of thought, the
world of freedom and the world of act are all
embraced within that purview and each is envisioned
in the light of the whole.   Analogy permeates every
realm and runs like a thread through the whole
thought of St. Thomas.   (St. Thomas and Analogy,
2-3)

It is not merely the modern view which sees synthetic
thinking as "presented with the assuredness that it embraces
the whole [but which] turns out in the end to be the expression

of the narrowest provincialism" (Mannheim, Ideology and Utopia, 94). To the contrary, William Matthews' descriptions of typical crimes alleged against the Warwickshire Malory indicate that Malory specifically and maliciously attacked forces which he perceived were unjustified in their authoritarian positions. His malice suggests a decision to rank personal needs and judgments above the law, and his attacks, therefore, are upon the order or the synthesis which forms the basis of the law. It is not important whether Malory was consciously aware of the ultimate aim of his rebellion, and indeed we shall never know. What is important, however, is that the effect of his actions and the actions of a few others constituted a social process of violent reaction which initiated further repressive responses from the authorities, increasingly hardened polar positions, thus further social disruptions, and eventually the abandonment of the medieval synthesis as an explanation of the order of life. One very clear example concerns an attack upon Thomas Cowper, the Prior of the Carthusian Monastery at Axeholme, who had secured a writ from the Duke of Buckingham for the arrest of Thomas Malory until such time that Malory could find guarantors that he would do no damage to the prior and the convent. The writ is dated July 13, 1451. Matthews continues:

> If Malory knew of this writ, his next reputed operation must have been prompted by insolence. For on July 20, according to a later charge, he broke into the park at Caludon, which Buckingham owned jointly with the Duke of Norfolk and the Archbishop of Canterbury. There he is said to have done damage extraordinary, with swords and sticks-- the amount of it was estimated at the outrageous sum of L500--and carried off six does that had graced their lordships' pleasance.

The raid on Caludon took place on Tuesday (July 20), and on the following Sunday Malory was arrested by Buckingham and Warwick. He was incarcerated at the manor house at Coleshill, notable for its strong walls and moat. But as Matthews reports, "Two nights later, on Tuesday, Malory broke out, swam the moat, and rejoined his band at Newbold." Any ordinary outlaw would certainly have hidden himself for a while, nor would a criminal have raided the garden of the very man holding a warrant for his arrest.   But "According to the records, their sally the next day (Wednesday, July 28) was the most violent and comprehensive of all their ventures to date."   In short Malory and his band rifled and vandalized the abbey of Blessed Mary at Coombe (21-22).   Here Malory looks like what we would call today a guerrilla, a terrorist, or a revolutionary. The motive for the crimes was not profit; at Coombe he smashed down eighteen doors and shouted insults at the monks. To be sure, money and valuables were taken, but the emphasis of the attack seems to be on destruction, particularly the symbolic act of breaking down the door.   Why would one need to break so many doors?   Malory's real interests, it appears, were in destruction and aggressive self-assertion for the sake of belittling and humiliating the authority he must have hated in the depths of his heart.   The same insolence appears dominant in his destruction of the park at Caludon.   As it eventually comes to be in his romance, the institutional authority and the individual are in irremediable opposition so that the survival of the individual depends upon his destructive acts against the ideology and its enforcers.   Malory is preparing the way for a new ideology which would make the individual an end or value in and of himself.   He is attacking the medieval synthesis which in both the secular and religious domains--in imitation of each other--explained life in terms of transcendental principles. Nothing in the here and now, medieval religious and political theory taught, was inherently valuable since the perfection of it was to found in the transcendental world.   Orthodox explanations of reason taught men to focus their lives upon perfection and the future (especially the life after death) and, hence, scorn the corrupt and mutable world.

The origin of such thinking, at lest for the medieval ideology, is in the writings of the Church Fathers, particularly St. Augustine who taught that man needed no concept of self-love because

> Among all these things only those are to be enjoyed which we have described as being eternal and immutable; others are to be used so that we may be able to enjoy those.   In the same way we who enjoy and use other things are things ourselves.

A great thing is a man, made in the image and likeness of God. . . . Thus there is a profound question as to whether men should enjoy themselves, use themselves, or do both. For it is commanded to us that we should love one another, but it is to be asked whether man is to be loved by man for his own sake or for the sake of something else. If for his own sake, we enjoy him; if for the sake of something else, we use him. But I think that man is to be loved for the sake of something else. In that which is to be loved for its own sake the blessed life resides; and if we do not have it for the present, the hope for it now consoles us. But `cursed be the man that trusteth in man.´

But no man ought to enjoy himself either, if you observe the matter closely, because he should not love himself on account of himself but on account of Him who is to be enjoyed. For he is the best man who turns his whole life toward the immutable life and adheres to it with all his affection. (On Christian Doctrine, 18)

Malory´s King Arthur, King Mark, and the Round Table require of the knights just such constant self-abnegation and manipulation of others as St. Augustine defines. For Malory, the Round Table is Christianity and the medieval synthesis in their institutional forms--the totality of the known world. At one point on the Quest for the Holy Grail, the Queen of the West lands comments to Sir Percival that "Merlyon made the Rounde Table in tokenyng of rowndenes of the worlde, for men sholde by the Rounde Table undirstonde the rowndenes signyfyed by ryght" (541). The great feast of the inception of the Round Table society is, of course, Pentecost, the feast of Church Militant. The knights who participate in such an institution or mystical body receive worship or grace and a position in the hierarchy of knights, depending upon, as St. Augustine advises, the degree to which they are wholly devoted to the "immutable life." Worship is Malory´s term for the knight´s secular value in the same way that grace is the church´s term for the value of an individual to God. Both terms measure individual worth from the perspective of the institution as creator, and they function as the only measure of how an individual feels about his self-value.

It is apparent that in Malory's version Lancelot's love for Guinevere is a function of his position as most radically devoted knight. As best knight he must love the best lady and no other, if he is to support the hierarchical explanation of life and love. Lancelot's story, as Malory tells it, is the tragedy of perhaps the most beautiful and most ennobling world view. Pushed to its limits so that the knight's life approaches an aesthetic as well as metaphysical ideal, the synthesis becomes absurd and the destroyer of all knights. We are never allowed to forget that while Lancelot is the best knight, he is also the worst of all knights.

For all the philosophical and aesthetic perfections of the synthesis, the knights live meaninglessly. While the full discussion of this point will have to wait for Chapter Two, here it is enough to say that they are taught to strive with all possible personal abandon for a goal which is by definition always beyond their grasp. They believe that the transcendental perfections of God are absolutely beyond man's grasp, but at the same time they are the only things worth living for. The clearest example of a knight destroyed by a system which separates him in this manner from his God is Palomides:

> 'Lord Jesu, what may this meane?' seyde sir Palomydes. And thus he seyde to hymselff: 'A, Palomydes, Palomydes! Why arte thou thus defaded, and ever was wonte to be called one of the fayrest knyghtes of the world? Forsothe I woll no more lyve this lyff, for I love that I may never gete nor recover.' (473)

Palomides loves, of course, Isode, but she stands in relation to his identity as one of the best knights exactly as does St. Augustine's God to the best of men: "for by her, and bycause of her, I have wonne the worshyp that I have; for whan I remembred me of the quene Isode I wanne the worshyp wheresomever I cam" (474). She is his creator, and his whole life is lived for her sake. Gottfried, Dante, and Wolfram as well as a host of courtly love writers had long established the psychological equation between Lady and God. As creator, the Lady becomes the source of identity and value. Palomides' wish for death results not from his failure to perform as a good knight, but rather from the psychic or mythic void created by the absolute separation of God from nature or from man himself. He realizes, simply, that nothing he does--and Palomides tries everything--will get him any closer to what he desires most, except his death. His worship is a meaningless consolation for a life of worthless striving. Palomides' life disproves St. Augustine's assertion that "that which is to be loved for its own sake [is] the blessed life . . . for it now consoles us."

As long as Christian symbols and mysteries--or chivalric ones for that matter--remained mythically viable, there was no problem; the dividing line between the world of the soul and the world of the body might easily be overcome by repeating the rituals of a coherent system which asserted in both physical terms (i.e. hierarchical) and metaphysical terms (i.e. St. Thomas' analogy of being) the unity of two. Actually, one never noticed the division since a living mythology or religion is not "believed in" but rather acted or lived. One's focus is on the macrocosm (as St. Augustine advises) because no life-enhancing reason exists for distinguishing it from the microcosm. Life is enriched or made meaningful by grace, the sacraments, and symbolic devotions all of which confirm the direct relationship between man and God; just as tournaments, shields, swords, and names establish the relationship between the knight and his lord. It is no small irony that Lancelot usually fights with a covered shield and refuses to give his name. He is specifically denying the tools which sustain the relationship between the individual and the group or the microcosm and the macrocosm because the rituals have become absurd. Lancelot's awareness of the absurdity and his penchant for enhancing it, as fighting in "a maydyn's garment," demonstrate the failure of the symbolic value of the knight's acts.

During the course of its development as institution, especially as a result of the four Lateran Councils (which coincide with the period of Romance), the Roman Church seized control of the sacraments and rituals. The literal and tangible institution took up its position on the dividing line between the individual and his ultimate goal or creator; "the Church is set," as Pope Innocent III declared, "in the midst between God and man, below God, but above man" (cited by Thompson, VI, 635). Myth became morality.   Acts that simply and unquestionably originated within the individual in response to his environment became conscious laws, and the notion that one cannot be saved without grace became the Church's ultimate sanction against those who failed to repeat laws which were continually making less and less sense on the personal level.   The claim that man can not be saved without grace is actually no more than a metaphysical interpretation of the overtly political claim that "There is one universal church of the faithful."   Pope Innocent III's proclamation at the Fourth Lateran Council of 1215 is true only because the Church had made itself the exclusive dispenser of grace.   This underlies the knight's desperate need for worship, but to Malory the rituals designed to produce grace are merely institutional constructs and in reality have no power to connect a knight with his creator, only with the institution itself.

The cultural crisis which this study explores concerns precisely that condition.   For Palomides, it means an entire career of striving for salvation, or in Malory's term, worship, with methods or acts that have no ability to achieve it.   What he seeks, as any rigorous Augustinian should, is the highest form of the Good, and he wagers his soul against the accumulation of worship, for he will not be Baptized until he has accumulated the worship due the best knight of the world.   His failure to win the "gre" at any tournament where Lancelot, Tristram, or Lamerok are present prevents him from achieving the highest Good, and yet all he knows is that nothing else is worth living for.   It is not that Palomides is incompetent, but rather the method for enhancing one's life is false and instills false goals. Any social system which defines success in terms of codes or rigid hierarchical patterns creates automatically a class of losers.   It is the loser who ratifies the winner's success, and Palomides represents all those losers who through no fault of their own are caught in a system which simply needs failures to make its successes seem valid and to make membership in the institution all the more desirable.

The incredible tension in Palomides' psychological breakdown is well exemplified in his constant ambivalence toward his sword, toward the instrument for gaining worship:

'Alas!' he seyde, 'Why live I so longe?'
And than he gate his swerde in hys honde and
made many straunge syngnes and tokyns, and so
thorow the rageynge he threw hys swerd in that
fountayne. Than sir Palomydes wayled and wrange
hys hondys, and at the laste, for pure sorow, he ran
into that fountayne and sought aftir hys swerde.
Than sir Trystram saw that, and ran uppon sir
Palomydes and hylde hym in hys armys faste.' (324-
25)

Tristram thinks that Palomides is going to drown himself in the
fountain, but it is clear to the reader that Palomides' sword is
his destroyer and yet he cannot live without it. The means of
establishing his value have become the means of separating him
from the worship he so badly needs. The same attitude, of
course, appears in the writings of the Reformation theologians
toward the Roman Catholic tools of salvation: good works,
sacraments, rituals, indulgences, and sacred images. And the
same attitude appears in the writings of Renaissance scientists,
such as Copernicus, Galileo, or Bacon, toward medieval
epistemology and methods in science. But the general situation
suggests precisely what Erik Erikson has called the "identity
crisis." A crisis exists when one reflects upon himself--as
Palomides does--and discovers that "this is the real me" and "I
am not worth the life I live." Identity emerges only in social
situations as a dialectic between a source (i.e. God, ideology,
society, tradition, etc.) and an individual. Identity is synthetic
and it fails when the individual perceives that he has been
hopelessly cut off from his source or his creator; that is, when
his actions follow established codes or behavioral patterns but
rather than producing the feeling of self-confidence and
closeness to the source, they produce the opposite: self-
denigration, despair, and a loss of central control over himself
(Identity, Youth and Crisis, 15-19). The final destruction of
Palomides' identity occurs when "the laste day [of the
Tournament of Lonzep] she [Isode] gaff me the grettyst rebuke
that ever I had, which shall never go fro my harte" (467). And
yet Palomides earned the rebuke by trying desperately to win
worship and therefore Isode's favor.

The method being used here to understand the degeneration of Palomides, and in fact all of Malory's knights, is modern and psychoanalytic. What Erikson sees in his twentieth century patients and Malory in his fifteenth century knights is the human condition of mal-adaptation to its environment, a motif as old as the loss of the garden of Paradise. Man, as Adam, is separated from his God, the source of perfect bliss and identity, and condemned, therefore, to wander and suffer in order to earn his way back to the blessed life. The fall-redemption archetype is exactly the structure of the identity crisis, and it is, as we shall see in Malory, the medieval conception of identity formation. The function of myth and religion--and now psychoanalysis--is to fill the psychic void created by the separation of God from nature and man himself. But by the later Middle Ages, the Church's methods for filling the void had become rather methods simply for enhancing itself as institution and thereby, in effect, increasing the void. In an effort to dispose men to devote themselves more and more fully to the immutable life, the Church pushed God farther and farther away from men's lives thus making grace and moral codes (its own devices) all the more necessary and prominent.

> God in this system [writes Joseph Campbell] is a kind of fact somewhere, an actual personality to whom prayers can be addressed with the expectation of a result. He is apart from and different from the world: in no sense identical with it, but related, as cause to effect. I call this kind of religious thinking 'mythic dissociation.' The sense of an experience of the sacred is dissociated from life, from nature, from the world, and transferred or projected somewhere else--an imagined somewhere else--while man, mere man, is accursed. . . . The sacred is now not secular, of this world of mere dead dust, but canonical, supernaturally revealed and authoritatively preserved. (The Flight of the Wild Gander, 204)

The prime cause of mythic dissociation, but which is offered as its remedy, is, as Campbell goes on to describe, "social identification." Social identification and the counterfeit religious experience it offers account for the phenomenal growth of the Roman Church as institution, and it is the principle upon which the Round Table is an imitation of the Church. It is often noted that Malory increases the number and prominence of references to the Round Table and specifically its Codes of Knighthood, but this is precisely because the Round Table society like the Church has replaced the experience of the sacred with moral laws and the quantities of grace or worship. The early books of Le Morte Darthur, when Merlin is directing Arthur in the establishment of his society, represent a time when experience was sacred. What Arthur does is seldom very knightly or moral, but he acts with the direct authority of some creative power. Merlin insists that it is God: "'There nys none other remedye [for the sickness of King Uther],' seyde Merlyn, 'but God wil have His wille. But loke ye al barons be bifore kynge Uther to-morne, and God and I shalle make hym to speke'" (7). The important point is the active role of God in the activities of men. Moral codes and ritualistic actions replace the active God, and as Palomides finally learns, they are worth nothing in establishing a healthy society; they cannot achieve a relationship with a source with creative powers. All that they can win for a knight is worship, and it is clear that Isode's love which is a creative power is bestowed on Tristram for reasons other than worship. In fact, Lancelot spends most of his time trying to deny his worship.

The writers of courtly love and Arthurian Romance, by equating the Lady and the battle with the experience of the sacred, show that the central cultural crisis of the late Middle Ages was the failure of institutionalized religion to fill the psychic void with an effective and living link between the sacred and the profane. Without such a link, as the case of Palomides shows, life is meaningless and worthless, but I shall have more to say on this point in Chapter Two. What Malory does for the human psyche is to establish the source of meaning within the human heart of the individual by attacking and destroying the institution which had claimed for itself the unique power of dispensing the feeling of value to its members. Malory implies that by making itself the mediator between the knight and the mythic source, the Round Table becomes the destroyer of all knights. While the phrase, "the destroyer of all knights," is used by Malory for King Mark only, it will be apparent that the analogy between Mark and King Arthur in their relationships with their principal knights, Tristram and Lancelot, is not one of opposition. In spite of Arthur's outward benevolence and his apparent love for his knights, his role in the process of social identification makes him, eventually, just as effective an enemy of Lancelot as Mark is of Tristram. How many times, at the various tournaments, does Lancelot say, "at that justys I woll be ayenste the kynge and ayenst all hys felyship" (622)! Such is the irony and the horror of the tragedy.

Palomides recovers from his identity collapse, and it is symbolized by his finally consenting to be Baptized--though he had long believed in God in his heart. Believing in one's heart is not enough for the terms of social identification; one must submit to and be a member of the institution by repeating successfully and exclusively its rituals. But Palomides finds a way of making his own heart his creative source. He will be not be Baptized until he is totally defeated in all of his attempts to merit the system's worship by using others. He repudiates the quest for social identification by abandoning the quest for the highest Lady, the seven battles for Christ, and the most worship at a tournament. He leaves the romance (Palomides does not go on the Quest for the Holy Grail) following the Questing Beast, no longer even planning to achieve it or gain worship by it (use it), but mythically identified with it and enjoying it as his personal and individual adventure, his own and uniquely unfolding fate. From the beginning, it had been his adventure; it was only interrupted by a worthless attempt at social identification. Once while following the Questing Beast, Palomides even outjousts both Tristram and Lamerok, but, of course, it does not matter here: "he smote down sir Trystramys and sir Lamorak bothe with one speare, and so he departed aftir the Beste Glatyssaunte" (296). Tristram, more importantly, transcends the meaninglessness and the incipient tragedy of social identification by loving and enjoying Isode for her own sake--St. Augustine's very definition of cupidity.

The statement Malory is making is no less radical than that of Wolfram who insinuates that Parzival has "forced God by defiance to make His infinite Trinity grant your will . . . for it had never happened that anyone could ever fight his way to the

Grail, and I would gladly have dissuaded you. Now it has turned out otherwise with you, and your gain has increased" (Parzival, 416). Or Gottfried who discovers that the individual can be larger than the institutionally and logically conceived Christ: "Thus it was manifest and confirmed to all the world that Christ in his great virtue is as pliant as a windblown sleeve" (Tristan and Isolde, 248).   While Malory is just as defiant, he is more perceptive in his understanding of the sociology of knowledge and the religious experience. No longer does he assert the value of the individual in contrast to Christianity itself, but rather he presents the psychological struggles of his knights to find meaning in their lives. While the problems of the meaning they find must be held for the next chapter, it is enough here to say that Malory discovers that the origin of the value of life belongs intrinsically in the individual irrespective of worth to the institution. When this is not the case, as he perceived it was not in the late stages of the Middle Ages, tragedy follows. In this sense he brings new mythic life to original Christian myths: "The kingdom of God is within you" (Luke 17:21).

Certainly the culmination of the analytic tradition is in the Reformation theologians, and perhaps the best depictions of the emerging individualism are to be seen in the discoveries of Martin Luther, about which I will have more to say toward the end of this book. Here it will suffice to note Erik Erikson's description of Luther's discovery of Christ, the God-man:

> Yet now, in finding Christ in himself, he establishes, an inner position which goes beyond that of neurotic compromise identification [social identification]. He finds the core of a praying man's identity, and advances Christian theology by an important step. It is clear that Luther abandoned the appreciation of Christ as a substitute who has died `for'--in the sense of `instead of'--us; he also abandoned the concept of a Christ as an ideal figure to be imitated, or abjectly venerated, or ceremonially remembered as an event in the past. Christ now becomes the core of the Christian's identity: quotidianus Christi adventus, Christ is today here, in me. The affirmed passivity of

suffering becomes the daily Passion and the Passion
is the substitution of the primitive sacrifice of
others with a most active, most masterly, affirmation
of man's nothingness--which, by his own masterly
choice, becomes his existential identity.
.   .   . [He] now said that Christ's life is God's
face: Qui est facies patris. The Passion is all that
man can know of God: his conflicts, duly faced, are
all that he can know of himself. The last judgment
is always the present self-judgment. Christ did not
live and die in order to make man poorer in the fear
of his future judgment, but in order to make him
abundant today: nam judicia sunt ipsae passiones
Christi quae in nobis abundant. Look, Luther said
at one point in these lectures (IV, 87 [Lectures on
the Psalms]) how everywhere painters depict
Christ's passion as if they agreed with St. Paul that
we know nothing but Christ crucified. The artist
closest to Luther in spirit was Durer, who etched
his own face into Christ's countenance. (Young
Man Luther, 212-13)

The cultural milieu in which Malory lived--whether he
was the Warwickshire or the Yorkshire man--was one in which
Christian explanations permeated every facet of live. As
Huizinga remarks, "Individual and social life, in all their
manifestations are imbued with concepts of faith. There is not
an object nor an action however trivial, that is not constantly
correlated with Christ or salvation. All thinking tends to
religious interpretation of individual things; there is an
enormous unfolding of religion in daily life. This spiritual
wakefulness, however, results in a dangerous state of tension,
for the presupposed transcendental feelings are sometimes
dormant . . ." (Waning, 151). Even more dangerous than the
occasional failure to be moved or spiritually excited by
religious iconography is the preception that such conventional
images have lost totally their ability to stimulate
transcendental feelings--or in clearer terms--establish a
healthy identity through mythic association. This is the
experience of explanatory collapse. A moment ago it was
mentioned that the fall-redemption archetype forms the basic

structure for the knight's quest for meaning.   But as the
following example shows, the redemptive force comes not from
orthodox re-incorporation of the knight with his creator--his
liege lord--though that happens with disastrous results, but
rather the redemption comes from chaos.   Briefly, Tristrams'
madness represents, as madness always does in Malory, a
separation of the individual from his value source; that is, an
identity crisis or a death of the self occurs.   Tristram has
already been betrayed by Mark, and now he discovers letters
written by Isode which seem to indicate her love for
Kayhedens.   The discovery of the letters completes his madness,
and he leaves Cornwall to live in the woods with shepherds.   In
the woods--the metaphor for madness and chaos--he is visited
by various individuals who attempt to heal him.   Malory invokes
the death-resurrection archetype three times, often enough to
indicate that Malory is aware of the theme he is using:

> Than sir Trystrames within a whyle mette with a
> knyght of hys owne . . . such sorrow he [Sir Fergus]
> was in three days and three nyghtes.   (304)

> And than hit was three dayes or that she coude
> fynde hym [Tristram], and than she broute hym mete
> and drynke, but he woulde none.   (304)

> So they [Kayhedens and Palomides] rode into
> foreyste, and three dayes and three nyghtes they
> wolde never take lodgynge, but ever sought sir
> Trystram.   (305)

To follow the archetype, Tristram should have remained
spiritually dead or in the tomb for the three days and nights
and then return to life, as for example in "Come and let us
return unto the Lord: for he hath torn, and he will heal us; he
hath smitten, and he will bind us up.   And after two days he
will revive us; in the third day he will raise us up, and we shall
live in his sight" (Hosea 6:1-2).   But that is not the case.
Some special means are required to affect Tristram's
resurrection, and, as we shall discover in the course of this
study, those means are violent and chaotic self-assertion.   Not
until after the Tournament of the Castle of Maidens where

Tristram "began so rowghly and bygly" that an anonymous knight thinks that "he ys a devyll and no man" (322) does his psychic health begin to return. The basis for the new identity is empowerment and the subsequent judgment of the intrinsic value of the individual. Tristram tells Dynadan after the Tournament and after simply ignoring the official ascription of value associated with winning the "pryce" or the "gre" that "never drede you, sir Dynadan, for I am harte-hole, and of this wounde, I shall sone be hole, by the mercy of God!" (327).

1.2 Art, Culture and Order

The approach to Le Morte Darthur being developed here suggests that Malory is not so much interested in chivalry and the usual themes associated with Arthurian Romance as he is with the crisis in individual response to social systems such as chivalry and a thorough deconstruction of those systems of orderly behavior. Since this approach is not at all like the usual approaches to Malory's or almost any other romance, the present study necessitates a somewhat different set of assumptions about art and about the Middle Ages than is usually taken. Before going any further, then, it is necessary to examine the various approaches to Le Morte Darthur and the assumptions upon which they are built because, in spite of what should have occurred, the publication in 1947 of the Winchester Manuscript of the romance has not been the occasion of the critical revolution that Charles Moorman, among others, suggests it has been (The Book of King Arthur, xii). Generally critics have rightly concerned themselves with the problem of the unity of the work (or works), but have not, in my estimation, arrived at a satisfactory conception of what the essential unifying principle might be. Clear understanding of any work--any Gestalt--depends upon the perception of what unifies it, what makes it one thing. The discovery of the principle of coherence, moreover, tells us something about the deep psychology of both the artist and his culture and about us, because it emerges from an interaction of reader and text.   S. S. Stevens pointed out long ago that the nature of any science or interpretive act is conditioned by the nature of the human observer ("Psychology as Propaedeutic Science").   Unity, therefore, is as relevant to our assumptions about art as it is to Malory's intentions.   No study of Malory can avoid this important point about unity, as Beverly Kennedy in the most recent book on Malory confesses that she could not: "It was not my intention when I began this study to solve the vital question of the unity of Malory's work; however, it is clear to me now that the `key´ to that unity is Malory's representation of knighthood" (7-8).   But, of course, the "key" to her discovery of unity is the fact that she had just conducted a very intense study of knighthood.

Malory's version of the Arthurian legend has always been the one most widely read, and comments from nineteenth century readers such as Walter Scott, Robert Southey, or Alfred Tennyson show that it was appreciated not for its craft or structure but for the "many fine things in it."   This is exactly the position Eugène Vinaver has taken, as we shall see later. But in spite of the fine things, those readers failed, as Larry Benson puts it, to observe "the organic unity that a successful work required" ("Malory's Le Morte Darthur," 81).   The position of Vinaver's opponents was also available in the nineteenth century.   Among the supporters of a whole book theory was George Saintsbury who in the 1890's began asking the same question which Charles Moorman and R. M. Lumiansky would ask in the 1960's: not how well does Malory conform to our conceptions of art, but how well does he do what he intended to do?   It was also Saintsbury's idea that Malory alone made "of this vast assemblage of stories one story, and one book" (cited in Works, I. xli).   But even that is not saying a great deal since every sensitive reader cannot help feeling the cumulative effect of the repetition of parallel episodes such as tournaments and recurrent individual fights or simply the growth in complexity and consistency of the characters' lives. And even if Saintsbury were only responding to Caxton's emendations of the works, as Vinaver thinks he was, his whole book theory cannot account for the inconsistencies between individual tales and the disproportionate treatment of the seemingly less artistically successful "Tristram" and "Grail" sections. But Saintsbury did not try.

The problem of unity in Malory's work, then, has been and remains overwhelmingly crucial, but it has not produced a critical revolution or even a major breakthrough precisely because of the assumptions about artistic unity that various critics have been working with. All of Malory's critics have begun with the unanalyzed assumption of a structural correspondence between artistic unity and an orderly explanation of human action. We need to look at unity more closely because in Malory the orderly explanation of life is intensely problematic. The felt cumulative effect suggests that Malory is attempting to write a complete romance or an organic Arthuriad just as do several of his direct comments about his work: "Here is the Ende of the Hoole Book of Kyng Arthur and of His Noble Knyghtes of the Rounde Table . . ." (726). Let us begin by merely asserting that Malory wanted to write some kind of "Hoole Book." It is the parts that will be difficult to reconcile. T. C. Rumble in his chapter of Malory's Originality has pointed out that all that is necessary for a complete Arthuriad is a Merlin, a Quest of the Holy Grail and a Lancelot (145). He is followed by Larry Benson who observes that "all Arthurian cycles are tripartite, for all tell the story of birth, life and death of Arthur, and the accompanying rise, flowering and fall of the Rounde Table" (Malory's Morte Darthur, ch. 1). But in Malory we never get a flowering, a tale of Lancelot, even though it is often remarked: "Wellcom, sir Launcelot, the floure of knyghthode, for by the we shall be holpyn oute of daungere" (478). Even though Benson argues that "The Noble Tale of Sir Lancelot du Lake" and "The Book of Lancelot and Guinevere" constitute a Lancelot segment (81-84), it seems rather that when compared with what we get of Tristram, the tales of Lancelot are fragments meant to establish Lancelot as the central hero but specifically to avoid telling much about his career. The reasons for this will be apparent in a moment. What Malory gives us is "The Book of Sir Tristram de Lyones," by far the longest, least appreciated, and least understood section of his work, but perhaps the section closest to his own heart. No where in the romance does Malory indicate his special concern and love for a character as he does in the

"Tristram." Malory's attitude toward Lancelot and Guinevere is tragic pity, but for Tristram he feels a deep, unconscious identification. While Tristram resides at the Joyous Garde, Malory remarks: "All maner jantylmen hath cause to the worldes ende to prayse sir Trystram and to pray for his soule. AMEN, SAYDE SIR THOMAS MALLEORRE" (416). It would be well worth considering the problem of unity, then, from the perspective of the tale of Sir Tristram. Most analyses work from the point of view of the rise of the Round Table and the "enfances" of the various knights, since, as Moorman points out, unity is "decreed from within by a seminal principle of growth" (Book of King Arthur, xxiii). Gareth becomes the paradigm, and Lancelot's centering orientation--a concept to be developed in the next chapter--provides the model for the evolution of the society and the development of the romance itself. But Malory shows no special concern or interest in Gareth's career once Gareth has completed his quest and earned his place at the Round Table. And the pattern of Lancelot leads only to tragedy.

If the tripartite structure of Arthurian Romance corresponds to the rise, flowering, and fall of a civilization, then how are we to account for the fact that the "Tristram" section, universally condemned by critics as the low point of work, must be the flowering of the Round Table society? Tristram overtly avoids the Round Table as much as he is able! Moreover, if Malory were as aware of the cycle tradition as Benson believes that he was (ch. 1), then he must have been consciously violating not only the tripartite structure by composing an Arthuriad of a Merlin, a Tristram, a Grail Quest, and a Morte d'Arthur; but also the coherency of the movement by including the Tristram. The importance of cycle literature in is the encyclopedic and coherent nature of the world it represents. Each episode should be part of the history of whomever the cycle is about, and the whole cycle implies a coherent and comprehensive explanation of the world by tracing some character or theme from beginning to end. By including "The Book of Sir Tristram" with all of the incoherencies that it contains, Malory seems to be doing something really new in Arthurian Romance, and our task is to discover what it is.

About the purpose of the "Tristram" section critics are divided; about the value and artistic achievement of it they are fairly unified in condemning it. Thus they destroy, it seems to me, the chance of a fruitful understanding of the remainder of Malory's work. The purpose of this study, then, will be to establish "The Book of Sir Tristram" as the center of Malory's romance and the proper perspective from which to view the remainder of the tales. It seems to be Malory's most complete and overt attempt to rework the history of King Arthur, and in the new telling suggest some truth about his own culture. If the "Tristram" has not been well received by the critics, it is not due to Malory's failure, but rather the result of the fact that Malory was doing something beyond the normal, synthetic, artistic performance of his time. Those critics who have thought the "Tristram" dull and inartistic have misinterpreted their feelings or responses to the tale. The "Tristram" is profoundly frustrating. After reading the preparatory tales of Merlin, Gawain, Marhalt, Torre, Lancelot, and especially Gareth, the reader expects to hear of the flowering of the society which is being set up. As readers, we are indoctrinated with the values and expectations of individual and political growth just as the knights are. We want to hear more about the Round Table, but we get a "Tristram" which frustratingly disrupts the natural progression and order of the narrative as well as the development of the Round Table. In the "Tristram" the focus shifts from the values and ideals of knighthood to the individual men and women and the psychological problems they have living under such a system. Malory's view of his narrative material changes from cultural synthesis and a focus on ideals to analysis as he moves into the "Tristram." The first significant thing Tristram does is to kill Marhalt, one of the best knights of the Round Table. Symbolically, this act tells us that Tristram's relationship to the Round Table as the center of the culture will not be harmonious. Immediately following the tale of Tristram, the Round Table begins to fall apart in an open and inexorable way. The "Tristram" attacks and deconstructs the Round Table sections. So also does the Grail section, as we shall see.

Medieval scholars very often take the sentimental view of the Middle Ages, thinking that it was a pious and serene age in which ideals of perfection were contemplated, sought, and sometimes achieved; while corruption and vice were castigated and satirized. In many ways it was, but for every pious ideal there existed an opposite anti-ideal, what Carl Jung has called "enantiodromia": that is, a crossing-over or a conversion to the opposite. The medieval histories are full of examples of blasphemous parodies of sacred rituals, and they would be even fuller had not a tremendous effort on the part of the orthodox culture suppressed nearly all of the records of the Gnostics, Manicheans, and the Cathars. The opposition is not good versus evil as the orthodox writers held, but rather a tension within the good itself. Johann Huizinga is astounded at the penchant for swearing, particularly blatant denials of God and the benefits of the Redemption: "Je renie Dieu." The most famous example of enantiodramia in Arthurian Romance is that of Parzival who kills the Red Knight only to put on his armor and become the Red Knight himself. But what is the cause of such overt inversion, of such disorder? Huizinga's answer is that "[it was] a spontaneous reaction against the incessant and pressing call of faith, arising from a culture overcharged with religious images and concepts" (Waning, 164). A page earlier, Huizinga remarks that, "Even the stupid sin of blasphemy has its roots in a profound faith." This same syndrome, it seems to me, underlies Malory's apparent violation of what his readers expected in romance or cycle literature. In a culture saturated with idealism, religious or chivalric, no attempt is made to dispute rationally with the controlling ideology; it is too pervasive and powerful. The most daring thinkers simply negate it--a restless and sportlike tearing down of culture which they perceive as oppressive and dissociated from their lives. The final result of this movement from mythic association to social identification is, as we shall see, frustration, psychosis, and tension in individuals and destruction for the civilization. And therefore, we do not get a tale of Lancelot and an exemplification of the flowering of the Round Table, but rather a tale of Tristram who negates it, even while he appears to be its representative hero.

Eugène Vinaver is his Rise of Romance tells us that according to Marie de France and Gottfried von Strassburg romance grew out of an attempt to explain further, to gloss or to exemplify Christianity. Indeed, Caxton recommends Le Morte Darthur for the moral lessons that it presents:

that noble men may see and lerne the noble actes of
chyvalrye, the jentyl and vertuous dedes that somme
knyghtes used in tho dayes, by whyche they came to
honore, and how they that were vycious were
punysshed and ofte put to shame and rebuke. (xv,
see headnote to this chapter).

Much of the criticism of Malory has been concerned with the
problem of interpreting those vicious acts in the light of what
is assumed to be the moral center or ethos of the work. The
question of the critic becomes "how can we harmonize the
violent murders and adulterous loves of the major knights with
norms we all assume to be true?" Such an interpretive act
rests upon certain assumptions about human behavior and about
the function of art within a culture. Whether Tristram and
Lancelot are taken as sinners or secular saints, any
interpretation of their acts works upon the assumption that
behavior is related to a body of doctrine which explains it,
evaluates or legitimates it, and therefore largely controls it.
The individual's relationship to the doctrine is taken as
positive; he seeks to act out the social paradigm in his life,
thus aiming himself at virtue. If he fails he sins and may suffer
certain consequences (as Caxton notes), but even in sin the
doctrine remains unquestioned in its authority to explain and
guide behavior. D. W. Robertson has suggested that romance
functions in relation to doctrine in the same way as preaching.
He writes,

As a poet, Chrétien had far more reason to entertain
his audience than had an ordinary preacher.
Although he had no obligation to supply the Word of
God to that audience, as had the preacher, he did
have, in accordance with traditions concerning
poetry handed down from antiquity, an obligation to
instruct them as well as to entertain them. And this
instruction--the 'bread' in his fables, as Boccaccio
called it later--was quite naturally derived from the
same philosophical traditions employed by the
preacher. These were, in fact, the only
philosophical traditions which he could expect his
audience to use as a basis for inferences concerning

his meaning, the only ones with which they were familiar. At the same time, references to those traditions offered a natural opportunity for satire, comedy, and humor. For these all result from the portrayal of deviations from reasonable behavior presented in such a way that their implications are not immediately serious; and the standards of reasonable behavior were, throughout the Middle Ages, those established by the Church.   (Preface, 88-89)

By including a "Tristram" rather than a "Lancelot," Malory makes such standard approaches to his romance inapplicable. When a doctrinal (or moral) approach is taken to the "Tristram," Malory appears not to be in control of his material. He seemingly cannot maintain Tristram as the model of the "clean knighthood" and at the same time give fair treatment to Dynadan, Lamerok, Segwarde's wife, or even Isode; all of whom Tristram involves in some very unknightly actions.   But with a different conception of the way art functions in relation to standards of reasonable behavior, the "Tristram" section shows Malory in even greater control of his material than elsewhere since here the narrative is moved along by the force of Malory's perception of the psychological sickness of his age.   It does not need a strong plot, as in "Balin," or a thematic pattern, as in "Gareth," because plots and themes exemplify explanations or systems and those are precisely the problem in the "Tristram" section.   Plots and thematic patterns depend upon logic and causality and those qualities belong to established rational explanations and orthodox positions.   In the "Tristram" Malory is anti-explanatory and thus sometimes a-logical and a-casual.

The positive relation of individuals to doctrine, upon which Robertson's interpretation is based, need not obtain in all art.   Many scholars of myth and literature have noted a cyclic pattern in the kinds of stories and heroes that dominate the literature of a certain historical period.   Why, for instance, did Milton in the seventeenth century reject the matter of Arthurian Romance for his great epic, while it was accepted by Wagner, Tennyson, and others in the nineteenth century. Morton Bloomfield refers simply to "a pattern of up and down in

the history of the tragic hero [as opposed to the epic hero],"
and he feels that "the later medieval period is a down period
[for the epic hero] in comparison with the early Middle Ages
and the high Renaissance. He has called these heroes of late
medieval romance "drastically ambiguous," suggesting that there
is something "powerfully wrong" with them that seriously
compromises their heroism (given standard definition rooted in
epic heroism) and conceding that evaluative interpretations of a
knight such as Gawain in Sir Gawain and the Green Knight are
frankly impossible. Almost any hypothesis within the range of
condemnation to praise is supportable by the text, Bloomfield
points out ("The Problem of the Hero," 33). The criticism of
Malory's knights shows as well that any hypothesis within the
range of praise to condemnation is supportable by the text.

Down periods seem to be periods of at least ambiguity,
perhaps more, in the relation of human behavior to the
doctrines or standards against which it is evaluated. This up
and down cycle is the subject of at least two books by Mircea
Eliade, Cosmos and History and The Myth of the Eternal Return,
which name it "the cosmogonic cycle": a mythic structure found
in all cultures that treats of the destruction of the world
followed by a new creation and the establishment of a new age-
-soon enough followed by another destruction and another new
age. These myths are familiar to readers of Hesiod or Ovid and
also the Bible. They are the myths of cultural evolution, and
historically, at least for the West, they are the periods of major
changes in human imagination associated with Socrates, Jesus,
the Renaissance, and post-modernism. In the Middle Ages, they
were listed by Peter Abelard and Hugh of St. Victor as the ages
of Adam, Moses, and Jesus.

If we think about cultural evolution and ambiguities of
the sort Bloomfield sees in Arthurian Romance, we are led to
the problem of how romance literature fits into the social and
philosophical developments of the late Middle Ages which
concern specifically the articulation of norms and doctrine.
Arthurian Romance--and, indeed, Arthurian Epic (Geoffrey of
Monmouth, Wace, Layamon)--emerges about the middle of the
twelfth century, just following the time of Peter Abelard's Sic
et Non, of Peter Lombard's Sentences, of the founding of the
school of Canon Law at Bologna, and great movements within
the church to synthesize, stabilize, and universalize doctrine.

In reading the romances, however, one begins to feel that the assumptions about human behavior and how it is legitimized, mentioned by Caxton, Vinaver, and Robertson, do not obtain; that is, the relationship between the major knights and the Round Table--itself a symbol for the world or the civilization, as Merlin says--is not a positive one but rather a negative, tension producing relationship. Milton belonged to an "up-period" and felt compelled to tell the story of a new creation after a fall, a story which would justify the ways of God to men; he must have recognized that Arthurian Romance is inherently the story of the destruction of a civilization and, therefore, one in which God's ways because they are the fundamental principles upon which that civilization is based cannot at all be justified.

The notion that one's civilization or culture, particularly its grounding values, provides the individual with guidance and functions as an ideal for virtue, happiness, and psychological health is an up-period assumption and it underlies all critical approaches to Malory--as Kennedy's discovery of "Knighthood" as the key to unity of the romance demonstrates. This general tendency toward cultural and explanatory harmony is indeed the position of orthodox medieval theology and psychology, but it is not what happens in much Arthurian Romance, especially Malory. Rather in romance, we get a psychic state described by Sigmund Freud, the great philosopher of the down-period of the twentieth century: "what we call our civilization is largely responsible for our misery. . . . It was discovered that a person becomes neurotic because he cannot tolerate the amount of frustration which society imposes upon him in service of its cultural ideals" (Civilization and Its Discontents, 33-34). Freud defines a relationship between the individual and his culture that D. W. Robertson tells us did not exist in the Middle Ages. Robertson writes, "To conclude, the medieval world was innocent of our profound concern for tension. We have come to view ourselves as bundles of polarities, in which, to use one formulation, the ego is caught between the omnivorous demands of the id on the one hand and the more or less irrational restraints of the super-ego on the other. . . . But the medieval world with its quiet hierarchies knew nothing of these things. Its aesthetic, at once a continuation of classical philosophy and a product of Christian teaching, developed artistic and literary styles consistent with a world without dynamically interacting polarities" (Preface, 51).

Again, this is certainly true for orthodox culture, especially in the light of St. Augustine's doctrine of Charity which is, in fact, a program for maintaining psychic health through a unified way of interpreting the world. St. Augustine writes in the Confessions, "Truly it is by continence that we are made one and regain the unity of self which we lost by falling apart in the search for a variety of pleasures. For a man loves you [God] so much the less if, besides, you, he also loves something else which he does not love for your sake. O Love ever burning, never quenched! O Charity, my God, set me on fire with your love! You command me to be continent" (233). Continence--he might well have said continuity between the individual and a coherent view of the world (doctrine). But if anything, the essential experience of the knights--that is, their relationship to the grounding principles of the civilization--produces discontinuity and tension. St. Augustine's positive evaluation of continence and the resulting coherence in personality are not the aim of Arthurian Romance, especially not for a writer like Gottfried von Strassburg who addresses his Tristan to those readers who are prepared to endure the essential tension:

> Thus I have undertaken a labour to please the polite world and solace noble hearts--those hearts which I hold in affection, that world which lies open to my heart. I do not mean the world of the many who (as I hear) are unable to endure sorrow and wish only to revel in bliss. (Please God let them live in bliss!) What I have to say does not concern that world and such a way of life, their way and mine diverge sharply. I have another world in mind which together in one heart bears its better-sweet, its dear sorrow, its heart's joy, its love's pain, its dear life, its sorrowful death, its dear death, its sorrowful life. To this life let my life be given, of this world let me be a part, to be damned or saved with it. (47)

As Gottfried tells us there exists a split in culture with one segment aiming toward bliss and tension reduction and the other aimed toward or at least able to endure great tension. In Malory, there exits a similar split in the structure of the romance, one which we must read as an essential tension within the work and the culture--not as merely an artistic flaw in the work.   The only way to do this is to see the Morte within a theoretical model for cultural evolution, and credit Malory with a great deal more originality and artistic perceptivness than those who demand moral lessons from art are generally disposed to do.

T. C. Rumble, in a chapter of Lumiansky's Malory's Originality, is essentially of the same opinion, but he reaches far different conclusions than I shall. He notes that since there is such a tremendous variation among the extant manuscripts of the prose Tristan, either Malory must have worked from a version which did not survive or we must credit him with a great deal more originality than is generally done (131). Aside from the tales which so far as we know are Malory's own inventions ("Sir Gareth" and "Sir Urry"), the "Tristram" is Malory's most original tale in that he reworked the career of Tristram from a rebel tragically opposed to Christianity and its moral codes to an epic hero who transcends the dead codes. It is significant that Malory begins Tristram's tale in medias res and ends at the high point of his career. Tristram does not undergo the same kind of training or social experience as do the other knights and he does not, therefore, suffer the fall that is the fate of all other knights (except Palomides). A new method, therefore, will have to be devised for analysis of the "Tristram." It must be based upon what the knights actually do in the work itself and not upon general conceptions of what a romance should be.

The headnote of this chapter reproduces the substance of Caxton's introduction to his 1485 edition of Le Morte Darthur in order to show what were his interests in art because they represent, to a significant extent, the prevailing modern approaches to Malory. Even Beverly Kennedy's recent study, Knighthood in the Morte Darthur accepts and builds upon Caxton's up-period assumption about the work: "William Caxton was right," Kennedy argues, "about the didactic purpose of Le Morte Darthur; however, I would argue that that purpose goes beyond an ethical intention to inculcate desirable social virtues in the governing class. . . .   [Malory's] hap motif rings throughout the `Death of Arthur' like a death knell, suggesting the providentialist view that these political disasters might have been avoided if men making the crucial decisions had not cut themselves off from the grace of God" (11).   But this is just straight Caxton.   According to Caxton, art induces moral actions in men by exemplifying the ultimate victory of truth in life; i.e., that good deeds eventually succeed and evil ones finally fail.   The desire to see justice and some Divine Plan-- Providence--prevail in the end bespeaks man's overwhelming craving for order.   In the words of Harry Berger, the desire for an orderly interpretation of life is the foundation of all culture: "at least as far as western civilization is concerned--all periods of human culture arise as responses to a single perennial human need, namely, the desire for order" ("The Ecology of the Mind"). Caxton, then, is interested in orderly interpretation of his own times, and for this interpretation he looks back to the model of orderly societies: King Arthur and the Round Table.   He goes to great lengths to demonstrate the historical validity of Arthur's world since if that picture of order is to induce moral action, the perceivers of art must, as Caxton knows, willingly suspend disbelief in the fictionality of the legend.   The weakness of Caxton's argument lies in the fact that the reader must be predisposed to accept an orderly interpretation even before experiencing the event of history.   The identity of truth with specific acts, moreover, will last and insure order only so long as those acts are unquestioned and repeated exactly as they existed in the original archetype.   Once variations set in or incoherencies are perceived, the present acts become merely symbolic and lose the power to maintain real order in the phenomenal world.   To be sure, Caxton's readers were predisposed to accept the orderly interpretation of England's past, but nothing within art itself demands that the artist produce an orderly tale.   Order is a social demand placed upon the artist by the art perceiver or critic, just as humans in general demand order in the natural world.   Science or natural philosophy is the name given to that demand.   Caxton, therefore, resorts to the strongest coercion of the disposition that he can think of: "al is wryton for our doctryne."

Psychologists tell us that all is not written for our doctrine; doctrine is just all that we see. Perceivers do not approach the world or their experiences (including a text) objectively and they never take in all of the information that an experience presents. Rather they are interested in only a very limited amount of information; only enough to construct a pattern or Gestalt is accepted by the mind as significant. Thus the perceiver knows his experiences by selecting data and conferring upon essentially ambiguous or unorganized situations some meaning that accords with a larger mental image of the world he holds in his mind. Ulrich Neisser in his Cognition and Reality argues that "without some pre-existing structure, no information would be acquired at all" (43). Phrased another way, this is to say that without a paradigm all sensory stimuli would seem equally relevant and perception could not be much more than chaotic. Any experience would contain an almost infinite amount of data. Cognition is the process by which this pre-existing structure is used to select out only the significant data from the abundance of data of any experience in a mental act that suggests the individual is comparing or matching perceptual stimuli to his mental model of the world.

This is not to say that we experience the world only subjectively, but rather that the world we do know and experience is, in fact, a social or cultural construction, and because it is shared and inherited individuals experience the paradigm and culture as objective, pre-existing themselves, and subsisting--although this would be ontologically impossible. To become aware of and pre-occupied with one's perception of the world, as are many a character of modern fiction, is to become alienated from the culture and the shared paradigm, and it suggests to anyone interested in art and psychology a serious cultural crisis of the sort Eric Erikson has discussed in Identity: Youth and Crisis. We tend to begin analyzing perspectives, heuristics, or our "selves" only when they do not work very well at making our experiences intelligible and we feel, therefore, cut off from a reality that is stable and palpable. This seems to be the relation between the individual knight in Malory's romance and the accepted codes of his culture; the relation is not one of increasing order in the world, as it would have been for an epic hero, but rather one of increasing chaos. For a simple illustration, Chrétien's "Knight of the Cart" works well. The background or the paradigm against which Lancelot's quest must be measured is the story of Christ's Harrowing of Hell as know in the Gospel of Nicodemus. This story defines the essential structure of the experience of the Christian Hero, but Lancelot's experience is simply his adulterous affair with Guinevere. Behavior and paradigm are irresolvably dissonant and yet consonance is implied by God's support of Lancelot in the judicial battle with Meleagant.

Thus Caxton's intentions are not necessarily those of Malory. The difference is subtle but crucial. Caxton and recently Kennedy interpret the vicious and sinful acts of the knights as superficial, merely corruptions and human weaknesses on the surface of a perfectly valid and coherent deep structure. The argument I am making is that the deep structure of the culture itself is fatally incoherent and thus becomes, in fact, the cause of the unexplainable behavior on the surface. We can see this in the fact that throughout the Morte runs a constant leitmotif of the ultimate victory of the unjust side in spite of and sometimes as a result of the Good. There simply is no providentialist's view that causes any good in the Morte. We see it overtly in Brunes Sans Pité who, in spite of a number of encounters with knights of the Round Table, is never finally conquered. Even more forthright is King Mark's victory over Sir Amant in a trial by battle. The conclusion of the battle is thus:

> And so lyghtly the kynge [Arthur] commaunded them
> to do batayle. And by mysadventure Kynge Marke
> smote sir Amante thorow the body; and yet was sir
> Amaunte in the ryghtuous quarell." (364, emphasis
> mine)

True, this is the short run, but the element of mysadventure, the hap theme Kennedy refers to, is so prevalent throughout the Morte--from Arthur's begetting Mordred upon his own sister, to Balin's "dolerous stroke" which kills his own brother, to Lancelot's killing by accident Gaheris and Gareth, and finally to the anonymous knight bitten by a snake at the worst possible moment--that we wonder whether or not any principle of good underlies creation. What Caxton failed to recognize (or did not want to) is that Le Morte Darthur is tragedy and as such depicts the process of disordering or disintegration of what was at one time highly ordered--at least ideally so. The romance does not support a providentialist view, but rather refutes the notion that the world is finally and ultimately good. The deep structure of the world is indifferent to human wishes for order.

It seems to me that Malory focuses on the very occurrences of "mysadventure," "mysfortune," and "myshappe." The meaning of the tragedy, then, is the inability of the best men to employ their inherited wisdom to understand the world and thus anticipate or predict the outcome of any experience. The limited world view, the highly selective collection of observations that comprises the culture's explanatory synthesis, simply overlooks important facets of the world (that is, the snake, for example) which will not finally be subdued by explanations. The purpose of explanation or of explanatory efforts as a whole is to provide theories about the world and human experience so that when one confronts a situation or an object he can immediately refer that phenomenon to its proper theoretical category of the explanation and thus by reasoning analogically and deductively predict the meaning, the outcome, or the value of the phenomenon and his own appropriate response. In this way the world becomes understandable and the more one is successful in interpreting and predicting phenomenon the more he believes in his explanatory super-structure and the more moral he becomes. But Malory shows that the explanatory categories are simply inadequate for real life; what in theory could a snake have to do with peace negotiations. In life, as the romance shows, everything.

The recognition of Malory's emphasis upon those cases where the interpretational method fails suggests that Malory is not interested in the inducement of a moral disposition but rather in the analysis of the failure of a cultural ideal and its moral codes to explain adequately, and hence order, life. In itself the number of occurrences of terms meaning "mysadventure" implies that the judgment is customary--we should think of such events as if they were happenstance and not an integral or predictable part of the explanatory category--but taken together too many happenstances mean that Malory is, as Robert Synder puts it, "Too tough minded and inquisitive either to postulate an arcane Providence or to concede all to an equally obtuse Fate; Malory insists upon human accountability" ("Malory and Historical Adaptation," 144). What emerges from Malory's tragic portrayal of Arthur and his Round Table "in tokenyng of the rowdnes of the worlde" is the necessity of a new epistemological and metaphysical order. His predecessor here is Wolfram von Eschenbach whose Parzival brought about the death of a system controlling the Grail Castle when he "forced God by defiance." Actually all that he defied was Trevrizent's rather inadequate conception of God which as an orthodox explanation had claimed to control all approaches to the Grail Castle. And Malory is followed by Martin Luther who perceived the inability of an individual to survive in a social system which places its codes and explanations above individual men. Such is the dilemma of the Round Table knights; they must uphold the code, even if it means the destruction of their way of life. Tristram, on the other hand, as Malory makes clear, comes to represent good faith in a direct contrast to the growing faithlessness, on all levels, of the rest of the knights.

It would have been especially pertinent for Malory to have been concerned with analysis since fifteenth century English society was itself interested in reviving and imitating the Arthurian ideal. Roger Sherman Loomis tells us that "Oscar Wilde's paradox about 'life merely hold[ing] the mirror up to art' has seldom been better exemplified than in the reflections of Arthurian Literature on the practices and pageantries, as well as the plays, of our Medieval ancestors" (ALMA, 553). The literature to which he refers is the courtly and chivalric romances written two to three hundred years before Malory's time. But others, Huizinga, Kennedy, Ferguson for instance, present good evidence to show that the imitation of Arthurian ideals was even more intense in the fifteenth century than in the twelfth or the thirteenth. The point is that by the fifteenth century chivalry had become a conscious, overt ideal with dubious practical application. The rage for chivalry as a behavioral ideal approximating the social role of manners can be seen in the increasing appearance in English translation of courtesy books and instruction manuals: The Book of Noblesse (1448) and The Boke of the Order of Chivalry (Caxton, 1484), to name two. But the interest in chivalry was of a particular sort--different from the interest of previous centuries. As Arthur Ferguson in The Indian Summer of English Chivalry points out, The Book of Noblesse was addressed to "this aggressive and naively patriotic public" and that the story of Arthur (as Englishman) strongly appealed to the emerging sense of nationalism.   I have already intimated that Malory was a dissenter from the ideal structure being revived and yet in order to exemplify the fallacy inherent in the synthetic attempt to explain the present by the past he had to work stylistically and thematically within the tradition. He presents the ideal structure, but with all the misadventure of human diversity, it simply does not work--and beyond that, the structure itself is what condemns life.

It was mentioned earlier that a critical revolution did not occur after 1947, but it should have.   If the nature of the critical responses to Malory's Le Morte Darthur did not significantly change, what did change was the cogency of the work. Finally with the publication of Eugène Vinaver's edition of the Winchester manuscript, we have the work in a form significantly free from Caxton's moral overlay and closer, therefore, to what Malory probably intended.   The term intended is important because the heart of the problems in Malorian scholarship rests upon various opinions of what Malory must have intended. We know Caxton's intentions in publishing the work, and they are both conscious and rational: "that noble men may see and lerne the noble actes of chyvalrye" (xv).   But Caxton's intentions need not necessarily correspond to Malory's The term, intentions, is problematic because it raises the debate about whether or not a work of art is a consciously created object or whether or not the reader can have access to the writer's private intentions. Conscious creation, however, is not the essential aspect of art; it is merely the aspect of art which is craft and certainly the least important and least interesting part of art, though because codifiable and amenable to quasi-rational standards of taste and proficiency, the aspect of art most frequently discussed. But it is not what lies at the center of the works of artists and not, therefore, the seminal principle of unity.   Art, as it were, speaks two, languages simultaneously.   It speaks the language of the conscious mind, but it also speaks the language of the unconscious.   The language of the unconscious consists of symbols, images, and actions which are responses or interpretations of experience, just as conscious language, but on a level beyond the range of logical understanding. The attempt to understand consciously what the unconsious knows about the world by using theories of motif, archetype, dream, symbol, and actions are inherently inaccurate, but they are about the best that can be done. The knowledge of the unconscious which is manifest in actions rapidly becomes conventionalized, but this is not to deny that such activity was genuine unconscious knowledge to begin with. The basic action of Arthurian Romance is the quest, and it represents a search which suggests both the perception of inadequacy and failure and the hope for something new and different from what presently prevails.

Jacques Maritan, a medievalist and a Thomist, in his Creative Intuition in Art and Poetry argues that "at the root of the creative act there must be a quite particular intellectual process, without parallel in the logical reason, through which Things and the Self are grasped together by means of a kind of experience or knowledge which has no conceptual expression and is expressed only in the artist's work" (29-30). He calls the unconscious faculty the "Illuminating Intellect" which makes symbols for a unique perception and response to the world (and that is all that the conscious intellect can do as well) which is manifest in works and acts, not ideas. Since the Romantics, the faculty or imagination has been deified, as Maritan himself tends to do. But as Carl Jung and his group of psychologists see it, the role of the unconscious is that of an intellectual faculty complementary to the rational or conscious intellect whose function is to perceive the world as "pure nature" quite free from the limits of explanation, ideology, logic, and sensory perception to which the reason is always subject (Man and His Symbols, 297). The unconscious by its very nature appears chaotic and ineffable because not only are order and verbal constructs products of the reason, but also to organize and to explain mean to limit and to define (de+finire, to finish, to bring to an end). But the world of pure nature is indefinable or infinite, and, from our human point of view, it is ultimately unknowable. Perhaps the unconscious is only that which knows that what the conscious knows is inadequate. In other words, since the conscious intellect can never know anything absolutely, all its knowledge is hypothetical. The unconscious, then, is aware of the "gap" between the hypothesis and the thing itself. And while it is hopeless to explain what that gap is, the unconscious becomes the source of some rather puzzling behavior, the "enantiodromia" for example.

The Christian who knows, for example, that "I believe in God" also knows that "I deny God" because of inexorable inadequacy of whatever he knows about believing in God. The Triplex Via of Dionysius the Areopagite is a sophisticated form of this complementarity of the unconscious and the conscious intellects. In knowing things about God, the way of Affirmation must always be immediately countered by the way of Negation because whatever man can affirm about God is certainly not God Himself. The value of the unconscious, then, is in establishing a connection with the infinite (whether it is God or simply some transcendental feeling). The connection is the root of the mythic association, mentioned a moment ago, and it provides a certainty that the world and life itself have some purpose and direction beyond the immediate level. The conscious reason can never feel certainty; it can only doubt and enforce its order.

If we admit that art can have unconscious as well as conscious intentions, the problem of intentions raised by W. K. Wimsatt and Monroe C. Beardsley vanishes. To be sure, we can never know Malory's conscious intentions. But his unconscious intentions are--especially after Vinaver's edition--manifest in the only manner that they can or could ever be known either by Malory or the modern reader. The artist, like the dreamer, observes the product of his unconscious from the same remote point of view as any other viewer. To be sure rational intentions can influence the work and even totally annihilate the unconscious, as in the case of much eighteenth century poetry. But clearly that is not the case with Malory. After 1947, Malory's work was suddenly substantially freed from the conscious and rational intentions of Caxton, but critics were not responding to it. They continued to see the Morte through Caxton's bias, reading unconscious symbols and patterns of actions as if they were conventional symbols, icons, or allegories. No one knew quite what to do with all of the little inconsistencies and seemingly inartistic excesses that flawed an otherwise perfectly rational development of a theme. A study of Le Morte Darthur has yet to be produced without forcing upon the work conceptions of what a medieval romance should be. Working from the aesthetic assumptions of conscious

creation and craft, the inconsistencies could only mean that
Malory was sometimes an inept artist. But if we accept that
art has an unconscious component, that art may very well be
the expression in images of instincts and impulses that are
misinterpreted, repressed or sublimated by the conscious mind,
then we make ourselves able to respond to what the knights
actually do in the romance.

The role of the unconscious in medieval art was
particularly strong because of the high degree of control of
thought exerted by religious and social explanations. While this
point will be developed more fully in the next chapter, it is
useful to mention again the enantiodramia and also Gottfried
who at the outset of his Tristan announces that his romance is
directed only to those who can respond to the unconscious: "I
have another world in mind which together in one heart
[unconscious region] bears its bitter-sweet, it dear sorrow, its
heart's joy . . . its dear death, its sorrowful life. To this life
let my life be given, of this world let me be a part, to be saved
or damned with it." As Freud writes in An Outline of
Psychoanalysis, "The governing laws of logic have no sway in
the unconscious; it might be called the Kingdom of the Illogical.
Impulses with contrary aims exists side by side in the
unconscious without any call being made for an adjustment
between them" (53). The same tensions and inconsistencies
abound in other writers of the period; Petrarch, Dante,
Chaucer, Chrétien, and Guillaume are a few of the poets whose
work is an expression of the knowledge of the unconscious. But
as already noted, the knowledge of the unconscious rapidly
becomes conventionalized and transformed into a conscious
technique for achieving rational ends, as is the case of the
difference between Petrarch and the Renaissance sonneteers.
Critics of our period make a grave mistake when they approach
the works of these unconscious artists armed with theories
about the conventional use and meaning of paradox, oxymoron,
and inconsistency that have been derived from the conscious
artists of the Renaissance.

John F. Benton has discussed this same problem with
reference to courtly love in medieval works. The tendency, he
concludes, is to work backwards; that is, approach the work
from a fairly complete concept of what the theme of the work
should be ("Historical View of Medieval Love," 24-29). The

same pattern applies, of course, to all phases of the study of works of the past, but the solution is not, as D. W. Robertson suggests, to refer to historical, philosophical, and theological records of the period.   Such records suffer to the highest degree from the control of the thought-police of logic, ideology, and explanation.   Art, because it is essentially fiction and therefore potentially free from the control of rational thought processes, is a unique record of culture and needs an approach based upon, not ideas, but what the characters actually do in the work.   Elizabeth Pachoda has summarized the inconclusive nature of Malory studies as the result of a logical and necessary process.   It was necessary for critics to establish that Malory was an artist in his own right, not simply a translator, before any theories of structure might be offered.   And naturally enough, she points out in Arthurian Propaganda, critics had to be sure that the work was internally consistent and devised with some overall plan before discussions of themes might be offered (3-6).   Thus the scholarship consists of three concerns or responses all of which are controlled by concepts extraneous to the work: source studies, structural analyses, and theme studies.   It cannot be that the principle of unity lies in any of these.

But it seems to me that the problem of discovering the principle of unity is still more deeply rooted and that the problem stems from the very nature of the descriptions and actions that Malory's unconscious intentions have produced.   C. S. Lewis, who is always a sensitive reader and honest enough in the midst of the structural battles to admit that "Malory eludes me," writes: "I find in it . . . an unforced reverence not only for courage (that of course) but for mercy, humility, graciousness, and good faith" ("The English Prose Morte," 9).   Indeed Caxton's preface suggests the moral intentions of the work, and modern commentators have generally corroborated his opinion.   P. E. Tucker notes that in spite of the sources "what is his own [Malory's] is the strong moral tone which pervades his accounts of chivalrous conduct and makes its various aspects coalesce into a single sentiment" ("Chivalry in the Morte," 65).   While it is perfectly true that a sincere moral tone pervades the Morte, one would be hard pressed, indeed, to name even one character whose actions are thoroughly moral and ethical.   Certainly not Arthur.   Sir Gareth is often suggested, but we must overlook certain of his acts in his own tale and at the Tournament of Lonzep where he attacks Lancelot from behind. The same holds true for Sir Bors. Galahad might qualify if he were not an ascetic and if he operated in the secular domain. It is significant that Malory chose not to retell any of Galahad's secular adventures. The moral tone is not, then, a judgment of what happens but rather is Malory's longing for psychic health. This is especially true since the basis of the moral tone is not empirical but in desire, a craving for the simple "good faith"--something which becomes tragically ironic in the last section, "The Most Piteous Tale of the Morte Arthur Saunz Guerdon." What seems to exist is a profound disparity between tone and action, between what is believed and hoped for and what is done. One passage that has caused a great deal of trouble for critics is Malory's statement of what actually exists in his romance:

> `What?´ sayde sir Launcelot, `is he a theff and a knyght? And a ravyssher of women? He doth shame unto the Order of Knyghthode and contrary to his oath. Hit is a pyte that he lyvyth!´ (160)

And yet he does live, and in the case of Sir Brunes Sans Pité, outlives King Arthur and his knights. No one can know the truth of Lancelot's horror better than Malory himself, and yet this profound dissonance between what the mind conceives of reality and what experience the world presents is exactly the condition which pervades the Morte.

Critics have not yet been bold enough to call Malory's heroes patent hypocrites, but it will occur and even prevail as an interpretation for a time. Maureen Fries comes close to it in her recent article on "Malory's Tristram as Counter-Hero to the Morte Darthur," but I will show later that any theory crediting Tristram with hypocrisy or with excesses which expose the cause of the fall of the Round Table is absolutely untenable. Tristram's role in the Morte is finished before the downfall proper begins and the cause of the fall is much more within the meaning of the Round Table itself, an institution he avoids as much as possible. The tension of the disparity is ubiquitous. For example, with Galahad's dubious begetting and Lancelot's subsequent repudiation of him, who would expect him finally to occupy the Siege Perilous?   Why could the institution not use its own great heroes?   And even worse, it is clear that only the best knight in the world can heal Sir Urry's seven year-old wounds, but Malory places "The Healing of Sir Urry" immediately after "The Knight of the Cart" in which Lancelot is guilty of adultery, blasphemy in calling God to witness a false oath and trial, and the murder of Meleagant.   Still, it is only Lancelot who can heal Sir Urry!   The knights of the Round Table condemn their own actions by their beliefs, and yet in their misguided quest for social order they can neither stop acting nor believing.   Finally we must confront what Charles Moorman calls "an insuperable paradox."   "How," he asks, "could a writer who set out certainly to praise, and perhaps even to revive a dying chivalry, have concluded by so effectively damning it" (A Knyght There Was, 99).   The truth is that he never set out to praise any explanatory or ideological system. Rather, as Malory knows, moral codes and ideal political systems can do nothing to make life meaningful and valuable. They are finally, as in Galahad's case, not relevant to the important things in this life; they belong, really, as Galahad does, in another world.

The recognition of the disparity in tone and action leads to an important discovery, one which exposes clearly the heart of the problems with structural and thematic unity.   We look for unity, continuity, reference, and order.   As human beings we prefer unity to disunity, order to disorder.   But the occurrences of mishap, injustice, and brute force in Malory suggest that life is not so well ordered, unless we condemn most of the knights as hopelessly corrupt.   Carl Jung observes that

> The sad truth is that man's real life consists of a
> complex set of inexorable opposites--day and night,
> birth and death, happiness and misery, good and evil.
> We are not even sure that one will prevail against
> the other, that good will overcome evil, or joy
> defeat pain.   Life is a battleground.   It always has
> been.   (Man and His Symbols, 75)

Such a perception would lead instantly to suicide if there were not some way to make life orderly; as had been said before, the rage for order is basic.   A romance like Malory's gives us the choice between orderly theories and the chaos of real humans. We must choose for we cannot have both. Art is often defined as the creation of unity or order from the chaos of experience. The artists' function, we are so frequently told, is to make life understandable, and therefore stable and comforting, in terms of universal patterns of action.   St. Augustine explains away evil as nothingness and enables himself to see the world as good. The process is simply one of ascribing value (being) to actions and theories which produce order and denigrating (denying being) those which lead to chaos.   But choosing the orderly explanation of the world is a false quest.   Thus Lancelot is the best knight and heals Sir Urry not because he is personally moral or just but because he preserves the order of the Round Table, and order in the explanatory center is taken to be the source of health and happiness in life.   Imagine the consequences if Meleagant had been allowed to enforce the truth of his charge against Guinevere!   But such order is a human construct and dangerously moves men away from their condition in nature toward an artificial life.   We are beginning to see that order works in opposition to what Malory would have called no more than "good faith."   The best example of Malory's good faith is the relationship between Tristram and Palomides; I will have much to say about this later on but here it is enough to point out that they are simultaneously the best of friends and the worst of enemies.

If art is unified, then understanding a work of art involves no more than, as Helen Gardner puts it, "the discovery of the work's centre, the source of the life in all parts, and response to its total movement."   The idea that a work of art contains a unified explanatory center, or centripetal force as Northrup Frye calls it, means that it is unified in all its parts (if the artist is competent) by a principle which applies to both the action of the art and to life.   John Leyerle calls the center a nucleus, and he defines it as "both seed, implying origin and growth, and center, implying the surrounding structure of the poem. . . . In this analogy the nucleus is the nodal point about which the manifest structures of a narrative poem are organized" ("The Game and Play of the Hero," 49-50).   The assumption that the purpose of art is to be unified goes unquestioned; so much for the human bias!   The logical implications are, moreover, astounding: life must also be unified or explainable in a coherent and internally consistent manner, just as art. Without exception Malory's critics, even Vinaver, have assumed that his work is unified by a centering ethos of religion and chivalry combined, but which is in a corrupted form in the "Tristram" section. All that should be necessary for understanding, then, is to explicate the "surrounding structure." Why has it proved to be so difficult? Is Malory an incompetent artist? I would contend that the problem is infinitely more complex; with Malory we get a work of art whose center is profoundly disunified! In Malory, we get simultaneous movements inward toward the explanatory center which consists of the rage for order and which is producing the tragedy and is, therefore, chaotic. On the periphery or the surrounding structure, there exists an outward movement, an escape from the civilization into the individual, and here we find a high degree of order which gives the work its moral and noble tone.

Tragedy in the highest sense grows out of man's highest efforts to impose order on a world which is itself chaotic or, at least, beyond the reaches of the order of the human mind. Nature fights reason with instances of mishap, chance, and randomness. Tennyson's perception of the tragedy in the Arthurian story is perhaps definitive:

> The old order changeth, yielding place to the new
> And God fulfills himself in many ways
> Lest one good custom should corrupt the world. . . .
> For what are men better than sheep or goats
> That nourish a blind life within the brain.

The recognition of this disparity or discontinuity will be of utmost importance in approaching the Morte and the culture to which it is a response. And because this incoherence is the nature of the "Tristram," we must adopt the "Tristram" as the nucleus of the entire work.

Perhaps we are now able to understand the importance of Vinaver's position, set forth in the introduction to the Works, that Malory intended to write eight separate romances, not a single tale. Vinaver, like those who have disputed with his theory, is responding with the particular bias toward order, only he has been a little more perceptive and honest than his critics. It seems to me that Vinaver perceived the impossibility of subsuming all of the books, tales, and episodes under a single coherent structure and center, and therefore, in desperation to put a halt to the emendators who suggested excising certain incompatible parts, he offered his separate romances theory. Vinaver was afraid of the very thing which occurs in Stephen Knight's The Structure of Malory's Arthuriad. Knight sets out to demonstrate the unity of the whole work and ends by admitting that Malory failed in the "Tristram" to measure up to the standards of the rest of the work. He writes: "it is aesthetically disturbing to find two quite different kinds of structure in a work when there is no union between them" (86-95). We have to wonder about an aesthetics which presumes unity and consistency. Where does it come from? Certainly not from a very close observation of art or of the world. Although Beverly Kennedy acknowledges this profound dissonance as "one of the qualities of Malory's fictional world which has proved most troubling to modern critics: there is more that one ethical point of view within that world, more than one set of moral criteria by which a man may be judged" (8), she resolves the dissonance by reducing the disparate moral viewpoints into a typical medieval hierarchy of knighthood: the Heroic, the Worshipful and the Christian knight. Such a typology or hierarchy serves the purpose of critical order, not necessarily romance. It weeds out, so to speak, those aspects of knightly behavior which one finds distasteful according to an absolute moral code and places them in a lower order of being where they can be accepted.

All Vinaver is saying is that since no one can discover a single, coherent raison d'etre or all embracing dramatic or ethical unity, the tales must be regarded separately in order not to lose the richness and diversity of each tale. In this Vinaver is perfectly correct, and no amount of "inconsistencies resolved" (see Rumble and Moorman) will ever generate a coherent center for the Works. That is not to say, however, that an incoherent and disunified center can not be found which would eliminate the need for the separate romances theory by justifying the existence of the surrounding structure on internal grounds. Vinaver as well as his opponents have simply lacked the critical approach necessary for understanding the kind of literary work which Malory has written. Their aesthetic principles originate in the conscious intellect and therefore must conform to the structures of logic and reason. But let us approach the <u>Morte</u> with a different assumption; how will the problem of unity be resolved if art originates in the unconscious and works on principles (impulses would be a better word) that are pre-rational and pre-logical.

Since Vinaver's original introduction, several theories have been advanced to demonstrate a dramatic and thematic unity for the work. For my own part, none is any more convincing than D. S. Brewer's simple insistence in his essay "'the hoole book'" that we feel the cumulative effect of each and every episode. The "Tristram" section, of course, provides the greatest obstacle to unity. T. C. Rumble has called the "Tristram" a development by analogy, while Donald Scheuler and Maureen Fries have gone a little further and considered it as antithesis or contrast to the Lancelot and Round Table sections. In this way unity is achieved since analogy and antithesis are sub-forms of a higher unity and explainable in that higher synthesis. Only paradox, negation, and contradiction are disunified or incoherent and admit of no orderly or ennobling explanation. For example, everyone excoriates Tristram for his affair with Sir Segwarde's wife or for striking Lamerok while the two of them are conversing. They do so because he violates the rules of noble conduct, but nevertheless Tristram loses no worship for his deeds, except in the eyes of a reader biased toward a uniform and consistent application of the principles of chivalry. In other words, those who condemn Tristram are responding to a conception of order which Malory is showing to be inoperative, and the concept prevents them from seeing what actually happens in the romance. Such a reader, if he were to be consistent, would have to condemn the whole Round Table from Uther's rape of Igraine to Lancelot's abduction of Guinevere. But no such condemnation takes place in the work. In fact, Tristram's reputation constantly increases whatever he does. That cannot be explained without viewing Malory's world as hopelessly corrupt. But what about the moral tone and Caxton's intentions? Vinaver offers a similar argument in objecting to Rumble's "Development by Analogy." Rumble, because he presumes that a unified set of values control the entire work, is constrained to conclude that Tristram is finally an evil knight. But as Vinaver points out, Rumble's conclusion contradicts direct statements that "all that the noble sir Tristram does is through clean knighthood" (Works, xli).   We can, on the other hand, read Tristram's actions as an expression of Malory's subtle perception that the ideological (i.e. rational) controls on his life make it increasingly difficult to live at all, that paradoxically what is offered as an ethical code for promoting life actually destroys it, and that Malory's own world had become a living death.   It is only by violating all that the culture stands for that he is able to gain the inner worship indicative of psychic health.

More recently Vinaver in an article called "The Questing Knight" has suggested that we cannot begin to understand medieval romance unless we have more than a passing acquaintence with the absurd and surreal art and literature of the twentieth century.   What marks both these periods--down periods, to recall Bloomfield's terms--is a tremendous pre-occupation with the arbitrary and conventional nature of knowledge and ultimately a shift in fundamental world views: for the medieval period from the Christian world to the modern world and for the twentieth century from modernism to post-modernism.   Writers of post-modern absurd fiction and writers of medieval romance perceive a significant inability to employ the inherited knowledge of their culture in a way that will make their lives or their art characterized by coherence and rational order.   Rather than rational order in life, what emerges in Arthurian Romance is the aggressive assertion of the individual in an attempt to impose his own unique way of ordering experience after the collapse of the orthodox way. What makes Lancelot finally the greatest of knights is not, as moral approaches must imply, that he most fully exemplifies the culture's ideals, for he does not, but rather that he is the biggest and fiercest fighter of all.   Aggressive self assertion directed frequently against the center of the institutional order itself, as loving the King's wife suggests, becomes the knight's way of resolving the essential tension created by the collapse of the explanatory center.   Its violence means also, tragically, the death of the knights themselves, but that violence injects into the highly ordered world of the late Middle Ages significant levels of explanatory disorder that would make modification of the explanatory synthesis possible and necessary for later thinkers such as the early scientists or Montaigne, Erasmus, and Michaelangelo.

It is to be my contention, then, that the tension produced from the reader's expectation of unity and order and the disunity and disorder which actually exists (on a ideological as well as dramatic level) is exactly Malory's intention in the work. Whether this calculated disunity is to be called structural unity matters little. What is important is that the ethical center of the work is not likely to be what a reader coming from a literary and aesthetic standpoint should expect from a romance, and it can only be approached by a careful study of surrounding structure-- what the knights are actually doing. It will be seen that Malory, a man living in the last stages of a culture which focused all its efforts on devising a thoroughly coherent explanation of the world, perceived as does Othello that when "chaos is come again" it will come from the very center of the old unity. Most importantly, disunity will prove to be the redemptive force. Malory perceived a profound incoherence within the values implied by the ideals of his culture and its explanation of itself, so much that Tristram by seeking chaos or separation from his culture finds at least a personal salvation in love and death. "But this is not death as a last judgment," Joseph L. Henderson writing in Carl Jung's Man and His Symbols points out. Rather, this kind of death is a symbol of transcendence: "it is a journey of release, renunciation, and atonement, presided over and fostered by some spirit of compassion" (150). In Malory there is little compassion but Tristram's death stabilizes him as the lover of Isode and saves him from the total degeneration in which the rest of Arthur's knights simply kill each other.

I will have more to say on Tristram's death as transcendence in Chapter Three, "The King and the Knight," but perhaps here it will be helpful for a moment to examine a similar approach to the declining stages of the Middle Ages. C. S. Lewis, in his The Discarded Image, observes that the most important cultural effort of the Middle Ages was to devise an explanation of life which would make the apparent chaos of experience seem orderly and teleological. Actually it is no more a phenomenon of the Middle Ages than it is of any other period, but it is always easier to observe in the past. Lewis writes that the impulse was to make "the whole organization of their theology, science, and history into a single, complex, harmonious mental Model of the Universe" (11). Lewis is not alone in this observation, as we have seen on several occasions in the present discussion. In Malory, the tension is not only between the Model and the actions of the characters but most importantly within the Model itself. While the discussion of the Model is the subject for the next chapter, here it is important to determine Malory's relation to model making. Lewis divides the great writers of the Middle Ages into two groups: those who delight in exemplifying the Model and adding to it, and those whom Lewis calls "experts" whose task it is to tear the Model apart. Although Lewis would certainly not place Malory among the experts, it seems to me, as we shall see, that he must be considered a dissenter from the medieval synthesis. Lewis' words express what is going on in Le Morte Darthur: "Every Model is a construct of answered questions [explanations in my terms]. The expert is engaged in either raising new questions or in giving new answers to old one. When he is doing the first, the old, agreed Model is of no interest to him; when he is doing the second, he is beginning a process which will finally destroy the old Model altogether" (18). The second function is Malory's. A great deal has been written about the transition from the Middle Ages to the Renaissance (although not in connection with Malory), and I think that Malory's perception that the Model, by the time of the fifteenth century, had become hopelessly incoherent and absolutely unable to inspire men to good faith in present social situations suggests that what happened in the transition was simply the adoption by Renaissance men of a new Model, the modern or scientific world. It is a truism that myth, itself the ultimate Model, will not stand up to analysis. If the process of the knight's training, so well exemplified in the tale of Gareth, is what sustains the synthesis, then it is clear that the life of the Model depends upon the knight's perceptions of the world being controlled by his conceptions of the world. Malory's Tristram is prophetic in the sense that while "mad" he learns to see the world in a new way. Before turning to the discussion of the Model which forms the ideological and rational center of Le Morte Darthur, it is still necessary to consider two more critical problems.

1.3 An Approach to
Le Morte Darthur

The first of these problems concerns the environment in which Malory must have written. We know that Malory was a prisoner during the time which he wrote most of the Morte. A great many details, however, especially in the "Tristram," equate exile to incarceration so that William Matthews' Yorkshire Malory who may have been an exile or prisoner of war at some French court (he favors Jacques d'Armagnac) might well be the man (Ill Framed Knight, 137-44). But it is also possible that Malory felt himself to be a prisoner of culture and the responsibilities its order and codes impose upon men and women. Elizabeth Pachoda has described this condition as the implicit propagandistic nature of Arthurian Romance: "that the ideal of personal perfection is coincidental with social fulfillment" (Arthurian Propaganda, x). This is an important recognition, for it means that no identity exists outside of the institution, and while I will have more to say about this point later, here I can only note Sir Alexander's predicament when he finds himself charged with the responsibility to avenge his father's murder but also bound by his promise to remain with Morgan Le Fay for one year: "for now I stonde as a presonere be my promyse" (395). All of the knights, of course, have taken the oath of knighthood at Pentecost which they perceive to be good; Alexander's case presents a good oath in new circumstances turning oppressive, exactly in the sense of William Blake's Marriage of Heaven and Hell: "Prisons are built with stones of Law" and "One Law for the Lion & Ox is Oppression."

The problem which needs to be examined here is the possibility of the Morte being revivalistic, the possibility that Malory was interested in further articulation of laws and codes to regulate behavior. The need for a revival of a prevailing spirit of justice, mercy, good faith, and nobility (which we have noted consititutes the tone of the work) is certainly apparent when one considers the historical accounts of the numerous baronial skirmishes, the incessant wars with France, the War of the Roses, and the growing restlessness and independence of the peasant and craftsman classes. That violence and brute force make up the ultimate standard of authority, even within the Morte itself, is also apparent from even a superficial reading. Though Roger Ascham may have been a conservative and stuffy pedant whose greatest pleasure lay in tormenting students with double translations, he is absolutely correct in observing that "The whole pleasure of this book standeth in two special points, in open manslaughter and bold bawdry. In which book those be counted the noblest knights that do kill most men without any quarrel, and commit the foulest adulteries by subtle shifts" (cited in Matthews, 49). Of this period, Edward P. Cheyney writes:

> Popular revolts often begin leaderless, springing from some petty incident. They soon take on larger proportions and eventually some man arises with the qualities of leadership. . . . The `Shepards´, the `Sicilian Vespers´, the `Jacquerie´, the Parisian `Mailotins´, the English `Peasants´, the `Ciompi´ of Florence, the `Matins of Bruges´ and successive risings in Flanders were only a few of the most prominent of these sudden outbreaks. There is scarcely a country, a province, a city which does not have in its annals the record of some wild outburst of popular turbulence. They were as grim as they were sudden. The reprisals of those who claimed to represent law and order, or who at least

had enough force in their possession to put down the risings, were hardly less barbarous than the most repulsive acts of the rebels. They have left a dark record of human rage, revenge, cruelty and futility. What is the cause of this epidemic, so characteristic of the fourteenth and fifteenth centuries? (Dawn of a New Era, 110-11)

But was Malory interested in counteracting the violent and chaotic tenor of his times by reviving a responsible form of chivalry? Larry Benson in Malory's Morte Darthur, among others, thinks that he was and reasons that "Chivalry is, among other things, a moral code, and those who admire chivalry are by definition moralists. Morality, of whatever sort, was always better in the past, is always sadly declining in the present, and is therefore always in need of revival. That is why the history of chivalry is a history of revivals" (145). While Malory affects this attitude in admonishing the "greate defaughte of us Englysshemen" (708), his admiration for his most morally imperfect hero, Lancelot, who provides the occasion for the default, remains unqualified to the end: "'A, Launcelot!' he sayd [Sir Ector], 'thou were the hede of al Crysten knyghtes'" (725). I find no irony in Sir Ector's threnody, and, as Vinaver tells us, it does not appear in the French source and is thus very likely Malory's own composition. Malory's admiration for Tristram is unparalleled, and yet we must remember that Tristram is a traitor and an abductor of his king's wife. That Mark is to us or to Tristram ignoble and contemptible is merely a matter of perspective. He succeeds in enhancing the strength and independence of Cornwall by a series of shrewd, but successful, political maneuvers beginning with the rebellion against Ireland. Political leaders--from the standpoint of ideology and national interest--are not judged personally. History is full of such examples. The men of the fifteenth century worshipped Henry V as nearly a saint, but as Sidney Painter concedes, he was no more than a bloodthirsty and ambitious conquerer (French Chivalry, 61).

Malory is just too interested in the immoral acts of his principal knights to take Benson's analysis straight, for in his case it appears that vicious behavior in the past becomes admirable in the present in the sense that the development of the mythologization of the hero tends to place those acts into a larger significance or frame of reference--the archetypal battle with the forces of disorder or even simple national interest-- and thereby make them seem noble or heroic. Malory, with his subtle paradoxes, allows the mythologization of heroes to take place, just as Benson and Caxton, for that matter, would have it, knowing full well, as Huizinga does, that "There is not a more dangerous tendency in history than that of representing the past as if it were a rational whole and dictated by clearly defined interests" (Waning, 94). Although Malory never directly blames his heroes, he constantly places them in situations which demonstrate their moral culpability: Morgan Le Fay's shield which Tristram carries in front of Arthur and Guinevere, or Lancelot's casuistry in defending Guinevere from Meleagant's charge of adultery--to name two. Lancelot is always both the best knight and the worst, and yet the mythologization of Lancelot makes everyone think only the best of him and therefore unable to discover the source of the great evil in the Round Table. Imitation of a mythologized past produces individuals in the present like Lancelot who habitually condemns his own present moral condition but is finally unable to draw upon his own resources to resolve his problems.

    If one significant cultural movement in the fifteenth century were an attempt to achieve a stable social structure based upon and justified by an historical ideal, then we must determine Malory's attitude toward the movement of historicism and revivalism. Beverly Kennedy and Larry Benson place him within the movement. More acutely, Elizabeth Pachoda reads Malory in opposition to it, noting that "by turning to the story as a potential cultural solution, in making it serve as a conscious cultural ideal, Malory . . . accomplished two things: he exposed the true nature of the moral demands implicit in Arthurian chivalry; and in showing their ultimate failure, he demonstrated the fallacy of consciously reviving the moral demands of the past to try to control the present" (104). Fifteenth century historicism as a cultural phenomenon bespeaks a belief that the only means of understanding the nature of a people or of a national identity and assessing its value is by considering the people in terms of origin and process of development. In order to justify contemporary actions and ideals, therefore, they must be traced back to their origin in a perfect state or at least one that has a completely indisputable foundation; that is, a state ordained by God, as Arthur's state seemed to have been. Romance literature and Courtesy books as well as much of the political philosophy of men such as Henry of Bracton, John Fortesque or earlier John of Salisbury and even St. Thomas Aquinas became the vehicles for the historical method of explanation and evaluation. Certainly for Caxton, the story of Arthur represents history in this sense: "And I . . . have doon sette it in enprynte to the entente that noble men may see and lerne the noble actes of chyvalrye, the jentyl and vertuous dedes that somme knyghtes used in tho dayes" (xv, emphasis mine). It was not until the studies of the Renaissance Humanists such as Vico or Petrarch in philology and the ancients as ancient instead of contemporaries that anyone realized the difference between history and romance. One hundred years after Malory, Sidney and Spenser had no problems viewing the Arthurian material as fiction. But as Malory's critics have quite correctly observed, he has handled the material of his sources in such a way as to increase the historical nature of the story. That is precisely what men of the fifteenth century wanted because they needed to see the moral codes presented in the form of historical truth.

The sudden appearance within a culture of an increased interest in history suggests an attempt to analyze its own cultural situation by measuring it against what can be more clearly understood in the past. It suggests a crisis in confidence of present institutions, in the legitimacy and efficacy of what individuals are doing and who they are. How Malory reacts to this cultural phenomenon and the implicit tragic nature which he sees in it are best seen in his narrative style. P. J. C. Field, in a study of Malory's style, Romance and Chronicle, rightly observes that Malory by writing a romance in the form of a chronicle has endowed his story with the aura of "flat truth" (37). But where this truth resides is the crucial point. Indeed Malory's basic narrative statement is precisely the basic statement of history: at a certain time . . . and then . . . and then . . . and then . . . and then. . . . For example, though the pattern is so common that an example is hardly needed, the opening phrases of the first ten paragraphs of "Alexander the Orphan" are: "Now turne we to another mater . . . So hit befelle . . . And or it were day . . . Whan Kynge Mark wyste . . . And thus . . . So whan . . . And therewith . . . Than the lady . . . Than was there . . . So La Beall Isode . . ." (388-89).

The style in its simple coordination of fact after fact is meant to de-emphasize analysis of personal emotion and agency, and emphasize cause-effect relationships of the most literal and objective sort: post hoc, ergo propter hoc. What is emphasized is simple chronology; this follows that. And what should move the chronology is the unanalyzed nature of the actors, Divine Providence, or at least a universal plan of history. History itself is silently taken to be inherently meaningful and necessary, a sort of "manifest destiny"--manifest to all those who belong to the culture. But in terms of the whole work, we again perceive a fundamental incoherence. There is too much mischance for such a cause-effect style. While the style of narration emphasizes chronological simplicity, the content exemplifies a complex and illogical order, characterized finally by happenstance and the nonchalant "So hit befelle." What, then, does this mean in terms of Malory´s endorsement, or putative endorsement, of historicism?

If we compare the style of Malory, who was writing legend, to that of Jean Froissart (1337-1410), who was writing history, it is apparent that Malory is the more historical. Not, however, in the sense that Malory is more accurate; to the contrary, Malory is less sure and clear about his material than is Froissart. A solution to this problem is offered by Eric Auerbach in his Mimesis: The Representation of Reality in Western Literature. He claims that "To write history is so difficult that most historians are forced to make concessions to the technique of legend" (20). In the Chronicles in an attempt to fill out the story and make history more personal, uniform, and comprehensible, Froissart has converted history to legend. Froissart gives the reader a great sense that history is controlled by an overall plan or plot in the same way that legends are controlled by thematic unity. The reason for this is that in the Chronicles we are almost always sure of the motivations of the participants; at least there is no doubt that the actors feel no problems about what and why they do whatever they do. Froissart always tells us what his characters know, and he allows us to see into their thoughts and feelings. For example, from "The Siege of Breteuil and the Poitiers Campaign" we are told:

For their part, the Prince and his men knew nothing of the enemy's movements and had no way of knowing. . . . When the Prince and his commanders learnt that the King of France was in front of them with his army. . . . When he knew the truth--that his enemies, whom he was so eager to meet, were behind him and not ahead--he was highly pleased. . . . The Prince was in no way disturbed by this, but said: `May God be with us!'" (126-27)

Malory is doing just the opposite; there is always great doubt about what his characters know and what their motivations are (see Field, 40). Malory is converting legend to history by concealing the thematic unity; events simply happen. The most common occurrence in Malory is that one knight is suddenly aware of another knight; he does not know who he is or why they will fight, only that they must fight. That Malory is aware of this lack of rationale in human action is confirmed by the questions Dynadan raises about the motivations for fighting. Dynadan always asks, as it were, why are we about to do what we seemingly must do? Froissart's figures always have the answers, but Malory's characters seldom do. For them the past and the rationale for present actions are as inscrutible as a certain lord's "custom" that errant knights thoroughly beat-up his own men before they can be given lodging for the night:

> `Sir,' seyde the herdemen, `hereby ys good herberow in a castell, but there ys such a custom that there shall no knyght herberow there but if he juste with two knyghtes . . . for and ye be beatyn and have the warse, ye shall nat be lodged there, and if ye beate them ye shall well be herberowed.' (312)

This "custom" makes no sense to Dynadan who responds, "There ys shrewde herberow . . . Lodge where ye woll, for I woll nat lodge there." History in relation to the present holds for Malory the power of custom--a practice not very rational, sometimes quite destructive, but always enforced with the sort of personal recriminations that Tristram inflicts upon Dynadan: "Fye for shame . . . ar ye nat a knyght of the Table Rounde?

Wherefore ye may nat with your worship reffuse your lodgynge"
(312).

In comparing the styles of the Old Testament to the
Homeric Poems, Auerbach discovers that the Homeric style
tends to externalize all phenomena: "The Homeric style knows
only a foreground, only a uniformly illuminated, uniformly
objective present." In contrast, the Old Testament style or
historical style, because it claims the status of truth or
"universal history" and is therefore never completely knowable,
is "fraught with background." "What he [the Biblical writer]
produced, then, was not primarily oriented toward `realism' . . .
it was oriented toward truth" (7-16). The difference between
Froissart and Malory is similar, and it lies in the difference in
orientation toward background (Malory) and foreground
(Froissart). On Froissart's foreground his actors merely have
some difficulties in carrying out what they believe--
background--without doubt. With Malory, the foreground is
certain but the background is much more complex and
problematic. Lancelot could easily achieve anything he desired,
if he only knew what he really believed in. Joan of Arc and
Henry V have no trouble knowing what they believe in; their
problems lie in carrying out their beliefs. In both cases, as in
most art, the writer focuses on the area of greatest problem.

Auerbach goes on to say, "As compositions, the Old
Testament is incomparably less unified than the Homeric poems,
it is more obviously pieced together--but the various
components all belong to one concept of universal history and
its interpretation." Finally Auerbach concludes his comparison
with a statement which might well be applied to Malory's
stylistic performance: "Abraham, Jacob, or even Moses produces
a more concrete, direct, and historical impression than the
figures of the Homeric world--not because they are better
described in terms of sense (the contrary is the case) but
because the confused, contradictory multiplicity of events, the
psychological and factual cross-purposes, which history reveals,
have not disappeared in the representation but still remain
clearly perceptible" (20). The facts or events which appear on
the surface need not be self-explanatory but gain reality
because some universal principle or rational history lies behind
them. That the principle exists, the knights assume, is evident
from the existence of the fact. We will see in a moment how
Malory questions the principle.

The sense in which Auerbach uses the term "realism" is our modern, scientific sense, meaning the presentation of perceptual attributes as much as possible as they appear to a particular viewer. But Malory would have had a different meaning for "realism" which was no less _real_ and true for him, and his style shows him being as consciously _realistic_ as possible. Medieval philosophic realism, the descendent of Platonism, held that reality resided in the ideal, the Form, or the perfect Model which informed all phenomenal, contingent existents. While in Froissart or the Homeric Poems "Delight in physical existence is everything . . . and their highest aim is to make that delight perceptible to us" (Auerbach, 13), in Malory the delight is in the Form, the category, or the Model. His style is best described as _Formalistic_; that is, objects, actions, and situations stand primarily for the Form or the Ideal which lies behind them (background) and only secondarily for themselves. Malory's Formal style is the equivalent of medieval philosophic realism, and by claiming this ultimate reality and truth for pseudo-history, he achieves the same sense of background as did the Biblical writer. Thus we are never told what Tristram or Isode looks like, except in terms of the Forms. Tristram is "the good knyght," and that tells all, provided we all agree and are certain about what the category knight includes. Isode is "the Fair," and we should not be surprised at all when we learn that she is even more beautiful than Guinevere (see 461). The Formal style, in locating reality in universals behind individual acts, is exactly the process of mythologization. It is the pattern or the archetype which is important, not the external manifestation of it. The more fully a knight exemplifies the archetype revealed in history, the better he is, and Lancelot as the flower of knighthood exhausts the form of the knight.

Larry Benson makes a mistake when he writes that Malory's realism (he means the modern sense, but see below) can be seen in the lifelike details such as Guinevere's expenditure of 20,000 pounds in the search for Lancelot, Tristram's blood which stained "bothe the overshete, and the nyther-sheete, and the pylowes and the hede-shete," (245) or in Mordred's use of "grete gunnes" in the siege of Canterbury (_Malory's Morte Darthur_, 197). This is not at all "realism" in the sense in which Malory is attempting to represent reality.

Malory's "realism" is his Formalism because he perceived that the thrust of fifteenth century historicism was an attempt to bring present social conditions in conformity with the historical ideal. The structure of such a cultural phenomenon suggests a belief that the Form is more real and more true than the individual trait or event. The details Benson points to are used by Malory whenever a character acts a-typically, in a manner inconsistent with the Form, as the anachronistic use of siege guns suggests. The conception of a knight would simply not permit his using guns, and, of course, we know that Mordred is far from being a good or noble knight according to the Form. The most real acts are the most typical of the Ideal. Gawain's taste for apples and pears is not a personal touch but a suggestion of weakness or a flaw in character, and what trouble he reaps for it: "And thys sir Pyonell hated sir Gawayne bycause of hys kynnesman sir Lamorakes dethe; and therefore, for pure envy and hate, sir Pyonell enpoysonde sertayne appylls for to enpoysen sir Gawayne" (613).

In short, then, Malory has invested the Arthurian world with the authority of Universal Truth. He has done so by diminishing the attributional qualities of the foreground in favor of the more real--that is, more true--background. I have insisted on equating Formalism to philosophic realism to describe Malory's style since even though it appears quite different from modern realism it, in fact, satisfies the same intellectual or psychological demand as does modern realism. What Formalism and modern realism suggest is a response on the part of the artist to a cultural demand for close examination and thorough exemplification of Truth (reality) wherever it is believed to reside--in Forms or empirical phenomena. The men of the fifteenth century wanted to know more fully the situations and circumstances which the categories chivalry, love, religion, and society informed, and the only method which they had for getting at the truth was a process of regression to higher and higher universals balanced by more and more elaborate exemplification of those universals. The political implications of such an epistemology are profoundly inadequate, as Pachoda's book Arthurian Propaganda makes clear. Political theory develops in the manner explained by the Levi-Strauss structural approach to myth; contradictions and antinomies are resolved on the theoretical level so that the ideal of the

Arthurian world becomes one of perfect social cohesion, but the reality of that world is quite different (102-106). Thus Malory's realism is that Lancelot is the best knight, and Tristram and Isode are true lovers. Their lives exemplify a universal Truth that has become crazy. Morton Bloomfield, while trying to figure out what is "powerfully wrong with these later Medieval heroes which seriously limits their heroism," suggests that a continuous widening of the category or Form Hero made it difficult to conceive of heroic individuals. He notes that "Sir Hector finds it difficult to describe the heroic; the Beowulf poet had no such problem." The effect of the expanding category causes "a drive to de-heroize literature--to create groups of heroes" ("The Problem of the Hero," 33-37). The question which Malory seems to be asking--and here he is playing the deconstructionist's role to the extreme--is just how much heterogeneity will the category subsume and therefore give truth to before it explodes! It is certain that we can never cease calling Lancelot the flower of knighthood, and yet he is guilty of almost every unknightly act imaginable: adultery, murder, lying, blasphemy, and treason.

As has been pointed out all along, tension and incoherence lie at the center of Le Morte Darthur, and thus it is important to note that Lancelot knows that the expansion of the category of the Good (knighthood equals the good life) has destroyed it, and hence he avoids the ascription of the Round Table's highest value whenever it is accorded to him. The healing of Sir Urry is a good example: "And ever sir Launcelote wepte, as he had bene a chylde that had been beatyn" (668). The simile connotes punishment or the de-ascription of value. One beats a child for wrong or improper acts, and yet all Lancelot did was to heal Sir Urry, something which could only be done by the greatest knight in the world. Lancelot seems to perceive a hollowness or perversion at the heart of his position as best knight. He weeps because he alone knows the absolute truth of his statement that Sir Urry was healed by God's miracle: "by the grete virtu and grace of The, but, Good Lorde, never of myselff" (668). And yet the structure of the explanation of reality persists in demanding that the background (God's miracle) ratifies the foreground (Lancelot's act and character). It is significant that Malory places "The Healing of Sir Urry" immediately after "The Knight of the Cart" in which

Lancelot calls upon God to witness a false oath (though technically true) and the murder of Meleagant. If God's miracle ratifies Lancelot's position as best knight, then the category of Knighthood must also include the actions of murder, adultery, and blasphemy. Lancelot alone perceives the discontinuity between the background and foreground. His penchant for fighting in disguise, refusing to identify himself, lying, adopting humiliating names ("Le Shyvalere Ill Mafeete") and giving equivocal answers to any personal questions suggests a profound desire to lose or deny his identity. As the flower of knighthood, Lancelot's career is the tragedy of medieval philosophic realism which is described by Huizinga as a tendency to forget "that all things would be absurd, if their meaning were exhausted in their function and their place in the phenomenal world" (Waning, 201). Lancelot is Malory's answer to the desire of his age to know fully what the Form of Knighthood includes, and certainly he means for us to see Lancelot as absurd when he appears at the Tournament of Surluse in "a maydyns garment" (410). And yet it is upon Lancelot that the whole Round Table depends to exhaust the Form of Knighthood and prove once and for all that humans are at least potentially capable of resolving all the political problems they face.

In the Morte, therefore, Malory is not trying to revive the ideals implicit in the fellowship of the Round Table; to the contrary, he has pushed those ideals to the furthest extreme so that the survival of the society is directly related to the ability of the knights to exhaust the Forms through their actions. If the empirical world were as elegantly coherent as the philosophical explanation of it, certainly the Round Table would have been a new Eden and never have fallen apart. The knights perform well enough, but Malory sees something implicitly tragic in the attempt to perfect the world by imitation of a Form or, in its fifteenth century manifestation, the attempt to explain the present by the past, to understand life in terms of its origin. Such an attempt produces absurd results and becomes, in fact, the source of great destructiveness. How many times are destructive and corrupt acts such as Tristram's senseless killing of Sir Darras' two sons justified because "all that ye ded was by fors of knyghthode, and that was the cause that I wolde nat put you to dethe"

(338)? That Malory is aware of the absurdity of historical redemptivism is apparent from his telling of the Quest for the Holy Grail. Malory's Galahad is the redeemed or perfect knight. If philosophic realism were successfully employed as a behavioral model, Galahad would be the result, surpassing even Lancelot his father. Arthur welcomes Galahad with these very telling words:

> Sir, ye be ryght wellcom, for ye shall meve many
> good knyghtes to the queste of the Sankgreall, and
> ye shall enchyve that many other knyghtes myght
> never brynge to an ende. (519)

By "enchyve," Arthur envisions the redemption of the Round Table. The movement of the Grail Quest, however, is away from the Round Table, as Arthur tragically discovers in his "all hole togydirs" speech. Percival and Galahad lead the knights away from the Round Table to regions that can not be recognized as earthly. No one returns with the Grail to the Round Table. Eventually--and herein lies the real failure of historical redemptivism--"hit [a hand from heaven] came ryght to the vessell and toke hit, and the speare, and so bare hit up to hevyn. And sythen was there never man so hardy to say that he hade seyne the Sankgreal" (607). Thus no tangible link exists any longer between the world of men and the heavens; the continuity between the individual and the Form has proved to be a false quest, one which no one will any longer claim. The past as ideal remains inaccessible and unrecoverable. In a world saturated with symbolism and Formalism, Malory is beginning to discover what Carl Jung phrases so well: "The individual is the only reality. The further we move away from the individual toward abstract ideas about Homo Sapiens, the more likely we are to fall into error. In these times of social upheaval and rapid change, it is desirable to know much more than we do about the individual human being, for so much depends upon his mental and moral qualities" (Man and His Symbols, 45).

Robert Snyder has demonstrated this point in reference to the opening reverdie of "The Most Piteous Tale of the Morte Arthur Saunz Guerdon." The climax of the tragedy begins with a passage that Malory did not find in his sources:

In May, whan every harte floryshyth and burgenyth (for, as the season ys lusty to beholde and comfortable, so man and woman rejoysyth and gladith of somer commynge with his freyshe floures, for wynter wyth hys rowghe wyndis and blastis causyth lusty men and women to cowre and to syt by fyres), so thys season hit befelle in the moneth of May a grete angur and unhappe that stynted nat tylle the floure of chyvalry of alle the world was destroyed and slayne. (673)

Synder observes that "The irony of this passage, original with Malory, stems from its inversion of an expected consonance between the macrocosm and microcosm. . . . Nature, the seasonal trope, is made to undercut itself, in effect to pronounce itself as a false assurance" ("Malory and 'Historical Adaptation,'" 136). This Spring men will not be rejuvenated along with the rest of nature. The fortune of human endeavors, therefore, does not correspond to the orderly (cyclic) progression that nature seems to follow. In fact no discernible governing principle is perceptible in the course of human history other than the simple "hit befelle." While Synder warns that we should "beware of imposing too modern a consciousness" on Malory's historical perceptions, that is, those of Schopenhauer, Spengler, or Toynbee, it is certainly reasonable to think of Malory in the tradition which produced the anti-medievalism and the anti-mythicism of Luther, Machiavelli, Montaigne, and Bacon-- all of whom lived within one hundred years of the writing of Le Morte Darthur.

The points I have been making so far all suggest the paradoxical or incoherent nature of the center or deep structure informing Malory's work. But in another sense and on another level, the surface, the Morte is highly structured and symmetrical. Larry Benson tells us that Malory is particularly fond of groups of four. There are the four best earthly knights--Lancelot, Tristram, Lamerok, and Palomides--who, according to Benson, are replaced by the four best celestial knights--Galahad, Percival, Bors, and Lancelot--who are finally replaced by the four remnant knights--Ector, Blamour, Bleoberis, and Bors (Malory's Morte Darthur, 32-35 and 108). Each group converges with the preceding group at a single point. Thus the celestial knights converge with the Round Table knights at the point or in the person of Lancelot; similarly Bors provides the continuity between the celestial and the remnant knights. The groups interpenetrate, but not fully. Lancelot's attempt as a member of the four best earthly knights to achieve the Grail Quest is ultimately unsuccessful. In the new domain he is not fully competent. Each group is hierarchically structured within, and externally, the top position of one group is the lowest position of the succeeding group with the celestial knights being the highest group. On the surface, the foreground, a high degree of order pervades the Morte. The end of "Sir Gareth of Orkney" gives us a clear picture of that order:

> So the fyrste day there justed sir Lameroke de Gelys, for he overthrewe thirty knyghtes and dud passyng mervelus dedis of armys. . . .

> Also the secunde day there justed sir Trystrams beste, and he overthrewe fourty knyghtes, and dud there mervelus dedis of armys. . . .

> Than the thirde day there justed sir Launcelot, and he overthrewe fyfty knyghtes and dud many dedis of armys, that all men wondird.   (225)

In addition, the career of each knight is developed as a response to the behavioral demands of a four-fold controlling explanatory system or Model: Knighthood, Governance, Love and Christianity. The historical ideal is itself four-fold, and just as the four best knights, these four categories of behavior also converge upon one another and interpenetrate or overlap in the sense that they completely fill up and exhaust the entire range of possibilities for noble or valuable human action. What primarily interests me in this study is how individuals respond to such cultural demands, but first we must determine what kind of demands these are. Carl Jung in his study Psychology and Religion points out that a four-fold symbol has usually been associated with God: "the four is an age-old, presumably pre-historic symbol, always associated with the idea of a world creating deity." "The four symbolize the parts, qualities, and aspects of the One" (71). Thus the culture itself replicates the religious experience, as it becomes the creative source of whatever identity an individual attains. Acting out the ideal on all levels purports to place one in contact with God. We shall see later that the fall of the Round Table results, not from excesses or immoral behavior, but from an attempt to be all inclusive, to be One, and respond to the demands of the system as if it were a compatible and coherent whole. Charles Moorman has written that as the Morte progresses the tension increases as a result of the increased frequency of plot connections, interactions of characters, and fulfillment of foreshadowings (The Book of Kyng Arthur, xxviii). I would add also that the increasing tension results from the increasing amounts of energy, both psychic and physical, required to keep the Round Table "all hole togydirs"; that is, increasing force is required to prove that the world of action is isomorphic with the Model in the face of not only conflicting instructions coming from an essentially disunified Model but also a world which is simply constructed of human diversity and desire. As we learn from physics, order requires inputs of energy.

Pairs, doubles, mirror analogs, and bracket tales also form part of the structural symmetry of Le Morte Darthur. Maureen Fries has already suggested that Mark and Arthur are inverse mirror analogs in which Arthur represents the maintenance of social order and explanation by the growth of justice and mercy while Mark represents precisely the opposite--brute force. My analysis will suggest that they are simply mirror analogs, that brute force is characteristic of both realms. The difference is rather that the Round Table presents a rationalized and sublimated form of force, while Mark acts directly and openly. Arthur's genuine love for Lancelot and the knights is matched by Mark's genuine need for Tristram and the knights, but they both are enforcers of the historical ideal and both finally destroy their knights. Even a superficial reading shows that ultimately there is no justice or mercy in the Morte; the past is unforgiving. But the doubling goes much further. Isode of the White Hands provides a double or a complement for La Belle Isode and offers Tristram an occasion to do everything related to love which he is not able to do with La Belle Isode--that is, marry her. Within the combination of the two Isodes, Tristram achieves a complete and conventional love-relationship, but in the reality of his life he must face a fragmented existence.

Lancelot is offered the same option in the two Elaines, the daughter of king Pelles and the "Fayre Maydyn of Astolat." Lancelot, however, proceeds very differently with the ladies than does Tristram; he rejects the opportunity for a love-relationship which is his own and unique and chooses to sustain his orientation toward the explanatory Center or court. Lancelot always acts to sustain the harmony of the four-fold explanatory system, while Tristram eventually seeks to resolve the tension and allow a new system to develop. His decision to marry Isode of the White Hands represents a significant negation, and Lancelot, characteristically, condemns him for it. Lancelot will never marry, not even Guinevere. And finally, Tristram and Lancelot mirror each other. There is no way of telling how many times Malory invites comparison between the two: "sir Trystrames ys called peerles and makeles of ony Crysten knyght, and of his myght and hardynes we know none so good a knyght but yf hit be sir Launcelot du Lake" (268).

From the point of view of Caxton and other revivalists, the structural symmetry reflects the age's, the perennial, desire for exemplification of a coherent and harmonious Model of the world, but it also suggests something else, something more important for us. The consensus of critical opinions agrees that Malory's work is in Mark Lambert's words "strikingly apsychological" (Style and Vision, 92). D. S. Brewer simply remarks, "Certainly, Malory was not interested in subtle analysis of courtly feeling, but it is fruitless to blame him for this" ("'the hoole book,'" 47). But the structural symmetry suggests, in fact, Malory's supreme interest in the analysis of psychological issues. Malory is a superb psychologist, and yet critics have been looking for the wrong kind of psychological interest. The study of emotions is not even very psychological, but if we consider the characters in the light of objective or behavioral psychology (i.e., not subjective or introspective) and psychoanalysis, they become profound psychological cases. T. C. Rumble suggested the objective approach, without perhaps even knowing it: "It is primarily actions that count; people are seen for what they are in terms of what they do, and their actions are allowed to stand silently symbolic of the causes which are constantly at work bringing about the ruin of the world" ("Development by Analogy," 147).

The final problem in critical approaches to Malory, then, is psychology. Since romance is the presentation of people in action, no criticism at all is possible without some theory of human behavior. All critics, before they can be anything else, are psychologists; psychology is "propaedeutic"--preparatory-- as S. S. Stevens says to the study of everything else. For Malory, we need to understand two radically different kinds of psychology. The first is the psychology of the unconscious or psychoanalysis. The world has always had rather elaborate and highly developed theories of the unconscious. It is interesting to note how much of Jung's own theories are derived from medieval topics and records, particularly alchemy, mysticism, and Catholicism. In medieval times the unconscious was recognized as soul, spirit, or for secular situations as eros or heart, as when Tristram sees himself as "harte-hole" (327). It is well accepted at all times that the heart has its own knowledge (albeit difficult to talk about) just as the brain or the rational faculty; only the knowledge of the heart is generally manifest in action or desire rather than discourse and logic. We need merely to observe what the characters of romance desire and do. The second kind of psychology is cognitive or rational psychology, the essential premise of which is that what men know about the world and hence what informs their behavior is a rational and social construct, an explanation, or a myth--all of which is perceived to be true, of course. Peter Berger and Thomas Luckmann, in The Social Construction of Reality, point out, "Humanness is a socio-cultural variable. In other words, there is no human nature in the sense of a biologically fixed substratum determining the variability of socio-cultural formations. . . . While it is possible to say that man has a nature, it is more significant to say that man constructs his own nature, or more simply, that man produces himself" (49).

This humanness is transmitted in social situations through normal interactive behavior, the core of which is a shared and increasing ability to decode the symbolic environment (a semiotic matrix) in a manner that enhances adaptation to the physical environment and the smooth interation with other members of the community. When this occurs one begins to feel fully human, he gains an identity. Analysis of this socially constructed humanness reveals two very useful theoretical substrata of the person: the individual and the self. The stimulus-response model of the behavioral psychologists exposes the dialectical relationship of the substrata. Consistency of response to stimuli or situations (i.e. social order) occurs as individuals gain proficiency in abandoning random responses to stimuli and limiting themselves to only the socially legitimated response. Social order demands that individuals perform roles, acquire selfhood. These roles are maintained by redundancy of experience and positive reinforcement, as the ascription of "worship" and the highly repetitive nature of any romance makes clear. Humanness is created, controlled, and conventional but never complete. The self, therefore, is not really the individual, as George Herbert Mead argues, but rather the self is a construct of social roles, something learned or acquired in the process of action and reaction within an environment of others (Mind, Self, and Society, 200-01).

The individual, on the other hand, can be seen in the judgment that exists between the stimulus and response, not the sort of conscious rational judgment that leads the knights to conventional choices and socially legitimated careers, but rather the element of randomness, stubbornness, refusal to participate, and all that is anti-cultural or deviant, as Lancelot's perception of the hollowness of his acts shows. He responds or acts conventionally; nonetheless, he feels or judges that his acts are not working at providing a stable or healthy society or identity. This is not deep reflection or introspection. Palomides is the only character who operates on that incredibly high mental level, and he does it because he has a vantage point, outside of the Model; he is a pagan, and he approaches the Round Table and its behavioral demands from a conscious and analytical perspective. Rather, what I am calling the individual and judgment represents the source of random (i.e. non-conventional) responses to stimuli and hence the origin of innovative behavior. Sometimes in the romance it will appear as simply a "gap" between socially constructed humanness and the needs of the human for survival in the world. This is frequently Dynadan's case. In other words, the individual judges that the socially offered role does not suit his own and unique needs but rather only those of the institution. In the present context, the individual is a random and unaccountable entity but something with great yet unspecific desire.

In Malory, the socially presented self comes to be seen in contrast to the individual; as mentioned earlier, identity results from the synthesis of the individual with some creative source, in the case of Malory's knights, the explanatory Model with its ability to offer roles or selves to the knights. Thus identity is constituted from the individual and the self, and it exists within the tension of a dialectic, an inherently unstable from. The great goal of humankind has always been to construct social situations so that the tension of the dialectic results in an equilibrium and the greatest possible personal and social stability. In Malory, however, the tension only increases; he presents a failing civilization, whose tragedy raises the issue of which substratum of humanness will motivate the course of human history. In psychological terms, the tragedy results from the culture's demand that the knights deny or repress absolutely their individuality. His romance as tragedy discovers, as we shall see, what Norman O. Brown has found in his Life Against Death: "The riddle of History is not in Reason but in Desire; not in labor, but in love . . . repressed Eros is the energy of history" (16-17). Le Morte Darthur looks forward to the mythologization of the individual that has characterized the modern world.

Malory's psychological interest, then, centers upon what we call today identity construction and identity crisis. He presents all phases of identity from the very healthy and stable Gareth, to the failure of Palomides, to the psychotic and destructive Lancelot. This approach looks for patterned responses or actions in similar situations. For example, beginning with R. M. Wilson's studies of Malory's characters, it has become customary to speak of Malory's characters as stylized, but it has not been pointed out that such stylization is entirely in character with medieval philosophic realism and Catholicism, which in the Middle Ages increasingly defined virtuous behavior in terms of universals and transcendental principles rather than pragmatic goods, as Huizinga has remarked: "The [medieval] mind is not in search of individual realities, but models, examples, norms" (Waning, 216). From the standpoint of social cohesion and the isomorphism of personal and social fulfillment, nothing could be more inappropriate than characters concerned with their own, unique interests and problems. Wilson is correct when he writes that "Minor peculiarities, such as Gareth's size and Gawain's taste for apples and pears, are unimportant rarities" (Characterization, 120)--unimportant, except in that these rarities as manifestions of the randomness of the individual eventually undermine the Model in that they cannot be accounted for, predicted, or subsumed.

It might be charged that modern psychoanalysis and sociology are irrelevant to literature written more than five-hundred years ago--as D. W. Robertson does so thoroughly in his Preface to Chaucer--but, as suggested earlier, what the modern analyst sees in his patients is exactly the same as what the romance writer sees in his knights. The problems facing humans as social beings have always been much the same. We now have more problems and more complex ways of addressing those problems--that is, sophisticated tools which in themselves can be problems--but the fundamental issues are not very different in kind from those that faced the men of the Middle Ages or Ancient World. As Tamotsu Shibutani, a social interactionist, writes, "Human beings are neither creatures of impulse nor heedless victims of external stimuli; they are active organisms who guide and construct their line of action while consciously coming to terms with the demands of an ever changing world as they interpret it" (Human Behavior, vi). There is simply no reason to suspect that they have not always been so. Our task as analysts of human nature in what ever conditions it is observed--romance literature or the couch--is to discover what the line of action is and what goals it is directed toward. This task of ours just turns out, as most of Malory's critics have seen, to be the theme of the "Tale of Sir Gareth," but it also underlies the careers of the greater knights: Tristram, Lancelot, Palomides, and Lamerok. The sum of individuals constructing their lives out of lines of action is what constitutes society--a paradoxical construct since while society is fully human produced, no one experiences it subjectively. Berger and Luckmann explain it this way:

An institutional world, then, is experienced as an objective reality. It has a history that antedates the individual's birth and is not accessible to his biographical recollection. It was there before he was born, and it will be there after his death. . . .

> The institutions are there, external to him, persistent in their reality whether he likes it or not. He cannot wish them away. . . . Since institutions exist as external reality, the individual cannot understand them by introspection. He must "go out" and learn about them [i.e. the quest], just as he must learn about nature." (Social Construction of Reality, 60)

What primarily interests me in the chapters that follow is an analysis of the knights as they experience and respond to the objective reality of the Round Table they have created. We are confronted in Malory with the situation in which these lives, these quests, and these lines of action lead to destruction and death; our task is to discover why.

A very clear example of the correspondence between the aims of the modern analyst and the aims of medieval philosophy is a comparison between the basic assumptions of Marsilius of Padua, a theologian and political philosopher of the fourteenth century, and Alfred Adler, an associate of Freud and later the head of his own branch of psychoanalysis centering around ego psychology. The important point of these aims is just how commonplace they are, and yet how many literary critics ignore them in studying medieval literature. In the Defensor Pacis Marsilius writes:

> Let us therefore lay this down as the principle of all things which are to be demonstrated here in this treatise, a principle naturally held, believed, and freely granted by all: that all men not deformed or otherwise impeded naturally desire a sufficient life, and avoid and flee what is harmful thereto. This has been acknowledged not only with regard to man but also with regard to every genus of animals, according to Tully in his treatise On Duties, Book I, Chapter III, where he says: 'It is an original endowment of which nature has bestowed upon every genus of livng things, that it preserves itself, its body and its life, that it avoids those things which seem harmful, and that it seeks and obtains all those things which are necessary for living.' (12)

This sounds a great deal like Freud's Pleasure Principle or Eros, an underlying principle in organisms which guides the construction of a line of action and thus a life. As the comment from Norman O. Brown, cited a moment ago, asserts, desire motivates history. This is a basic assumption of psychoanalysis, as in Herbert Marcuse's Eros and Civilization, but it is just as fundamental in the writings of, for example, St. Augustine. Marsilius' Defensor Pacis examines the ways in which the basic human impulse is frustrated by society much in the way Freud treats repression, neurosis, and sublimation. But while Freud is more interested in the negative influence of society upon the individual--and this focus makes him useful for understanding Tristram, Palomides, and Lancelot--Marsilius is more concerned with the positive role of society in helping men achieve the sufficient life and thus healthy identities. We note only a difference in "up-period" and "down-period" orientations. For Adler, who broke with Freud over just this emphasis, the individual is guided by a constructive "I wish to be a complete man" (Neurotic Constitution, ix). Adler sees the human condition as itself a neurosis: "To be a human being means the possession of a feeling of inferiority that is constantly pressing on toward its own conquest" (Social Interest, 73). What Adler describes is precisely the desire for a sufficient or meaningful life and it is, above all else, the central motif of Arthurian Romance. We see it clearly in Palomides, whom Isode calls "this unhappy Sarezen" (267), Gareth, and La Cote Male Tayle, but it is also the quest of the great knights: Tristram and Lancelot. The problem for the great knights is that they have achieved the sufficient life in the society's highest identity, and yet it does not work very well in sustaining their lives and resolving the neurosis.

Malory's interests are best seen in the light of psychoanalysis and sociology--whether modern or medieval--for in his romance he shows the normal desires of normal men to achieve happiness and maturity, and the unhappiness, frustration, and psychosis that can occur when the goals presently existing in the society require of the knight a degree of self-abnegation which makes the feeling of fulfillment impossible and rather reinforces the feeling of inferiority and insufficiency. After all, the complete man or knight is a culturally determined identity or goal--"the guiding fiction in every neurosis, claiming higher reality values than even the normal [i.e. personal] psyche," Adler says--toward which one's actions might aim; it is not, as Palomides' Questing Beast is, a personal adventure. At this point the objectively experienced society becomes the enemy of the individual in that it demands repression of impulses toward pleasure and happiness which are individual or deviant rather than orthodox and conventional. Many medieval scholars refuse to see such a tension in the Middle Ages and look to St. Augustines' resolution of his own psychosis and the City of God as evidence for the essential harmony of goals in individuals and society, but it was such theories as St. Augustine's which required the repression of the individual's erotic energy in favor of the higher unity and harmony, as the Confessions makes clear, and it was against such repressive controls that the writers of courtly and Arthurian romance so strongly reacted. St. Augustine defined the basis of sin as "cupidity," a love of oneself or the things of the world for their own sake. The writers of courtly love and Arthurian romance present to us St. Augustine's greatest sin, but the context of the romances shows it to be the greatest good, precisely because sin becomes, in the view of the writers of medieval romance, the only possible area of human behavior where one can continue the innovation required to pursue truly the quest for the sufficient life.

For the knights, all experience and individuality must be justified and validated by the ideolgy of the Round Table society, its mental model of the real world. The Model, because it gains as all models do its authority by claiming to represent an immutable human nature and world, remains static and demands only a repetition of the acts which brought it into being. Failure in repetition is a failure in identity, and yet how often is the repetition absurd and destructive. The perception on the part of individuals that the actions sanctioned by the Model are not good should lead to negation and innovation. When it does not, as Lancelot refuses to do, the Model is held together by pure force and tragedy follows. The tension builds to a point when the Model simply explodes, and the members turn upon their creator and kill it and then each other in the most horrible and chaotic anarchy. That Malory is aware of this pattern is apparent in the dream of Sir Bors which encapsulates the story of the Round Table from beginning to end:

> Ryght so furthwythall he sawe a dragon in the
> courte, passynge parelous and orryble, and there
> semyd to hym that there were lettyrs off golde
> wryttyn in hys forhede, and sir Bors thought that
> the lettyrs made a sygnyficacion of `knyge Arthure'.
> And ryght so there cam an orryble lybarde and an
> olde, and there they fought longe and ded grete
> batayle togydyrs. And at the laste the dragon
> spytte oute of hys mowthe as hit had bene a hondred
> dragons; and lyghtly all the smale drgons slew the
> olde dragon and tore him to pecys. (484)

The destruction of the Model will come from within the Model, from incoherencies never perceived within its purview but which arise in the individual selves it had created.

The case I am making for the interpretation of Malory's Le Morte Darthur is that Malory as a man living in the last stages of the Middle Ages perceived that the ideological structure of his age was no longer able to make life meaningful in the full and far-reaching sense of the term. Huizinga tells us that the tendency of the Middle Ages to transform ideals to entities had the effect of giving a rigidity both to its conceptions of the world and to the sorts of behaviors that were validated (Waning, 214). By the middle of the fifteenth century social conditions had changed so much that a revival of Chivalry or the old values was indeed an historically existing movement. Malory, however, is not didactic but analytic, and he sees that the failure of any ideology to change necessitates tragedy. Therefore in contrast to Brewer, Benson, Kennedy, and others, Le Morte Darthur must be seen, not as the portrayal of a golden age or of a "well-nigh perfect civilization," but rather as the portrayal of golden men and women trapped in a age of lead. I think finally that we can account for the perplexities of both Lewis and Vinaver about the sustained admiration Malory shows for his characters in the recognition that it is the system which fails, not the knights. What Malory presents, finally, is what William James has called the "Nightmare view of life" whose "great reflective source has at all times been the contradiction between the phenomena of nature and the craving of the heart to believe that behind nature there is a spirit whose expression nature is. . . .   What result can there be but inner discord and contradiction" (Will to Believe, 40).   Malory's is a grim recognition, for well he knows of the cravings.   To those cravings, we now turn.

`Now God have mercy on hir soule!´ seyde sir Percyvale. "Hit sore forthykith me; but all we must change the lyff. Now, fayre awnte, what ys that knyght? I deme hit be he that bare the red armys on Whytsonday.´

`Wyte you well,´ seyde she, `that this ye he, for othirwyse ought he nat to do but to go in rede armys. And that same knyght hath no peere for worchith all by myracle, and he shall never be overcom of none erthly mannys hande.

`Also Merlyon made the Rounde Table in tokenyng of rowndnes of the worlde, for men sholde by the Rounde Table undirstonde the rowndenes signyfyed by ryght. For all the worlde, crystenyd and hethyn, repayryth unto the Rounde Table, and whan they ar chosyn to be of the felyshyp of the Rounde Table they thynke hemselff more blessed and more in worship than they had gotyn halff the worlde.

`And ye have sene that they have loste hir fadirs and his modirs and all hir kynne, and hir wyves and hir chyldren, for to be of youre felyship. Hit ys well seyne be you, for synes ye departed from your modir ye wolde never se her, ye founde such felyship at the Table Rounde.

`Whan Merlyon had ordayned the Rounde Table he seyde, "By them whych sholde be felowys of the Rounde Table the trouth of the Sankegreall shold be well knowyn." And men asked hym how they myght know them that sholde best do and to encheve the Sankgreall. Than he seyde, "There sholde be three whyght bullis sholde encheve hit, and the two sholde be maydyns and the thirde sholde be chaste. And one of thos three shold passe hys fadir as much as the lyon passith the lybarde, both of strength and of hardines.´

--The Queen of the West Lands
to Sir Percival

2.

The Meaning of Meaningful
or the Quest Without End

2.1 Explanation and Action

Before even beginning a chapter which purports to discuss the meaning of "meaningful," it must be acknowledged that while the term and concept are grossly abused in popular discourse, we cannot, as historians of human endeavors, do without them. It is not, moreover, only the twentieth century which is beset with Man's Search for Meaning--to borrow a title from Victor Frankl--but it is mankind. Human beings, if we think about it, cannot possibly exist or merely act in the naive manner of the animals; they must know or simply feel that behind their acts lies some cogent reason which insures that the actions are real (whatever that is); their lives must relate to something, mean something. Humans must risk James' nightmare. Talcott Parsons predicates his Evolution of Societies upon the point that human behavior is inescapably meaningful (4-5), that human acts are purposive beyond the mere needs of survival; they attempt to recreate on the plane of human action some perceived deeper level of reality. The merely physical world is taken as symbolic of something ontologically prior. This point is attested to even by such radical empiricists as William James, who writes: "It is as if there were in the human consciousness a sense of reality, a feeling of objective presence, a perception of what we may call

`something there,´ more deep and more general than any of the
special and particular `senses´ by which the current psychology
supposes existent realities to be originally revealed" (Varieties
of Religious Experience, 61). Or from another point of view,
Carl Jung observes, "The fact is that certain ideas exist almost
everywhere and at all times and they can even spontaneously
create themselves quite apart from migration and tradition.
They are not made by the individual, but rather they happen--
they force themselves upon the individual´s consciousness. This
is not Platonic philosophy but empirical psychology" (Psychology
and Religion, 4).

   The purpose of this chapter, then, is not to propose a
"meaning" or a content for the meaningful; such a task would be
as misguided as it would be fruitless. Rather in the recognition
of the fundamentally religious structure of human action (re +
ligare, to bind back to origin), we can discover something
important about both the creation of the Round Table as an
institution and its collapse. We are always searching for
meaning, but meaning is nothing in itself as an a priori Divine
providence, even though this is inevitably the way it is both
experienced and described. Hypostatizations or even
conceptualizations of meaning always lack meaning in the full
sense of the term. To the contrary, meaning is in the doing,
and yet such action is inevitably creative of institutions which,
as pointed out earlier, attain an ontological status independent
of the individuals who created them, as the Round Table comes
to be. The philosophers of this group, moreover, are always
engaged in the act of defining meaning or in the creating of
knowledge about the institution in an attempt to gain a more
certain access to meaning, to discover its content, and thereby
promote optimal behaviors in individuals. The result of this
sort of activity is social order. Peter Berger and Thomas
Luckmann, in The Social Construction of Reality demonstrate
that

> Social order is not part of `the nature of things,´ and
> it cannot be derived from the `laws of nature.´
> Social order exists only as a product of human
> activity. No other ontological status may be
> ascribed to it without hopelessly obfuscating its
> empirical manifestations. Both in its genesis (social

order is the result of past human activity) and its existence in any instant of time (social order exists only and insofar as human activity continues to produce it) it is a human product. (52)

What interests me is the paradox at the base of the development of the Round Table and all social institutions. They are fully human created but experienced as objective and a priori, as Jung's comment asserts; that is, while the actions of the knights are ineluctably creative, they perceive their own actions as merely responsive or adherent to an a priori providence or institutional policy. Strictly speaking, the Round Table exists only in the consciousness of the knights, but as James finds in The Varieties of Religious Experience, "All our attitudes, moral, practical, or emotional, as well as religious, are due to the 'objects' of our consciousness, the things which we believe to exist . . . they elicit from us a reaction; and the reaction due to things of thought is notoriously in many cases as strong as that due to sensitive presences. It may even be stronger" (58). Thus in our analysis of Le Morte Darthur we observe a continuum of reactions to prior actions that have created what the knights are conscious of as real; the continued reactions further create the social order, and yet the overall direction of this creation is tragic and destructive. Malory seems to see political life and the historico-religious nature of any institution as inherently tragic, and we need to understand why. How can it be that acts which at the outset of Malory's Le Morte Darthur were perfectly meaningful and productive of healthy individuals and society become by the end meaningless and destructive. The tension which the last chapter noted at the center of Le Morte Darthur can now be seen as an antinomy of forces within any institution. What I am working up to is an assertion that the creation of order itself in institutions that attain an objective relation to their human creators is a process that destroys the human lives of those creators. Karl Marx called it alienation. Berger and Luckmann phrase it this way: "Reification implies that man is capable of forgetting his own authorship of the human world. . . . The reified world is, by definition, a dehumanized world. It is experienced by man as a strange facticity. . . . That is, man is capable paradoxically of producing a reality that denies him"

(89). This, it seems to me, is what happens to the Round Table. It is also Tennyson's view, who in The Passing of Arthur has Arthur finally understand that "I perish by this people which I made."

Before going any further, it is necessary to establish certain distinctions about the meaningful which make the creation of institutions its result. The first distinction is that the category of the meaningful is empty; the world itself is indeterminate and open to human acts and desires. The second distinction concerns the product or the effect of meaningful acts. So far these effects have been called a healthy society (i.e. smooth interaction of the members) and healthy individuals. This chapter will attempt to make those terms more clear, for it is apparent everywhere that when acts are meaningful a mysterious joy--wholly extrinsic to the act itself--overwhelms the actor. For example, in the unlikely context of metaphysics, we find: "in the realm of metaphysical abstraction, there is light and vision--the light and vision which comes with that rush of understanding, that burst of insight, in which one knows and realizes, with sudden vivid intellectual joy, that being belongs intrinsically to all that is and to each and every thing analogically, that is, in proportion to its nature" (Phelan, 8). This is a special kind of joy. Its structure suggests a participation in what the actor believes is the ultimate level of reality. The same kind of joy is to be found wherever the term meaningful is appropriate, regardless of the content of the reality. Another seemingly contrary instance, for example, is Albert Camus who discovers that being does not belong intrinsically to all and yet finds the same joy: "One does not discover the absurd without being tempted to write a manual of happiness. . . . All Sisyphus' joy is contained therein [futile sufferings]. His rock is his thing . . . . The absurd man says yes and his effort will henceforth be unceasing" (Myth of Sisyphus, 90-91). The joy here is the same as the metaphysician's, and we would call these meaningful actions or moments. This joy is properly the perception of self-value, the perception that a creative source apart from man freely and inexplicably affirms the value of the individual's acts and now becomes a part of himself. Self-value becomes the core of identity and humanness, it makes further action possible and desirable, and such identities become the heart of society.

The feeling of self-value will be of utmost importance to this analysis of Malory because of his concern for "worship" and because, as the Queen of the West Lands makes so clear, "whan they ar chosyn to be of the felyshyp of the Rounde Table they thynke hemselff more blessed and more in worship than they had gotyn halff the worlde" (541). Hereafter I will refer to it as the "feeling of the numinous," borrowing the term from Rudolf Otto's The Idea of the Holy. The religious context is appropriate because we are dealing with the individual and a source which he feels related to as his creator or origin; that is, we are concerned with the psychology of homo religiosus. By "numinous" Otto means the category of the "wholly other," the divine, or whatever is completely beyond any and all rational concepts of the good, the moral, or the holy. It is, as Otto refers to it, simply a category, empty insofar as the reason would perceive it, but accessible through acts. The individual thus experiences himself as a victim of the numen, and the feeling of the numinous occurs when his acts place him in direct contact with the category: "there must be felt a something 'numinous', something bearing the character of a 'numen' to which the mind turns spontaneously; or (which is the same thing in other words) these feelings can only arise in the mind as accompanying emotions when the category of 'the numinous' is called into play. The numinous is thus felt as objective and outside the self" (11). The original Latin term numen suggests a spirit or divinity which inhabits a worldly object or individual. There is no need to restrict the spirit to the presence of God since whatever is mysterious, unknowble, or wholly other, and beyond man is interpreted as spirit. Certainly "worship" refers to this sort of secular spirit. We can even refer to the spirit or the ethos of the Round Table or knighthood which motivates an individual knight. Otto's category of the numen is an outgrowth of G. W. F. Hegel's Absolute Spirit as developed in the Phenomenology of the Spirit. The Absolute Spirit would perhaps be a better term here and for Otto, but in discussions of this kind where we are concerned with the construction of a particular reality--the Round Table--it is necessary to avoid all of the content which has been ascribed to the Absolute by philosophers since Hegel. Certainly Otto wants to avoid the content. We are interested in the actions by which men project themselves against an empty category, and therefore the relatively free and connotationless term numen seems right.   Thus men are seldom trying to be moral, noble, or whatever other rational system might be attributed to human behavior; they are, rather, seeking the feeling of self-value from the deepest possible source of it. Since, as Otto makes clear, the feeling of the numinous is itself unexplainable but experienced when certain conditions are fulfilled, homo religiosus inevitably believes that the connection of the feeling with certain acts discloses the numinous object. In this way, the numinal becomes the deeper underlying reason for habitual action or patterened responses to the physical environment and thus the origin institutions and knowledge.

The third distinction in the meaningful is the dualistic, synthetic, or symbiotic structure of it.   The relationship has been called one of creator to created, and indeed Otto considers the feeling of the numinous to grow out of "creature-consciousness or creature-feeling": "It is the emotion of a creature, submerged and overwhelmed by its own nothingness in contrast to what is supreme above all creatures . . . an overpowering, absolute might of some kind" (10).   The character of the symbiosis follows the mystical formula that the way up is the way down, that the way to self-value is through loss of individuality.   In the examples cited above, the metaphysician has his being, he is the creature of being; while Sisyphus is the creature of his rock.   The structure is always the same.   The individual by himself is nothing; he becomes something only in the experience of being created by the mysterious category of the numen.   It will be charged that I am invoking Jean-Paul Sartre's formula about existence preceding essence, and yet if we consider Gareth who appears at the Round Table as a "no-man" and only becomes Sir Gareth as a result of certain actions and experiences, Sartre's formula is quite appropriate.   Gareth's actions transform or re-create him from the meaningless "Beaumains" to the meaningful Sir Gareth. The condition of being Beaumains is pain, subjection, and valuelessness: "thus he was putt into the kychyn and lay nyghtly as the kychen boyes dede" (179).   Upon arriving at the Round Table, Gareth requests three gifts: food, lodging for a year, and when the year is up he asks to be allowed to undertake a certain adventure or quest.   The first two requests fulfill simple animal needs; the third will initiate a process through which he will attain humanness. One becomes human only by relating himself to the transhuman plane (see section 2.2 for a full discussion of Gareth).

The pattern of Gareth's initiation suggests what Mircea Eliade has called a movement from profane to sacred time and space: "an object or an act [or an individual] becomes real only insofar as it imitates or repeats the archetype. Thus reality is acquired solely through repetition or participation; everything which lacks an exemplary model is 'meaningless'; i. e., it lacks reality" (Eternal Return, 34). Or in The Sacred and the Profane : "Religious man wishes to be other than he is on the plane of his profane experience. Religious man is not given; he makes himself. . . . One becomes truly a man only be conforming to the teaching of the myths, that is, by imitating the Gods" (100). Thus it is Gareth's acts which create him, but those acts are not merely any acts. They have the creative power to give Gareth identity and humanness because they are, as Eliade puts it, ab origine. These acts comprise the original set of acts which as history shows were responsible for the creation of the Round Table society. They were acts which got the necessary work done; that is, they extended the original knights' domination of their environment. Successful repetition of these aboriginal acts constitutes the conditions under which Gareth will experience the numinous which confirms the value of his identity as knight of the Round Table. In this way, each knight believes that the Round Table and the set of acts of which it is composed are called out and ordained by God--an absolute might of some kind. The Queen of the West Lands can say that the knights are "blessed" when they join the Round Table because, as the structure shows, the institution itself--as all institutions do in the minds of their members--resides in "sacred space" as opposed to profane or meaningless space.

As institution, the Round Table consists of defining and creating acts, the acts which at the outset were responsible for bringing the society itself into being. For the knight, the general character of such acts is the quest for order and the battle against enemy forces. Repeating such acts creates the identity of the individual and also sustains the creative source as creator; that is, by repeating the aboriginal acts one creates the institution. The initial quests are quests for order because the knights are learning to bring the great variety of actions they might do under social control.   (I return to this point in greater detail in 2.2.)   Institutions emerge as individuals give up their plurality of interests and work toward the attainment of common or shared goals; in this case, those of Arthur and Merlin.   The knight begins to think, "this is what I ought to be doing."   His acts come to be seen as typical, and that is all any institution is: a collection of typical or normative ways of behaving together with the power of legitimation and enforcement.   In this way the numen is filled in with content, and it is tacitly assumed that these acts and no others are called out by the Divine.   When the symbiosis works and the feeling of the numinous results, we say that life is fraught with meaning.   The act of the numen in creating men is the same act as men creating the numen; that is, men filling out an empty category with specific schemes and codes designed to produce the feeling of self-value and meaning.   Any knight may say to himself: the world makes sense through me.   There obtains a unity of history and biography.

A crucial insight of Karl Marx is that human knowledge grows out of human activity or labor.   The process of the institutionalization of human action is inherently one of narrowing or limiting behavior: certain acts will be rewarded with worship--gain legitimacy--and certain others will not. Institutionalization always involves the reduction of randomness in behavior, and it is precisely this production of a higher level of order which makes knowledge possible at all.   From a behavioral standpoint, knowledge is the process of signification, the production of signs which represent kinds or types of things. Lancelot's knowledge that Guinevere "ys a trew lady untyll her lorde" is not the fact of Guinevere's behavior but rather Lancelot's way of signifying what he knows about her behavior to himself and others--that is, what type or category of women she belongs to.   His knowledge is of the type, not of the woman Guinevere.   This is essentially the understanding of St. Augustine in On Christian Doctrine, a seminal work for medieval conceptions of knowledge and of the interpretation of signs made by others.   In that treatise, he writes, "All doctrine concerns either things or signs, but things are learned by signs. Strictly speaking, I have here called a thing that which is not used to signify something else, like wood, stone, cattle, and so on. . . .   From this may be understood what we call signs; they are things used to signify something" (8, emphasis mine).

All signs are categorial. The verbal signifier "trew lady" subsumes a vast variety of different individuals and actions into a single category of true ladies. As Jerome Bruner points out in A Study of Thinking, categorizing is behaviorally a response to "discriminably different things as the same kind of thing, or as amounting to the same thing" (4). St Thomas points to categorizing as the fundamental act of the reason: "For it is distinctive of reason to disperse itself in consideration of many things, and then to gather one simple truth from them" (Division, 63). Cognitively, the category comes to signify not the range of discriminable differences, not the richness and variety of life, but precisely the opposite: only the essential property that all members of the category hold in common. A tendency to move upward toward categorial simplicity and universality pervades institutional thought, what I call synthetic thinking as a cultural movement. St. Thomas is, again, in The Division and Methods of the Sciences very clear on this point: "the ultimate end of analysis in this process [categorization or abstraction] is attainment of the highest and most simple causes . . . because what is more universal is more simple. Now that which is most universal is common to all beings; and so the ultimate end of analysis in this process is the consideration of being and the properties of being as being" (64).

This is a point of utmost importance, as will be seen at the end of this chapter, for it explains why Lancelot's empirically false statement and his insistence upon it even to the extent of war embodies the tragedy of political life. The development of knowledge within an institution--what will be termed ideology in a moment--proceeds by destroying information. The signifier "true lady" contains far less information than does the woman Guinevere herself standing before Lancelot and Gawain. The cultural problem posed by Malory is which of these two phenomena--"trew lady" or Guinevere--should one's behavior be a response to. Social order requires that people respond not to individual realities with all their variety but only to the category or the type of situation. St. Thomas himself says that we should understand particular cases by reasoning downward from universal principles and the categories of the mind. Obviously, Lancelot with his enduring orientation toward the center of the institution responds to the category "trew lady" and not Guinevere, for simultaneous with the growth of categories is the development of value ascriptions and behavioral imperatives. The category "true lady" produces order among all ladies who exist and because it creates order it calls out the feeling of the numinous and is itself, therefore, subsumed by a higher level abstraction "the Good." A considerable bias within the ideology of the Morte and medieval culture stipulates that the higher the universal the more good it contains. St. Thomas´ "being" terminates the explanatory and valuational regress for created things. These values, however, are based only upon the essential or formal property of the category itself. Thus anything else Guinevere may be besides a true lady is irrelevant; she will always possess the essential property of a true lady--she helped create the category of true ladies. Knowledge, the production of signs, is the mechanism by which institutions arise and, of course, it presents the learned man with certain explanatory and behavioral powers not possible for the unlearned. Only in language (the primary mode of knowledge) is it possible to generalize or to collect actions into typologies and thus to choose optimal behaviors in situations that can be recognized as of a certain type or to predict the behavior of others. In language, also, these can be passed to a younger generation of knights more efficiently than would be possible without knowledge. Palomides is especially shrewed at this and may be the most astute man of the romance: "`Nay,´ seyde sir Palomydes, `I woll nat juste, for I am sure at justynge I gete no pryce" (370). Knowledge, however, serves the ends of the institution as a reified entity; its province is compliance and legitimation, and therefore while it may enhance the attainment of certain goals it does so at the expense of the great variety of goals that may be required in emergent situations. Analogus to the principle of the inherent loss of information in the reasoning process, is the growth of narrowness in institutions. We can see how this works by considering, for a moment, perception. Ulrich Neisser asks the question: "The information in any real situation is indefinitely rich. There is always more to see than anyone sees, and more to know than anyone knows. Why don´t we see it?" The answer is that individuals do not perceive the vast amount of data of any situation because they are not equipped to do it.

The knights--and everyone else--are trained to think categorically. Categories point to only the data which is relevant to their formal constitution; the rest of the world is filtered out. As Neisser puts it in Cognition and Reality, "Selection [of information] is a positive process, not a negative one. Perceivers pick up only what they have schemata [i.e. categories] for, and willy-nilly ignore the rest" (79-80).

The thinking of the knights, moreover, follows an explanatory hierarchy, a regress to ever more general and all inclusive categories, each of which legitimizes those beneath it and all of which terminate in God. A typical process of thought might be this: an act is legitimized because it is done for the sake of knighthood; knighthood is legitimized because it is practiced for the sake of the Round Table; the Round Table is legitimized because it exists for the sake of the Good; the Good, finally, exists for the sake of God; therefore, God's will must be in this act. The tragedy implicit here is that as one moves higher and higher along the explanatory regress, more and more information about the empirical world is filtered out and, in fact, destroyed, thus making men less and less able to face adequately the problems of their daily lives which originate in random, un-categorized details. They may perform exceedingly well in legitimized behavior--as is Lancelot's case--but those acts are really useless in resolving the problems that are causing real social tensions. They simply do not have the mental ability to isolate aspects of the environment that cause problems. The more fully one is socialized, the less he is able to perceive the rich variety of the world. Lancelot, as the "floure of knyghthode," can only see "trew lady" when he looks at Guinevere; he cannot see a great many other things she is as well--things that he would have to see to avoid the tragedy.

The terminology being used so far is, although precise, highly abstract. Abstraction is necessary and appropriate, however, because we are concerned with things which do not themselves exist. There are no numina that we will ever know anything about--St. Thomas even admits this, "God is beyond the comprehension of every created intellect" (Division, 65). There are only humans and actions and the social products of these--institutions which have no ontological status of their own but are some "thing" nonetheless which people respond to. The category of the numen is only a useful term for observing the origin and structure of human institutions. The category of the numen enables us to talk about early legitimations that are felt rather than rationalized, the difference that one can see in the socialization of, say, the Confessions of St. Augustine and the Summa Theologica of St. Thomas Aquinas. Early in his career, St. Thomas found it necessary to write something called The Divisions and Methods of the Sciences; St. Augustine, as we shall see in section 2.3, required no such conceptual or rational frame for legitimzing his behavior. Malory depicts the thrust of late medieval culture as a search for meaning in earnest; that is, an attempt to articulate fully a rational structure of culture as if it were derived from a facticity with certain properties and not an ineffable category. The primary difference between St. Augustine and St. Thomas (which is also an important difference between the early and late Middle Ages) is that St. Augustine is truly responding to an experience of the numen and he creates order from that; St. Thomas responds to the institution and he articulates meaning--he does not create it. This difference is crucial, for it also defines the turning point in the Morte, when in its development the Round Table ceases to be a creative activity of a group of knights and becomes a reified institutiion to which the behaviors and values of individual knights must conform.

Reification means that the numen and therefore the derivative institution exist objectively with fixed properties. These properties are asserted to be universal for all members; the ineffable numen is replaced by categories of the mind. The inteilectual process of legitimation replaces creative work; one now knows the value of his acts by determining which category will subsume the act. The question of what to do with one's time is answered by making deductions from the properties, as if those mere attributes were, in fact, true and universal characteristics of the numen. They must be true, so the reasoning goes, since we are what we are today because of some ontologically or historically prior cause. At this point, it is possible to observe a crisis in culture. All institutions reach a point of maturity when the nature of institutional behavior changes from active participation and creation to maintenance. The problem of existence is no longer creation of order but compliance with the established order. This is the point at which the group is no longer engaged in constant modifications of behavior in response to the environment but now responds to the institution as reified entity. The Tournament replaces the battle. Charles Warriner points out in "Groups Are Real" that institutions often have interests that cannot be traced to the private interests of any of the individual members. The "group" exists and develops on its own and yet commands certain behaviors. This split in culture--precisely the one alluded to by Gottfried von Strassburg--means that the institution now develops on a course independent from the private and pluralistic interests of the members. The institution's growth is taken over by professional philosophers and politicians who guide it according to principles of thought, logic, and the conceptualized original intent of the institution itself. There emerges a separation of knowledge and action, and the important, still creative people of the world, are seen as deviant and suppressed.

This brings us to ideology. In his important work, Ideology and Utopia, Karl Mannheim defines ideology as the socialization of knowledge; that is, ideology names man's perennial belief that his social institutions are isomorphic with the entire world--as the Queen of the West Lands so clearly points out, "Merlyon made the Rounde Table in tokenyng of rowndnes of the worlde, for men sholde by the Rounde Table undirstonde the rowndenes signyfyed by ryght" (541, see headnote to this chapter). Whether it is romance or fantasy, the knights inhabit a world that is real to them. But this is a socially constructed reality, a "known world" of typical behaviors and situations. The knowledge which the knights possess is, strictly speaking, of an interpreted world, not the entire world itself, just the world that is known to them. This world, moreover, increasingly excludes the complexity and diversity of individuals because it defines itself categorially.

For us the term ideology is important, especially because in its history it has had the connotation of the lie or the hopeless ideal. It was used by partisans, such as Francis Bacon who coined it, to condemn the knowledge-action structure of the Middle Ages. In Bacon's case, the Idola (essentially the categories) of medieval thinking were no longer applicable to the new world he was beginning to discover with his new empirical and inductive methods of science. During the nineteenth century, ideology was attached to French socialists whose reforms were seen as something unreal or inapplicable to real-life situations. In current usage, from an analytical rather than a prescriptive point of view, the term ideology has come to denote precisely what of our knowledge of the world really exists on the social plane, the level of institutional behavior. Ideology concerns the knowledge which is not speculative, worn-out, sui-generis, or irrelevant, but rather knowledge which is vital in controlling and informing human behavior. Ideology is political knowledge in the sense described by Peter Sederberg is his recent book The Politics of Meaning: "Politics consists of all deliberate efforts to control systems of shared meaning" (18). Ideology is always the knowledge of the institution; when we speak of the codes of knighthood or love we are referring to part of the ideology of the Round Table. But it is knowledge that will pass; it is not the knowledge of the totality of the world; in fact, it specifically excludes all that is wholly other, numinal, random or impossible to categorize. The experience of the numen involves the relationship between actions and the wholly other; ideology describes a connection between actions and the institution; in the terms suggested by Joseph Campbell, the difference is between mythic association and social identification. The structure of the meaningful which requires that human action relate to something transhuman is retained, but the ineffable numen is replaced by a scheme of concepts controlled by human reason.

Ideology possesses behavioral imperatives both because it represents the only reality known and because of the reward of the meaningful (though, as we shall see, this is the counterfeit reward of social identification, essentially the destructive emotion of patriotism). In ideology, as in the psychology of religion, the emphasis is on the usefulness of the knowledge in controlling the individual's decision to do a certain act rather than an almost infinite number of other acts. The reason for doing the particular act is, indeed, cogent; a certain act is chosen because by doing it and not something else the individual realizes his own value. This is not simply reinforcement; rather the individual's act is his affirmation of the scheme of knowledge which his culture had devised as the best explanation of the world, man, and the category of the numen. The feeling of value is not simply reward but the hard-nosed and practical perception of doing something "real." In Psychology and Religion, Carl Jung observes that "A great many ritualistic performances are carried out for the sole purpose of producing at will the effect of the numinosum by certain devices of a magic nature, such as invocation, incantation, sacrifice, meditation [and so on]" (4-5). Institutional behavior is, as we see, essentially ritualistic. And, rituals are to believers the most real acts. Ideology is to secular institutions what doctrine and liturgy are to religious institutions.

What can be said of all the knowledge and actions that lie outside of the narrow scope of ideology. Utopia, in Mannheim's analysis, denotes what is incongruous with the socially constructed reality; that is, knowledge which has no direct relationship with legitimated acts. Utopia is the world of knowledge for its own sake, the wholly other, randomness, personal insights, heresy, and, most importantly, deviation and innovation. This is not to say that utopian (other world) thinking which does inform behavior is not part of ideology. The utopian mentality of, for example, the medieval Christian who looks forward to a life after death constitutes a part of ideology, and it does inform his behavior; the life after death is clearly a vital part of his social reality--whether it is phenomenally real or not. Strictly speaking, utopia denotes knowledge which does not inform actions that are institutionally validated (Mannheim, 73).

The value of Mannheim's methodology for the student of works such as Malory's Le Morte Darthur is that now he can trace the collapse of a once vital and meaningful society, not to corruptions of men which would imply that the knowledge-action structure was left intact, but rather trace it to the explanatory system itself. For as Mannehim points out, the theory of ideology and utopia enables the social historian to identify the interrelationship between an intellectual point of view and the social conditions which, in a manner of speaking, are its precipitates and to identify within those social conditions the ultimate sources of antinomous forces. Ideology is inherently conservative and enhances the stability of institutions, while utopic knowledge is innovative and pushes institutions beyond what they presently are. The theory of ideology and utopia enables us to see social groups as dialectics and sites of confrontations among pluralities of interests; we can now see the great aim of social cohesion and world peace articulated by medieval political thinkers from St. Augustine to John Fortescue to be a false good and one Malory himself must have viewed as inherently tragic. Reified institutions, because they are experienced objectively and are the object, therefore, of knowledge, acquire their own growth pattern which follows the direction of a reduction in variety and plurality and thus is independent from the needs of humans. Thus it is possible in a romance like Malory's to trace the separate development of the ideology of the Round Table and the utopic actions and desires of particular knights. (I take up this point fully in Chapter Three.) The end occurs when the ideology and its fanatical adherents like Lancelot are simply no longer able to recognize the existential world they live in. They hold, as Tennyson puts it, "A blind life within the brain." To repeat the conclusion of Berger and Luckmann: "man is capable paradoxically of producing a reality that denies him" (89). In Lancelot's "reality" Guinevere is a true lady, but this is clearly not the empirical world in which he must perforce continue to live-- unlike his son Galahad.

   The concept of the numen, moreover, allows us to discover the origin and structure of the intellectual point of view. It places full responsibility for the creation of institutions upon the shoulders of humans and it allows for significant innovations or cultural evolution by abolishing the limits of a fixed human or Divine nature. Thus if man's knowledge of himself and the world is inaccurate and incomplete, his derivative social institutions contain the liklihood of eventually becoming incoherent with each other and with man's needs for a meaningful existence. The openness of the numen gives us a way of showing that knowledge will always be incomplete. The decision to do the "right" or moral thing in circumstances which could not be foreseen at the origin may, in fact, be destructive. Failure of the explanatory synthesis, of ideology, to be unceasingly modified by new experiences, by utopic desires, results in a gap or disparity between what men actually do and what they believe, or between the demands of the situation and what they know how to do. When the gap grows large enough to be perceived by certain sensitive individuals, ideology lapses into utopia itself (a longing for the more moral past) and we are confronted with the meaninglessness of the situation which prevails in the latter half of Malory's Morte. The knights know perfectly well what they are doing, but it is not working at preserving the Round Table and producing the feeling of self-value in them. Given the perfections of the Code of Knighthood--which, of course, is not all that perfect but was believed to be by the knights and many revivalists--we are shocked when Malory tells us that Lancelot after defying Arthur, killing Gareth and Gaheris, and abducting Guinevere "rode hys way wyth the quene, as the Freynshe booke seyth, unto Joyous Garde, and there he kepte her as a noble knyght shulde . . . and many full noble knyghtes drew unto hym" (684). The statement "as a noble knyght shulde" has lost all meaning, become destructive, and lost its ability to produce in Lancelot the feeling of the numinous. It exists here because the institution and its ideology now have their own inertia and subsist irrespective of what the knights do. Taking the Queen "knyghtly away," as Sir Bors advises (681) can be legitimated on purely ideological grounds, the only grounds upon which Lancelot will ever think.

Shortly later, Lancelot changes the name of his castle to the "Dolerous Garde" (698). His knowledge about what he should do prevents him from doing something innovative that might actually resolve the problem he faces, and he feels terrible about his conventional acts, even though he believes that he is doing the right thing. We know that whatever Lancelot does will be "knyghtly"--but "knyghtly" acts no longer resolve the problems of existence. For Lancelot knighthood has become a disease, a psychosis. In the present circumstances, the code, the explanatory model, is being called upon to explain and therefore validate actions which are well beyond its original intentions. The stability of the Round Table depends upon the knights' adherence to the code which stipulates "allwayes to do ladyes, damesels, and jantilwomen and wydowes socour: strengthe hem in hir ryghtes . . ." (75). Lancelot, therefore, has no other way of understanding and choosing his action than as Sir Bors puts it "that ye knyghtly rescow her" (680). The category "knightly" contains only the essential information stipulated by the code. In the computation and application of that category all other information has been suppressed and destroyed. But how much, much more is

Lancelot doing as well! The specific circumstances and unusual conditions of Lancelot's case could not be predicted at the time the code was solidified, and we are driven to the paradox in which doing the "right" thing is the most destructive thing of all; we are driven to the tragic disparity between explanation and action--meaninglessness. And yet, as we shall see, this situation grows directly out of the code itself, not from Lancelot.

The conditions which prevail at the end of Le Morte Darthur exemplify an ideology which has broken down. Not only are there independent developments in knowledge and action, but also the various propositions of knowledge and the behavioral imperatives which follow have become incoherent with each other. The knowledge by which actions were to be explained has become useless, and the actions by which the knowledge was to be affirmed are simply no longer done; that is, the conditions demonstrate that the world has returned to the state of chaos. The category of the numen has departed from the world of the Round Table. We see this growing meaninglessness in the Quest for the Holy Grail, itself a numinal symbol, which moves away from rather than toward the Round Table and finally departs altogether: "Also thes two knyghtes saw com frome hevyn an hande, but they sy nat the body, and so hit cam ryght to the vessell and toke hit, and the speare, and so bare hit up into hevyn. And sythen was there never man so hardy to sey that he hade seyne the Sankgreal" (607). What will emerge from this situation is a new stage in the evolution of culture; a new institution and counter-reality (we move into the modern period which institutionalizes the individual--individualism) will develop around the actions which are responses to the failing institution, and the old institution will persist only as sedimented knowledge and a source of incoherence at a later time.

The final conference between Lancelot, Arthur, and Gawain called by the Pope in an attempt at reconciliation shows clearly the condition of meaninglessness. It is, in fact, an argument among the knights about how their actions are legitimated; that is, what category their acts were to have exemplified, and about how to interpret certain terms and concepts which should be used to explain (subsume) actions. The discussion is worth quoting at length because it illustrates the social chaos which occurs when it is discovered that the categories or the ideology is inherently incoherent.

`My moste redouted kynge, ye shall undirstonde, by the Popis commaundemente and youres I have brought to you my lady the quene, as ryght requyryth. And if there be ony knyght, of what degre that ever he be off, except your person, that woll sey or dare say but that she ys trew and clene to you, I here myselff, sir Launcelot du Lake, woll make hit good uppon hys body that she ys a trew lady unto you.

`But, sir, lyars ye have lystened, and that hath caused grete debate betwyxte you and me. . . . [H]ad nat the myght of God bene with me, I myght never have endured with fourtene kynghtes, and they armed and afore purposed, and I unarmed and nat purposed; for I was sente unto my lady, youre quene, I wote nat for what cause, but I was not so sone within the chambir dore but anone sir Aggravayne and sir Mordred called me traytoure and false recrayed knyght.´

`Be my fayth, they called the ryght!´ seyde sir Gawayne.

`My lorde, sir Gawayne,´ seyde sir Launcelot, `in their quarell they preved nat hemselff the beste, nother in the ryght.´

`Well, well, sir Launcelot,´ seyde the kynge, `I have gyvyn you no cause to do to me as ye have done, for I have worshipt you and youres more that ony othir knyghtes.´ (694-95)

Lancelot and Gawain attempt to place Lancelot´s killing of Aggravain into its proper category: knightly or traitorous. Lancelot rehearses the explanatory and legitimatory regress all the way to its termination in "the myght of God." Lancelot includes the political subsumption that he deserves the greatest worship because he has done more for Arthur than any other knight, the personal or fraternal subsumption in reminding Gawain of an oath of perpetual loyalty he made after Lancelot had rescued him from Tarquin, and at the bottom-line the physical subsumption that Lancelot can defeat any knight in battle. The essential aim in such an explanatory regress is social cohesion, and it should signify or call out specific responsive behavior in Gawain to interpret the event in the culturally orthodox way. But in fact, it ignores certain percepual attributes of the situation (i.e., destroys information) that have forced their way into Gawain's consciousness, and he attempts an explanatory regress of his own based upon those perceptual attributes that Lancelot's explanation required him to ignore. Gawain's reply invokes a part of the ideology built around different categories and is, therefore, irresolvably incoherent with the construction of explanations Lancelot has pursued:

> `Sir, the kynge may do as he wyll,´ seyde sir Gawayne, `but wyte thou well, sir Launcelot, thou and I shall never be accorded whyle we lyve, for thou hast slayne three of my brethryn. And two of hem thou slew traytourly and piteuously, for they bare none harneys ayenste the, nother none wold do.´ (695)

Lancelot offers several alternative subsumptions for the deaths of Gareth and Gaheris and makes large offers of penance and restitution. When legitimations are not shared or when knowledge becomes suspect, bribery may induce cooperation. To these Gawain replies:

> `Sir Launcelot,´ seyde sir Gawayne, `I have ryght well harde thy langayge and thy grete proffirs. But wyt thou well, lat the kynge do as hit pleasith hym, I woll never forgyff the my brothirs dethe, and in especiall the deth of my brothir sir Gareth. And if myne uncle, kynge Arthur, wyll accorde wyth the, he shall loose my servys, for wyte thou well,´ seyde sir Gawayne, `thou arte both false to the kynge and to me.´
> `Sir,´ seyde sir Launcelot, `he beryth nat the lyff that may make hit good! And ye, sir Gawayne, woll charge me with so hyghe a thynge, ye muste pardone me, for than nedis must I answere you.´

'Nay, nay,' seyde sir Gawayne, 'we ar paste that
as at thys tyme. . . .' (696)

Gawain here attacks Lancelot's legitimations as mere language
(ideology in the pejorative sense) and goes on to explain that
forgiveness and world peace are only the Pope's ideas and no
longer possible. Blood vengeance for the death of a family
member is an equally possible solution. Lancelot continues to
urge the social bonds between himself and Gawain such as
forgiveness, knighthood, mutual loyalty to Arthur, and finally
the strongest of all--the duty to preserve "Moste nobelyst
Crysten realme" (697). What is at stake here is literally the
social order itself. If individuals cannot be brought into
agreement and their thoughts and actions controlled, there
cannot be said to be any degree of order in the world. The
meeting ends upon a note of pure chaos.

'Do thou thy beste,' seyde sir Gawayne, 'and
therefore hyghe the faste that thou were gone! Any
wyte thou well we shall sone com aftir, and breke
the strengyst castell that thou hast, uppon they
hede!'
'Hyt shall nat nede that,' seyde sir Launcelot,
'for and I were as orgulous sette as ye ar, wyte you
well I shulde mete you in myddys of the fylde.'
'Make thou no more langayge,' seyde sir
Gawayne, 'but delyvir the quene frome the, and pyke
the lyghtly oute of thys courte!'
'Well,' seyde sir Launcelot, 'and I had wyste of
thys shortecomyng, I wolde a advysed me twyse or
that I had come here. (697)

Lancelot's last words confirm the futility of the knights'
attempt to agree upon the meaning of actions and, conversely,
which acts verbal constructs legitimately point to. What will
now resolve problems is not meaning but brute force. We call
it "brute" not because it will be any more violent than the
force used to maintain institutional stability, but rather because
it arises from an incoherence in the ideology and, therefore,
destroys not only individuals but also the ideology's power to
order life. In the end nothing will remain because the

explanatory model has become so incoherent that it places one knight in direct opposition to another without providing any means for resolving such conflicts since it rules out innovative behaviors.   Innovation is always initially socially deviant, criminal, and destructive of institutional order, as Galileo or Giordano Bruno well knew.   No unity or reconciliation is possible because Arthur, Gawain, and Lancelot are, it is still true to say, trying to preserve the social order and stability, and therefore each one acts from the position of right and justice.   Gawain argues from the position of truth just as surely as Lancelot does.

Hence it is in practice that moral codes, which are the behavioral imperatives of the knowledge of the properties of the category of the numen, are inherently inadequate expressions of human experience.   This is necessarily so because the original experience of the numen is always infinite and ineffable, but the codes are definite and by nature simply deductions from the properties attributed to the numen.   If, as argued before, categories emerge at the cost of the destruction of information, then it is likely that experience will become recognized as incoherent with the general principles.   In order to satisfy one code, Gawain or Lancelot would have to violate another.   The problem is not only that the intellect is incapable of knowing the world absolutely and therefore incapable of predicting situations in the future with certainty, but also that laws and knowledge develop much slower than experience.   Small variations in behavior accumulate so that when the law is put to the test, as Gawain does here, it is found to be inoperative. Gawain asks Lancelot to think <u>down</u> the ladder of abstractions (rather than upward) to the phenomenon that "trew lady" existentially points to, and he discovers that there is no reality to Lancelot's words.   As mentioned before, ideology is a process and within society there is always a conflict between established codes and the anomalous information personal experience inevitably generates.   Gawain's anger about the deaths of Gareth and Gaheris is experience and information that Lancelot's orthodox interpretation regards as inessential.

Once knowledge has been codified, moreover, it becomes an objective facticity in the present world of experience which is, indeed, now a different world from that which existed before the law was conceived.   Once an institution has become reified, it becomes something which the knight must respond to that was not in existence before the knights created it. Laws, therefore, make possible new situations and new problems which were not possible before the inception of the law, and yet the law still exists to inform and control behavior in the present world in a now outmoded way. The code to defend all ladies works this way. Before its inception it would not have been morally possible for a knight to defend a lady against his king or, indeed, the wife of the king against him. The law emerged before Arthur was married, but the law now makes defending Guinevere imperative and moral. Lancelot's dilemma is the result of an inherent inconsistency that could never have been predicted when the law was contemplated--it was not part of the experiential tension which necessitated and gave rise to the law.

It is a large, but worthwhile, generalization to say that valid knowledge grows out of the perception of problems in experience. No matter how detached and abstract some philosophies may seem, they can always be traced to some tension in experience. Knowledge which seems to exist for its own sake seems so only because we have forgotten the tension which gave rise to it. By the time tensions are resolved and the strategies used in their resolution have become sedimented into knowledge, the problems have, naturally enough, ceased to cause any real tension in the lives of those expected to use the knowledge to make their actions valid and their lives ordered. Arthur Ferguson sees this principle at work in the ideal of knighthood in the late Middle Ages: "As a military force he [the knight] passed away with the French wars and the War of the Roses, driven from his monopoly of the military profession by the yeoman archer, gunpowder, and the professional captain. . . . Knighthood in the stricter sense had, in fact, ceased to have anything necessarily to do with the political or administrative life of the community" (Indian Summer, 3-4). And yet, Ferguson goes on, "Chivalry had perforce to continue to do what it had been doing since the twelfth century, namely to supplant for the purposes of secular life the great body of Christian ethical teachings" (32). The interests and practical lives of individuals move on to new and more pressing problems (i.e. gunpowder), but knowledge remains as an abstract and detached model which certain individuals will always seek to revive or continue

to enforce as a way of solving the social problems indicated by
the ideology itself. On the ideological level, it is assumed that
knowledge is valid because the solutions to problems which are
no longer current problems must have been complete and
comprehensive. This sort of thinking in the face of present,
overpowering problems underlies the notion, as mentioned in
Chapter One, that the past was always a more noble time, and
it, of course, underlies revivalism. But for contemporary
society, the presence of old explanatory models presents, in
actuality, a source of chaos in the guise of order. Lancelot
cannot stop seeing the defense of damsels in distress as the
crucial problem of his existence. In reality, he faces a much
greater problem, but he has no way of identifying it.

Gawain's refusal to forgive Lancelot for the deaths of
Aggravain, Gaheris and Gareth can be validated by invoking an
even older piece of sedimented knowledge: the code of blood-
vengeance for crimes committed against one's family and
possessions. H. M. Chadwick, in his The Heroic Age, tells us
that this code arose as a strategy for preserving social order
and the security of family and possessions (344). The code
developed in a period (at least for the Anglo-Saxon version of
it) before the idea of repentance and forgiveness had been
raised to a significant ideological level by Christian teachings.
Later, forgiveness should have replaced vengeance in sustaining
order and protecting individuals from one another. And yet a
great deal of the old code of vengeance persisted into Christian
times, especially, as we see in Arthurian Romance, in the codes
of Chivalry. Hence the situation which confronts Gawain can
be interpreted by him in two ways with very different
outcomes. He can follow the "popis commaundment" for
forgiveness and reconciliation, or he can look back to times
when justice and security seemed more effective and direct.
Both codes are available as modes for preserving social order,
and yet they are mutually incoherent. Lancelot's large offers
of restitution call out for a response from Gawain, but they are
not requited because Gawain has valid ideological support for
his choice of action. Gawain perceives in Lancelot's willingness
to lie about his affair with Guinevere a distinction between his
(Lancelot's) actions and the ideology he is calling upon to
validate his acts, and Gawain revives, therefore, what appears
to him a more coherent and more natural method for achieving

justice. When he tells Lancelot, "we are past that as at this tyme," he means that forgiveness has not been comprehensive in solving all the tensions that experience might produce. Gawain feels that Lancelot's offers of restitution are simply too cheap for the lives of his brothers, and forgiveness, therefore, is an inadequate way of solving the problem confronting him. The dilemma of Gawain, then too, grows out of incoherencies within present ideology, a problem which the culture itself never bothered to resolve completely because it had moved on to new and more pressing problems, while the vengeance-forgiveness incoherence was causing no real tension. But now Gawain perceives the tension. The doctrine of forgiveness is seen to have no useful relation to the situations of real life. Then suddenly the old way rises again, and no one can say that Gawain is not just in his actions.

The nature of the final discussion between Lancelot, Gawain, and Arthur is chaos. No one can agree on the meaning of the terms used to place actions within the explanatory structure, and no one can reliably predict the response of another to the signs or gestures he offers. Each member returns to the most basic and chaotic social mode: stability by brute force. This situation arises, Malory perceives, from the fact that the Round Table society had assumed that its ideology was consistent and coherent. Lancelot's shock, early in the romance, that a knight who is a murderer and a thief is nonetheless a knight gives away his belief that such things could not occur within knighthood. Such beliefs imply that the explanatory system of a society represents a complete understanding of life and the world. But as Malory shows, the search for knowledge and understanding of the world is infinite and unceasing, and the endless character of it is what makes life meaningful. The chaos at the end results, more than anything else, from a tacit agreement among the knights that they had achieved the quest for knowledge, and now that the quest is at an end all that is left to do is live the derivative social order. If we accept the relationship between knowledge and society, as Mannheim describes it, then why should the quest for social order not be unceasing and infinitely undetermined? Any notion of fixed social order and fixed behavioral or moral codes is inherently incompatible with the conditions of being human. Fixed doctrines rob present individuals of reality in their lives when it can be perceived that present situations do not conform with the historical or metaphysical model.

The substance of Lancelot's tragedy is, finally, in his attempt to exhaust the fixed ideological structure of the Round Table society, to bring into the clear light of the present the order, purpose, and meaning of the origin. The horror of the tragedy which follows is not the result of Lancelot's corruption or incompetence but rather of the failure of the ideological structure to be perfectly coherent after he has achieved the "flower of knighthood." The Round Table, which was ordained by Merlin "in tokenyng of rowndness of the worlde," comes finally to symbolize a rigidity that places one knight against another in a struggle which is both demanded by honor and right and yet destructive of life. The knights see clearly this paradox, but they never perceive its origin. To the very end Lancelot remains faithful to Arthur; he remains the perfect knight <u>and therefore</u> cannot see why he is the cause of all the destruction. For Malory the origin of the destruction was in the medieval world itself which had, especially in theology, assumed that its knowledge and doctrines should be fixed and stable because, as St. Thomas explains, the understanding of any particular must be deduced ultimately from the nature of a fixed and universal Creator. In his treatise <u>On Kingship</u>, St. Thomas makes deductions about the political domain from his concept of an intelligible and universal God. This is just what the second generation knights do; they make deductions about the present from Merlin's original concept of the Round Table. The hidden assumption, of course, is that Merlin knew perfectly well what he was doing or that he was an agent of God who intended to establish a perfect society. But the assumption is clearly false; it grows out of Arthur's successful use of force in subduing his enemies as a confirmation of Merlin's apparent prophecies. Though I will have more to say about this later, the second generation knights make their history--their origin--a source of their social codes and values. For these knights, life itself is destroyed in the process of identifying themselves with the socially constructed reality of the Round Table.

2.2 The Quest for Civilization and Selfhood

Perhaps the greatest difficulty in understanding the Round Table is that it must be approached in two different stages of its development, but these stages are structurally identical and the transition from mythic association to social identification is only subtly perceived by the four best knights. The remainder of the knights, and indeed many readers, never perceive that ideology replaces the world openness of the numen, and they persist in seeing the Round Table as a stable fulfillment or socialization of the truth of what the Middle Ages knew about the world (perhaps undermined by corruption or bad fortune). A real difference, however, exists in the nature of the institution in its early and mature phases. We cannot, for example, explain Uther Pendragon's conquest of Igraine by deceit in terms of the moral ideology that prevails later on. Rather, Uther is erotically drawn to the beautiful and seeks to possess it by the enforcement of his will: "Thenne for pure angre and for grete love of fayr Igrayne" (3). It is pointless to make moral judgments about Uther's act, and Malory makes that clear by casting the situation so that Uther's actions are precisely on the borderline between adultery and not-adultery. From a later point in time and more highly developed ideology, moreover, Uther's rape of Igraine is seen as history, the

107

temporally and ontologically prior events which are the causes of the present social conditions. After the destruction of a certain amount of the original information, the act is interpreted in a larger frame of reference and becomes, according to Merlin, part of the will of God. Such actions which exist as Eliade calls them "ab origine" are thus taken as definitive of the present institution. They represent--in spite of the dubious moral quality--what Eliade identifies as "the irruption of the sacred into the world, an irruption narrated in the myths, that establishes the world as reality" (Sacred and Profane, 97).

Both the medieval Roman Church and the Round Table saw themselves as historical institutions. For the Church, the Old Testament and the life of Christ comprised the history, in illo tempore, and St. Augustine in a function similar to Merlin's (i.e., careful destruction of information) explains in his writings how such information should be interpreted and thus used as a guide for present behavior. Malory is consummately aware that he is writing the history of the Round Table, and he coordinates the events in the rise of the Round Table with the feast days which comprise the history of the Church and thus account for its rise. It is not merely that such coordination was a common or conventional method of dating used in the Middle Ages; rather Malory's romance is a response to the kind of objective culture Christianity had become, and he sees a profound distinction between the actions done before and after the maturation of the institution, that is, before and after Pentecost. His conclusion is that historically based institutions (political life itself) are inherently tragic because they rob the present of reality and meaning except insofar as the present imitates the past. Only imitations of acts done as Caxton says "in tho dayes" have reality in themselves; the present acts are informed or given value insofar as they can be interpreted in terms of the historical acts. The present, as is the case with the tournaments, becomes ritualized in the worst sense of existing only to commemorate the past. Thus the history of the Round Table is of paramount importance, and Merlin insures it is recorded and interpreted:

> And so he departed and com to hys mayster [Bloyse]
> that was passynge glad of hys commynge. And there

he tolde how Arthure and the two kynges had spedde
at the grete batayle, and how hyt was endyd, and
tolde the namys of every kynge and knyght of
worship that was there. And so Bloyse wrote the
batayle worde by worde as Merlion tolde hym, how
hit began and by whom, and in lyke wyse how hit
was ended and who had the worst. And all the
batayles that were done in Arthurs dayes, Merlion
dud hys mayster Bloyse wryte them. Also he dud
wryte all the batayles that every worthy knyght ded
of Arthurs courte. (25, emphasis mine)

The history of the Round Table centers around the feast
days of Pentecost and the Assumption, and the correspondence
with the liturgical year shows why. Alan Watts in his Myth and
Ritual in Christianity explains that the Church interpreted its
history in terms of a yearly cycle. The Church sees the portion
of the year composed of Advent, Christmas, Epiphany, Lent,
Crucifixion, and Resurrection as representing the actions "ab
origine"--the defining mythic actions which essentially describe
a cycle of birth, death, and rebirth into a new realm. The
segment including Easter, Pentecost, Assumption, and a great
aray of Saint's feasts defines the present institution as
responsible for carrying on the acts done originally by Christ.
Pentecost is the key feast of the Church as historical
institution, and it is, of course, also the day of Arthur's
miraculous assumption of kingship and thereafter the feast day
of the Round Table. Watts goes on to point out that Pentecost
is the inversion of the Tower of Babel story. The attempt of
man to penetrate the heavens of his own volition (what I call
the conquest of the numen) is frustrated by God's imposing upon
men a confusion of tongues (i.e., the pluralism, diversity, and
meaninglessness that must exist before an institution emerges).
The resulting chaos from an inability to agree upon meaning
causes complete social disorder, abandonment of the conquest,
and the dissolution of a single race into many tribes. The same
disorder prevails in England after the death of Uther Pendragon
who was "kynge of all Englond." But even when Uther was
king, no institutional solidarity bound men together, for there
was no political control of meaning and no socially conscious
selves; rather Uther ruled by force and personal domination.

When Uther, the dominant member dies, the kingdom simply falls into chaos; there exists no objective social order outside of the person of the king and no social continuity: "for every lord that was myghty of men maade hym stronge, and many wende to have ben kyng" (7).

Pentecost reverses the Tower of Babel story by replacing the chaos with semantic order. The final result of Christ's coming to earth is the descent upon the Apostles of the Holy Spirit, one of whose gifts to the Apostles is the gift of tongues. This is the second event of the irruption of the sacred into the world, which as Eliade observes, establishes a new order of reality. Now the Apostles are able to begin rebuilding the Tower, but with the key difference that the new Tower and group effort required to build it find an origin in historical and defining acts. The message of Pentecost is that mankind once divided semantically is now united through a shared meaning of experience. In short, the institution is still a conquest of the heavens and the net effect is a kingdom on earth made possible by stability in verbal behavior; that is, meaning and explanation find stability by tracing themselves to the historical acts of Christ and the revealed word of God. Pentecost corresponds to the Jewish Feast of Weeks or celebration of the wheat harvest; thus it is a time of "gathering in" and the Church becomes the communion of the faithful. Later in Jewish history, the Feast of Weeks commemorated the giving of the Tablets of the Law to Moses on Mount Sinai. Pentecost historically commemorates the birth of the group and the inception of ideology or law. What makes an individual a member of the group is the presence of the "word" of God in him or his choice to accept the "word" and reject other possible words (Watts, 186-90).

In Malory the miraculous unanimity of the presence of the word (i.e., the now univocal interpretation of an event) occurs on Pentecost as the sudden recognition that Arthur is God's appointed agent and shall be king:

> And at the feste of Pentecost all maner of men assayed to pulle at the swerde that wold assay, but none myghte prevaille but Arthur, and he pulled it oute afore all the lordes and comyns that were there. Wherefore all the comyns cryed at ones,

> `We wille have Arthur unto our kyng! We wille
> put hym no more in delay, for we all see that it is
> Goddes wille that he shalle be our kynge, and who
> that holdeth ageynst it, we wille slee hym.´ (10)

The problem of facing the confused people is one of decoding or interpreting Arthur´s pulling the sword from the stone. The nobles refuse to grant that it meant that Arthur was to be king; we need only recall the doubts of Thomas and other Apostles as well about the nature of Christ after the Crucifixion to see how natural their position is. Variability and randomness in response to events and stimuli make institutional activity impossible. But on Pentecost--when all are gathered, while they had been dispersed and subject to an even greater variety of stimuli on previous occasions--there occurs a sudden infusion of unanimity of interpretation. A single stimulus emerges as dominant. Everyone forgets all the disparate information such as Arthur´s youth, his uncertain parentage, and his servant upbringing. The inception of an institution, just as a revolution, requires an initial focusing event which a significant number of people agree to respond to in the same way. Malory´s misgivings about the putative divine origin of the institution are made clear in the cynical equation of meaning stability and force; all those who do not interpret the event in the now true way will be killed. Though Malory sees danger ahead, he understands clearly that the institution finds its origin in a created truth; that is, the forced (whether by miracle or sword) stabilization of meaning, response to stimuli.

This truth thus acquires the status of <u>aboriginal</u> act and is eventually taken over as the institution´s history. In the later stages, the collection of such acts become the historical rationale for the laws and codes of the institution. It is assumed all along that the laws and codes are true simply because they are derived from the origin which is true. Merlin´s comment after Pentecost suggests the necessity of the emergence of an institution from the infusion of truth. Concerted human action ineluctably is creative of institutions:

> And, who saith nay, he shal be kyng and overcome
> alle his enemyes, and or he deye he shall be long
> kynge of all Englond and have under his obeyssaunce

Walys, Yrland, and Scotland, and moo reames than I
will now reherce. (11)

The occasion of control over the meaning of things is also
the birth of knowledge. As section 2.1 pointed out, valid
knowledge emerges from problems duly faced. The conditions in
England before Arthur's kingship illustrate the sort of human
problems that call for truly innovative and culturally
transcending solutions: "Thenn stood the reame in grete
jeopardy longe whyle" (7). Nothing in the ideology of Uther
Pendragon's time could provide a viable solution. Various
barons simply fought each other for dominance. Uther's
ideology itself, grounded in personal dominance, had by now
become the problem. To any problem, a very great number of
genuine solutions exists. Since the problem is social, the
persistence of competing solutions actually only exacerbates the
original problem. Somehow a single solution needs to emerge
and become adopted by enough people to drive out competing
solutions. It can never be proven that the chosen solution is
inherently better than any of the competitors, but what we can
observe clearly is that it was chosen, not for intrinsic merit,
but rather because of extrinsic circumstances. In an analogus
manner, Thomas Kuhn concludes that in the history of science
new scientific paradigms are not chosen for their greater
explanatory power (scientific reasons) but largely for political,
economic, or aesthetic reasons (The Structure of Scientific
Revolutions). Thus in Malory, Merlin's solution that Arthur will
be king and unify all England gains acceptance because he is
able to construe or present it as a miracle, something
authorized by God. His solution gains power from the
transhuman numen; no one else can claim that. Malory tells us,

Thenne Merlyn wente to the Archebisshop of
Caunterbury and counceilled hym for to sende for all
the lordes of the reame and alle the gentilmen of
armes, that they shold to London come by Cristmas
upon payne of cursynge, and for this cause, that
Jesu, that was borne on that nyght, that He wold of
His grete mercy shewe some myracle, as He was
come to be Kynge of mankynde, for to shewe somme
myracle who shold be rightwys kynge of this reame.
. . .

Soo in the grettest chirch of London--whether it were Powlis or not the Frensshe booke maketh no mencyon--alle the estates were longe or day in the chirche for to praye. And whan matyns and the first masse was done there was sene in the chirchyard ayenst the hyghe aulter a grete stone four square, lyke unto a marbel stone, in myddes therof was lyke an anvylde of stele a foot on hyghe, and theryn stack a fayre swerd naked by the poynt, and letters that were wryten in gold about the swerd and that saiden thus: `WHOSO PULLETH OUTE THIS SWERD OF THIS STONE AND ANVYLD IS RIGHTWYS KYNGE BORNE OF ALL ENGELOND.´ (7)

We cannot know how the great stone got into the church yard; perhaps Merlin himself hauled it there and carved the inscription on the sword. No voice from heaven speaks to the lords and Merlin's rather precise analogical argument deducing Arthur's kingship from Christ's looks more like the planting of a suggestion than a word he received from God. The way the lords interpret the stone derives from the whole context-- something Merlin has very carefully constructed. The lords were brought in to pray all day with the expectation (Merlin's suggestion) of a miracle, and suddenly a stone with a sword stuck in it appears in the yard. How else could they decode the event? In an essay on how meanings come to be seen as literal, natural, obvious, and what goes without saying, Stanley Fish asserts that

There always is a literal meaning because in any situation there is always a meaning that seems obvious in the sense that it is there independent of anything we might do [an uninterpreted meaning]. But that only means that we have already done it. . . . [An object or statement] always has the meaning that has been conferred on it by the situation in which it is uttered. Listeners always know what speech act is being performed, not because there are limits to the illocutionary uses to which sentences can be put, but because in any set of circumstances the illocutionary force a sentence [or a stone] may

have will already have been determined.   ("Normal
Circumstances," 250-264)

Merlin's interpretation of the sword miracle is accepted not
because he has any guarantee of a better institution built
around Arthur (we will see that the opposite is the case), but
because his solution acquires extrinsic powers for persuading
people in general to accept it and reject others: "Thenne the
peple merveilled and told it to the Archebisschop" (7).   Part of
the extrinsic power is the threatened force: "payne of
cursynge."   We will see a pattern in Merlin's ability to
manipulate the situations in which perceptual stimuli acquire
meanings that augment his promotion of Arthur as King of all
England.   As Fish's essay makes clear, the lords brought with
them into the church the meaning that the stone eventually
acquires.   But the most important extrinsic power involves the
relation of Merlin's meaning to an explanatory regress that
terminates in God.   Talcott Parsons in his Evolution of Societies
argues that no social system can be self-legitimating (8).
Phrased another way, Parson's thesis argues that without
extrinsic legitimation, no social system at all could emerge and,
in fact, neither could any stable meaning for any sign.   The
relation of Merlin's interpretation to the explanatory regress
that is already known by the lords also means that the lords
can now rationalize or explain to themselves Merlin's meaning.
    In Mind, Self, and Society, George Herbert Mead points
out that society arises only when an event is experienced by a
group of individuals who during the event observe or analyze
their own behavior and the situation from the point of view of
what Mead calls the "generalized other" (32-34).   The social
process is nothing more than the agreement among individuals
about the meaning and hence their reactions to events, words,
and situations.   This agreement occurs because everyone, as the
lords do, agrees to adopt a single point of view with regard to
the event in question.   Merlin's point of view toward Arthur is
not presented as his own but as a perspectiveless, uninterpreted
meaning, what goes without saying--the word of God.   Thus
production of likeminded individuals within an institution
depends not on the domination of a single person's meaning (as
in Uther's days) but on a transhuman perspective and meaning.
And that is certainly the case with the Round Table as well as

the Catholic Church; all events must be interpreted from the now institutional or group created point of view, what is always attributed to the will of God, though in actuality it is nothing more than Merlin's point of view. The structure suggests, as mentioned a moment ago, a death of the individual and a rebirth into a new kind of reality. Though I will get to the point later, this process is what Malory sees as root of the tragedy inherent in institutions. Eventually individuals will lose the ability to recognize one another as unique and independently existing beings, for the institution will demand that individuals face each other only in terms that serve the interests of the institution. Self-consciousness comes to mean conscious of one's self from the perspective of the institution. Balin, for a quick example, in this way loses the ability to recognize his brother, Balan.

The course of events following Pentecost concern Arthur's living the <u>aboriginal</u> acts, Merlin's constructing contexts in which a particular response appears inevitable or Divinely ordained, and the developing self-consciousness of the knights. This stage comprises the mythic time of the creation of the institution out of chaos by the putative will of God.   Its end point is not the death of Merlin as is usually thought, but rather the proposed marriage of Gareth to Lyones on the feast day of the Assumption of the Virgin Mary.   The marriage actually takes place on Michaelmass day, the feast of the Archangel Michael, at a Tournament which illustrates and commemoratively recreates the social order and cohesion that Arthur and Merlin have created. The Tournament at Michaelmas has always been well understood, but its real importance lies in its contrast to the Tournament on Assumption Day, for the difference in these two events indicates the difference in the social conditions of an emerging and meaningful institution and a mature repressive one. The essential difference lies in the creation of order rather than the enforcement of order.   The Tournament on Assumption Day permits a far greater level of pluralism and personal contribution than the following one.

The Assumption as a feast day marks the last occasion of the direct participation of the numen in the acts of men.   In terms of Church History, Mary--as God--leaves the Apostles on their own.   The Roman Catholic has generally, though covertly, accepted Mary as holding the fourth position in the quaternine

God. No theologian ever officially declared Mary to be God, but to grasp the popular spirit one needs only to consider the numerous Cathedrals dedicated to Notre Dame, at for example Chartres or Paris, in which the position of Mary is not as the human mother of Christ but as an equal to the Father and Son. The unconscious drive to place Mary in a position that demonstrates her equality with the original persons of the Trinity appears more openly in popular works or works by minor or provincial artists who normally possess substantial freedom from direct supervision of an authority who might recognize and challenge the theme. The works of marginal members of an institution, moreover, express more faithfully the popular beliefs rather than the strict doctrine. A painting of Nicola of Pisano (1499-1538), for example, shows Christ and Mary jointly handing keys to St. Francis. Mary and Christ are dressed in a similar fashion, scarlet and blue robes, and they stand on the same level, above St. Francis. Or, John Audeley's hymn to Mary which calls her "thou quene of maydens mo, / Lord of heven and earth also." The importance of Mary as God demonstrates that the essential feature of the quest for meaning is the necessity of mankind having some role in creating his creator or God. Mary is the most powerful and creative human; at once created and the mother of God. Another English poem points out this advantage clearly:

> Thou my sister and mother
> And thy son my bother--
>   Who then should drede?
> Who-so haveth the king to-brother
> And eke the quene to mother
>   Well ought for to spede.

The import of this little digression on Mary is that what she represents is required in institutions that can be said to be meaningful. What departs from the Round Table after the feast of the Assumption and after the "Tale of Gareth" is Arthur's unself-consciousness and the mythic association of the knights as individuals with the institution. After the Assumption, they only repeat as ritual the acts which brought the society and hence themselves as knights into being. The feast of the Archangel Michael has implications directly opposite to those of the Assumption. Michael is the policing or warrior angel whose task it is to enforce heaven's rules on those such as Lucifer or Adam who refuse to submit. The problem facing mature institutions is not self-creation but rather compliance and maintenance of stability. Michalemas and the final tournament of Gareth' tale celebrate an established order that the members will fight to the end to defend. Immediately following the Assumption, Malory turns to the "Tale of Tristram" in which the problem of meaninglessness appears and gradually undermines the institution.

During the time before the Assumption and Gareth's marriage, it is inappropriate to speak of the knights' acts in terms of codes and laws. We see the process of acts being transformed into codes, but it is well to point out the essential randomness of Arthur's acts, and that a great deal of what Arthur does cannot be understood in terms of any cultural construction. The actions of Arthur comprise the mythic archetype for acts which are later regulated and explained by the codes. Goethe had this sort of insight in mind when he has Faust re-write the Gospel of St. John:

Is mind the all-creating source?
It ought to say: In the beginning there was Force.
Yet something warns me as I grasp the pen,
That my translation must be changed again.
The spirit helps me. Now it is exact.
I write: In the beginning was the Act.
(Kaufmann, trans., 153)

Goethe's famous "Im Anfang war die Tat" is crucial. Arthur originates in random activity--chaos. But certain of his deeds are more effective at making himself the master of his environment: both the environment of the physical world and of other competing lords. Arthur has no ability, however, to distinguish self-creative acts from self-destructive acts; that is Merlin's role. The nature of Arthur's actions is naive response to the interests of the moment, but from these actions Merlin selects certain ones which become definitive. When at a tournament on New Year's Day, for example, Sir Kay has lost his sword, Arthur responds by providing a new one: "I will ryde to the chirchyard and take the swerd with me that stycketh in the stone, for my broder sir Kay shal not be without a swerd this day" (8). His next act which becomes an archetype is the giving of an office: "by the feith of my body, that never man shalle have that office [seneschal] but he [Kay] whyle he and I lyve" (9). The giving of a sword and an office, as they occur here, lack the ideological and symbolic implications that they will have later on. Here Arthur merely responds to the simple necessity of the day (some part of which is certainly guilt for upstaging Kay), and he can mean no more than Uther or Ector could by his acts. Kay's sword is lost; Arthur finds him a new one and pledges family loyalty to his brother. Later on, these acts will be transformed into rituals and interpreted symbolically as the core of the society and constituent of the knight's identity. The knight's sword, as mentioned earlier, becomes the tool for the maintenance of the knight's worship, and thus without it no social value is possible. The office becomes a seat at the Round Table. And the harmony of the whole society comes to depend upon each knight repeating these archetypal acts by keeping and using his sword to maintain his place at the Round Table. Thus in creating themselves the knights create the society.

As the institution develops, more and more elaborate means of initiation are required for the granting of a sword or office, as in the case of Gareth. The earning of these two gifts becomes the process of socializing the individual. George Herbert Mead defines this creation of self as "the importation of the conversation of gestures into the conduct of the individual organism, so that the individual organism takes these organized attitudes of others called out by its own attitude, in the form of its gestures, and in reacting to that response calls out other organized attitudes in the others in the community to which the individual belongs" (Mind, Self, and Society, 186). And so it goes on, a reciprocal process of both self and culture creation. Thus Gareth's earning of his name involves not a personal quest but an interaction between himself and the group, represented by the Dame Lyonet. He must learn to interpret his own actions in the manner of the other members of the group, particularly its leader Lancelot. This process involves a diremption of the individual into, as Mead puts it, an "I" and a "me." Pre-social man is a monad; institutional man is dyadic. The "me" is the socially determined or acculturated self of which one is conscious when he thinks about "me" as fully a knight with a certain known reputation. The statement "This is `me`" means the organization of explanations and behavioral models that have been assimilated by the individual. In other words, a knight´s acceptance of a sword indicates his assimilation of the set of attitudes of the "general other" toward himself and to his world; he is now able to view and interpret his own actions in the same manner as would any other person. When a knight gives his name and adds that he is a member of the Round Table, he is defining "me" by calling out an organized set of attitudes--the ideology of the Round Table--in both himself and the other person. "Me" is the self one is conscious of. The importance of self-consciousness is, of course, that it is the foundation of moral action and it makes possible stable institutions. At the outset, however, Arthur cannot be either moral or immoral because he has no such means of analyzing his actions. He cannot observe himself acting from the standpoint of a behavioral model or generalized other, which is the pre-condition for moral behavior.

The "I," on the other hand, represents the incomprehensible element of the individual which responds to the essentially dutiful actions of the "me" in ways that cannot be accounted for in social explanations. The "I" is the element of the unconscious insofar as that term represents simply a category of unanlyzable and unpredictable judgments ranging from simple mistake to unmotivated deviance. One is not conscious of these judgments until after they are acted out (Mead, 173-78). One cannot, of course, think the unthinkable which the "I" is, but doing the unthinkable is entirely possible, and if action is the origin of thought, we can become aware of the "I" component after the deed. Hence the "I" appears as little more than the element of unpredictability in the individual, but in Malory this element is of utmost importance. In the early stages, Arthur is all "I." He lacks an historical perspective in the sense of a naive child, that is, a pre-social individual. One of the major objections to Arthur´s kingship is that he is a child: "for it was grete shame to all them to see suche a boye to have a rule of soo noble a reaume as this land was" (11). Malory even makes a point of comparison between Arthur´s growing beard and his emerging society. At one point, he has to defend his "bearde [that] ys full yonge" against King

Royens of North Wales (36).   The point is significant because only through interaction with the group does the individual gain an historical or social perspective on himself, and therefore, fighting King Royens is just what Arthur needs in order to grow up, but such fighting also defines the nature of the subsequent institution and in such a way limits the range of behaviors that the knights may legitimately engage in.   For the knights, the granting of the sword and office becomes the socializing process because the sword as the instrument of activity and, indeed, interaction provides the opportunity for an individual to do the things which make him a part of the community.   The developing self-consciousness of the knights through interaction is precisely, during this stage of mythic time, the process of the development of the society.   As Mead puts it:

> One must take the attitude of the others in a group in order to belong to a community; he has employ that outer social world taken within himself in order to carry on thought.   It is through this relationship to others in a community, because of the rational social processes that obtain in that community, that he has being as a citizen.   (199)

Hence Gareth must remain the denigratory Beaumains until he has the opportunity of interacting with the knights and thereby defining himself as knight.   No one is born with knighthood or humanness.   And Arthur, since he is of the origin, has somehow to invent the stature of Arthur before he can become king.

We must recognize, however, that in the opening episodes until about the death of Merlin Arthur acts unself-consciously; that is, he possesses no method, no categorial model, for understanding and therefore judging, predicting, or even knowing the outcome or that there might be an outcome of what he does.   He has, moreover, no means of perceiving inconsistencies between several of his acts.   He has no social mind.   Arthur simply acts upon his environment or surroundings with the sort of personal domination that characterized his father, Uther Pendragon.   He appears much like the Adam and Eve of Genesis who because they had no experiential knowledge of good, evil, or death had no way of knowing the outcome of their decision to eat the fruit of the forbidden tree.   God's threat of death was meaningless to the unself-conscious Adam who had no experience with death. The tree, however, as a part of his experience with historical inter-relatedness called out the response that other trees did: eat. It is best to see Arthur as pure and unregulated energy. Placed in a situation he will do something and not stop until he controls his surroundings or he is forced by a superior power to cease. He is unregulated aggression. He falls in love with every beautiful woman he meets whether it is his own sister Morgause, whom he does not recognize, or Lyonors with whom "the kynge had ado . . . and gate on hir a chylde" (26), or whether it is finally Guinevere. At one point he attempts to follow the Questing Beast, a wholly inappropriate quest for King Arthur, but he discovers the quest and immediately wants to pursue it. And when the Lady of the Lake presents him with the sword Excalibur and its miraculous scabbard, he characteristically, though imprudently, tells Merlin that he likes the sword better. Arthur himself is the chaos of pure energy. This is Merlin's apprehension of him:

> Thou hast never done. Hast thou nat done inow? Of three score thousande thys day hast thou leffte on lyve but fyftene thousand! Therefore his ys tyme to sey 'Who!' for God ys wroth with the for thou woll never have done. (24)

Merlin goes on to say that if allowed to continue, Arthur will soon destroy himself. What is Malory suggesting? Mead's concept of the "I" as "biologic individual" is useful. Though he avoids the term "will" in discussing the origin of societies in Mind, Self, and Society, Mead suggests that the human being as organism, and indeed all organisms, can do nothing else but impose its will on its surroundings in the sense of feeding off of them. Humans cannot be still; inevitably to live means to do something with the things surrounding one. This notion is very nearly the same concept of the will as appears in medieval discussions, particularly St. Thomas who sees the will as the spontaneously active faculty that Arthur is. But for St. Thomas the will has a teleology; its proper object is the good, toward which the will automatically turns once it has been informed by the reason. Arthur's problem, as I have said, is an absence of reason or mind, and he does not know what is good because reason and a hierarchy of goods are cultural products. No orientation is present in Arthur. Neither is his will aimed at bodily pleasure as St. Augustine understood the will. It requires, rather, a very modern theory of behavior to approach Arthur. Arthur simply and unaccountably acts. It is true that sometimes he chooses what appears to be the good--that is he appears to think out his actions--as, for example, when he orders the massacre of all male children born of nobility on the first of May, since Merlin had prophesied that a child born on Mayday would eventually destroy the kingdom. Here the good is the survival and the preservation of the kingdom which from Arthur's, and, let's face it, any king's or government's, point of view is a higher good than preserving the lives of some children. But another pattern of events shows that Arthur does not act to preserve himself or his emerging kingdom. He is quite like a moth drawn to a flame which very likely--but not necessarily--will be his destruction. At one point Arthur drives off three churls who were bothering Merlin. Arthur believes that he has demonstrated his strength: "`A, Merlion!´ seyde Arthure, `here haddist thou be slayne for all thy crafftis, had nat I bene.´" But Merlin replies:

> `Nay,´ seyde Merlyon, `nat so, for I cowde a
> saved myselffe and I had wolde. But thou arte more
> nere thy deth than I am, for thou goste to thy dethe
> warde and God be nat thy frende.´
> So as they wente thus talkynge, they com to the
> fountayne and the ryche pavillion there by hit.
> Than kynge Arthure was ware where sate a knyght
> armed in a chayre. (33)

Arthur's apparent socially positive choices are in reality no more than reactions to his first doing something which placed him in imminent peril, as the Mayday massacre makes clear, and are thus properly a response to a new situation, one which he helped create. His act of begetting Mordred upon his sister Morgause creates circumstances which call for further action. Taken together, actions for survival and for destruction demonstrate that no teleology governs Arthur's actions. He simply and necessarily interacts with his surroundings, having no ability to devise a policy which would ensure his survival. We can see this clearly in the strange case of Sir Grifflet, a man just knighted by Arthur and then nearly killed by him in a battle that "sitthyn I [Arthur] muste nedis, I woll dresse me thereto" (32).

Malory does not allow Arthur to answer Merlin's comment about his (Arthur's) approaching destruction. Rather he shifts immediately to an adventure which exemplifies Merlin's meaning. Briefly, as just cited, Merlin and Arthur come upon a fountain and an armed knight apparently relaxing in a chair. Arthur challenges the knight, saying that he will force the knight to abandon his custom of defending the well; that is, he will impose his own will upon the environment of the knight. Malory presents Arthur as always fighting against whatever environment he finds himself in. They fight, and the nature of the battle is revealing. Three times Arthur and the knight joust and each time the spears are shattered, whereupon Arthur draws his sword and offers to finish the battle on foot. But the knight insists upon getting new spears until finally Arthur is knocked to the ground. Now the knight will fight on foot. The advantage changes hands repeatedly, and, as it almost seems, unceasingly. First the knight has the advantage, but Arthur overthrows him and tears off his helm; before he can strike, the knight wrestles Arthur under him and tears off Arthur's helm. All the while Merlin watches, as the two "hurteled togydirs lyke too rammes that aythir felle to the erthe" (34). Finally, Merlin calls a halt to the battle just before the knight can kill Arthur--or perhaps there would have been another reversal of advantage. Instead of relief and gratefulness, Arthur is angry:

> `Alas!´ seyde Arthure, `what hast thou do, Merlion? Hast thou slayne thys good knyght by thy craufftis? For there lyvith nat so worshipffull a knyght as he was. For I had levir than the stynte of my londe a yere that he were on lyve.´ (34)

What Merlin sees in Arthur is that life for men is a continual struggle, a battle with the environment or with forces that simply appear at every turn. Though he is sometimes successful, Arthur has little means of defending himself, not even much desire to do so (this too is cultural), and almost no knowledge of what sort of actions would enhance survival. What concerns him is the interaction with whatever confronts him and the assertion of his will or in better, less teleological terms, the expenditure of his energy in immediate confrontation with problems which occur at any moment. And yet as the example shows, such interaction is structureless; it does not favor Arthur; and in fact, it may just as well destroy him. When he is actually fighting a knight, whether the knight is a foe or one of his own men, Arthur fights to kill. But if he defeats the knight, he laments. Merlin's point is that Arthur is near death, and the example shows, too, that the more successful Arthur is in asserting his will and dominating his environment, the closer he approaches death. For if the fundamental biologic condition of man is activity or interaction with the environment, then total domination of the environment would mean his death in the sense that activity would stop. Arthur is most himself not in victory but in battle. To be near death is the inherent condition of biologic, pre-cultural man, condemned to an absurd activity the result of which may or may not be his destruction. The conclusion of the battle with the knight of the fountain is that Arthur loses his sword. Merlin directs him to Excalibur, but when Arthur tells Merlin that he prefers the sword to the scabbard, we see in Merlin's answer the helplessness of Arthur, endowed with only innate or biologic capacities:

> `Ye ar the more unwyse, for the scawberde ys worth ten of the swerde; for whyles ye have the scawberde uppon you ye shall lose no blood, be ye never so sore wounded. Therefore kepe well the scawberde allweyes with you.´   (36)

Soon enough, of course, Arthur loses the scabbard. Arthur's preference for the sword identifies him with the sort of aggressive energy that has been named by psychoanalysts various things such as eros, libido, or primal instincts, and in a special sense the self-preservation instinct and the pleasure principle. Of utmost importance, however, is the distinction between this raw energy and such teleological principles as self-preservation which is in the present context associated with Merlin rather than with Arthur. Rather this energy is best understood in terms developed by Carl Jung in his The Theory of Psychoanalysis (1912) and later, more fully, in On Psychic Energy (1948). Jung describes this human inability to be inert or this propensity for aggression as an undifferentiated energy similar to the meaning of energy in physics, that some force or expenditure or energy lies behind every motion or change in phenomenon. Some undirected energy funds life itself but it cannot preserve life. In his autobiography, Jung explains the background of his concept: "I conceived the libido as a psychic analogue of physical energy, hence as a more or less quantitative concept, which therefore should not be defined in qualitative terms. My idea was to escape from the then prevailing concretism of the libido theory--in other words, I wished no longer to speak of the instincts of hunger, aggression, and sex, but to regard all these phenomena as expressions of psychic energy" (Memories, 208). Jung defines the human condition as evolutionary, but not in the sense that some final condition or overall direction underlies the process; rather the human condition is a permanent process which demands of an individual constant adjustments or adaptations in order to remain at a relative equilibrium with the environment. All of these adjustments require psychic energy, but the consciousness of what enhances equilibrium or destroys it is cultural. Without social institutions, then, the expenditure of energy can be no more than random. What Arthur represents, in this early stage, is the psychic energy in a pure and unregulated form. The basic insight in Malory is the same as in much twentieth century psychoanalysis: this psychic energy or eros is the ultimate source of civilizations, and the great problem facing all civilizations is finding a means for regulating the level of and channeling the direction of the expression of this energy into goals that promote the life of the species. A civilization must be perpetually creating itself; defining social goals so that energy expenditure is directed into specific objects or actions and survival becomes more probable than destruction.

We come now to Merlin and how it is that Merlin changes the fundamental condition of absurd activity into the meaningful and teleological institution of the Round Table. Merlin is culture; he provides direction and control. This chapter began with a discussion of a process or movement from an experience of the category of the numen to knowledge to ideology and finally to moral codes. In terms of the present events, the movement is from aboriginal acts to interpretation to institution. Merlin's goal throughout is Arthur's survival. Merlin's function is that of interpreter or ideologue, the one who affects the transition from energy to society, from random interaction to controlled behavior. In a sense, his role corresponds to the tongues of fire which enabled the Apostles to explain the puzzling events of Christ's life in a way that was to shape the actions and regulate the energies of thousands of men and women into the institution of the Church. Merlin's preservation of the history of Arthur's life has already been noted, and it will be recalled that the history of the deeds done "in tho dayes" becomes an archetypal and mythic model for the moral and ethical codes of the present. But not all acts. Merlin, claiming to know the will of God, chooses only those acts which further the ends of the new society he is creating. Thus Arthur acts randomly (the "adventure" below) and Merlin sets those actions into historical and valuational contexts (the "grace") so that psychic energy comes under the control of knowledge.

> In the begynnyng of Arthure, aftir he was chosyn kynge by adventure and by grace, for the moste party of the barowns knew nat he was Uther Pendragon son but as Merlyon made hit opynly knowyn, but yet many kyngis and lordis hylde hym grete werre for that cause. But well Arthur overcom hem all: the moste party dayes of hys lyff he was ruled by the counceile of Merlyon. (59, emphasis mine)

Merlin is often called a witch (e.g., 12) and Ninive believes him to be a devil's son (77), but these names result more from the fear various people have of him than from his real nature. Comments such as a knight's that "Beware . . . of Merlion, for he knowith all thynges by the devylles craffte" (74) indicate that no obvious or universally accepted reason exists to believe Merlin's own claim that he works by the will of God. What makes Merlin so fearful is his power, not the will of God. King Lot, for example, learns to regret his sarcastic remark that "Be we wel avysed to be aferd of a dreme-reder" (12).

Lot's comment is instructive because it contains all three essential elements of Merlin's nature: fearfulness, counsel, and interpretation. Taken together these qualities comprise the prophet as Merlin is usually taken to be, but it must be understood that the sort of prophet Merlin is does not foretell the future; rather the prophet in this sense is the historian who arranges objects of the present experience in spatial, temporal, hierarchical, and causal relationships so that it becomes possible to respond to an organized environment and thus by controlling response predict the future. The prophet, as the ideologue of the institution, creates the future by controlling the meaning of the present world. Merlin's organization of the present experience enables Arthur to discern when to fight and when to retreat. Merlin begins in Arthur the practice of regarding his knights hierarchically according to chivalry, an act which becomes a major ideological algorithm in the future:

> `I shall say you,´ said Merlyn, `I warne you al, your enemyes are passyng strong for yow, and they are good men of armes as ben on lyve. And by thys tyme they have goten to them four kynges mo and a myghty duke, and onlesse that our kyng have more chyvalry with hym than he may make within the boundys of his own reame, and he fyghte with hem in batail, he shal be overcome and slayn.´ (13)

Merlin establishes the acquisition of chivalry as a cultural goal, and so through the efforts of Arthur by the time of the War with the Five Kings we discover "Ye knowe well that sir Arthur hath the floure of chevalry of the worlde with hym" (78).

Thus in Malory, as opposed to his French sources and previous tales of the rise of the Round Table, Merlin has a much more vital role in planning and bringing about the formation of the Round Table society. He works with Arthur's acts pushing them into the future by defining and giving meaning to each act and thereby creating a self-conscious group of knights who are able to choose productive acts over destructive acts. The rage for order is the rage for definition and meaning since, as the problem of interpreting Arthur's pulling the sword from the stone shows, consistency of interpretation provides for stability of response to stimuli and thereby solidarity among people. But as the coronation of Arthur again shows, stability of meaning is established by some form of training or miracle, and if those fail, force. This is a crucial point in understanding the emergence of an institution. It forms the thesis of Morse Peckham's important work Explanation and Power, in which he asserts that "the basic unit of human behavior is sign response, not the individual organism. Sign response is not genetically transmitted, and therefore it must be learned, and it follows that it must be taught" (162). Peckham concludes that "force is the ultimate sanction for maintaining response behavior. . . . Economic deprivation, imprisonment, the infliction of pain, and killing are the ultimate sanctions for the validation of any semiotic link between sign and meaning" (169). What Merlin does is regulate and direct Arthur's energy so that it becomes the force which stabilizes in all men a certain interpretation (response) of the present events (stimuli) which Merlin sees as productive of social order. Peckham rightly sees reward as power accepted positively or covert force, and thus Merlin teaches Arthur to reward his men who successfully perform certain behaviors:

> And therefore withdraw you unto youre lodgynge and reste you as sone as ye may, and rewarde youre good knyghtes with golde and with sylver, for they have well deserved hit. There may no ryches be to dere for them, for of so fewe men as ye have there was never men dud more worshipfully in proues than ye have done to-day: for ye have macched thys day with the beste fyghters of the worlde. (24)

In addition to stabilizing responses to signs, Merlin operates in the manner of what Sigmund Freud calls "the reality principle"; a process of repressing, displacing, or postponing the expenditure of psychic energy (libido or eros for Freud) so that immediate action is waived in favor of a later action. For Freud the object of energy is always pleasure, but neither Jung nor Malory limit the object to pleasure except in the very strict sense of pleasure accruing from the mere expenditure of energy. The reality principle enables one to choose a greater pleasure over a smaller one or a constructive pleasure over a destructive one. It becomes the origin of the reason or the super-ego. In Beyond the Pleasure Principle Freud writes, "We know that the pleasure principle is proper to a primary method of working on the part of the mental apparatus, but that, from the point of view of the self-preservation of the organism among the difficulties of the external world, it is from the very outset inefficient and even highly dangerous. Under the influence of the ego's instincts of self-preservation, the pleasure principle is replaced by the reality principle. This latter principle does not abandon the intention of ultimately obtaining pleasure, but it nevertheless demands and carries into effect the postponement of satisfaction, the abandonment of a number of possibilities of gaining satisfaction and the temporary toleration of unpleasure as a step on the long indirect road to pleasure" (4). The result of the working of the reality principle is the development of an ability to predict and plan ahead, and therefore it enables individuals to avoid the self-destruction that would attend absolute and uncontrolled pursuit of pleasure. Merlin's task is to regulate Arthur's energy in this manner, as he counsels mid-way through the war with the Eleven Kings: "Therefore hit ys tyme to sey 'Who!' for God ys wroth with the for thou woll never have done. For yondir eleven kynges at thys tyme woll nat be overthrowyn, but and thou woll tary on them ony lenger thy fortune woll turne and they shall encres" (24).

The emergence of an institution is always associated with the discovery that a specific act, rather than other acts, satisfies what is taken as the collective interest rather than any personal interest. The act can be repeated with expectations of a similar satisfaction whenever the now typical situation again presents itself. The biologic individual, Arthur, cannot make this discovery, for it is really the emergence of mind, as the individual becomes conscious that his behavior has a pattern or is habitual in certain situations. This emerging consciousness takes the form noted by Berger and Luckmann, "'There I go again' as he starts on step one of an operating procedure consisting of, say, ten steps. . . . Habitualization carries with it the important psychological gain that choices are narrowed. . . . This frees the individual from the burden of 'all those decisions,' providing a psychological relief that has its basis in man's undirected instinctual structure" (Social Construction, 53). The creation of conscious individuals is

Merlin's task who, in effect, repeats to Arthur, "there you go
again" or "do that act again" until Arthur begins to see himself
the way Merlin does and habitualize his response to certain
situations.   In this way, Merlin transforms the tremendous
energy that Arthur initially is into power--that is, energy
directed to do productive work.   Order requires directed inputs
of energy.   Merlin's constant attribution of his counsel to the
will of God is much better understood as the difference between
Arthur's pure energy and his power.   When Merlin directs his
energy, the seemingly miraculous change feels as if it were, to
use Eliade's term, an infusion of the sacred into the realm of
the profane.   Looked at another way, Arthur's power is now
traceable through an explanatory regress to the might of God;
it is, of course, the power itself which will maintain that
explanatory regress.   Such are the metaphysical and cultural
implications of the psychological gain when choice is narrowed.
What I am describing is the way in which institutions emerge
around optimizing habituations, a principle, which as we shall
see, continues to narrow the range of behavior throughout the
life of the institution.   Merlin teaches Arthur that one kind of
behavior is more effective or optimal than any other kind.   But
an act can only be optimal in terms of achieving already chosen
goals.   Merlin's decision to create a civilization with Arthur as
king and center becomes the goal against which every act has
to be measured.
    This principle is well exampled in Arthur's war with the
Eleven Kings, where a physically greater force (the Eleven
Kings) is overcome by the vastly greater power Merlin confers
upon Arthur.   The character of the wars is initially much the
same as Arthur's battle with the knight of the fountain, a back
and forth struggle between opposite forces.   The war actually
destroys both sides.   The war originated as a refusal by the
Eleven Kings to accept Arthur as their king.   Although they are
told by Merlin that "he is kyng Uther Pendragons sone borne in
wedlock, goten on Igrayne, the dukes wyf of Tyntigail" (11),
they do not accept this definition of Arthur.   "`Thenne he is a
bastard,` they said al" (11).   Malory clearly shows that the war
grows out of the instability of the meaning of Arthur; as he puts
it:

> Some of the kynges had merveyl of Merlyns
> wordes and demed well that it shold be as he said,
> and some of hem lough hym to scorne, as kyng Lot,
> and mo other called hym a wytche.   (12)

The Eleven Kings exhibit a wide range of responses to their
confrontation with Arthur.   The situation is chaotic.   But the
Kings are themselves a situation to which Arthur must respond.
In this sense the Kings represent "reality," the environment, or
the human condition against which the individual will must
thrust itself but which is often impossible to meet directly with
much hope for success.   Merlin advises Arthur to hold back, to
postpone his aggression and choose his acts:

> `Syr,´ seyde Merlyn to Arthur, `fyghte not with the
> swerde that ye had by myracle til that ye see ye go
> unto the wers; thenne drawe it oute and do your
> best.´   (12)

And when Arthur finally draws Excalibur and begins to vanquish
his enemies, Merlin again advises him to hold back:

> `Thou hast never done. Hast thou not done inow. . .
> Therefore hit ys tyme to sey "Who!"´   (24)

The greater good to be obtained here is, of course, the co-
optation of Kings Bors and Ban.   But Arthur cannot see it
himself; he is only directed toward immediate domination of
whatever affronts him.   Sometimes that dominance may result in
a long range disadvantage, for those enemies that Arthur is
intent upon killing might some day be brought over to Arthur's
side and into the Round Table, as happens importantly with the
sons of King Lot.

Merlin also works upon the Eleven Kings.   Merlin's
comments to them are attempts to unify their responses to
Arthur by any means short of battle.   He claims to represent
the will of God, to be a prophet, and he uses reason in pointing
out the superior power of Arthur's forces: "Ye were better for
to stynte, for ye shalle not here prevaille, though ye were ten
so many" (12).   But Merlin is clearly lying.   He has no way of
knowing the outcome of the battle with the Eleven Kings;

rather he attempts to forestall the battle by intimidating the kings with false prophecies and claims about the will of God. When the battle takes place, it is an even fight until, luckily enough, the common people arise and drive off the forces of the Eleven Kings with sticks and clubs. It will be recalled that the meaning of Arthur had been stabilized in the common people long before on the feast of Pentecost. Even though Merlin is telling the truth about Arthur's origin, he knows that truth by itself is not enough to make it universally accepted; it is clear to him, in spite of all his admonitions about the will of God, that "your [Arthur's] enemyes are passyng strong for you" (13). Merlin is Arthur's orientation and teleology, and in order for him to push Arthur into the future, he manipulates Arthur's force by advising an alliance with King Ban and King Bors of France, knowing that "onlesse that our kyng have more chyvalry with hym than he may make within the boundys of his own reame, and he fyght withe hem [Eleven Kings] in batail, he shall be overcome and slayn" (13). Indeed we should not think of Merlin as being able to see the future, but rather as willing to say whatever is necessary to organize within the kings a set of attitudes such that they respond to similar situations in a similar way.

Predicting the future is, therefore, the same effort as stabilizing meaning in the present. If, as we have seen, random response is the natural condition, then the only means of stabilizing the behavior of a group is to develop self-consciousness so that the knights can observe their actions from the single point of view, in this case, the teleology of the emerging society. When Arthur is able to view himself as a role in the development of the society, he begins to be prudent about selecting actions which augment the growth and avoiding those which hinder the development. The same must be true for other knights. But self-consciousness is only acquired through experience and interaction with a group. This is why Merlin allows the war with the Eleven Kings to take place at all; surely he could have employed some means of magic to vanquish the Kings, as he did in the case of the knight of the fountain. But the war is good experience, and Malory sees that socially minded individuals arise only through experiencing the social process itself. Thus Arthur and Merlin are not merely fighting insurgents they wish to annihilate, but more importantly they are educating or socializing their own men by forcing the men to experience the self-creating acts. The social process of war which at one level appears only as self-defense on another level creates the culture in which Arthur's ends must be defended.

The exchange between Merlin and Sir Ulfins over the cause of the war makes clear that the war is a situation Merlin has constructed. Ulfins charges Igraine: "thys quene Igrayne ys the causer of your grete damage and of youre greate warre, for and she wolde have uttirde hit in the lyff of Uther of the birth of you, and how ye were begotyn, than had ye never had the mortall warrys that he have had" (30). Igraine in turn explains that only Merlin knew the whereabouts of the child Arthur since "whan the chylde was borne, hit was delyvirde unto Merlion and fostred by hym." The debate goes on:

> Than Ulphuns seyde unto Merlion,
> `Ye ar than more to blame than the queene!'
> `Sir, well I wote I bare a chylde by my lorde
> kynge Uther, but I wote never where he is becom.'
> (30)

The last quoted statement appears as if it should have been spoken by Igraine; after all, she bore the child by Uther and it would be impossible for Merlin not to know what became of the child. He delivered the infant Arthur to Ector, and it was "by advys of Merlion" that the stone with the sword is set up in London. He must have known that Ector continued to foster the child. Moreover, Merlin is the first to identify Arthur, though few people believe him at the time of Arthur's pulling the sword from the stone. But the last quoted statement is Merlin's. Ulfin's charge is directed to Merlin, and the denial of knowledge must be Merlin's response. Here Merlin's outright lie is tantamount to an admission that he is responsible for the war, given the causal relationship established by Ulfins just previously. But on the other hand, without the war, without experiencing the social process itself, the knights could never learn to respond to Arthur as king by discovering themselves in terms of Arthur's mission or by becoming conscious of their own habitual response.

Another example shows more clearly how the social process--orchestrated by Merlin--organizes the attitudes of individuals by giving them experience in viewing objects or events not from a personal but from a collective point of view. The collective point of view becomes the ideological norm or code for interpreting any event or object, and the degree to which individuals uniformly view their own personal experiences from the ideological point of view marks the degree of order in the society. For Malory, this process is inherently tragic, for it brings the individual paradoxically to his highest civilized state but it also brings him to his death by denying him. As we shall see in the story of Balin and Balan, the Eleven Kings are finally defeated by Arthur's most highly self-conscious knight, Balin, but the brothers Balin and Balan also destroy themselves. Here, however, we are concerned with the rise of self-consciousness. As mentioned before, Arthur's wars with the Eleven Kings are an even-handed struggle. There are great losses on both sides, but also some great heroism on both sides. At one point King Bors and King Ban pause to reflect upon the course of the battle. They see great heroism on both sides, and their personal admiration of valor and dedication to knighthood itself results in a attitude which disposes them to sympathize with the enemy. In fact, given the terms of knighthood, there is no reason why the Eleven Kings should even be classed as enemies. They are noble men and to be loved or admired for it.

> `A, sir Arthure,´ seyde knyge Ban and kynge Bors,
> `blame hem nat, for they do as good men ought to
> do. For by my fayth . . . they ar the beste
> fyghtynge men and knyghtes of moste prouesse that
> ever y saw other herde off speke. And tho eleven
> kyngis ar men of grete worship; and if they were
> longyng to you, there were no kynge undir hevyn
> that had suche eleven kyngis nother off suche
> worship.´ (23)

The problem here is that from a personal point of view, there is nothing to keep Bors and Ban on Arthur's side. They might well refuse to kill such noble opponents or might join them. Knighthood, prowess, and heroism by themselves cannot dispose an individual to adhere to Arthur, for those qualities are found everywhere, even among enemies or strangers. Arthur, however, must get Bors and Ban to view the Eleven Kings from the point of view of his emerging ideology, and therefore make knighthood or prowess a judgment dependent upon first determining institutional adherence. He replies to Ban and Bors: "I may nat love hem . . . for they wolde destroy me" (23) The analytical point of view of Bors and Ban changes immediately. Instead of an objective or personal analysis of the Eleven Kings, they now interpret them as enemies or destroyers, no longer even noble or men of prowess: "they ar your mortall enemyes, and that hathe bene preved beforehande. And thys day they have done theire parte, and that ys grete pyte of their wylfulness." Once the beauty of the Eleven Kings is seen as willfulness (a vice or sin), the battle can resume with the assurance of solidarity on the part of Bors and Ban. What has happened here? Essentially Arthur has taken over Merlin's technique of selecting only a part of history, only a small segment of information of the present situation, and responding to that as if it were all that existed or all that mattered. Information is destroyed in order that power and solidarity be created. Now it is no longer possible or desirable to be conscious of the manifold beauties of the Eleven Kings. We move into a human created reality that necessitates blocking out of consciousness all such un-real possibilities as the goodness of an enemy.

The growth of self-consciousness--and we must recall that the "self" is presented only in social situations and thus what one is conscious of is a social construct of attitudes and behavioral modes--which is brought about within Arthur's knights by Merlin is, in fact, what makes Arthur finally victorious over the Eleven Kings. Arthur's knights make themselves stronger as a society by increasing their level of social mindedness. On the side of the Eleven Kings, just the opposite takes place. There is no movement within the psyche toward social self-consciousness, but rather solidarity is brought about by oath and will which do not create "selves." Immediately following the passage in which Bors and Ban interpret the Eleven Kings, Malory tells how the Eleven Kings understand their own position: "Than all the eleven kynges drew hem togydir" (23). King Lot offers a plan for the battle, encouraging more bravery and greater physical exertion. Each king responds with an oath of solidarity; Malory even names each king who "swore they wolde never fayle other for lyff nother death, and whoso fledde all they sholde be slayne" (24). The society of the Eleven Kings may be said to be organized upon a "social contract" of essentially autonomous individuals. When the battle abates, each king simply returns to his own castle to defend it.

The fact is simply that the forces of the Eleven Kings are militarily superior to Arthur's forces; as Malory comments repeatedly, "for well he [Merlin] knew that and knyge Lotte had bene with his body [his forces united] at the first batayle, kynge Arthure had be slayne and all hys peple distressed" (48). King Lot, however, can never get his forces together in the same sense that Arthur can. The social contract binds individuals for both personal and communal interests, but it does not change or create wholly new socially minded individuals. The Kings remain essentially separate entities, and no institution develops around them because they lack an inner coordination that can be perceived as an objective point of view. No historical self, no "me," emerges in the Eleven Kings, and they do not define themselves in terms of their history and origin; rather they live in an eternal present, confronting each situation on its own terms and thereby projecting nothing into the future. At the last battle, just before he dies, King Lot understands what Merlin has accomplished: "'Alas,' seyde kynge Lotte, 'I am ashamed; for in my defaute there ys many a worshipful man slayne; for and we had ben togyders there had ben none oste undir hevyn were able to have macched us. But this faytoure [i.e., impostor] with hys prophecy hath mocked me" (48). We know, as Lot now does, what prophecy entails.

In actual history rather than fable, the Eleven Kings remind us of pre-Carolingian Europe or of the social system in Beowulf, in which various tribes would form alliances from time to time for specific reasons but remained essentially distinct peoples without historical or national identity. And even in Feudal Europe, the sense of national or social identity did not replace local individuality until the period of the Hundred Years War. The Magna Charta of 1215 is an example of resistence to the emergence of national consciousness, and it is well to note that the Round Table itself, as Malory sees it, is not an institution which looks back to primitive times, but rather forward, much beyond feudalism, to the nationalism openly advocated by the Tudors of the sixteenth century. But of course, the Tudor spirit was a product of the social experience of the Hundred Years War. In writing about that war from the point of view of France, Joseph Calmette observes the emergence of what he calls a "popular instinct" manifest in the popular saying of the time: "Never shall reign in France an English King" (Cambridge Medieval History, VIII, 240). This is, of course, not instinct. It is rather social self-consciousness, the habit of mind of seeing oneself and one's experiences from the point of view of France. If the Round Table looks back, its model is the Roman Church which from about the time of Pope Leo IX (fl. 1049-54) had succeeded in producing an institution with an ideology comprehensive and pervasive enough to make itself the exclusive core of the Christian's identity. (This point is treated more fully in section 2.3.) Secular states did not achieve the sort of social self-consciousness that the Church achieved until the eighteenth, nineteenth, and finally, tragically, the twentieth centuries.

I have been calling Merlin an interpreter, and it may be useful to consider another sense in which that term is appropriate. The theories being used to analyze Merlin's affect upon Arthur's knights come, of course, from twentieth century social theory, but Malory would have had just as clear a model for the rise of an institution or civilization by means of interpretation and developing self-consciousness in Christianity and the method of Biblical exegesis developed by the Church Fathers. The problem facing Ambrose, Jerome, and Augustine, for example, is much the same as Merlin's problem: how to transform a chaotic, or even corrupt, human nature into a Christian being pleasing in the sight of God. The solution to the problem is civilization, the production of self-conscious individuals. In order to do this, St. Augustine suggests that signs--phenomena, texts, or situations--be interpreted literally and spiritually. The literal meaning is the thing existing unaccountably in itself and open to infinite possible meanings. For St. Augustine the literal is worthwhile only as a similitude or analogy to the spiritual meaning: "The letter killeth while the spirit bringeth life" (2 Cor. 6, cited often by Augustine). What St. Augustine advises, then, is seeing God's providence or creative plan in the phenomena of the world; that is, seeing normal human experience from the point of view of God's conception of human life. For example, he writes in On Christian Doctrine that "Human institutions are imperfect reflections of natural institutions or are similar to them" (62). Thus, attention is directed to the spiritual or numinal world which is felt to lie behind and inform the everyday world. He goes to great lengths to refute superstitions, conventions, pseudo-science, and faulty knowledge of language--all of which cause men to interpret phenomena from a false worldly point of view. Christian doctrine is, rather, the superstructure in terms of which all realities should be interpreted, for "He is a slave to a sign who uses or worships a significant thing without knowing what it signifies. But he who uses or venerates a useful sign does not venerate what he sees and what passes away but rather that to which all things are to be referred" (86-87). Merlin merely offers the same advice: refer all things to the goal of creating Arthur's civilization. Augustine concludes:

> To this warning that we must beware not to take figurative or transferred expressions as though they were literal, a further warning must be added lest we wish to take literal expressions as though they were figurative. Therefore a method of determining whether a locution is literal or figurative must be established. And generally this method consists in this: that whatever appears in the divine Word that does not literally pertain to virtuous behavior or to the truth of faith you must take to be figurative. Virtuous behavior pertains to the love of God and of one's neighbor; the truth of faith pertains to a knowledge of God and of one's neighbor. For the hope of everyone lies in his own conscience in so far as he knows himself to be becoming more proficient in the love of God and of his neighbor. (87-88, emphasis mine)

For St. Augustine, meaning results from a process of first determining that a phenomenon is a sign, then placing that sign in either the category of literal or figurative signs, and if figurative, then within a doctrinal category. All phenomena which do not directly articulate or exemplify doctrine must be taken figuratively, and therefore related to the explanatory regress. Interpretation becomes nothing more than subsuming any phenomenon by its proper category. Though St. Augustine refers specifically to the Word of God or Scriptures, to say that his method did not apply to all aspects of human experience is to deny that ideas have consequences.

If we return to the example of Bors and Ban, they are initially slaves of the phenomenon of the Eleven Kings in that they admire or "worship" the Kings in and of themselves, and they mistake figurative attributes such as heroic behavior for literal or plainly meaningful ones. No matter how brave their actions might appear, they simply do not pertain, as St. Augustine would have phrased it, to the truth of faith. Arthur's comment instructs Bors and Ban to place the Kings in the category "enemy," and thus the Kings can be responded to from the ideological point of view and in a manner which will contribute to the development of civilization. The noble acts of the Eleven Kings now become figures for willfulness or pride. As the process continues, categories such as Knighthood, Governance, Love, and Christianity--which I shall discuss in section 2.4--acquire meaning and power by subsuming an ever greater range of actions. The knights come to view every act from the point of view of, for example, knighthood. At one point, we even see that Gareth eats in a knightly manner: "and full knyghtly he ete his mete and egirly" (219). The question Malory is asking throughout the Morte and the question which demonstrates the tragic nature of such endeavors as Merlin's is how much heterogeneity will the category subsume before it explodes. Lancelot's incredulity about the knight who is also a thief and a murderer results from his unwillingness to subsume nobility, thievery, and murder within the same category. The assimilation of the organization of categories and their contents by the knights is, finally, what constitutes the socializing of the individual. As St. Augustine recognizes, the hope of every individual lies in his becoming more proficient in loving God and his neighbor; that is, interpreting his actions and conceiving of himself in terms of Christian doctrine which is the schematization of the love of God.

Arthur is eventually victorious over the Eleven Kings, and Malory makes it clear that the triumph is one of self-conscious individuals over a group of socially contracted individuals. The victory is achieved by Balin and Balan; that is to say, the knight with the dual-psyche, the first of Arthur's great self-conscious heroes, and Malory's closest analysis of the diremption of the individual into a "I" and a "me" brought on by the acquired mental capacity to view himself and his actions from the point of view of the culture itself. Merlin predicts the battle, but again it is not a case of reading the future. Rather Merlin explains his own present plan for civilization through developing self-consciousness which is built around the teleological principle that the more one experiences the social process the more socially minded he becomes and, therefore, the more he seeks to experience the social process even further. Institutions possess their own inertia, and, unfortunately, as the case of Balin shows, its direction is toward the center of ideology and a reduction of sensitivity to everything that lies outside the purview of culture. In Merlin's prophecy, only the names belong to the future, and they are added by Malory:

> For thes eleven kyngis shall dye all in one day by the grete myght and prouesse of armys of two valyaunte knyghtes,'--as hit tellith aftir. Hir namys ben Balyne le Saveage and Balan, hys brothir, that were merveylous knyghtes as ony was tho lyvynge. (27)

Through the "I"-"me" diremption brought on in the process of socializing the biologic individual Malory moves his treatment of the theme of the rise of culture one step further, and what he adds shows us how he feels about the creation of selves within the social process. Balin's two swords as well as the two brothers are, in this analysis, the two components of Balin: "I" and "me." His own sword, the "I," and the brother Balan do not originate in Arthur; his own defines him as Arthur's enemy, a violent and irresponsible sword which earns Arthur's wrath "for sleyng of a knyght which was cosyne unto kynge Arthure" (39). This sword identifies Balin as "poore and poorly arayde"; that is, lacking in the accouterments of a well socialized knight, but, we are told, Balin even as pre-social, biologic individual "was a good man named of his body." He starts out with--as apparently all humans do--a deep desire for meaning and the sufficient life: "in hys herte he was fully assured to do as well, if hys grace happed hym, as ony knyght that there was" (39). The second sword, the "me," is acquired in the process of interacting within the group; effectively it is a gift from Arthur for it was brought to Arthur's court to be given to the best knight. Though the lady who brings it advises Balin not to keep it, Balin does, and it transforms him from "a poore knyght . . . that had ben presonere" to "a passynge good knyght and the beste that ever y founde" (39).

Balin understands clearly the sort of transformation the sword will mean for him, as he explains his reasons for wanting it:

> `A, fayre damesell,´ seyde Balyn, `worthynes and good tacchis and also good dedis is nat only in araymente, but manhode and worship ys hyd within a mannes person; and many a worshipfull knyght ys nat knowyn unto all peple. And therefore worship and hardynesse ys nat in araymente.´ (39)

The sword and by extension civilization will enable Balin to attain the humanness that exists potentially within his person, but with this sword also Balin "shall sle . . . the beste frende that ye have and the man that ye moste love in the worlde, and that swerde shall be youre destruccion" (39-40). Thus from the beginning of Le Morte Darthur, Malory sees tragedy inherent in social identification, for throughout the romance it is the sword, and by extension, the grantor of the sword, the Round Table society and Arthur, which is the destroyer of the knights, precisely because it is also their creator. It creates social individuals who are devoted to categories to the extent that they can no longer recognize the simple things of the natural world such as their own biologic condition; this process destroys both nature and the individual. Malory, like Luther fifty years later, saw this ideological over-determination as the essential character of the late Middle Ages.

The tale of Balin and Balan is, after "The Tristram," Malory's most puzzling tale, and space permits me to mention only the outlines which place it in the frame of Arthur's actions, Merlin's interpretations, and the rising self-consciousness of the knights.   Balin is the first great self-conscious knight; the first to raise his individuality to the level of full identity as a knight of Arthur's and Merlin's civilization. Above all, Arthur and Merlin are concerned with existence itself, mere survival.   The knights raise the question of mere existence to the level of culture, but it is through Arthur and Merlin that they do so.   At the outset Malory sees a perfect symbiosis and interchange between the individual and the group. The group or society comes into being simultaneously as self-conscious individuals come into being.   The symbiosis has the form of individuals defining themselves as knights or citizens from the perspective of the group.   In the case of Balin, he controls his actions and attitudes from Arthur's point of view: that is, he does what he thinks Arthur would want him to do. This ability to assume the point of view of a "generalized other" towards oneself begins immediately after Balin is released from prison and given his second sword. We should see socialization as initially empowerment and freedom.   At this point, he meets quite by coincidence (or is it?) his brother Balan.   Their exchange is revealing:

> `Truly,´ seyde Balyne, `I am ryght hevy that my lorde Arthure ys displeased with me, for he ys the moste worshypfullist kynge that regnith now in erthe; and hys love I woll gete othir ellis I woll putte my lyff in adventure.   For kynge Ryons lyeth at the sege of the Castell Terrable, and thydir woll we draw in all goodly haste to preve oure worship and prouesse uppon hym.´
> `I woll well,´ seyde Balan, `that ye so do; and I woll ryde with you and put my body in adventure with you, as a brothir ought to do.´   (44)

Balin wants Arthur's love, and he is the first knight to seek it by, as St. Augustine would have advised, making himself more proficient in defining his life in terms of Arthur's ends. This is the quest for social identity, and as the passage indicates Balin requires that Balan, the biologic individual or "I," subject his body to a pattern of actions designed to call out the response of love or ascription of value from Arthur. He can optimize his behavior only by being able to mentally imagine the position of Arthur, that is, to view himself as he believes Arthur would, and to call out of himself, thereby, the actions that Arthur would call out if he were present at every moment.   Balin internalizes or intellectualizes the "other" or the ideology.   In the tale, this self-analysis and emerging self-consciousness is guided very closely by Merlin who, of course, has a special interest in Balin.   The result of Balin's quest is just what he sought, the infusion of the feeling of value from a trans-personal source: "And kynge Arthure seyde hymself they [I and me] were the doughtyeste knyghtes that he ever sawe" (47).   But the result is also a radically self-conscious Balin; that is, he is now pre-occupied with analysis of his whole life from a purely social point of view.

This feature of social identification enables the brothers to defeat the Eleven Kings.   The brothers, the core of society, make Arthur more powerful than the Eleven Kings who have no such core.   The new socially created being, indeed, appears miraculous in the final battle: "they dud so mervaylously that the kynge and all the knyghtes mervayled of them.   And all they that behelde them seyde they were sente frome hevyn as angels other devilles frome helle" (47).   The ambiguity about whether this new fighting machine is from heaven or hell must be taken seriously.   After the climactic battle, Arthur asks Merlin to ensure that the brothers always remain with him. Merlin's reply indicates what has happened to the original individual and points out the source of the tragedy: "And as for Balyne, he woll nat be longe frome you.   But the other brother woll departe: ye shall se hym no more" (49, emphasis mine). This is not prophecy; it is simple explanation of what has already happened in the creation of a radically self-conscious Balin.   Merlin will not even mention the name of Balan, the "I" component which has been totally overruled and annihilated. George Herbert Mead, my authority for much of the present discussion, writes, "Social control is the expression of the 'me' over against the expression of the 'I'" (Mind, Self, and Society, 210).

In the tale of Balin and Balan, Malory raises for the first time the dangers of social identification.   The quest for civilization is so intense that even though it makes Arthur socially (for a war society, militarily) superior to the Eleven Kings, it occurs at the expense of the uniqueness of the individual. Again, as Mead so acutely understands, "an institution is, after all, nothing but an organization of attitudes which we all carry in us, the organized attitudes of others that control and determine conduct" (211). These attitudes of the general other--here of Merlin and Arthur--drive out whatever unique "I" may have originally existed. The identity or self that Balin achieves, or is now aware of, is no longer the awkward but unique "poore knyght"; it is rather a social construct organized around Arthur whose raw energy is being manipulated by Merlin into a force for domination of the environment. Balin becomes conscious of himself as a dominating force, a questing knight, and loses the ability to be conscious of anything outside of Arthur's goals. In spite of Balin's apparently noble intentions, after he is separated from Balan, he causes destruction and suffering where ever he goes. For example, Balin is responsible for wounding King Pelles and creating the "wasteland" which follows:

> So he rode forthe thorow the fayre contreyes and citeys and founde the peple dede slayne on every syde, and all that evir were on lyve cryed and seyde,
>   `A Balyne! Thou hast done and caused grete vengeaunce in thys contreyes! For the dolerous stroke thou gaff unto kynge Pellam thes three contreyes ar destroyed. And doute nat but the vengeaunce woll falle on the at the laste!´ (54).

Balin's responsibility for the wasteland condition brings up again--and it is essential to recall the discussion of meaning--the paradox underlying the quest for civilization: that humans are capable of creating institutions which destroy them. Arthur's best knight is a social automaton, a plague released upon the countryside. Balin, it should be stressed, is not corrupt; he is highly devoted and moral. The problem is rather inherent in the civilization itself. As Carl Jung points out, "The educated man"--he means the civilized man who affirms an objective hierarchy of values--"tries to repress the inferior one in himself, without realizing that by this he forces the latter to become revolutionary" (Psychology and Religion, 95).

We might rightly ask what would have been Malory's model for such a concept of civilization and selves. To be sure, it was the aggressive and acquisitive nobility whose exploitation of their position at the center of ideology and exploitation of the resources of the land created both the high culture of chivalry and the popular revolutions that mark the fourteenth and fifteenth centuries. The ultimate model for the development of self-conscious individuals was, of course, the Catholic Church. We must recall St. Augustine's constant assertion that man's only hope lies in his viewing his life from the point of view of Christian doctrine. As the doctrines, liturgy, and rituals of the Church became more elaborately solidified and uniform in the late Middle Ages (as we shall see in the next section), the "I" component lost the privilege to modify and, indeed, create the individual's own Christian identity. The condition of meaninglessness suggests that the "I" component has lost God's acknowledgement in the sense that through the Church God demands total attainment of personhood within the purview of doctrine. This is what happens to Balin and Balan; Balin's quest for social identity is so intense that Balan is forced to give up his right to influence Balin, and, of course, at this point Balan disappears from the tale. Over-determination, which means that all feelings of self-value originate in institutional rituals, demands stable meanings to mysteries such as the Eucharist or even Kingship and therefore permits no individual participation in the sense of individual input into the mystery. The result is complete social control of identity through a self-consciousness that, because meaning is stable, can see only doctrinal order in the world, nothing else. Innovation, the random response of the "I" to environmental stimuli disappears, and yet as we saw earlier innovation is the absolute ground of human existence. The dualistic or symbiotic structure of the meaningful is abolished because the "I" component is always the source of the unpredictable and disorder. St. Thomas Aquinas in the Summa Theologica plainly condemns "private individuals who have no business to decide matters of faith" (II, ii, q.1, a.10). Erik Erikson sees this social principle as the origin of Martin Luther's rebellion against his inherited historical-consciousness: "The Roman Church, more than any other church or political organization, succeeded in making an ideological dogma--formulated, defended, and imposed by a central governing body--the exclusive condition for <u>any</u> identity on earth" (<u>Young Man Luther</u>, 181). The Round Table will eventually do the same thing to the knights so much so that Tristram, in pronouncing the heroic <u>I will not serve</u>, cannot even find a way to stay alive outside of the institution. He simply submits to death.

Malory tells the tale of Balin and Balan early in his romance, and its theme sets the stage for what eventually happens to Lancelot, Tristram, Lamerok, and Palomides. The number of foreshadowings in this tale exceeds any other, and, therefore, the conclusion of the tale is important. Balan disappears from the community of knights; there is no physical or ideological place for an element of the personality which responds to the environment and other humans from the point of view of the absolutely unique individual. The quest for society simply destroys what Balan represents. But at the end of the tale, the brothers meet again; the "I" comes back as a revolutionary and an enemy. This time Balan and Balin are unable to recognize each other, so changed is Balin by the the social process. The battle that ensues is well known; it begins the "dolerous stroke" theme which recurs throughout the romance and suggests that a knight fights or destroys what is dearest to him. The cause is always the same: adoption of an identity that makes the individual himself unrecognizable to those who did not also go through the social process. Malory tells us:

> `O, Balan, my broder! Thow hast slayne me and I the, wherfore alle the wyde world shalle speke of us bothe.´
>
> `Allas!´ sayde Balan, `that ever I sawe this day that thorow myshap I myght nat knowe yow! For I aspyed wel your two swerdys, but.bycause ye had another shild I demed ye had ben another knyght!´
>
> `Allas!´ saide Balyn, `all that maade unhappy knyght in the castel for he caused me <u>to leve myn owne shelde to our bothes destruction.</u> And yf I myght lyve I wold destroye that castel for ylle customes.´ (57, emphasis mine)

The "unhappy" knight who gave Balin an unrecognizable shield is not alone in the blame; he is merely the last step in a process that had begun long before. Balin's new identity--symbolically, the shield--had made him unrecognizable to Balan. In this sense, the "unhappy" knight is also Merlin who instigates the process of social identification by promulgating self-consciousness. Balin as Arthur's first fully self-conscious knight is the first knight to organize his entire life from the standpoint of the ideology of the Round Table, and this is why the tale is filled with so many foreshadowings; organized behaviors enable one to predict a response in a certain situation. It looks forward to the meaninglessness of Lancelot and Tristram, the murder of Lamerok, to the vengefulness of Gawain, to Galahad who is the second to carry Balin's sword, and finally to the "dolerous stroke" and "dolerous day" when Arthur himself is destroyed by the forces of Mordred who comes from within Arthur himself, not from Arthur's society for Mordred repudiates its values, but from within the repressed elements of Arthur's personality, the chaotic "I" elements that Merlin ostensibly refined out of Arthur. By the very end, even Balin has become revolutionary, swearing to destroy the castle (the Round Table) and its custom (ideology).

Merlin directs the growth of civilized men through selective repression, and, naturally enough, it is he who recognizes immediately the destructiveness of Mordred. Merlin represents the drive toward order, explanation, categorization in the same sense that St. Augustine advises men to devote themselves fully to God by directing their lives toward God and away from the temporal things of the world. Neither Merlin nor St. Augustine could anticipate the possibility that in such radical devotion men might well lose the ability to recognize each other as unique human beings and lose the innovative ways that lie outside of the ideological purview. Lancelot in his radical devotion to the highest lady loses the ability to recognize his actions as simple adultery; he explains it to himself in another way--with cultural legitimation. At one point in On Christian Doctrine St. Augustine unwittingly defines the tragic potential in the quest for civilization and selfhood, "For when He said 'With thy whole heart, and with thy whole soul, and with thy whole mind,' He did leave any part of life which should be free and find itself room to desire the enjoyment of something else" (19). And thus when Balin encounters his brother after long separation, he cannot recognize him because his faculties for doing so have withered away; he is totally consumed with devotion to the social mode. As he rides away from the castle carrying his new shield, he thinks to himself: "what adventure shall falle to me, be it lyf or deathe, I will take the adventure and that shall come to me" (56). A moment later when he meets an anonymous knight, Balin organizes his stimulus field in the way he knows how and categorizes the configuration as an "adventure," never considering that it might be his own brother. It is not inappropriate to borrow Malory's frequent comment: "And alle that wrought Merlin."

When Balin and Balan are buried--significantly in one tomb-- a lady knowing only Balan's name writes only that one name on the tombstone. But as Malory tells us:

> In the morne cam Merlyn and lete wryte Balyns name on the tombe with letters of gold that 'here lyeth Balyn le Saveage that was the knyght with two swerdes and he that smote the dolorous stroke.' Also Merlyn lete make there a bedde, that ther shold never man lye therin but he wente out of his wytte. (58)

Merlin makes no mention and has no interest in Balan, nor is he likely to since his function is to raise the self-consciousness of the knights by providing them with historically based identities to be conscious of. The magical bed is the tomb of Balin and Balan, now re-united. The influence of the "I" component will finally assert itself, and yet Merlin sees this condition as insanity. He follows here St. Augustine who writes, "cursed be the man who trusteth in man" (Christian Doctrine, 18).

The trap which makes the importation of the social perspective into individuals eventually destructive grows out of two seemingly natural conditions. First, society appears to precede selves, both temporally and ontologically, and therefore society becomes the origin of thought in that society provides the individual with the criteria for making judgments about his own behavior. As Mead puts it, society is the origin of mind: "if . . . you regard the social process of experience as prior (in a rudimentary form) to the experience of mind and explain the origin of minds in terms of the interaction of individuals within that process, then not only the origin of minds, but also the interaction among individual minds (which is thus seen to be internal to their very nature and presupposed by their existence or development at all) cease to seem mysterious and miraculous" (Mind, Self, and Society, 50). The problem here is that only individual minds can innovate, and to the extent to which anyone is socialized he loses the ability to innovate significantly new responses to the environment. This common sense analysis leads to something else. The second feature of the development of selves is the meaningful; one now knows the meaning or value of his acts because his mind is filled out by the social process. Balin's mind becomes filled to the extent that he could recognize nothing outside the social process, but Balin, of course, looks forward to the end of the romance. Here I want to stick to its rise. More in line with the emerging civilization is Gareth, the conclusion of whose social experience is the full recognition of him as Gareth, the brother of Gawain. Though it will eventually be a destructive trap for Gareth, initially the objective feeling status of the institution causes the symbiosis to work well: "'Alas! my fayre brother,' seyde sir Gawayne, 'I ought of ryght to worshyp you'" (222). Malory suggests that Gareth acquires mind and value only after he has passed through the social process of experience.

The overwhelming appearance of psychic health acquired in the symbiosis of institution and individual is confirmed by the conclusion of Gareth's quest--his marriage to Lyones. Marriage is the model for symbiotic identity, for it is only the husband who can make a woman a wife, and, naturally, it is only a wife who can give the status of husband to a man. This is the point of the conversation between Gareth and Lyones just before their marriage, but it is, in fact, an imitation of the exchange between Gareth and the Round Table:

'My moste noble kynge,' seyde dame Lyonesse, 'wete you well that my lorde, sir Gareth, ys to me more lever to have and welde as my husbonde than ony kyng other prynce that is crystyned; and if I may nat have hym, I promyse you I woll never have none. For, my lorde Arthure,' seyde dame Lyonesse,

`wete you well he is my fyrste love, and he shall be the laste; and yf ye woll suffir hym to have his wyll and fre choyse, I dare say he woll have me.´
    `That is trouthe,´ seyde sir Gareth, `and I have nat you and welde you as my wyff, there shall never lady nother jantyllwoman rejoyse me.´   (223)

The "Tale of Gareth" is above all a quest for meaning and the feeling of the numinous which is produced by the performance of meaningful acts. The meaningful identity Gareth earns reproduces in him--as biologic individual--the content of the category of the numen. More than any other knight, Gareth becomes the archetype for everything that the Middle Ages understood about the attainment of a sufficient life, and, what is more, in Gareth the attributes of the numen exist harmoniously in an individual. This is precisely the reason why the tragedy becomes inexorable when Lancelot kills Gareth, and why Gawain cannot forgive and reconcile with Lancelot; once Gareth as the model for healthy identity formation is dead, there is no going back.
    Critics of Malory have had particular trouble with this aspect of the "Tale of Gareth."   Eugène Vinaver calls it "Malory´s most puzzling work," and he surmises that much of the sense of the tale is lost in Malory´s adaptation of a much more coherent "romance of Gaheret" (Works, III, 1427-30). No such French romance survives; rather it is more likely that Malory invented his own tale of Gareth based upon the numerous models of the enfance provided in the narratives of Perceval, Tristan, Ipomadon, Lybeas Desconus--as Larry Benson has argued (Malory´s Morte Darthur, 92-108). Malory needed a tale which would raise to a metaphysical level the process of developing self-consciousness as related on a behavioral and social level in the adventures of Torre, Gawain, Ywain, Pellinor, Marhalt, Balin, and, of course, Lancelot. The tale of Gareth comes after the adventures of all the major knights of the Round Table and serves as a summing up and a pronouncement on the metaphysical significance of what all these knights have been doing. The special context of Gareth´s battles gives us a first clue as to what Malory is up to:

'Hit may well be,' seyde the dwarff, 'but this knyght hath passed all the perelouse passages and slayne the Blak Knyght and other two mo, and wonne the Grene knyght, and the Rede knyght, and the Blew Knyght.' (195)

Critics have been hesitant to interpret the knights whose names are colors, assuming that the key has been lost with the original tale. But I think we need not be so timid; the battles with the color-knights form the deep structure of Gareth's simultaneous quest for civilization and selfhood. The quest is, moreover, set in the context of an even deeper psychological battle against Lyonet, the Lady who observes Gareth's actions and denigrates him. Thus he fights physically with the color-knights but psychologically the more difficult battle is with the Feminine and with the point of view of the general other as observer of his actions. Throughout the ordeal Gareth is mocked and ridiculed (de-valued) by Lyonet until he is triumphant over the four color-knights which is simultaneously a victory over Lyonet who now begins to praise him:

'A, Jesu! mervayle have I,' seyde the damesell, 'what maner a man ye be, for hit may never be other but that ye be com of jantyll bloode, for so fowle and shamfully dud never woman revyle a knyght as I have done you, and ever curteysly ye have suffyrde me, and that com never but of jantyll bloode' (191)

The victory is followed a day later by Gareth's meeting Lyones, Lyonet's sister, and his instantly falling in love with her. The quest, then, suggests an initial tension between the male and female principles, or to use Carl Jung's terms anima and animus, and Gareth succeeds in harmonizing them (Psychological Types, 594-96). On an internal level, the battle is within Gareth's psyche to determine the inner attitude of his psyche. The debate over the implications of the name "Beaumains" is substantially resolved if we consider Gareth's quest as a search for harmony between the anima and animus, or in less hypostatized terms, the ultimate bundle of antinomies that is both the world and the psyche. Gareth must organize male and female traits--symbolically, all the forces of the world--so that his overall dispositon or attitude is male.   This is not to suggest that any such universal male attitude exists, but rather that Gareth must bring his self-concept in line with the prevailing social concept of maleness rather than femaleness, for the pre-minded or pre-social individual is really neither male nor female except in the biologic sense.   Though I will get to this more fully in the next section, civilization is inherently a tension reducing adaptive strategy--the bliss that Gottfried von Strassburg says most people only wish to revel in.

Gareth's only means of establishing his orientation is the social process of interacting with males and females.   The social plane is the only place such attitudes exist.   Gareth is a big and strong individual; Malory uncharacteristically makes a special point of his size, but the name "Beaumains" does not connote "fair-handed" in the sense of strength, as Vinaver thinks that it does.   Rather it suggests, as Kay intends, effeminacy.   Hence, Gareth's "Beaumains" means soft or pretty hands, and his role as kitchen-boy implies a disharmony within his psyche about anima-animus traits and their manifestations. The emergence of the dominant male attitude occurs only after experiencing the social process.   Gareth fights and defeats knight after knight, who begin to think of him as a pretty rough and courageous man.   In this way, Gareth assimilates the opposite knights' attitudes toward himself and discovers, of course, that he is a very powerful knight.   But he cannot do this without the point of view of Lyonet, for she denigrates him throughout the process.   For him to take her view of himself as weak, effeminate, and unworthy would mean an immediate abandonment of the quest and no knighthood for Gareth. Lyonet prevents Gareth from taking her viewpoint, from seeing himself as weak, by making her view denigratory.   Gareth learns that seeing himself as weak or as a kitchen-boy is painful and therefore to be avoided, more painful even than the bruises and wounds he can get in battle.   After the successful defeat of the four color-knights and the change in Lyonet, made possible by the expulsion or repression feminine traits in Gareth, the name "Beaumains" acquires a new meaning, but, naturally enough, the quest gives a new meaning to everything:

`But I mervayle,´ seyde she [Morgause, Gareth´s
mother], that sir Kay dud mok and scorn hym and
gaff hym to name Bewmaynes; yet sir Kay,´ seyde
the quene, `named hym more ryghteously than he
wende, for I dare sey he is as fayre an handid man
and wel disposed, and he be on lyve, as ony
lyvynge.´ (210)

The key to Morgause´s statement is that Gareth is now well
disposed.

We have yet to consider the color-knights. The key to
understanding Gareth´s quest lies in his harmonizing the anima-
animus. What he has done is organize within his mind or psyche
a set of attitudes or a disposition which reflects the content of
"maleness" rather than "femaleness." Attitudes are, in the
general sense, prerequisite to action, but they, too, arise in the
experience of the social process. Arthur may act without
attitudes but not Gareth. Jung´s definition of attitude may
help: "For us, attitude is a readiness of the psyche to act or to
react in a certain direction" (Psychological Types, 526-27).
Thus the process of civilization is the process of organizing
within individuals a set of attitudes. In this sense Gareth´s
quest goes beyond the normal "fair unknown" pattern and
explores the origin and content of the attitudes themselves.
Though most critics have tended to ignore the color-knights,
they were not ignored by Alfred Tennyson whose version of the
tale provides another key. Tennyson did not hesitate to
interpret the color-knights, and his perception of the anima-
animus complementarity was so strong that he was constrained
to have Gareth marry his direct complement, Lynette, instead
of Lyonors (Tennyson´s spellings). He writes,

Then Arthur mindful of Sir Gareth ask´d:
`Damsel, ye know this Order lives to crush
All wrongers of the realm. But say, these four,
Who be they? What the fashion of men?´
    `They be of foolish fashion, O Sir King,
The fashion of that old knight-errantry
Who ride abroad and do but what they will;
Courteous or bestial from the moment, such
As have nor law nor king; and three of these

Proud in their fantasy call themselves the Day,
Morning-Star, and Noon-Sun, and Evening-Star,
Being strong fools; and never a whit more wise
The fourth, who always rideth arm'd in black,
A huge man-beast of boundless savagery.
He names himself the Night and oftener Death;
And wears a helmet mounted with a skull,
and bears a skeleton figured on his arms,
To show that who may slay or scape the three,
Slain by himself, shall enter endless night.
And all these four be fools, but mighty men,
And therefore am I come for Lancelot.'
                    ("Gareth and Lynette")

For Tennyson--though his tone suggests that it is silly--Gareth's quest is clearly a cosmogonic myth, the same sort of creation of order form chaos story as told in Genesis where night is separated from day and the heavens from the firmament.   The old knights are lawless and therefore chaotic. The function of the Round Table is to crush, i.e., give order, to such disorder.   The nature of the acts of the old knights is very much like those of Arthur at the outset of his career; he acts spontaneously and chaotically, but with great energy.   The cosmogonic myth represents the transition from the primitive energy of chaos to the refined power of civilization and explanation.   The battle remains the central act of mankind but its character changes with the imposition of order.   Gareth is the last of Arthur's knights to experience the creation of the civilization first hand; from now on experience will only be ritual.   Tennyson describes the change as the difference between Arthur and Lancelot and the difference between battle and tournament:

For Lancelot was the first in Tournament
But Arthur mightiest on the battlefield.
                    ("Gareth and Lynette")

Tennyson is right.
    Malory takes the problem of the color-knights much more seriously than does Tennyson, and it is more difficult.   Instead of allegorical figures who represent night, morning, noon, and

evening, Malory presents pure symbols: Black, Green, Red, and Blue. In the next section in connection with the Romanesque and the Gothic I want to point out that symbols cannot have literal meanings because they stand for what is infinite, ineffable, or numinal in human experience. Here, we do not know the world of chaos; all the world we know is the order and the explanations that men have ascribed to it--an interpreted and meaningful world. And yet these knights are symbols of that chaotic world which is felt by the unconscious to be logically and temporally prior to the one that is known. Perhaps an example will be helpful because the knights stand for an empty category which is felt to be the origin of the organization of attitudes which eventually constitute civilized man. Chrism or sacramental oils are symbols for grace. No matter how much we talk about it, no one has seen or measured grace, and no one knows anything about grace itself. And yet most everyone knows the feeling of holiness or of the numinous derived from encounters with devices symbolic of grace. We cannot know whether or not grace actually exists, but the effects of the symbol on the individual are empirically observable. What the symbol does to the individual is call out an attitude already present, and we name this attitude or feeling grace. The sacramental oil works only so long as grace is believed to be something in itself. The power of symbols, and indeed their purpose, is in providing an occasion for the individual to organize or control his attitudes and thus direct his energy into culturally valid activity. The structure of symbolism--symbol and response--suggest what Malory is doing with the color-knights. These knights become symbols for the category of the numen. Gareth, therefore, is organizing within himself a set of attitudes as a response to the environment of the world (the knights) he encounters. At the same time, the converse is tacitly at work; Gareth is at war with the openness of the numen and, by attributing through his acts a content, meaning, or order to the category of the numen, he closes it. We know that the category of the numen has such contents or such a nature because we know what attitudes are organized in Gareth when he confronts it. In the same manner we know what grace is because we know what effects it produces in the individual.

There are initially four color-knights. As Jung tells us, four is always associated by the unconscious with the world creating Deity:

> The idea of those old philosophers was that God manifested himself in the creation of the four elements. They were symbolized by the four partitions of the circle. . . .
> The division into four, the synthesis of the four, the miraculous apparition of the four colors and the four stages of the work [of alchemy]: the nigredo, the dealbatio, the rubefactio and citrinitas, are constant preoccupations of the old philosophers. The four symbolizes the parts, qualities and aspects of the One. . . .
> The four is an age-old, presumably prehistoric symbol, always associated with the idea of a world creating deity. (Psychology and Religion, 70-71)

We cannot know if Malory knew anything about alchemy, but it is clear that Malory's Gareth is doing the same thing as the alchemists. Arthurian Romance and alchemy are two vastly different and yet parallel movements within the same cultural phenomenon of discovering the contents of the category that was believed to be the origin of the created world. Malory's colors do not match the alchemist's black, white, red, and yellow; but there need be no attributional consistency between symbols for the same category; when there is consistency in attributes, as in the case of four or in the use of colors, it is both fortuitous and fortifying. Both the alchemist and Gareth-- as representative of the cultural effort of the Round Table society--are on the conquest of what Chaucer, who did know alchemy very well, calls the "secree of secrees." The parallel between Chaucer and Malory is significant. A major theme of Chaucer's Canterbury Tales advises the abandonment of the quest for the "secree of secrees." Chaucer sees the conquest of the numen as the highest tragedy, for it makes the infinite and ineffably diverse world of things in themselves subject to the limits of human reason, the desire for order, and anxiety for truth. Though this is not the place to discuss Chaucer, the ending of the "Canon's Yeoman's Tale" sheds some light on the magnitude of what Gareth succeeds in doing:

`For this science and this konnyng,´ quod he
`Is of the secree of secrees, pardee.´
    Also ther was a disciple of Plato,
That on a tyme seyde his maister to . . .
`Telle me the name of the privee stone?´
    And Plato answerde unto hym anoon,
`Take the stoon that Titanos men name.´
    `Which is that?´ quod he. `Magnasia is the same.´
Seyde Plato.   `Ye, sire, and is is thus?
This is ignotum per ignocius.
What is Magnasia, good sire, I yow preye?´
    `It is a water that is maad, I seye,
Of elements foure,´ quod Plato.
    `Telle me the roote, good sire," quod he tho,
`Of that water, if it be youre wil.´
    `Nay, nay,´ quod Plato, `certein, that I nyl.
The philosophres sworn were everychoon
That they sholden discovere it unto noon,
Ne in no book it write in no manere.
For unto Crist it is so lief and deere
That he wol nat that it discovered bee,
But where it liketh to his deitee
Men for t´enspire, and eek for to deffende
Whom that hym liketh; lo, this is the ende.´
    Thanne conclude I thus, sith that God of hevene
Ne wil nat that the philosophres nevene
How that a man shal come unto this stoon,
I rede, as for the beste, let it goon.
For whoso maketh God his adversarie
As for to werken any thyng in contrarie
Of his wil, certes, never shal he thryve,
Thogh that he multiplie terme of his lyve.

Chaucer, who certainly had a better philosophical understanding of the conquest of the numen than Malory though a lesser psychological understanding, sees that the quest for explanation and civilization is a battle directly against God or the numen, and yet, as dangerous as this battle is, it is capable of transforming life. In fighting the four color-knights, Gareth experiences the feeling of the numinous which, it will be recalled, is a mysterious wonder resulting from a direct participation with the wholly other, but something very strange and potentially destructive occurs in the quest. Rudolf Otto explains,

> `The numinous´ is the object of search and desire and yearning, and that too for its own sake and not only for the sake of the aid and backing that men expect from it in the natural sphere. . . . This takes place, not only in the forms of `rational´ religious worship, but in those queer `sacramental´ observances and rituals and procedures of communion in which the human being seeks to get the numen into his possession. (Idea of the Holy, 32)

The context of Otto´s discovery that humans seek to possess the numen is a discussion of a transition in the feeling of the numinous from awefulness to wonderfulness and rapture. This characteristic is easily seen in the battle itself, which for Malory´s knights is always a numinal experience, (except for certain fights of the four best knights in whom the meaningful is failing). The battle places the knight in direct participation through his acts with the origin of his being as a knight; but as the institution matures and the knights come to know what to expect, they begin to feel a possessiveness that makes the numinal experience actually a product of human effort. Gareth´s battles are only a little more awe-inspiring and wonderful than battles elsewhere, but the possession of the numinous is well exampled:

> Than the Rede Knyght wexed wroth and doubled his strokes and hurte Bewmaynes wondirly sore, that the bloode ran down to the grounde, that hit was wondir to see that stronge batayle. Yet as the laste Bewmaynes strake hym to the erthe. And as he wold have slayne the Rede Knyght, he cryed,
> `Mercy, noble knyght, sle me nat, and I shall yelde me to the wyth fyffty knyghtes with me that be at my commaundemente, and forgyff the all the dispyte that thou haste done to me, and the deth of my brothir the Blak Knyght, and the wynnyng of my brother the Grene Knyght.´ (188-89)

The color knights, in short, symbolize the numen, the Divine, or the "secree of secrees" which is being imported into the knight's life. In fighting them Gareth places himself in contact with the Divine in the same way that the Christian does through the sacraments and the Mass. The important result in both cases is that the individual learns that these particular acts, and only these acts, are effective in relating himself to the Divine. The relationship is confirmed by the feeling of the numinous, and thereby the individual is transformed from a valueless and nameless human into the highly ordered and magnificent Sir Gareth--or saint. On an internal level, such acts organize within Gareth a set of attitudes which because they are called out by the opposing color-knights seem to demonstrate the meaning or content of the color-knights. The repetition of aboriginal acts, therefore, has the net effect of filling out or giving content to the category of the numen since it is these acts and only these acts which bring the Divine into the life of the individual. The knights feel that they can now state with certainty what the numen contains because they can see clearly what Gareth does as a response to the numinal symbols. Gareth is a fighter, he becomes a governor of the lands of Lyones, he is a husband, and he is a Christian who draws together all the components of his newly created self in a tournament and marriage on the feasts of the Assumption of the Blessed Mary into heaven and of Michael the Archangel. The Black Knight, the Green Knight, the Red Knight, and the Blue Knight come now to stand also for the ideology which the Middle Ages deduced from its experience of the numen as if ideology and numen were isomorphic. The components cannot be taken in an allegorical sense, but rather they represent the organization of interests within Gareth of Knighthood, Governance, Love, and Christianity. In short, the culture now feels that it possesses Truth.

We arrive now finally at the import of Gareth's conquest. Carl Jung, in Psychology and Religion relates his experience with patients whose dreams exhibit a quadrapartite structure, precisely the sort of experience Gareth undergoes. He discovers that most of his patients attribute the symbol to themselves: "I was careful, therefore, not to disturb them with my own opinions and as a rule I discovered that people took it [the experience of the four] to symbolize themselves or rather something in themselves. They felt it as belonging intimately to themselves as a sort of creative background, a life-producing sun in the depths of the unconscious mind. . . . The application of the comparative method indubitably shows the quaternity as being a more or less direct representation of the God manifested in his creation. We might therefore, conclude that the symbol, spontaneously produced in the dreams of modern people, means the same thing--the God within" (71-72). Gareth's story signals both the high-point of the Round Table as institution and the death of the numen as infinite and "wholly other." Now all spirit is contained within the institution itself; that is to say, there is no meaning outside of the Round Table and, in fact, the culture is the origin of Truth. Such experiences as Gareth's quest against the four color knights represents the production of a mandala, a quadrapartite circle suggesting the emergency of psychic health or wholeness after a state of psychosis or internal disorder. But just as the circle is four-fold it is also a unity; health and wholeness emerge when the many is contained or harmonized by the One. Hence the quest through the multiplicity of the color knights climaxes in Gareth's meeting with the Red Knight of the Red Lands, who subsumes the four color knights in the same sense that theologians speak of three persons in one God. Civilization is inherently a unifying and tension reducing process, but one that occurs only as the influence of the numen diminishes. Gareth's quest marks both the triumph of the civilization and the death of the numen. The Red Knight of the Red Lands is established by Malory as a type of sun-god or numen, precisely as Jung observes in his patients: "blow ye nat the horne [to start the battle] tyll hit be hygh none, for now hit is aboute pryme, and now encresyth his myght, that as men say he hath seven mennys strength" (197). Or later, "And, sir, now I woll telle the that every day my strength encresyth tylle none untyll I have seven mennys strength" (200).

The addition of this knight, who repeats and subsumes the preceding experiences, shows Malory's acute sensitivity to the psychological level of the knight's quest in that the social process is experienced piecemeal but forms an organized whole, a Gestalt, within the mind. As Chaucer also saw, this phenomenon of mind challenges and attacks God. The Red

Knight as the One is the numen or wholly other, and he also becomes at the high point of civilization the worst enemy of a society committed to the quest for order: "And so I ensured her to do all the vylany unto Arthurs knyghtes, and that I sholde take vengeaunce uppon all these knyghtes" (199-200). Committed as he is to Merlin's explanatory quest, Arthur's imposing order on the land is the same act as imposing definitions on the category of the numen. For as we have seen, "Merylon made the Rounde Table in tokenyng of the rowndnes of the worlde, for all men sholde by the Rounde Table undirstonde the rowndenes sigynfyed by ryght" (541). But what if the world is not round, and what about all the things the world may be that the Round Table is not interested in! The roundness comes finally to signify the closing down of the openness of the numen. Here, just before Malory turns to the real center of his work, the "Tristràm," he presents the institution at its highest moment of maturity, when the symbiosis of the numen and institution makes the members believe in an isomorphism between world and ideology. This is actually a turning point after which the ineffable numen becomes subservient to the ideology of the institution. God now belongs to man in the sense that his entire existence is fulfilled in the institution.

Malory sets Gareth's battle with the Red Knight of the Red Lands just below the window of Lyones, so that by defeating the sun-god Gareth can simultaneously adopt a new god and new source of warmth, light, and meaning. That is, Gareth replaces the god of unknown origin with another of his own choice and creation, but which just as effectively becomes the source of his identity as a civilized man. The radically extramental is replaced by Truth. Lyones becomes a rival sun, one whose strength grows as the strength of the other wanes. Eventually, because she is chosen by man, she will replace the sun-god that Gareth will soon with her aid destroy forever:

> And than sir Bewmaynes, whan his helme was off, he loked up to the wyndowe, and there he sawe the fayre lady dame Lyones, and she made hym suche countenaunce that his herte waxed lyght and joly. And therewith he bade the Rede Knyght of the Rede Laundis makes hym redy, `and lette us do oure batayle to the utterance.´ (199)

2.3 Historicization of the Numen

The growth of the Round Table as institution corresponds to (more precisely, is feuled by) an increasing feeling among the knights that the institution possesses Truth, its own inspirational sun at the center of being. In alchemy, medieval philosophy, aesthetics, and, indeed, in theology, whatever substance was imperfectly mixed or whose parts did not follow the laws of proportion became subject to decay and corruption. In the political sphere, therefore, the goal of the Round Table is to construct a society which approaches the immutable status of truth in perfect cohesion. During the formative period of the institution, Malory lets us overhear the following conversation:

> `What tydynges at Camelot?´ seyde that one knyght.
> `Be my hede,´ seyde the other, `there have I bene and aspied the courte of kynge Arthure, and there ys such a felyship that they may never be brokyn, and well-nyghe all the world holdith with Arthure, for there ys the floure of chevalry. (74)

I take "floure of chevalry" to mean the perfection of chivalry, and in this chapter I want to explore in both medieval theology and human psychology the question of why it is that leaders in the Middle Ages sought with such energy to move their institutions into the position formerly occupied (in the psychology of homo religiosus) by the numen and to define that perfection by cohesion and truth. In my own view, truth is really the wholly other, what we will never know, but medieval institutions developed in general along the lines of thought and doctrine rather than experience (when experience would seem all the more practical and useful), and the direction of this development is toward ideological tension reduction or coherence and, therefore, toward the condition of perfection and away from the necessities of experience. What occurred in the fourteenth and fifteenth century rage for historicism (to which Malory's romance is a reaction, as I maintain) was a precipitate of a more pervasive phenomenon of the conquest of the numen. The Middle Ages sought at the highest level to make ideology truth; that is, to know or to fill out the category of the numen in a way that would result in an isomorphism of institution and truth. The pattern of St. Thomas' making predications about the nature of God and then drawing deductions from them about the nature and moral proclivities of mankind has the same structure as the historicism implicit in both Merlin's construction of the Round Table ideology and in Caxton's preface to his edition of Le Morte Darthur. Historicism posits properties of the past (or any realm inaccessible to experience) and deduces the nature of present life from those. This is fundamentally a scientific way of thinking, and I want to explore why the Round Table directed its scientific research toward transcendentals rather than toward experience, when it would seem that an empirical orientation of the sort described in John Dewey's The Reconstruction of Philosophy, or most significantly Alfred Korzybski's Science and Sanity would better direct the institution. Dewey, Korzybski, and Malory (as I am arguing) point to transcendental orientations as the ontological root of tragedy.

As the last section pointed out, institutions emerge only when a number of individuals give up their own personal points of view and agree to interpret all their experience from the point of view of the group. In the philosophy of St. Thomas Aquinas, this structure is taken as natural, not human created;

Merlin's case shows it to be cultural and created. Aquinas, following Aristotle, asserts an identity of the natural and institutional. He writes, for example, in The Division and Methods of the Sciences that "As the Philosopher teaches in his Politics, when several things are directed to one end, one of them must be director or ruler and the rest directed and ruled. This is evident in . . . the powers of the soul, for according to the natural order the irascible and concupiscible powers are ruled by reason. Now all the sciences and arts are directed to one end, namely to the perfection of man, which is happiness. So it follows that one of them must be ruler of all the rest; and this science rightly claims the name of wisdom, for it belongs to the wise man to direct others" (86-87). If wisdom is to control the development of the institution, it is important to know the proper object of wisdom. Wisdom does not address experience or the things of the world, which are the objects of empirical reasoning; wisdom, rather, orients itself toward the categories of the mind. Wisdom is the science of ordering the mind, and, as we discovered in the case of Merlin, wisdom is also the epistemological center of the institution. In all cases, this sort of thinking constructs an analogical or proportionate relationship between the categories of the mind and the objects of the senses. St. Thomas goes on,

> `The most intelligible beings` [i.e., categories of the mind] can be understood from the viewpoint of the intellect's own knowledge. Because a being has the power of intellect owing to its freedom from matter, those things must be supremely intelligible that are most disengaged from matter. For the intelligible object and the intellect must be proportionate to each other and belong to the same genus, since the intellect and the intelligible object are one in act. Now those things are most separated from matter that abstract not only from individual matter (such as natural forms understood universally, which are the objects of natural science), but entirely from sensible matter; and these are separated from matter not only in thought, like mathematicals, but also in existence, such as God and the Intelligences. Consequently, the

science inquiring into these beings seems to be most
intellectual and the director or mistress of the rest.
(88)

The historicism or philosophic realism of the Middle Ages
meant simply that whatever was not material and was purely an
object of thought--a universal--held a position of priority over
mere sensible beings. If men wanted to know more about what
it meant to be human and wanted to pursue the one end of
happpiness, the established means for doing so was filling out
the attributes of "intelligible beings" or categories and deducing
behaviors from that. Wisdom or categorial thinking orders the
mind and creates social institutions whose ideology is,
consequently, categorial. The assumption is tacitly made all
along that nothing is lost in the process and that the ideology
fully expresses and explains the original experience; that, as St.
Thomas says, the intelligible object and the intellect are
proportionate and one in act.   What in experience that cannot
conform to the doctrine is cast out as evil or non-being, and
while it is never suggested that the world as a whole will ever
be without evil or non-being, the potential exists that any
individual (the microcosm) might ultimately mirror exactly the
infinite, the creative mind of God, and a selective group of such
individuals might become--"a felyship that they may never be
broken." Perfection ineluctably becomes the goal of thought
because both transcend matter.
The key perception of the writers of Arthurian Romance
suggests that St. Thomas is wrong; the writers conceive of
knights who are without evil and they construct political
systems that reflect the unity at the center of being. As it
turns out, such a world is merely a mental construction that
replaces the real one and blocks a knight's clear perception of
all the incoherencies that steadily convert perfection to
tragedy. The Queen of West Land's statement about Merlin's
making the Round Table as a symbol for the roundness of the
world has, as we see, the same structure as St. Thomas'
argument about intelligible beings, but if we understand the
construction of the Round Table through the selective
destruction of information of private experience we see that the
world is not round or perfect but only that both Merlin and St.
Thomas construct intellectual worlds by making predications

from the material world to the numinal. The openness of the
numen permits that, of course.

We need to look just a bit closer at the structure of this
thinking. Man is made in the image and likeness of God, St.
Augustine, among a myriad of others, writes, and therefore as
one understands the attributes of man--or of the roundness of
the Table--one knows, Merlin and St. Thomas feel, something of
the attributes of God--or of the world. The process of
historicizing or concretizing the numen works from the present
to the past or from the created to the creator, and yet it
claims priority for the realm of the numinal or intellectual over
the empirical. Psychologically, the reason for this is, as
pointed out in the last section, that no instituition is self-
legitimating and what Merlin and St. Thomas construct,
therefore, is an explanatory regress which reaches from the
present act to its archetype in the transcendental (whether
past or creative mind of God). The unanticipated effect of this
process is, however, a closure of the numen, something that will
make innovations beyond the original conception of the
institution impossible and, if they do occur, heretical and
destructive of the institution. St. Thomas in Concerning Being
and Essence illustrates very clearly the problem inherent in
wisdom:

> Indeed God has the perfections which are in all
> genera, and for this reason He is called perfect
> simply . . . but He has these (perfections) in a more
> excellent mode than other things, because in Him
> they are one, but in other things they have
> diversity. And this is because all these perfections
> belong to Him according to his simple existence; just
> as if someone were able by means of one quality to
> affect the operations of all qualities, so God in His
> very existence has all perfections. (29)

By compiling all the possible attributes and predications
about God that existed up to his time and rejecting erroneous
and inconsistent ones, St. Thomas in the Summa Theologica
hoped to articulate the qualities which taken as a whole must
constitute God--remembering, of course, that God is always
beyond each perfection, in the same sense that the present is

only the derivative of the more moral past. Even if the Summa were incomplete, the predications it, and a great many others like it, made about God became a body of logically and historically prior knowledge or truth from which deductions about the present conditions of the world could be made. Thus the ideology--the totality of knowledge of the socially constructed reality--came to be rooted ultimately in a fixed and absolute God Himself and, therefore, the derivative institutions operated with the authority that they were expressions of God's will or plan for creation. No other reality need be tolerated, and St. Thomas freely concedes that the community as a whole possesses the right to coerce individuals to accept the one true way.

Early Christian theology such as that of St. Augustine or Dionysius the Areopagite tends to emphasize the mystery and unknowable character of the origin; in contrast, late medieval theology, particularly in the hands of St. Thomas and the schoolmen, becomes a science whose first principles are absolute. The opening sections of the Summa Theologica set forth this radical position:

> I answer that, Sacred doctrine is a science. We must bear in mind that there are two kinds of sciences. There are some which proceed from a principle known by the natural light of the intellect, such as arithmetic and geometry and the like. There are some which proceed from principles known by the light of a higher science. . . . And in this way sacred doctrine is a science, because it proceeds from principles established by the light of a higher science, namely the science of God and the blessed [i.e., the numen] . . . so sacred science believes the principles revealed to it by God. (I, i, q.1, a.2)

Strictly speaking, St. Thomas uses the term "science" in the literal sense of "knowledge" without the connotations of method, but as Jaroslav Pelikan in his Growth of Medieval Theology notes Christian theology did indeed evolve toward the modern notion of science: "It was only slowly that `theology' acquired the specific sense of an organized and learned understanding of the data of revelation" (5). More generally, all ideology evolves this way. The term "Growth" in the title of Pelikan's four volume history refers to change and development, the nature of which is imitated by Malory in his own depiction of the growth of the Round Table. By the time of the late Middle Ages, and especially St. Thomas, theology or more generally ideology had become a science. The task of normal science (as opposed to the revolutionary science of, say, St. Augustine), Thomas Kuhn tells us, is articulation and exemplification. The scientist sees nature (or his object of study) as a puzzle for which there most certainly is a solution, not as a mystery or a wholly other for which there can be no final solution. The normal scientist avoids innovation and concerns himself rather with verification, extrapolation, and reconciliation of minor inconsistencies. This, as we see, is precisely the character of high medieval theology and of Malory's depiction flower of chivalry at the Round Table.

The crucial insight of Arthurian Romance, as just mentioned, is to fulfill Aquinas' hypothesis: "just as if someone were able by means of one quality to affect the operation of all qualities." The Round Table with Lancelot as its flower exemplifies precisely that. And while the full discussion of this point must wait until the next section, here it is enough that we notice the hopelessly incoherent nature of the perfect simplicity of the Round Table. The roundness "sygnyfyed by ryght" (541) suggests both inclusiveness and divisionlessness, but, as we discover, the society is marked by tension at its very heart. Lancelot who not only excels in all perfections, but indeed transcends all perfections, shows ultimately the incoherent nature of the explanatory model, and yet Lancelot, in the manner of abstract perfection, must sustain the material synthesis of knowledge. Aquinas suggests that in God there is no tension and no incoherence, but that cannot be claimed for the philosophy about God or of the institutions based upon it, even though it clearly was in many works featuring the presumptious title summa or more overtly in Gratian's twelfth century Concordantia Discordantium Canonum (The Concordance of Discordant Canons) and the school of canon law he began at Bologna whose purpose was "aimed at creating for the Church a law worthy of it as societas perfectas; canon law should be as complete, as perfect and as free from loopholes as Roman Law" (Heer, 243).

The final result of the historicization of the numen was an immense body of theology replacing the numen, and a reified institution legitimated by that theology, and "set," as Pope Innocent III claimed at the Fourth Lateran Council of 1215, "in the midst between God and man, below God, but above man." And yet at the moment of apparent triumph of the Church in the conquest of the numen during the period of the Lateran Councils and the High Scholastic philosophy of the twelfth and thirteenth centuries, the Christian world was never more beset with heresy, controversy, and religious warfare; so intense was the failure of the quest to produce the unity and order of the origin that nothing short of force and inquisition would hold the church together for the next three centuries. So much might be said of all institutions, for the normal direction of development of any institution or system is toward a reduction in variations of behavior and increasing narrowness of thought resulting from the needs of maintaining cohesion on both the mental and behavioral levels and the process of legitimizing both by means of an explanatory regress toward ever more universal categories. This reduction in the level of individual (i.e., random) participation leads finally to the production of a class of revolutionaries, counter-realities and civil war.

We ought now to turn to Merlin's counterpart in theology and the origin of such institutional life. The most important source for the conquest of the numen is found in the writings and teachings of St. Augustine, Bishop of Hippo. It is important to understand his institutionalization of his religious experience and the quantum increase in cognitive power and meaning he derives from it because Malory imitates this process in his version of the rise of the institution of the Round Table, and it is what initially makes life meaningful--provided that the quest does not end with a definition of the numen as fixed and fulfilled. We can see very clearly this quantum difference in St. Augustine's conversion from Manichaeism and its fundamental world image to Christianity and its different image. In the transition we see clearly that the Christian explanatory system arises because it resolves real problems St. Augustine faced, just as Arthur and Merlin do. The process begins with an inherited image of the world or culture--as St. Augustine says himself of Manichaeism, a reflection of the center of being. Manichaeism was felt to be coherent, integrated, and comprehensive not because it was fully articulated but because it provided the devotee with explanatory power--that is, a critical strategy or heuristic for selecting, evaluating, and organizing (i.e., explaining) perceptual data of experience.

St. Augustine became an "aspirant" to Manichaean sect at the age of eighteen because its doctrines seemed to explain creation and offer a process of self-development that would resolve the terrible anxieties he had about the presence of so much evil and confusion in the world. In this, he appears much like any young knight such as Gareth or Tristram. Very briefly, Manichaean doctrine held that before creation there existed two conflicting forces, light and darkness, each dwelling in its own realm and each committed to the extermination of the other. In the beginning of creation, the Father of Greatness or light sent man to battle with darkness; in the fight man was partially devoured by darkness and all creation thus became a mixture of particles of darkness and particles of light--good and evil. The devotee of Manichaeism enters a process of self-purification--actually, a continuation of the primal battle--and gradually purges from himself particles of evil. When complete, he returns to the primal separation of good from evil; death of the body means the release of the soul, which is light, from imprisonment in evil.

Because this fundamental image of the world so completely matched St. Augustine's daily experience, he felt the paradigm (a useful term here since it implies an image of reality which is employed algorithmically (see Kuhn)) to be real and sought in all areas of his life specific confirmations of its reality. This is the world of cultural synthesis, the bringing together of initially disparate areas of experience into a single and harmonious whole. The Round Table is itself a symbol for the synthetic activity of the knights. The quest of any particular knight or any tournament attempts to verify the paradigm by applying with increasing precision and proficiency the tenets of the Round Table in ever wider domains and ever increasing detail. For ten years St. Augustine followed the Manichees, studying their doctrines and seeking to incorporate other philosophies into Manichaeism. During this time, he wrote his treatise on Beauty and Proportion which asserts that true beauty is found in the proper proportion of separate things. St. Augustine establishes for culture and philosophy the same goals as he held in rhetoric: "It is always the same with parts that together make a whole. They are not present at the same time, but if they can all be felt as one, together they give more pleasure than each single part" (Confessions, 4.11). Unity is a purely mental phenomenon, and one that produces substantial pleasure in the reduction of mental tension; the principle of unity, therefore, becomes for St. Augustine the pivot upon which all matters turn: "I concluded that in goodness there was unity, but in evil disunion of some kind. It seemed to me that in unity was the seat of the rational mind and was the natural state of truth and perfect goodness; whereas disunion consisted of irrational life" (4.15).

While the Manichaean synthesis grew, so also grew his awareness of anomolies, or certain experiences that Manichaeism could not explain and which, therefore, threatened the cohesion of the paradigm. Research or questing inevitably produces anomolies even though its purpose is thoroughly synthetic. It requires, as Thomas Kuhn notes in his The Structure of Scientific Revolutions, the truly brilliant researcher to allow anomolies to gain much of his or her attention. For St. Augustine, frustrations with Manichaeism grew steadily, as he tells us in his encounter with Faustus, the great Manichaean teacher:

> I badly wanted Faustus to compare these [teachings of Faustus] with the mathematical calculations which I had studied in other books, so that I might judge whether the Manichaean theories were more likely to be true or, at least, equally probable, but now I began to realize that he could not give me a detailed explanation. . . .
>
> The keen interest which I had had in Manichaean doctrines was checked by this experience, and my confidence in other teachers of the sect was further diminished when I saw that Faustus, of whom they spoke so much, was obviously unable to settle the numerous problems which troubled me. (5.7)

This is the point of personal or cultural crisis, and it is certainly the state of mind in which Malory wrote the Morte. Certain individuals who have become aware of anomolies can no longer accept the paradigm as more than an artifice or convention which actually cuts them off from a more infinite and beautifully unified reality they can only at this point dream of. Tristram's longing for the perfect love of Isode exactly matches this state. The majority of mankind--Arthur's knights--continue to adhere to the explanatory system; but, once a critical mass of anomolies surfaces, the nature of their cultural action changes from expansion to defense and contraction in response to the threatening de-constructive arguments of the analytic movement. Lancelot's behavior in response to Gawain's charges, as noted in Chapter One, should be read in this light. It becomes safer to exclude recalcitrant members and reject as unreal data that cannot be easily subsumed than to continue to expand the synthesis. The narrowing of the institution actually exacerbates the essential tension of the analytic thinker. St. Augustine's emotional state at this point is the same state we find in the four best knights of the Round Table, especially Tristram, as we shall see in Chapter Three. St. Augustine describes himself as "falling apart" (10.29), "torn to pieces" (2.1), "eaten away with anxiety" (6.6), and feeling as if there were a war between nature and spirit inside of him. This psychic incoherence or identity crisis leads him to desperation, self-denigration and nearly to suicide. He says in the Confessions, "My inner self was a house divided against itself. . . . I was beside myself with madness that would bring sanity. I was dying a death that would bring me life" (8.8).

The metaphors are important: madness which brings sanity, death that brings life. Leon Festinger in his Theory of Cognitive Dissonance suggests that cognitive dissonance--the clinical term for the war inside of St. Augustine--is a powerful motivation for either cognitive reorganization or behavioral change because of the anxiety it produces. The mechanisms of these changes have been studied quite fully by Hans Selye in his works on what he calls the General Adaptation Syndrome. Stress, tension, or anxiety, Selye points out, is the common denominator in all adaptive reactions in organisms, including mental adaptations. Selye points to stress, an alarm reaction, as the first stage in adaptation in the sense that the organism registers its awareness that it is mal-adapted. The direction of all adaptive responses, Selye argues, is toward tension or stress reduction (The Stress of Life, 35-40). Cognitive dissonance is one such mal-adaptation; as we see, St. Augustine is unable to match the mental map of his explanatory system with his experiences in the world: "I was trying to find the origin of evil, but I was quite blind to the evil in my own method of research" (7.5). His method, his mind, produces disunion or evil, while he believes it to be a method for producing the opposite, unity and the good. Resistence and self-imposed alienation from tension causing situations comprise, according to Selye, the second stage. St. Augustine writes,

> The more I thought about the material world and the whole of nature, as far as we can be aware of it through our bodily senses, and the more I took stock of the various theories, the more I began to think that the opinions of the majority of philosophers [skeptics] were most likely to be true. So, treating everything as a matter of doubt, as Academics are generally supposed to do, and hovering between one doctrine and another, I made up my mind at least to leave the Manichees. . . . Nevertheless, I refused to entrust the healing of my soul to these philosophers. (5.14)

Faced with dissonance in the paradigm he knows and its intolerable anxieties, St. Augustine enters what I like to think of as a holding pattern of alienation during which he doubts all that he formerly knew and commits himself to nothing. A great deal of what Malory presents in the "Book of Sir Tristram" can be explained in terms of this holding pattern of alienation. We see in St. Augustine's Confessions that this period is characterized by violently conflicting emotions, excessive interest in passion and sex, randomization of behavior, experimentation with various life styles, and de-construction of whatever theory might be presented to him as truth. Cognitively, this stage denotes a priority of experience with the phenomenal world over the mind. Andreas Capellanus begins his Art of Courtly Love with the observation that love results from the sight of and excessive meditation upon the beauties of the opposite sex. A Middle English poem remarks that "Love is a selkud wodenesse"--a marvelous insanity, that results, as we now are able to see, when the sensory data of

the world hold a priority over the mind. This disordering of St.
Augustine's behavior, though regarded as madness or death, is,
in fact, search behavior and innovation carried on outside of
paradigmatic directives, and, as everyone knows, it leads him to
St. Ambrose who teaches him to interpret the Scriptures
allegorically and thus discover consistency in Christian
doctrine. His experience of conversion comes as he hears the
voice of a child saying, "take it and read, take it and read"
(8.12), but this is only after he has learned how to read from a
unified perspective. When this experience is formalized, St.
Augustine tells us, "We were baptized, and all anxiety over the
past melted away from us" (9.6).

Christianity provides St. Augustine with an heuristic with
seemingly infinite explanatory power and complete ability to
resolve psychic tensions by restoring beauty to the world
through a unified point of view. The core of the new heuristic
is charity which he describes as,

> the Light that never changes casting its rays over
> the same eye of my soul, over my mind. . . . What I
> saw was something quite, quite different from any
> light we know on earth. . . . It was above me
> because it was itself the Light that made me, and I
> was below this Light because I was made by it. All
> who know the truth know this Light, and all who
> know this Light know eternity. It is the light
> Charity knows. (7.10)

St. Augustine's discovery of this light or doctrine of
charity is a numinal experience, and it gives him a unified way
of interpreting not only all experiences he might encounter but
himself as well. He is re-created in the experience. He defines
charity as an orientation of the soul toward God so that one
knows and acts with the things of the world for the sake of
God. Charity enables him to refer all perceptual data to the
nature of God and arrange the world, therefore, systematically
and hierarchically. St. Augustine understands very clearly what
Charles Osgood calls the "Principle of Congruity in Thinking";
that is, the tendency in one's thought to develop in a direction
of increasing congruity with respect to a basic frame of
reference. In a similar manner, memories and new experiences

tend to drift in the direction of pre-existing cognitive structures so that the coherence of the cognitive structure is maintained and carried over into the diversity of the experiential or mnemonic data. With the doctrine of charity and allegory as heuristic, St. Augustine can begin again the work of cultural synthesis and resolve the problem of pluralism in belief and interpretation, as he attempts at the end of the Confessions and throughout On Christian Doctrine. The doctrine of charity is even powerful enough to dispose entirely of the Manichaean doctrine of evil as a paradigm competing with the paradigm of the good. Those things which imitate most closely the nature of God are good and those having the least of God in them are evil. Evil imitates the good; it can never be, he says, an independent force with its own orientation and thus paradigm, rather only a privation of the good. From the doctrine of charity grow medieval conceptions of "Ordo" and hierarchy as images of the world, as Chaucer's "Faire Cheyne of Love" in the "Knight's Tale" or even Malory's hierarchy of prowess.

Near the end of the Confessions, St. Augustine gives us a picture of his mind--his cognitive map of the world--that illustrates precisely the sort of cognitive consonance and order that result from a unified point of view and produce the psychic peace of the meaningful and that becomes the socially constructed world of the institution which follows:

> In the memory everything is preserved separately, according to its category. . . .
> In the vast cloisters of my memory . . . are the sky, the earth, and the sea, ready at my summons together with everything that I have ever perceived in them by my senses. . . . In it I meet myself as well. I remember myself and what I have done. . . . From the same source I can picture to myself all kinds of different images based upon my own experience or upon what I find credible because it tallies with my own experience. I can fit them into a general picture of the past, from them I can make a surmise of actions and events and hopes for the future, and I can contemplate them all over again as if they were actually present. . . .

The memory captures their images with astonishing speed and stores them away in this wonderful system of compartments [i.e., the categories of the mind], ready to produce them again in just as wonderful a way when we remember them. (10.8-9)

The synthetic mode asserts the priority of mind over experience or world. The mind is able to make such wonderful order out of things only because, as St. Augustine says a little earlier, the world "is only understood by those who compare the messages it gives them through their senses with the truth that is in themselves" (10.6). St. Augustine returns to psychic health when his mental image of the world, the truth that is within him, is felt to be isomorphic with the world of the senses or experience. In just this way, the lords bring the meaning of the stone with the sword stuck in it to the encounter at the church. Thus is created the interpreted world of the institution which carries with it all the implications of the meaningful, as St. Augustine himself so clearly understands: "in that brief moment my mother and I had reached out in thought and touched eternal Wisdom which abides over all things; suppose that this state were to continue and all other visions of things inferior were to be removed, so that this single vision entranced and absorbed the one who beheld it and enveloped him in inward joys in such a way that for him life was eternally the same as that moment of understanding for which we had longed so much" (9.10). From the discussion of St. Thomas above, it is well to recall that wisdom is architectonic; it supplies the system for organizing the categories of the mind which then, in turn, organize sensory data. What St. Augustine presents here is the same sort of numinal or religious experience that we saw in the previous section when "the peple merveilled" and "alle the comyns cryed at ones, `We will have Arthure unto oure kyng.´"

Somewhat skeptically, this process establishes order in one´s life only in this sense that mind informed by wisdom points exclusively to data that demonstrate one´s association with his chosen creator. Nevertheless, both St. Augustine and Malory describe what Eliade defines as a genuine religious experience, which differs from the ordinary experiences of everyday life. It is well to note that the term "religious" originates in the Latin word for binding up; one is bound by these acts to his origin. Eliade explains, "The 'religiousness' of this experience is due to the fact that one re-enacts fabulous, exalting, significant events; one again witnesses the creative deeds of the Super-natural; one ceases to exist in the everyday world and enters a transfigured, auroral world impregnated with the Supernaturals' presence" (Myth and Reality, 19). What Eliade describes is precisely the process of becoming a knight of the Round Table, but it is also the substance of St. Augustine's construction of Christian Doctrine upon charity. The newly emergent institution is, indeed, a different reality than what previously existed. The socially constructed reality is truly experience impregnated with the presence of the supernatural, as wisdom, numen, or God.

This is also a world that comes into being by destroying as much data as is created; certain acts and attitudes are exalted and others that do not serve the now institutional goals suppressed. As St. Augustine clearly acknowledges, "all other visions of things inferior were to be removed, so that this single vision entranced and absorbed the one who beheld it." St. Augustine, however, as any architectus, is not aware of the loss; so absorbed is he by the increase in explanatory power of the mind and newly found beauty in unity that, he tacitly assumes that because the chosen vision is effective in producing the feeling of the numinous, the derivative knowledge and institution must be true and as universal as the infinite wholly other.

Initially predications made of the numen are legitimated by feeling alone; the actions reduce psychic tension associated with cognitive dissonance. St. Augustine, like Arthur, feels joy and awesome power. From our standpoint, we see that the feeling derives from an increase in the level of order or unity the individual is able to impose upon his environment and his experience (interaction with environment). The feeling is of power, an imaginative power which Samuel Coleridge identified at the very root of all creation: "the living power and prime agent of all human perception, and as a repetition in the finite mind of the eternal act of creation in the infinite I AM. . . . [T]hat synthetic and magical power . . . revels itself in the balance or reconciliation of opposite or discordant qualities

(Biographia Literaria, XIII-XIV). This incredible power in discovering unity in complex and disparate phenomenon continues to feul the institutional modus operandi, and yet it inevitably denies pluralism of private experience and destroys competing world views, as we just saw. The pleasure of creation is also the pleasure of destruction; Malory, in the "Tristram" understands this point so well.

We need to examine a little more closely the faculty for producing the "inward joys" mentioned above. St. Augustine suggests that men possess two modes of knowledge: empirical and intuitive. He belittles empirical knowledge as limited to what the senses are capable of perceiving and therefore of knowing nothing beyond the changeable appearances of the world and producing no unity, no beauty, no goodness, and no pleasure: "Those who are given to bodily senses think the God of gods to be either sky, or that which they see shining most brightly in the sky, or the world itself." Such a limit, St. Augustine believes, makes empirical knowledge useless in discovering the really important aspects of life; that is, the unchanging reality which grounds institutions. On the other hand, he asserts that "Those, however, who seek to know what God is through the understanding place Him above all things mutable, either visible and corporeal or intelligible and spiritual" (Christian Doctrine, 11). St. Augustine's discussion of the understanding's ability to perceive the transcendental describes the religious experience of the numen, the simple but ineffable perception of the wholly other. Platonism had taught him that truth was not corporeal (Confessions, 7.20), and from mystical theology, he knew that God transcends all human expressions.   And yet he goes on to make some very definite deductions from a radically extra-mental category. The structure of the rational process is the same as that of historicism; the aboriginal time is just as immutable and wholly other as the transcendental God. Although the assertion that God is above all things mutable, corporeal, or visible quite clearly makes any predications dubious, the openness or emptiness of a transcendental God allows St. Augustine to establish his religious experience as the first principle for personal order and ultimately political order--to use his own words, The City of God. The dwellers in the City of God, the predestined, are those who have been able to bring their lives in conformity with Christian ideology; all others, the mass of perdition, reside outside of the institution.

What St. Augustine is actually doing is using the ingenuity of the mind to fill out the category of the numen and thereby explain the present in terms of inaccessible and irreproachable truth. In combating heretics in Hippo, St. Augustine employed the same strategies of constructing obvious interpretations of God's nature as did Merlin in the baronial wars before the emergence of the Round Table. In demonstrating, for example, that man can know transcendentals, St. Augustine writes,

> No one is so impudently stupid as to say, `How do you know that an immutable wise life is preferable to a mutable one?' For the thing he asks--whence I know--is commonly and unchangeably obvious to all who think about it. And he who does not see it is like a blind man in the sun who profits nothing when his eye sockets are infused with the brilliance of clear and immediate light. . . . Therefore, since that truth is to be enjoyed which lives immutably . . . the mind should be cleansed so that it is able to see that light and cling to it once seen. (On Christian Doctrine, 12-13)

What lies behind St. Augustine's certainty that an uninterpreted hierarchical meaning of life is accessible to all who think about it? And what is it that will cleanse the mind or restore sight to the blind? He knows it by intuition; there exists no empirical or rational demonstration but rather the insight is validated by intense feelings, the intensity of St. Augustine's religious experience. I am not implying that this condition is at all bad; to the contrary, it is what makes one's experiences meaningful. But it is necessary to distinguish sharply this kind of institutional association and belief generally available only to the innovators of the institution from that produced by physical or psychological coercion later on, a strategy St. Augustine advocates in The City of God as well as most other mainstream medieval philosophers. The point is, remarkably, that those who have the sort of numinal experience at the origin of an institution do not feel the world as ineffable or wholly other. St. Augustine clearly says, as would Merlin or Arthur, "God should not be said to be ineffable . . . [God] has accepted the tribute of the human voice and wished us to make joy in praising Him with our words.   In this way He is called Deus" (Christian Doctrine, 11).

Another example in On Christian Doctrine shows how St. Augustine's goes on to extrapolate the religious experience into a body of codes and laws--a science--that he believes with all the certainty of faith but which are designed specifically to substantiate the truth of his interpretation of reality to the exclusion of all others.   He implicitly contends that we know the transcendentals because the interpretation appears so complete and natural; that is, the present explanation is isomorphic with the original religious experience and hence isomorphic with the nature of the world or of God as the object of the original experience.   He writes,

It is perfectly clear to the most stupid person that the science of numbers was not instituted by men, but rather investigated and discovered. . . .   No one could because of his personal desire arrange matters so that three threes are not nine, or do not geometrically produce a square figure, or are not the triple of the ternary, or are not one and one half times six, or are evenly divisible by two when odd numbers cannot be so divided.   Whether they are considered in themselves or applied to the laws of figures . . . numbers have immutable rules not instituted by men but discovered through the sagacity of the more ingenious.   (72-73)

But it is more correct to say that the number system is not absolute or isomorphic with the world; rather it is a totally artificial construct attributed to things in the world for the purpose of organizing and relating them according to some human use.   There are no numbers in nature, merely unique and independent entities from which the purely mental category of numbers may (or may not) be abstracted.   Though there may be circular and square things in nature, none of them find their origin in mathematical formulas and none are so perfect as the mathematical circle or square.   It makes no sense in a purely natural context to multiply, add, or divide entities which exist unaccountably in themselves. Three oranges times five oranges remains a group of oranges that may be rearranged in various manners, but the result will never be fifteen oranges. I am tempted sometimes to think Shakespeare's clown Costard in Love's, Labor's Lost had a refutation of St. Augustine in mind when he points out to the pedantic scholar Berowne the differences between numerical abstractions and physical objects:

Cost.	O Lord, sir, they would know
	Whether the three Worthies shall come in or no.
Ber.	What, are there but three?
Cost.	No, sir, but it is vara fine
	For every one pursents three.
Ber.	And three times thrice is nine.
Cost.	Not so, sir, under correction, sir, I hope it
	is not so.
	You cannot beg us, sir, I can assure your, sir,
	we know what we know.
	I hope, sir, three times thrice, sir--
Ber.	Is not nine.
Cost.	Under correction, sir, we know whereuntil
	it doth amount.
Ber.	By Jove, I always took three threes for nine.
Cost.	O Lord, sir, it were pity you should get
	your living by reck'ning, sir.
Ber.	How much is it?
Cost.	O Lord, sir, the parties themselves, the
	actors, sir, will show whereuntil it doth amount.

(V. ii, 485-500)

The fact that we may measure different objects with the same method and achieve predictable results is not a feature of the regularity of the world but rather of the ingenuity of the mind and the ability of any organism to habituate its response to stimuli it regards as recurrent. All of this occurs at the expense of the destruction of a great deal of information. The underlying purpose is in resolving the problems of human need. And herein lies the key to St. Augustine's thinking. St. Augustine is not looking at the world but rather at his own mind and organizing it to best reduce mental tensions and anxieties. By using the same method and constructing seemingly consistent systems or methods within the mind, St. Augustine is able from his unified point of view to see human life as ordered and tending toward the immutable. What makes him able to know transcendental categories or able to cleanse his mind and restore vision to the blind is hermaneutics: the method, the systems of logic, of measures, and of reason. Here is the modus operandi of ideology; the knowledge that St. Augustine discovers is above all useful in controlling his behavior and solving his own problems which just happen to coincide with a much broader cultural crisis. "A large part of the social stock of knowledge," Peter Berger and Thomas Luckmann write, "consists of recipes for the mastery of routine problems. . . . My knowledge of everyday life has the quality of an instrument that cuts a path thorough a forest and, as it does so, projects a narrow cone of light on what lies just ahead and immediately around; on all sides of the path there continues to be darkness" (43-45).

St. Augustine's example of numbers is characteristic of his constructing Christian ideology by interpreting his experience according to a consistent method. His assertions about the content of the transcendental begin the process of filling in the category of the numen and producing a body of recipes and rituals which would comprise the Christian world. When complete, the human created abstract world actually replaces the physical world in the experience of the devotee. The implicit dangers--the darkness of information destroyed and discarded all around the beam of light--are well worth the risk for the process relieves the anxiety to believe that behind the unaccountable existence of independent and potentially hostile entities there lies unity and purpose which serve to enhance the group's potential for survival. The doctrines which express such order are felt to be grounded in the wholly other, and all that is necessary for social order is to encourage men by training and teaching to conform to the codes--that is, adopt the point of view of the institution. Thus individual human actions begin to fall under a body of knowledge, and the species moves out of the primitive stage of innovating domination of the environment into one filled with the problems of enforcement and compliance. At this point of maturity in the institution, human behavior becomes generally a response to a reified institution and an interpreted or meaningful world rather than the natural world itself. The discussion in the last section about Merlin's warning to Arthur that finally defeating an opposing knight would also mean his own death now becomes true in that individuals no longer perceive the natural or open world at all. Responding to the institution can do nothing to further the adaptation of the species to the natural environment or to each other because the institution is now the total environment. Mature institutions stifle human innovation because the ideology provides no behaviors that will enable individuals to take an oppositional stance to the institution itself and thus modify the institutional, the only, reality they know.

Mature institutions are described by Campbell as the movement from mythic association to social identification in which primitive acts of the individual imposing his will on the environment and the pleasure and increasing physical adaptation resulting therefrom are transformed into rituals which establish or confirm the continuity between the individual and the institution itself, without, however, continuing to develop further environmental adaptation. Rituals are designed to promote adaptation to the institution and thus institutional stability rather than continued change and adaptation to nature. At this point, the institution takes the place of nature or whatever is wholly other and becomes the problem that truly innovative thinkers must seek to resolve, but nothing within the ideology of the institution exists to enable them to identify the institution as a problem, let alone articulate the tensions someone like Tristram at this point feels. The individual now identifies with the institution rather than the numen which was the origin of the institution and which the explanations of ideology persist in telling the member his ritual performances relate him to. It is worth referring again to Pope Innocent III's rather open admission of this fact: "The Church is set in the midst between God and man, below God, but above man."

The institution and its rituals provide the individual with the feeling of value without his having to change or determine the environment--even the environment of the institution--any further. The Middle Ages cultivated to the extreme the practice of producing the feeling of the numinous in this humanly and practically useless way, and Malory imitates it in the tournaments which fill up a knight's time but do nothing to

create any further the institution or humanness of its members-
-let alone satisfy their present psychic needs. The rage for
relics, indulgences, pilgrimages, blessings, devotions, crusades,
and icons is often considered merely superstition, but
superstition is no small matter. All societies are grounded upon
superstition; fear, identity, or patriotism produced by any
totem, no matter how absurd it appears to the outsider, is the
real feeling itself. And the feeling produced by a splinter of
wood believed to have come from the cross of Calvary or a kiss
upon the hem of the Pope's robe means, for the believer, the
entrance into his own life by the sacred or the Divine. In his
biography of Martin Luther, Roland Bainton notes the extent to
which the purely ritualistic attempts to invoke the meaningful
had descended by the early sixteenth century: "the catalogue
illustrated by Lucas Cranach in 1509 listed 5,005 particles, to
which were attached indulgences calculated to reduce
purgatory by 1,443 years." He goes on to list some of the more
interesting items of the collection at the Castle Church at
Wittenberg, the supervision of which must certainly have driven
Martin Luther to his revolt against the institution. There was
a thorn from the crown of Jesus, St. Jerome's tooth, four pieces
of St. Augustine, four hairs of Our Lady, four pieces of her
girdle, and on and on. The list is remarkable; by 1520 Emperor
Frederick had increased the holdings by 19,013 bones. Bainton
calls it the bingo of the sixteenth century (Here I stand, 53).
      The existence of opportunities which allow the individual
to establish freely his own unique and personal connection with
whatever lies at the origin of his conception of himself is the
prime indication of a psychologically healthy society. Luther's
letters reveal his extreme devotion to the performance of
prayers, vigils, and other such rituals. It is not at all cynical
to say that a psychologically healthy society is one in which
the superstitions and symbols are working--with the crucial
proviso that the sum of such opportunities must actually
promote the survival of and the smooth interaction among the
human members. The problem, of course, arises when
individuals perceive that their superstitions and symbols relate
them only to the institution and do nothing whatever to satisfy
human needs, as Luther came finally to believe. We have
arrived at, perhaps, the most important insight about
institutions. The human needs which brought the institution

into existence do not continue to be the same needs at the maturity of the institution. If the institution is actually created, then it has resolved its originating human crisis. Generally, at the outset the crisis is disorder in life. St. Augustine repeats over and over that "I saw that what remains constant is better than that which is changeable. My heart was full of bitter protests [about his own condition of psychic instability]" (Confessions, 7.1). But for subsequent generations, those not present at the inception of the institution, the initial experience is an imposed and intractable order. Their psychic needs in responding to the reality they know are for precisely the opposite of order and stability. As we will see in Chapter Three, Tristram seeks disorder and chaos and these become salvific qualities. The recipe knowledge of the institution can only resolve the crisis of disorder, and no one any longer needs that sort of behaviorally reductive policy, just as the rituals of Catholicism at Luther's Wittenberg church were able to provide 1.9 million years of indulgence which no one really needed at all.

The desire to produce the feeling of the numinous became more and more intense in the Middle Ages as the rituals became less and less related to genuine human problems. It is, in fact, appropriate to call the efforts of theologians in the Augustinian tradition a conquest of the numen, the result of which could never have been any real truth about the numen but rather the increasing reification of the institution increasingly committed to the defense of its position as intermediary between man and God. The chief weapon in its defense became grace. St. Augustine is again the key figure in formulating the doctrine of grace. Grace, just as the feeling of the numinous, is the result of the religious experience, but it also, for the purposes of social identification, serves to distinguish those who have had the religious experience from those who have not, the predestined from the damned. In its first function, grace is the free gift of God. In its second, it is a tool of the Church for maintaining its primacy of power by coercion since for the individual the Church becomes the source, or at least the controller of the source, of grace. The first function--that of the free gift of God--describes mythic association in which individuals spontaneously and unconsciously participate in the Divine. Acts are not ritualistic; that is, they are not done for the sake of the rewards.   As Jung explains, the primitive religious experience is "a dynamic existence or effort, not caused by an arbitrary act of the will.   On the contrary, it seizes and controls the human subject, which is always its victim rather than its creator.   The numinosum is an involuntary condition of the subject whatever its cause may be" (Psychology and Religion, 23).   The second function, on the other hand, describes social identification in which primitive acts are interpreted and raised to the level of self-consciousness and volition.   The individual, therefore, ceases to determine his environment and rather chooses to affirm the one offered by the institution by performing the acts associated with doctrine and avoiding acts condemned by the doctrine.

In point of fact, St. Augustine devised his doctrine of grace as a means of combating the Pelagian heretics who sought to sustain a primitive religion by denying the effects of original sin and maximizing the individual's capacity for achieving salvation or perfection through his own efforts with a minimum of aid from grace.   For the Pelagian each individual is finally responsible for his own salvation, and, moreover, he possesses sufficient means to achieve it.   In asserting that original sin completely corrupted human nature, St. Augustine made it impossible for man to save himself; it was now necessary for some institution or exterior power to overcome the effects of a corrupt nature.   Salvation was possible, so St. Augustine argued, only through participation in the sacraments of the church, beginning with the baptism of infants.

The evolution of theology in the Middle Ages is a process of both the gradual increase in the importance of grace and the increase in activities designed to produce its effects.   Beginning with St. Augustine, the movement climaxes in the twelfth and thirteenth centuries in which grace is no longer the free gift of God at all, but rather a reward given by the Church for the devotion of its members.   We need not go as far as Henry Charles Lea in his History of the Inquisition who writes: "The affection of the population was no longer attracted by the graces and loveliness of Christianity; submission was purchased by the promise of salvation, to be acquired by faith and obedience, or was extorted by the threat of perdition or by the sharper terrors of earthy perdition" (5).   The inquisition, just as the final war between Lancelot and Gawain, only represents a last and desperate attempt to do what had been done earlier spontaneously and willessly--that is, maintain the unity of the institution.   The destruction of mythic association by the institution's assumption of a position between the individual and his God and thus the assumption of control over the dispensing of the feelings offered by the numen produced both fanatical adherents to the institution and rebels or heretics.   In both cases, rituals amount only to surrender and repression of individuality.

By the twelfth and thirteenth centuries, the individual's participation in the Divine had become no more than social order and repression.   By the time of the emergence of Arthurian Romance, the Roman Church was actively engaged in forcing individuals to adopt its faith and perform its sacraments to receive grace.   In 1184 in the decretal Ad Abolendum, Pope Lucius II declared heresy to be a revolt against ecclesiastical authority and formally instituted inquisition throughout Latin Christendom.   Pope Gregory IX's decretal of 1231, Excommunicamus, described the fate of those who for whatever reasons could not participate in the institution: "Those condemned by the Church will be relaxed to the secular arm where they will be punished by the debt of hatred" (Peters, 189).   Pope Innocent IV continued the normal development of institutions toward coercion in his decree of 1252 authorizing systematic torture to extract confessions from accused persons. One could, of course, avoid the pain by accepting the graces of God through the Church.   Lea's statement though cynical, is hardly too strong, and Alexander Thompson's analysis of the situation points to the inevitable problem in institutional association:

> At the same time, the abstract discussion of the process of grace was overshadowed by the visible organization of the Church and the benefits offered by its sacraments.   The elect and the reprobate were known only to God, but the means of grace were open to all. . . . Speculation upon the uncovenanted mercies of God could not alter the fact that the Church possessed only one means of entry to the way of eternal life, without which the infant was as helpless as the unbaptized adult whose apparent virtues were but splendida vita.

> The official teachings of the Church, therefore,
> laid all its emphasis upon the use of means of grace
> . . . [for] the only guarantee of salvation was
> membership in the visible Church. ("Medieval
> Doctrine," VI, 654-55)

The danger in St. Augustine's concretizing his religious experience is twofold: because the numen is ineffable and its experience gives unity to the sensory world, St. Augustine assumes that the derivitive doctrinal world will be coherent; that is, sacred doctrine which is the basis for identity will be tensionless. Thus the first danger is a shift in orientation from the real world to an abstract world, and with the shift comes a loss in problem solving interest and activity--which is what brought about the ideology in the first place. What had originally been concern for the problems of men became contempt for the mutable world and an abandonment of useful knowledge. We can see this general tendency of institutional life in the growing interest Malory's knights have in tournaments rather than in efforts to resolve the real tensions that steadily grow within their personal relationships. The institution is now, at the mature stage the knights' only real environment but their ideological training has disposed them not to see tensions within the ideology--just as Lancelot refuses to acknowledge that a man can be a thief, a murderer, and a knight. To see incoherence within the institution, as Tristram eventually does, requires alienation from the group and an oppositional stance of the "I" over against the institutionally determined "me." This condition, of course, is regarded by other members as sinful, insane, or heretical because it produces an increase in anxiety and a loss of identity. It should be no surprise, therefore, that the innovators of the modern world--Peter Abelard, Marsilius, Luther, Copernicus, Galileo--urged a radical empiricism, a method of turning toward the phenomenal world of the present and thereby necessitating the eventual abandonment of all intellectual constructs inherited from the Middle Ages.

But the process of building an ideology is both unavoidable and desirable for those who as Gottfried says "wish only to revel in bliss" in the sense that it stabilizes the religious experience, making it repeatable at will. The danger

here, the second, lies in the inadvertent creation of a class of
addicts, those for whom the institutional confirmation of self-
value becomes so essential that they give up the primitive
oppositional stance of the "I" in order to exploit the institution
and its rituals to produce greater and greater feelings of value
in themselves.   Mature institutions tend to produce heroes of
larger and larger status without those heroes having to do
anything substantive to develop further the civilization and
resolve real problems. They merely learn to play the game well
or they enhance the now repressive dominance of the
institution.   The late Middle Ages were affected with an
extreme need to produce the feeling of the numinous, and this
syndrome is imitated by the writers of Arthurian Romance,
especially Malory who in his romance constantly reports on the
relative ranking of the knights on the hierarchical scale of
value. Palomides is a knight who is driven nearly to suicide by
his fanatical devotion to the acquisition of institutional value or
worship.   Chaucer's Canterbury Pilgrims are other literary
figures who have learned to play their games supremely well.

The feeling of value becomes the core of the individual's
identity.   The giver of value assumes the position of the
creative source of identity. When it is discovered that ideology
can not be interpreted univocally, individuals are forced
nevertheless to adhere to their beliefs with all the intensity of
self-defense, for indeed one is protecting his source of self-
conception.   This situation made it all the more necessary to
persecute heretics because they undermined one's own identity.
Increasingly, no level of dissent from the institution could be
tolerated.   The condemnation of Marsilius of Padua and John of
Jandum by Pope John XXII illustrates the vehemence of the
defense: "We declare by sentence the above mentioned articles .
. . to be contrary to Sacred Scripture and enemies of the
Catholic Faith, heretic, or heretical and erroneous, and also
that the above mentioned Marsilius and John, will be heretics--
rather they will be manifest and notorious archheretics"
(Peters, 231).

In the twelfth and thirteenth centuries, it is apparent
that a tremendous development in the human psyche had come
of age. The success of the Church in filling out the numen and
controlling the feelings of the numinous permeated all phases of
life and created an institution that was aware of its own

unifying power. What interests me is the general and unconscious feeling of coming of age, that all parts of existence, just as all members of the Round Table, are now in place. This section opened with a statement about the attainment of perfection and the flower of chivalry, and that recognition seems to have been the nature of the twelfth and thirteenth century church. Pelikan tells us that "The precise meaning of the phrase, `the communion of saints (communmino sanctorum),´ had not been specified in the patristic era and remained ambiguous in medieval theology." But the power of the institution to subsume all disparate areas of life into a single unity was well understood by Peter Abelard, who in his Exposition of the Apostles´ Creed wrote that "we may take the word `saints´ [sanctorum] as a neuter, that is, as a reference to the sanctified bread and wine in the Sacrament of the Altar." He goes on to say that it also refers to "that communion by which saints are made or are confirmed in their sanctity (that is, by participation in the divine Sacrament), or to the common faith of the church, or to a union of love" (The Christian Tradition, III, 174). Thus the grace of the sacraments creates a perfectly unified people.

What is ambiguous in theology is often clear in art. The character of the religious experience in the High Middle Ages implies that dogma and institution of the church have attained the psychic tensionlessness of Truth and fully represent--at least in potential--the category of the numen. This is the feeling that the quest is now at an end; the end of the quest is the attainment of Truth. It has often been observed that the Round Table and, in fact, the style of Arthurian Romance in its subtle interlacing of details and episodes is a Gothic phenomenon. We now need to explore the reasons why, as the final link in the relationship between Malory´s romance and the culture to which it is a response. In his Idea of the Holy, Rudolf Otto describes the feeling of the numinous as the "mysterium tremendum"; that is, the terror of the absolutely mysterious. It is that quality of Truth which the Middle Ages sought above all. Otto points out that the "Gothic appears as the most numinous of all types of art." "Gothic," he goes on, "does instill a spell that is more than the effect of sublimity. But `magic´ is too low a word; the tower of the Cathedral at Ulm is emphatically not `magical´, it is numinous" (67-68).

Architecture, largely because of the great organization and expense required to produce it, is the art of the official establishment. The Gothic Cathedrals are the art of the Roman Church, and they exemplify the Church's final conquest of the numen. Otto von Simpson asserts that Abbot Suger, who more than anyone else is responsible for the innovation of the Gothic style, is "an architect who built theology" (The Gothic Cathedral, 133). The Gothic style, Simpson discovers, is not a linear development of the Romanesque, but rather a revolt against it.

> A work of art is created because an individual or a group is compelled to convey an experience that is particularly his or theirs. . . . The more significant a work of art the more marked will be the element of revolt, the destructive tendencies, even in regard to the work that served as a prototype. (The Gothic Cathedral, 61)

Using Simpson's principle, it is clear that what separates the Romanesque and the Gothic is a radical shift in Christian ideology, especially in its disposition toward the numina and the individual. As mentioned before, the shift is from mythic association to social identification; the institution replaces the myth or the numen. The Romanesque style with its heaviness and darkness suggests the preservation of the mysterious element or the wholly otherness of the numina. There exists both the "mysterium" and the "tremendum." Mystery and terror are present prima facie, and there is no suggestion that the builders of the cathedrals or the Church itself had any better access to the mysteries than the ordinary individual who experienced the church. The Romanesque Church provided an occasion for the religious experience but does not tell what the experience is--that remains a matter between the individual believer and his God. It is tempting to associate the Romanesque with the heresies of the Waldensians who were against both sacraments and the clergy and urged a universal priesthood of all men and women. With the Gothic style, however there is too much light; the thick walls have been replaced by windows of lace-like bar tracery and the feeling evoked by the Gothic is one of fulfillment and attainment of mystery, not preservation of mystery. By the time of the full development of the Gothic style, at for example Amiens, Ste. Chappelle, Chartres, or Rheims, Simpson reports that "no segment of inner space was allowed to remain in darkness, undefined by light" (4). "Mysterium" has become the "magisterium"--the authority of the church to promulgate doctrine.

The incredible increase in the sheer complexity and multifariousness of the design of piers, facades, arches, vaults, and walls which are reduced to lace is majestic, and it represents a revolutionary replacement of the truly infinite and wholly other with the human built infinite and wholly other. Certainly the Gothic is the closest to the infinite of anything man has built before the ages of computers and space; the stained glass is paradoxically a transparent wall just as the vertical force of the towers suggests a defiance of gravity. Gargoyles, monsters, and highly abstract designs reproduce the feeling of terror within the context of the holy. Of the Gothic style, Simpson writes:

> The content of Suger's Booklet on the Consecration [of his Cathedral at St. Denis] may be summed up as follows. It opens with the intellectual vision of divine harmony that reconciles discord among conflicting things and infuses in those who behold that concord the desire to establish it also within the moral order. The construction of the church is the subsequent realization of that vision both in the work of art and in those who have undertaken it from a desire `to be glorified by participation in the Eternal Reason´ [i.e., the conquest of the numen].  The work of `edification´ is consumated in the consecration of the completed sanctuary, the rite that enacts the sacrament of union between God and man to which the church itself is dedicated. (131)

What the Gothic style of architecture tells us is that the Church has finally totally established itself--at least feels as if it has--as the only access, the mediator, through which men are able to approach the Divine. From a psychological point of view, the role of mediatorship gives the Church exclusive possession of the category of the numen in the sense that what men perceive or feel of the Divine is now the Church itself. The shift in theology, then, is from the wholly other to a body of doctrine and an institution, for the feeling of the numinous now originates in the Church, its rituals, and its iconography. It is significant that Abbot Suger's Cathedral at St. Denis was named after Dionysius the Areopagite just as Suger took his inspiration for both the church and the explanatory Booklet from Dionysius' writings On Celestial Hierarchy, On Ecclesiastical Hierarchy, and On Divine Names. What Suger does to the theology of Dionysius is precisely what the Church as a whole has done to the religious experience of early Christians. For Dionysius all predications and knowledge about the Divine are hypothetical constructs or names used in order to be able to talk about the Divine, but in no way should these names be taken as content of the category of the Divine itself. The Divine must remain as an infinite and unknowable category. He writes, for example, in On Divine Names, "These mysteries we learn from the Divine Scriptures, and thou wilt find that in well-nigh all the utterances of the Sacred Writers the Divine Names refer in a Symbolical Revelation to Its beneficient Emanations" (56).

God should be named the highest Good, Dionysius argues, not because that is God's nature or any part whatever of God, but because as men we see God through the human mind which in giving order by explanation to the natural world has decided that the Good is the highest of things we know. For Dionysius and the tradition of mystical Christianity which followed him as opposed to St. Augustine's rational Christianity, human knowledge is a construct, a Weltanschauung, or an approach to an infinitely unknowable numen. It is appropriate to name God, but the names we give Him will never constitute the ultimately unknowable category of God. Transcendentals remain in a "cloud of unknowing" or a "divine darkness"--as is suggested by, of course, the Romanesque style. In The Mystical Theology, Dionysius has the unique habit among theologians of calling God "It" instead of the usual anthropomorphic "He":

> Once more, ascending yet higher we maintain that It
> is not soul, or mind, or endowed with the faculty of

imagination, conjecture, reason or understanding . . .
nor can It be described by the reason or perceived
by the understanding, since It is not number, or
order, or greatness, or littleness, or equality, or
inequality . . . nor can It be grasped by the
understanding, since It is not knowledge or truth;
nor is It kingship or wisdom; nor is It one, nor is It
unity, nor is It Godhead, or Goodness . . . nor does
It belong to the category of non-existence or to
that of existence. (Ch. V)

Dionysius goes on and on, but it is enough to say that the
only predication he will affirm is that God is the ultimate
cause, not because cause is a valid attribute of God, but rather
because men are created; our own "creature-consciousness" is
all that we know of God. Needless to say, no institution
emerged from Dionysius' theologizing about his religious
experience. What Abbot Suger has done is claim the status of
Truth for all of the names Dionysius uses to talk about his
religious experience. This process is a historicization or a
reification of the ineffable experience of the numen, and it
underlies not only the development of theology but also the
growth of the Round Table as institution and Weltanschauung as
truth.
By the time of Abbot Suger and even more especially St.
Thomas Aquinas, what had been mystical and symbolic
discussions of the wholly other are literalized and historicized
as truth. An infinite and ineffable God has become an "Eternal
Reason" or, in St. Thomas' more remote but equally concrete
term, "Esse." Man's institutions must imitate the
conceptualized God upon peril of failing to live in the image
and likeness of God. St. Thomas' treatise On Kingship is just
such a series of deductions about temporal cities and provinces
made from what he is now sure is the nature of God. For
example,

Just as the founding of a city of kingdom may
suitably be learned from the way in which the world
was created, so too the way to govern may be
learned from the divine government of the world.
(58)

We wonder how St. Thomas knows how the world is governed or, indeed, was created, and yet this is precisely what Suger has done with Dionysius; he has converted symbol into truth by taking Dionysius literally and historically. While the Romanesque is symbolic of the numen, the Gothic is metaphoric of it. The difference between symbol and metaphor is crucial. A symbol always "stands for" the infinite or the ineffable. It matters little what the literal manifestation or attributes of the symbol are since the focus is on the background and the background remains unknowable. Symbols are directed to the unconscious in that we simply feel that a certain object is symbolic of something we know not what for sure. Symbols are freely created as opportunities to rehearse the feelings that are appropriate to whatever the symbol stands for (see Jung, Man and His Symbols, ch. 1). Metaphor is very different. The vehicle or the phenomenon is important because metaphor asserts that some inner likeness or metaphysical likeness exists between the metaphor and what it represents. Coleridge, of course, defined metaphor as similarity within dissimilarity, and he is working in the long standing tradition whose highest statement is certainly St. Thomas' analogy of being. A metaphorical relationship or an analogy exists between God and man. The statement that man is made in the image and likeness of God means that man is a metaphor for God, and while God is certainly beyond anything that man is, St. Thomas asserts with the strength of logic and reason that the attributional similarity is true. The maker of metaphors, therefore, is bound to the truth of whatever the metaphor represents.

The transition from the Romanesque to the Gothic or the transition from symbol to metaphor suggests, finally, a movement from myth to dogma and the feeling that the literal institution possesses truth. The Gothic style is employed by the Church as a metaphor for the feeling of the numinous in order to enforce social identification. It is literally true that the Gothic style is "awe-inspiring," and it was designed to be so. If the Romanesque inspires awe, it is because of a relation between the believer and God. Art historians have long recognized that the Gothic represents the final merging of spiritual and temporal powers. For example, Otto von Simpson writes:

The consecration of the church [St. Denis] was but
the first liturgical ceremony in which the
monarchical and theological spheres were to
converge--one might say, to the glory of both.
Suger certainly had this politico-religious function of
his church in mind when he designed his sanctuary
as a typos of the Dionysian vision of heaven. . . .
The reader of the Booklet on the Consecration
becomes aware of a curious and bewildering
ambivalence, or a 'shuttling back and forth' between
the moral and aesthetic spheres and between moral
and aesthetic values.   (140)

The shuttling back and forth is indeed apparent in the building
itself, for the aesthetic is designed to confirm the moral.   The
beautiful is exactly the same as the unified, the good, and the
true.   It should be clear by now that what had happened to
Christianity in the late Middle Ages but was indeed latent from
the time of St. Augustine was a process of literalizing and
institutionalizing the meaningful; that is whatever acts could
now be called meaningful came under the control of the
schematized knowledge of the Church's codes and doctrines.
Dogma and moral law are asserted to be the meaningful; that
is, living the law produced the feeling of the numinous.   One of
the prime means for producing the feeling was the Gothic style
itself.   This process accounts for the success of the Church as
institution, but the number of imitative revolts against it
indicates that social identification builds institutions not men.
We must always bear in mind that at the moment of its greatest
political power and its greatest doctrinal expression, the
Church was challenged by more heresies than ever before.

It seems that the more comprehensive the doctrine and
the more intensely it is asserted as truth and the origin of the
meaningful, the more pervasive are the heresies that undermine
it.   This is not only because the more thoroughly articulated
the doctrine and canon law are, the better churchmen are able
to recognize and prosecute heresy; but chiefly because the
more complete the doctrine, the more completely it limits and
distorts the openness and variability of life and the more
individuals law cuts off from the beauty of the meaningful and
sufficient life.   Deductions made from numinal explanations and

applied to real life situations quite frequently will simply not work out; the knowledge is seen to be useless and abstract--utopic. The inquisition which followed the highpoint of the Church and, in fact, replaced the Gothic represents a desperate attempt to produce the same effects of the feeling of the numinous about the Church's doctrines. The feeling of the numinous is properly directed to the unconscious, but when the Church made its transition from its mythic role to a temporal and rational power, it began to address its feeling-stimulants to the emotions. Thus the feeling offered by the Gothic style is to the emotions not to the unconscious as it is with the Romanesque style. Even art historians find less to talk about with the Romanesque than the Gothic because the aesthetic appeal of the Romanesque is to mystery and darkness--things hardly amenable to reason, measure, and discussion. The Gothic, on the other hand, appeals to the emotions; it is clearly awe-inspiring and its terrible-joy is analyzable into specific images that affect the perceiver and produce certain emotions because he has learned the recipies. By the time of the inquisition, the feeling-appeal had been degraded to brute fear and terror, produced not by images but by real or threatened physical pain. Alan Watts in Myth and Ritual in Christianity calls this progression "myth debased to science," and he sees its purpose as social control, a phenomenon which necessitates the loss of meaning:

> Thus `theologized' myth is unable to liberate western man from history, from the fatal circle of a past which repeats itself faster and faster, from a life which loses all touch with reality in its increasing absorption in the fantasies of abstraction. For the living God has become the abstract God, and cannot deliver his creatures from the disease with which he himself is afflicted. (76-77)

The problem we face here in the analysis of institutional behavior is that what Watts describes is inevitable in the growth of any institution. To be sure churchmen such as St. Thomas were still on the quest of the numen, the quest to make life meaningful, and to them this point described by Watts is not tragic but precisely the opposite--the point of fulfillment and attainment.   Carl Jung has observed that in the final stages of the healing of psychological disorders, arising from meaninglessness or mythic dissociation, patients will dream or produce in fantasy images of a quartered circle or similarly symmetrically divided circle.   He calls the image a Mandala from the Hindu word meaning "magic circle," and it represents what he calls the "nuclear atom" of the psyche, perceived by an individual or a group as whole and coherent rather than chaotic and dissociated. Abelard sees this occurring in the communion of saints, just as the knights see it in the Round Table. Mandalas are produced when the patient is unconsciously aware of "an inner peace, a feeling that life has again found its meaning and order" (Man and His Symbols, 230).   Jung's most radical interpretation of the production of mandalas is that the troubled psyche finally perceives that itself and God are one-- "the God within."   To be sure, Jung is following the Hindu tradition, but mandalas are to be found in the West just as often as in the East with no trace of influence or imitation. The process of St. Augustine's recovery of psychic coherence after feelings of disintegration, described earlier in this section, is of this sort.   The typical manner of thinking of the Scholastics--the dialectic--exhibits the sort of tension reduction that produces mandala images.   St. Thomas, for example, thinks in a pattern of thesis-antithesis and synthesis. He poses questions, raises conflicting viewpoints, and resolves the dissonance in a final reply.   This is inherently a tension reduction way of thinking; it aims at maintaining a perceived isomorphism between mind and reality, a perfect adaptation of organism to environment.

Jung describes the production of the mandala in terms of the meaningful as I have defined in this book: "They felt it as belonging intimately to themselves as a sort of creative background, a life producing sun in the depths of the unconscious mind" (Psychology and Religion, 72).   This structure, however, is identical to that of social identification, the difference being only that between myth as creative sun and ideology as creative sun.   It is no coincidence, therefore, that with the emergence of the Gothic style and the feeling of fulfillment and attainment of the quest for the numen, there appears the rose window as perhaps one of the most significant and socially prominent mandalas of all time.   It represents metaphorically the deepest and most sincere feelings that lay behind the philosophy and theology of St. Thomas Aquinas and the ideology of Pope Innocent III. St. Thomas wrote a great deal on virtually every subject, but one of his special concerns was aesthetics. The substance of his aesthetic thinking involves harmony, proportion, and radiance, and these are exactly the spatial and organizational equivalents of the feeling which underlies not only his own view of the world but also the rose windows as mandalas and the Weltanschauung of Pope Innocent III who writes:

> We firmly believe and openly confess that there is only one true God, eternal and immense, omnipotent, unchangeable, incomprehensible, and ineffable, Father, Son, and Holy Ghost; three Persons indeed, but one essence, substance or nature absolutely simple; the Father proceeding from no one, but the Son from the Father only, and the Holy Ghost equally from both, always without beginning and end. The Father begetting, the Son begotten, and the Holy Ghost proceeding; consubstantial and coequal, and coomnipotent, and coeternal, the one principle of the universe, Creator of all things invisible and visible, spiritual and corporeal, who from the beginning of time by his omnipotent power made from nothing creatures both spiritual and corporeal; angelic, namely, and mundane, and then human, as it were, common, composed of spirit and body. The devil and the other demons were indeed created by God good by nature but became bad through themselves; man, however, sinned at the suggestion of the devil. This Holy Trinity, in its common essence and in personal properties divided, through Moses, the holy prophets, and other servants gave to the human race at the most opportune intervals of time the doctrine of salvation.
>
> And finally, Jesus Christ, the only begotten Son of God made flesh by the entire Trinity, conceived with the cooperation of the Holy Ghost of Mary ever Virgin, made true man, composed of a rational soul and human flesh, one Person in two natures, pointed

out more clearly the way of life. Who according to his divinity is immortal and impassable, according to his humanity was made passable and mortal, suffered on the cross for salvation of the human race, and being dead descended into hell, rose from the dead, and ascended into heaven. But he descended in soul, arose in flesh, and ascended equally in both; He will come at the end of the world to judge the living and the dead and will render to the reprobate and to the elect according to their works. Who all shall rise with their bodies which they have that they may receive according to their merits, whether good or bad, the latter eternal punishment with the devil, the former eternal glory with Christ. There is one Universal Church of the faithful, outside which there is absolutely no salvation. In which there is the same priest and the sacrifice, Jesus Christ, whose body and blood are truly contained in the sacrament of the alter under the forms of bread and wine, the bread being changed [transubstantiatio] by divine power into the body, and the wine into the blood, so that to realize the mystery of unity, we may receive of Him what He has received of us. And this sacrament no one can effect except the priest, who has been duly ordained in accordance with the keys of the Church, which Jesus Christ Himself gave to the apostles and their successors.

But the sacrament of baptism, which by the invocation of each Person of the Trinity, namely, of the Father, the Son and Holy Ghost, is effected in water, duly conferred on children and adults in the form prescribed by the Church by anyone whatsoever, leads to salvation. And should anyone after the reception of baptism have fallen into sin, by true repentance he can always be restored [reparari]. Not only virgins and those practicing chastity, but also those united in marriage, through the right faith and through works pleasing to God, can merit eternal salvation. (Peters, 173-74)

This is a great moment for Christianity, one fraught with meaning as well as dangers. What Innocent's declaration, offered as the opening address to the Fourth Lateran Council in November 1215, attempts to do is establish absolute foundations upon which the whole body of Christian ideology, indefinitely expandable in exemplary detail, is based. This, now, is the absolute meaning of existence, the only reality, and the secure means to perfection. His comment about "ineffable" is simply part of the explanation and has no operational value. At the same council, Innocent III also declared "We excommunicate and anathematize every heresy that raises itself against the holy, orthodox, and Catholic faith which we have above explained; condemning all heretics under whatever names they may be known" (Peters, 175). Sigmund Freud's definition of Weltanschauung helps clarify what sort of psychological position underlies Innocent's vision: "By Weltanschauung, then, I mean an intellectual construction, which gives a unified solution of all the problems of our existence in virtue of a comprehensive hypothesis, a construction, therefore, in which no question is left open and in which everything in which we are interested finds a place. It is easy to see that the possession of such a Weltanschauung is one of the ideal wishes of mankind. When one believes such a thing one feels secure in life, one knows what one ought to strive after, and how one ought to organize one's emotions and interests to the best purposes" (Dictionary of Psychoanalysis, 165-66). This position places God in service of the needs of the institution in the sense that the intellectual construction of God is a response to the needs of men for a coherent and comprehensive understanding of existence. Such an understanding of existence is only required for institutional action. At this moment the Church becomes the creator of God and the god of men--it is at this point in history, the late twelfth century, that Arthurian Romance emerges as an imitative response to the church.

Jung's studies have shown him that the psyche in relation to "religious" matters always produces a fourfold mandala: "I cannot omit calling attention to the interesting fact that whereas the central Christian symbolism is a Trinity, the formula of the unconscious mind is a quaternity" (Psychology and Religion, 73). He goes on to point out various attempts to fill in the fourth position, as for example the Manicheans who suggested the Devil, or modern man who has placed himself in the fourth position. But it is clear from Innocent's proclamation that the medieval Church saw itself as the temporal extension of the eternal God. The notion of the Church as the mystical body of Christ also confirms this feeling. The rose windows represent an unconscious perception that finally, as it were, the Church has healed a deficiency in God by filling out the triune God to a quaternity. The Church, as mystical body, repairs the dissociation created by Christ's death and ascencion and returns men to the living continuation of the incarnation. The extreme self-confidence and power of this feeling is evident in both Innocent's letter and in the position of the rose windows. The windows normally appear on the facades just above the main portal. This is the focal point for anyone approaching or desiring to enter the cathedral, and the window announces metaphorically that just as it is the point of harmony among all the disparate and elaborately heterogeneous parts of the building, so too is the Church the point of unity, peace, and meaning among men.

Irwin Panofsky in his little book on Gothic Architecture and Scholasticism writes: "Like the High Scholastic Summa, the High Gothic cathedral aimed, first of all, at `totality` and therefore tended to approximate, by synthesis as well as elimination, one perfect and final solution. . . . In its imagery, the High Gothic cathedral sought to embody the whole of Christian knowledge, theological, moral, natural, and historical, with everything in its place, and that which no longer found its place, suppressed. . . . The second requirement of Scholastic writing, `arrangement according to a system of homologus parts and parts of parts,` is most graphically expressed in the uniform division and subdivision of the whole structure" (44-45). While Panofsky stresses the narrative and iconographical interpretation of the cathedral, he ends up talking about the whole effect. No one has ever worked out a very satisfactory narrative scheme for a Gothic cathedral, and even Abbot Suger's attempt to explain the narrative content of St. Denis suggests rather the importance of the whole, the Gestalt. For the whole produces the feeling of the numinous; that is, the building itself provides the Christian with an assurance that the body of doctrines, the Weltanschauung, which brought the building into existence is true and immutable. (This principle, too, accounts for the feeling of the whole or the moral tone in Malory's romance and yet no one can make the parts add up to that whole). The power of the style itself confirms the Christian's identity and existence by the feelings that it produces in him. The fact that rose windows usually contain more than four divisions, usually eight, twelve, sixteen, or twenty-four partitions which, of course, are multiples of four and are very often organized around a dominant quadrapartite theme, suggests that the producers of such mandalas have gone beyond the basic religious experience and have found meaning in the process of elaborating, enhancing, and schematizing the experience. The cathedral as a whole also suggests, because it is now the real source of the feeling of the numinous, that western man has gone beyond mythic and social indentification and the meaningful and created an institution which will deny his own being; eventually, he will turn upon his institutions which have become solidified as truth and begin to dismantle them in a new quest for meaning beyond truth, a new quest which will have no end.

2.4 The Model of the World

The theme of Malory's romance up to the "Tale of Tristram" imitates the history of Western civilization from St. Augustine up to about the twelfth century; the theme concerns what Peter Berger and Thomas Luckmann call the creation of a symbolic universe:

> Now, however, <u>all</u> the sectors of the institutional order are integrated in an all-embracing frame of reference, which now constitutes a universe in the literal sense of the word, because <u>all</u> human experience can now be conceived of as ta<u>king place within</u> it.
> The symbolic universe is conceived of as the matrix of <u>all</u> soically objectivated and subjectively real meanings; the entire historic society and the entire biography of the individual are seen as events taking place <u>within</u> this universe. . . .
> The symbolic universe provides order for the subjective apprehension of biographical experience. Experiences belonging to different spheres of reality are integrated by incorporation in the same, overarching universe of meaning. . . .

> This nomic function of the symbolic universe for
> individual experience may be described quite simply
> by saying that it `puts everything in its right place.´
> What is more, whenever one strays from the
> consciousness of this order (that is, when one finds
> oneself in the marginal situations of experience), the
> symbolic universe allows one `to return to reality´--
> namely, to the reality of everyday life. (Social
> Construction of Reality, 96-98)

As we turn to the "Tale of Tristram" and even already in the
adventures of Gareth (though not problematic for Gareth), the
institution of the Round Table in imitation of the medieval
Catholic Church is experienced by any individual as a concrete
and objective reality, a real thing out there around which all of
one´s own private actions revolve. Again, Berger and Luckmann
are so clear on the nature of secondary social experience (as
opposed to the primary creative experience): "This means that
the institutions have now been crystallized (for instance, the
institution of paternity as it is encountered by the children) are
experienced as existing over and beyond the individuals who
`happen to´ embody them at the moment. In other words, the
institutions are now experienced as possessing a reality of their
own, a reality that confronts the individual as an external and
coercive fact" (58).

We now need to investigate the nature of the experience
of responding to this crystallized institution, for it presents to
the knights of the second generation quite a different reality
and experience than that faced by Arthur, Merlin, Lancelot,
Gawain, Torre, Pellinor, Balin, Marhalt, Ywain, or Kay--all of
the first generation. The nature of institutional action, as we
saw in the progression from St. Augustine to Pope Innocent III
changes from creativity to universe maintenance and enforced
compliance. The history of the first generation, comprised of
behavioral and cognitive strategies they innovated for adapting
to the environment they faced, persists into the lives of the
second and subsequent generations as schemes of normative
behavior and thought they are bound, upon pain of real
punishment, to employ in adapting their own personal lives to
the world they encounter. But the generations face essentially
different worlds. My analysis of the the major knights

advances, therefore, generally along the lines of Lancelot and Arthur as model first generation knight and king, and Tristram and Mark as second generation society. The first generation experiences the sort of chaos we have seen in the cases of Arthur or St. Augustine; the only real world encountered by the second generation is that of the solid order of the oath of knighthood taken each Pentecost or the absolute dogma of Innocent III, elaborated in minute detail by a growing army of canonists and scholastics at universities throughout Europe.

We see in this diachronic analysis the fundamental tragic potential of historically based institutions; the terms chaos and disorder come in the mature phase to have new meanings. They now must be understood, not as pre-institutional or profane time and world, but as deviance from the institutional order and reality, as heresy and non-compliance. The power which brought the institution into being now turns from fighting the forces of chaos to fighting and beating its own members into compliance. The individual, the unaccountable "I," becomes the new site of chaos upon which the social order must be imposed, suggesting the sort of overt enmity between the individual and culture that exists in Cornwall. Louis Althusser in his For Marx points out the nature of the experience of society and ideology we must consider if we want to understand what Malory presents in his "Tristram" and "Grail Quest." For those not participating in the original quest for civilization, culture presents a facticity to be perceived, accepted, and suffered.

> Ideology is a system of representations . . . but it is above all as structures that they impose on the vast majority of men, not via their `consciousness´. They are perceived-accepted-suffered cultural objects and they act functionally on one in a process that escapes them. Men `live´ their ideologies as the Cartesian `saw´ or did not see--if he was not looking at it--the moon at two hundred paces away: not at all as a form of consciousness, but as an object of their `world´--as their world itself. . . .
> So ideology is a matter of the lived relation between men and their world.   (233)

If chaos changes meaning and location, so too does innovation. Innovation is an inescapable fact of human existence; human beings cannot stop innovating. What changes is the backdrop against which the act occurs. Tristram innovates against the backdrop of the perceived-accepted-suffered culture in the same manner that Malory's romance was written against the backdrop of late medieval culture, or Martin Luther's ninety-five theses were posted against the world of sin, good works, and indulgences. We never really face a world "ab origine"; we never really create order "ex nihilo" or out of chaos. Innovation is always circumscribed by culture and thus by order. Innovation within the symbolic universe moves man toward the margins of culture producing some level of disorder; innovation pierces through the sphere of culture, breaking the bonds or limits of reality and pushing mankind into larger worlds able, once again, to contain human eros. The aboriginal quest for meaning may, indeed, impose order on chaos, but the quest for meaning within any civilized world will, in fact, be just the opposite: rebellion, dissent, heresy, and the injection of pluralism into order. We must, therefore, draw out in some detailed the picture of the structure of the content of the ideology which resulted from the conquest for the numen, for the structure of the explanatory model shows an attempt to resolve all the tensions that might arise in experience; at the same time, the structure is imported into the life of the individual knight with the same promise of tension reduction. The knights "live" their culture. In the structure we are able to see direction of movement, and we will have to determine whether a knights actions are designed to move him toward the harmony and perfect adaptation of man to man and man to world that resides at the center of culture or whether they are designed to move him away from it toward the margin.

The following diagram is intended to show structure and direction. It must be acknowledged that any diagram has limitations; the text is vastly more rich and complex, but perhaps in simplicity there is some clarity.

The Quest for the Numen as the Quest for the Center

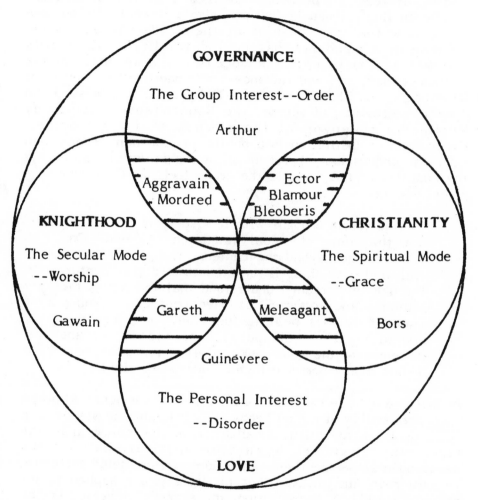

Fig. 1: On the quest for the numen, the direction or the meaning of any individual's act is a movement toward the center of being. The overall thrust of the synthetic tradition was to move culture toward harmony and tensionlessness among modes and interests of life at the center, for as theologians argues the world is a unity. Any individual may excel in only one area, but his orientation is inward and toward the center.

The diagram represents what the knights actually do in the romance, and the fact that their actions form a coherent whole--at least in potential--justifies a diagram which looks very much like a mandala (perhaps also a flower). My purpose is to show that the meaning of their collective acts is the meaning of a mandala; that is, the totality of their acts presents to the knights the unconscious awareness of the wholeness, harmony, and radiance that underlie the Summa of, for example, St. Thomas Aquinas. The general roundness of the diagram represents, of course, the Round Table ordained by Merlin "in tokenyng of the rowndnes of the worlde." Civilization or institution is a public or common dream, and when the unconscious apprehension of the structure approaches the qualities of the mandala the group feels, as Carl Jung says of his own dreams, that

> This dream brought with it a sense of finality. I saw that here the goal had been revealed. One could not go beyond the center. The center is the goal, and everything is directed toward that center. Through this dream I understood that the self is the principle and archetype of orientation and meaning. Therein lies its healing function. For me, this insight signified an approach to the center and therefore to the goal. Out of it emerged a first inkling of my personal myth. (Memories, 199)

We must be a little careful about using Jung's insights; although his understanding of human behavior is brilliant, he stands as a major figure in the institutionalization of the individual in the same way that St. Augustine institutionalized the transcendental perspective. When Jung writes "self," therefore, we must read "institution" when his insights are applied to the medieval world. The institution, the symboic universe, is the principle and archetype of orientation and meaning, not the "self" for medieval times.

The sense of the roundness of the diagram is that of metaphor; the Queen of the West Lands suggests that there is an attributional carryover between the Round Table and the world. The ideology of the Round Table, therefore, exhausts in potential the entire range of human actions; those actions which are validated and explained by the doctrines of the Table are moral (i.e., real) and those which are not are immoral. Disharmony or the personal failure of any particular knight is explained as "mishap" or accident, which of course preserves the essential harmony. Only negation of the explanatory model and alienation cannot be explained by the ideology, for they imply an oppositional relationship between the individual and the culture and a movement away from the center; from the institutional standpoint (and Jung's, too), that can only be understood as insanity. The direction of movement of the Round Table knights is toward the center, just as for Jung. The quest for the numen is the quest for the center; for at the center, tension--possible in a conflict between any two of the separate domains--is totally absent.

The harmony which appears at the end of the "Tale of Gareth" represents the tensionlessness of the center. Governance, Love, Knighthood, and Christianity are simultaneously and harmoniously at work controlling and organizing the knights' lives in a manner which suggests that they are fulfilling their own personal destinies. At the tournament, not only do the best knights overthrow the number of opponent knights which corresponds exactly to the degree of their respective prowess, but also opposites are reconciled in the simultaneous marriages of Gareth to Lyones, Gaheris to Lyonet, and Aggravain to Laurel--"wyth grete and myghty londys, wyth grete ryches igyffyn wyth them, that ryally they myght lyve tyll theire lyvis ende" (226). None of these knights, it must be noted, lives to a very happy or royal end, but the structure of the social organization establishes them as perfect knights, lovers, governors and Christians according to their positions on the hierarchy of perfection. No individual knight attains the center, although their lives are directed to it; rather at the center resides the apotheosis of mankind, the condition to which all men must aspire but not attain.

All of this set up on the Feast of the Assumption, the celebration of God's acknowledgement of the highest perfection ever attained by a human being. The feast commemorates Mary's assumption into heaven without having to die. The Assumption, therefore, completes the Immaculate Conception, a doctrine which explains that Mary alone among mankind was conceived without original sin. She could not die because she

had not inherited the wages of original sin--death. The
Assumption, then, fulfills the story of Adam's fall in the same
sense, discussed earlier, that Pentecost reverses of the Tower
of Babel story. But the Assumption is even more important, for
it overturns both disorder and the very origin of disorder in
original sin and man's subsequent alienation from God; the
Assumption commemorates the completion of Mary's earthly
quest to fulfill the first messianic prophecy, that the seed of
Woman shall crush the head of Satan who brought sorrow and
enmity into the world (see Genesis 3:15).

The modern, Darwinian, counterpart to original sin holds
simply that as organisms we are not perfectly adapted to the
natural environment. The species evolves in the direction of
enhanced adaptation. These same implications were the
attributes of original sin as understood in the Middle Ages.
Original sin explained why so many problems existed in
everyday life; it was, moreover, taken as a universal predicate
of human nature. Christian life, as all biologic impulse,
directed itself toward perfection. The Immaculate Conception
and the Assumption, therefore, situate Mary in the center of the
mandala of human experience. On the circumference may exist
suffering, ignorance, and corruption, but in the center resides
the conditions of Eden. In relation to the church calendar and
major feasts, the Assumption immediately precedes the
institution's feast day, Pentecost, the last day of the Easter
Cycle. The relation of the two feasts completes the Easter
Cycle in such a way as to suggest that the social organization
now upon Mary's departure takes over as its own center the
factual reality of the edenic condition of perfect and tensionless
adaptation to the environment.

Though the Immaculate Conception was not officially
made Canon Law until Pope Pius IX's bull Ineffablis Deus on
December 8, 1854, and the Assumption did not become an
Article of Faith until 1950, both doctrines had long been
believed and their necessity as the mythic deep-structure of
the historical institution was felt as early as the tenth century.
Peter the Venerable, abbot of Cluny from 1120 to 1156,
describes in his book On Miracles the Assumption and notes its
occurrence on August 15th. The Feast Day of the Immaculate
Conception, December 8th, was instituted in Malory's own time,
1476, and celebrations of her feast were common in England and

France or generally outside of Roman practices well before Pope Sixtus IV in 1477 and again in 1483 issued bulls urging the faithful everywhere to observe the commemorations but stopped short of making them dogma. Matters of faith or deep belief do not usually become law--or need to become law--until it is perceived that few people continue to believe in them. Law is the last stage of ideology when coercion and enforcement replace simple personal belief or need for behavioral direction.

In the Middle Ages, no law was needed to convince the people that the miracles of Mary were real; there was a sufficient amount of art, poetry, and liturgical commemorations to do that, such as Gautier de Coincy's thirty-thousand line poem on the miracles of Mary. He presents them not as fantasy but as fact. Though nothing is mentioned of the Immaculate Conception or the Assumption in the New Testament, the institution needed Mary at its center, and the conceptions arose probably, as Jaroslav Pelikan citing Peter Aureoli's Tractate on the Conception of the Blessed Virgin Mary notes, through "a progressive revelation of divine truths about Mary through successive periods of church history and setting it down as a hermeneutical axiom that Scripture was to be interpreted in such a way as to redound to her perfection, so that from the title 'Mother of God' it was possible for the church to 'infer all holines, all honor, all perogatives' for Mary" (The Christian Tradition, IV, 44). Medieval discussion of the Assumption tend to focus on the mechanics of how it took place; that it occurred was required as a vital link in the explanatory regress. The needs of ideological legitimation always precede exact articulation of dogma. Humans feel connections of this sort before they bother to prove them with arguments. This is demonstrated by the fact that after 1854 the church lived for one hundred years with a glaring inconsistency in its doctrine that did not seem to trouble believers, at least at first. If Mary were born without original sin, then she could not die and would have to be assumed into heaven, but it took one hundred years for the church to make that logical conclusion official.

The importance of the Assumption, then, is that it represents the final reconciliation between God and man after the fall. Pentecost implies a questing social structure, but the Assumption suggests rest and fulfillment--the end of the quest for meaning. The angel addresses Mary as "full of grace"--not as seeking grace. The combination of Pentecost and Assumption follows the Aristotlean and Thomistic rule of potency and actuality. The tournament which symbolizes the Round Table's potency occurs on Assumption day, but the actual marriages and establishment of the permanent hierarchy of the four best knights do not take place until Michaelmas, about six weeks later. Traditionally the Archangel Michael drove Adam and Eve from the Garden of Eden and protected its entrance against their return. Now with the marriages upon Michaelmas and Lancelot's defeat of fifty knights, Tristram's beating of forty knights, and Lamerok's downing of thirty knights; that condition of exile, labor, and potency is redeemed, and Michael, as it were, welcomes mankind to a recovery of unity and sinlessness. In some medieval legends, it is even Michael who carries the body and soul of Mary into heaven. The quest is the condition of exiled man in the sense of wandering and searching for his proper home, but after the battle on Michaelmas the quest is no longer felt to be necessary. This is, of course, just what happens in Le Morte Darthur; after the "Tale of Gareth" the battle is replaced by the tournament. The unconscious perception of wholeness and harmony, moreover, that is suggested by the Assumption is exactly the feeling-state that pervades the end of "The Tale of Gareth." This is the feeling of the numinous, the active participation of man in his God. Christ is God's offering of reconciliation to man; Mary is man's offering of reconciliation to God. When at the end of Gareth's tale the configuration of actions suggests a quadrapartite circle and this mandala occurs on the Feast of the Assumption, we must conclude that the knights now feel that they, through the ideology of the Round Table, have reconciled themselves with God and have, therefore, recovered the tensionless state of Eden. The Round Table has--at least in potential--attained the perfection of Mary.

Carl Jung is again so instructive on the feelings experienced by the society itself or the collective unconscious of the knights:

> The wholeness of the celestial circle and the
> squareness of the earth, uniting the four principles
> or elements or psychical qualities, express
> completeness and union. Thus the mandala has the

dignity of a `reconciling symbol.´ As the reconciliation of God and man is expressed in the symbol of Christ or of the cross. (Psychology and Religion, 96)

Though the context of Jung´s discussion is the modern world, his method for understanding the psychoses of his patients is derived from religion, both Hindu and medieval Catholicism, and it derives from the experience of men caught in the quest to resolve the problem of the fundamental emptiness and meaningless of the world or their fundamental mal-adaptation to their environments. Jung goes on,

A modern mandala is an involuntary confession of a peculiar mental condition. There is no deity in the mandala, and there is also no submission or reconciliation to a deity. The place of the deity seems to be taken by the wholeness of man. (99)

Again, we must read "wholeness of man" as the wholeness of the institution. Malory sees that the all-consuming effort of medieval institutions was to objectivate the paradox expressed in numerous theological tracts that, as St. Bonaventura puts it, the simplicity of Being "is entirely within and entirely without all things and, there, is an intelligible sphere whose center is everywhere and whose circumference is no where" (The Mind´s Road to God, 38). Although it is unlikely that Malory knew of this text, the movement of the society as a whole toward the center makes the center an everywhere. Thus institutional life must be taken in the same sense that St. Bonaventura takes Being: "Being, therefore, which is pure Being and most simply Being and absolutely Being, is Being primary, eternal, most simple, most actual, most perfect, and one to the highest degree" (36). The institution itself possesses the qualities of Being, and even a cursory knowledge of medieval theology reveals that these are the qualities of God. No individual knight attains the status of the center; we need not worry, as so many of Malory´s critics have, about Lancelot´s failure on the Grail Quest (see Ihle). Perfection is rather the sum of individual action or the institution itself. It is further asserted that although individuals may have different personal characteristics, they all possess the same "being," only in different degrees. In terms of the model, the ideology of the center controls even the circumference. Because it is felt to be thus unified and perfect, society cannot develop or grow as it did prior to the Assumption, for the quest is now at an end. The feeling is that of rest since its tensionlessness is permanent, but at this point the institution itself replaces the ineffable God or numen and actions lose the ability to create knights and a society as they had at the origin. It is, of course, significant that immediately after the festivities of the Assumption and Michaelmas, Malory turns to "The Tale of Tristram," a tale about the gradual loss of the meaningful.

The sub-circles of my diagram on opposite ends of either the horizontal or the vertical axis represent essentially different and mutually exclusive kinds of human behavior that are harmonized in the medieval symbolic universe. Hence Knighthood represents both modes and goals of life essentially opposed to Christianity. Knighthood has its roots in the pagan warrior ethos, in self-preservation, competition, hatred for others, vengeance, and its primary mode is overt force. In contrast, Christianity finds its roots in the self-sacrificial Christ, and its primary mode is love for others. A cynic might define Christian love as seduction, bribery, or covert force in the promise of redemption or the threat of damnation as the ultimate means of imposing the Christian order on the world. But that is a late, puritanical form of Christianity, not the Christianity of the New Testament. At the base, Christianity is a life of love or genuine concern for others irrespective of the worth or merit of the other. Though Knighthood and Christianity are both explanatory systems which may be said to address different aspects of the person (the temporal and the spiritual), people are whole beings and they thus are fundamentally incompatible and compete for control of behavior and social order. And yet after 800 when the warrior Charlemagne became the Holy Roman Emperor and especially after 1095 when Pope Urban III proclaimed the knight the fighter for the Prince of Peace, the two systems were forced to conflate; the modes and goals of each shpere were taken over and assimilated into the sphere of the other. The composite whole made possible the disaster of the crusades against the Moslem Turks which led to the crusades against domestic heretics such as the Cathars and finally to the inquisition. The end result of the harmony was the death of both Christianity and Knighthood as they were originally conceived.

On the other axis, Governance and Love are opposed. In Malory, the impossible quest for the center is undertaken by both Lancelot and Tristram whose fate it is, for reasons that shall have to wait until Chapter Three, to love the wife of their respective king. Ultimately the choice for each is between the beloved and the King. The choice of the beloved means the destruction of the kingdom. But on a more general level, the dichotomy suggests the irresolvable tension between the person as individual and the person as member of a group, community, or race. That Malory is aware of the emerging trend of individualism and the assertion of the private over the public concern is apparent in the fact that both Tristram and Lancelot choose their lovers over their kings. Love, then, is the private mode. If we accept C. S. Lewis' theory that courtly love represents a fundamental change in human sentiment, then the ultimate irreconcilability of the private and the public modes takes the form of a subtle rebellion against the feudal system of social identification. Erotic love forces the lover into secrecy and isolation, the result of which is the avoidance of his social responsibilities. The lovers feel themselves to be of a special status, one which alienates them from the socially prescribed identity. The Lady, sometimes called "Midons" (though not in Malory) which etymologically means, Lewis points out, "my lord," replaces the feudal lord as master, and Love becomes a collection of behaviors in parallel contrast to the state (Allegory of Love, 3).

In Malory love is always sexual and always seditious, even when it is not secret or adulterous. Gareth, for example, enters a conventional marriage and seems to harmonize Love with Knighthood and Governance, but by marrying he relinquishes his position as the fourth best knight of the world and ceases to extend Arthur's control. His interests gravitate to personal affairs. What is clear is that the knight cannot serve--i. e., respond to the demands of--both the private and the group concerns simultaneously, and yet the force of the quest for the center demands that the knight do so. It is for this reason that Lancelot will never marry, not even after Arthur is dead. And so, as governor, the king appropriately enough has little personal interest in Love. Mark uses Isode to control Tristram; he loves her no more than Guinevere is loved by the Arthur who tells his men: "And much more I am soryar for my good knyghtes losse [death of Gareth and Gaheris] than for the losse of my fayre queene; for quenys I myght have inow, but such a felyship of good knyghts shall never be togydirs in no company" (685).

In the shaded areas of the diagram, areas where two explanatory spheres overlap, the possibility exists that instructions coming from two systems will be mutually compatible. Thus Gareth is a good knight in that he fights extremely well (perhaps eventually sixth or seventh rank) and he is loyal to his comrades. He is also a good lover; he has one of the few successful love affairs in the entire romance, but Malory characteristically shows little interest in a successful harmonization of two systems. Gareth has little to do with the political or religious affairs of the Round Table. He is mentioned only once--and that just in passing--in the "Tale of the Sankgreal," (534) and in the final dispute between Arthur and Lancelot, Gareth sides with Lancelot, the knight, rather than with the social organization. Gareth finds a harmony between Knighthood and Love, but he remains essentially a private individual. Gareth, nevertheless, is not a rebel. He appears at the trial of Guinevere as Arthur requires him to do, but he appears unarmed so that he sides with Lancelot without overtly challenging Arthur. To his death, Gareth supports the harmony of the whole. He actually believes that he is supporting both Arthur and Lancelot at this final moment when there can no longer by any harmony between the two of them.

In contrast, Ector, Bleoberis, and Blamour operate in the realms of religion and politics, but ultimately have little to do with Knighthood in its personal sense. Their Knighthood is a function of political needs; they are soldiers or perhaps policemen whose concern is maintaining peace among the knights. They fight reasonably well, but never on the level of the four best knights and their battles are not undertaken on their own behalf as attempts to develop further their own personal sense of prowess and worship. They are reasonable and careful about considering the nature of a conflict, and they form the remnant knights, the knights who after the final destruction of the Round Table take up the cause of the Church and continue to defend the public or social concern by crusading against the Turks. Blamour, Bleoberis, and Ector present the Christian sense of love and loyality, what St. Augustine calls Charity. Their self-less and self-sacrificing love is given for the sake of the institution (ultimately God in the explanatory regress) or given as an individual for the sake of the higher moral laws he seeks to enforce. For Gareth as well as for Ector, Bleoberis, and Blamour, Lancelot and the magnitude of the quest he represents is finally destructive. It is of course Lancelot who kills Gareth, but Lancelot also forces Ector, Blamour, and Bleoberis to choose between the Round Table and the individual, a choice which without Lancelot they would never have had to face.

Meleagant's love for Guinevere is the extreme, seditious, and sociopathic kind that Malory always associates with Guinevere, though it is the kind that deeply interests him. But Meleagant harmonizes his love well with Christianity in the sense that if Christianity orientates men toward the Good, not for personal reasons, but for God's sake, then the Christian, it follows, must embrace some code of universal justice which emanates from God. Meleagant uses God's justice to validate his claim for the love of Guinevere and to invalidate Lancelot's love. In accusing Guinevere of adultery, he hopes above all to disgrace Lancelot by forcing him to take the unjust side of the quarrel. He calls upon God to defend his position for he knows that it is just: "yet sholde ye [Lancelot] be avysed to do batayle in a wronge quarell, for God woll have a stroke in every batayle" (659). Trusting in the reality of the conflation of Love with Christianity, he fights Lancelot thinking that surely God will not allow Lancelot to be victorious in an unjust cause. Here Meleagant's Christianity disrupts the social order, for by all rights he should defeat Lancelot whom the Round Table desperately needs as its best knight. But he does nothing to harm Christianity or Love. Meleagant is not a preserver of the social peace in the manner of Blamour, Bleoberis, or Ector. Rather if he can discredit Lancelot with the help of God, he will certainly move in and undertake an affair with Guinevere, as a Lover should do. But of course, no one defeats Lancelot, God's help notwithstanding, and yet in the outright murder of Meleagant (since Lancelot is in fact guilty of the crime no matter how imprecise Meleagant's statement of it is) what can be said of God's justice or His hand in every battle?   Can God read only the letter and not the hearts of men?

Complementary to Meleagant are Aggravain and Mordred. They also hate Lancelot, but find legitimate and just political means for achieving their ends.   While Meleagant appears to be fighting for God's justice, Mordred and Aggravain, when they surprise Lancelot in Guinevere's chambers, use the guise of political justice and social order to assert the power of the Orkneys over the family-clan of Lancelot.   They find a harmony between personal interest and Governance.   In all these cases, Gareth, Blamour, Bleoberis, Ector, Meleagant, Aggravain, and Mordred, the knights are trying to put into force the terms of their ideology.   In spite of the fact that their actions sometimes turn out badly, they all believe in the truth and appropriateness of the universal laws upon which their society is based.   In other words, their movement is toward the center of the explanatory model, and they believe in harmony on earth. They do not see the ideological significance of the tension their actions produce, but we who are privileged with an overview can see how their adherence to the terms of any particular part of the ideology eventually places them in a direct life and death struggle with some other knight who is only, in turn, performing his duties as he sees them.

The great heroes--Lancelot, Tristram, Lamerok, and Palomides --must operate in all four spheres; that is, they must find harmony through perfection of performance in Knighthood, Love, Governance, and Christianity.   But even within the four best knights there is a difference.   Lancelot and Lamerok always move toward the center forcing, as it were, perfection to prevail.   All the while the tension gradually builds.   Tristram and Palomides, on the other hand, move toward the center until they discover the emptiness of it and the inevitable destructiveness of the quest; whereupon, they repudiate the quest and move away from the center.   From the standpoint of the knight as a responder to the institution, each sphere, although unique in itself, is structurally identical to the others. Each provides an explanatory regress for certain kinds of behavior which are, in this manner only, held by the knights to be exactly what is real in their world.   The regress of categorial subsumptions terminates in the center where essentially different kinds of behavior are perfectly unified.   But on the periphery, the margin of reality, each explanatory system points to incoherent experiences. The orientation of ideology is toward the center which means that any knight must turn his back upon the plurality of his own marginal existence, exactly in the way St. Bonaventura describes the quest through the multiplicity of things in themselves to the contemplation of the unity of Being at the center of creation:

> In this consideration is the perfection of the mind's illumination, when, as if on the sixth day, it sees man made in the image of God. If then the image is an express likeness when our mind contemplates in Christ the Son of God . . . our humanity [is] now wonderfully exalted, now ineffably united, by seeing at once in one Being the first and the last, the highest and the lowest, the circumference and the center, the alpha and the omega, the caused and the cause, the creator and the creature, the book written within and without, it [the mind] arrives at a perfect being in order that it may arrive with God at the perfection of His illuminations on the sixth day . . . on which, by the elevation of the mind, its insights rests from all work which He had done. (Mind's Road to God, 42)

The contents of each system are derived from the deeds of history, the deeds believed to be responsible for creating men as they presently exist. The movement from the circumference to the center is a movement toward wholeness, harmony, and radiance--toward the ideal life of the mind. But, Malory sees, Lancelot when he acts most like an ideal lover, he acts most unlike a knight, a Christian, and most disloyal to his king. At the same time his code of love instructs him to be the best knight, Christian, and champion.

This profound incoherence at the center prevails no matter how the center is approached. The quest of all knights pre-supposes that at the center all the disparate elements will be united into a single vision. Their quests are to bring all the possible facets of life together and hold them in harmony at the center. Lancelot's love for Guinevere is a function of his quest for the center and without the quest he has no idea of what love might be. The quest upon which medieval romance is built is inherently research or illumination, to use St. Bonaventura's term, in that it is designed to bring to light the consonance between the ideology (the mind) and the phenomenal world. The kind of resolution found in St. Bonaventura, St. Thomas, St. Bernard, Gratian and many others should be the result of the scientific process of subsuming ever greater amounts of data under theory and it should be the result of the quest.   In Arthurian Romance, however, not even Galahad is successful in the quest considered this way.   He pushes the explanatory potential of the ideology into new and unknown areas to test the extent to which it and reality are isomorphic on the most essential level.   The question posed by the French Quest Del Saint Graal is whether or not the Christian life exemplified by Galahad is true.

Roger Sherman Loomis has traced the name Galahad to the Biblical Galeed, referring to a pilar of stones erected by Jacob and Laban as a symbol for the covenant between them establishing the borders and limits of each man's territory (The Grail, 179).   The name itself means "a heap of testimony" and Galahad in achieving the Grail Quest becomes a heap of evidence to the validity of the world view that divides life into secular and spiritual concerns and subordinates the secular to the spiritual, thus requiring men to interpret experiences from the spiritual point of view.   The spiritual functions as the unifying center because it emanates from a unified (i.e., divisionless) God, as St. Thomas argues in "Of the Simplicity of God" (Summa Theologica, I, ii, q. 3).   In establishing and accepting such a dualism and subordination, Galahad overcomes the tension between the two domains, just as the pilar of stones at Galeed ended the war between Jacob and Laban and began a period of peace (Genesis, 31:45).   His quest is a testimony to the potential for psychic satisfaction through the elimination of tension between mind and reality.   The structure of his resolution follows exactly that of St. Augustine and St. Bonaventura, but in Malory, because the Grail Quest occurs in the context of the politically disintegrating Round Table, the Christian life actually exacerbates the failings of the political sphere; especially in the way it negates Lancelot's perfections as a chivalric knight.

Tristram, in sharp contrast to Lancelot and Galahad, perceives the tragedy implicit in the quest for the center; in his experience the center does not project unity out to the circumference but rather only repression and a loss of being. Consequently, he moves in an outward direction, toward disintegration and alienation but away from the center of death that guides Lancelot and Galahad. The perception is possible for Tristram, but not for Lancelot, because for Tristram the fundamental incoherence of the model dominates his experience; his socialization is faulty and incomplete. He is, moreover, the representative of the analytic tradition, while Lancelot represents the synthetic tradition of medieval culture. As a second generation knight, his experience of the social process differs from Lancelot's in the manner described by Berger and Luckmann: "To put it simply, it is more likely that one will deviate from programs set up for one by others than from programs that one has helped establish himself" (Social Construction, 62). Tristram represents the "I" responding to the socially determined "me." For example, in the famous passage in which he, while bringing Isode from Ireland to Cornwall, hears that Lancelot knightly "toke sir Carados by the coler and pulled hym under his horse fete . . . and strake offe his hede" (262), Tristram is presented with conflicting behavioral programs. In order to affirm the political structure and the king-champion relationship, he must perform the "message" given him by Mark. For such work he will be worshipped by Mark. He is equally attracted, however, by the possibility of knightly fame with Lancelot: "Alas . . . and I had nat this messayge in hande with this fayre lady, truly wold I never stynte or I had founde sir Lancelot" (263). We know, of course, that the message (the bringing of Isode to Mark) will also destroy the possibility of a peaceful love between Tristram and Isode.

Tristram's inclinations as champion of Cornwall are to do the things that will move him toward the center just as are his desires to follow Lancelot and love Isode, but here Malory emphasizes the incoherence, the impossibility of performing all four roles harmoniously. By the end of his section, Tristram is secluded in the "Joyous Garde" with Isode, having repudiated his king. He maintains a diminished interest in Knighthood and he is instrumental in the Baptism of Palomides. The important point of Tristram's seclusion with Isode is that all of his behavioral controls come from a single explanatory source: Love. Rather than forcing unity, Tristram effects an oppositional stance of one category against another and marginalizes himself with respect to the needs of the institution (whether in Cornwall or Camelot). Dynadan is similarly marginalized, and the centering orientation of most readers makes for little understanding of the import of his influence on others. In a sense, Tristram has put his life in order by negating the quest for the center and rejecting the idea of universal order altogether. Malory has perceived the dissolution of the Medieval explanatory system in both the tragedy of Lancelot and in the self-imposed exile of Tristram.

The cases of Tristram, Palomides, and Dynadan provide a movement opposite to that of Lancelot and Lamerok and indeed opposite to the major thrust of medieval culture. The counter-cultural movement, therefore, requires that the diagram of the explanatory synthesis be filled in with different knights. In the new diagram, it will be seen that each knight attempts the quest for the center only until he perceives the incoherence of the explanatory synthesis; he then repudiates the synthesis and the quest which sustains it. The key figures here are Dynadan and Galahad who reveal most clearly the tragic destructiveness of the quest for the center.

The Quest For Selfhood as the Abandonment of the Center

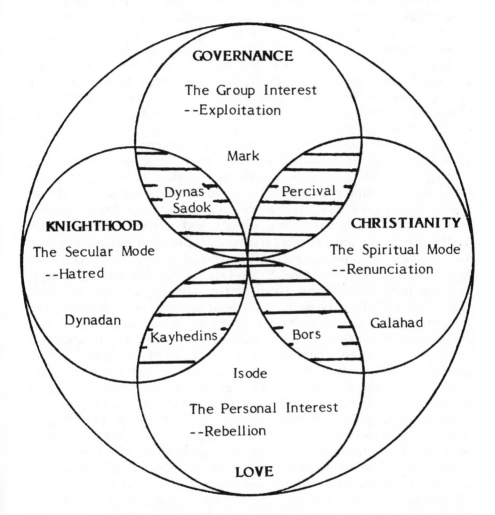

Fig. 2: Each person listed above moves toward the center and discovers the incoherence and life destroying tension that resides there. Upon that discovery, some continue on and submit to death, while others turn outward and begin a movement of rebellion away from the center toward pluralism, chaos, and self-ascription of value.

It can be seen that each character who occupies the central position in a particular sub-sphere of the Model violates the tenets of the sub-sphere that serve the unity of the model as a whole. Dynadan abjures Knighthood when it represents a frantic quest, Mark abuses his position as king by refusing to accord value to Tristram who has been his champion, Galahad undercuts Christianity by moving away from men toward asceticism and ultimately death, and Isode negates Love by loving Tristram for personal reasons, his own sake, rather than hierarchical and ideological ones. But the pattern of negation emerges only after considerable striving toward the center. It is certain that Malory did not have the degree of theoretical understanding of cultural negation that he shows for cultural affirmation. While models for affirmation and cultural synthesis were overwhelming in romance, devotional literature, political tracts, and every day experience, his only model for negation was his own experience, his violent and lawless behavior, and he had no analytical vocabulary to explain such behavior as we now have. His treatment of the theme of negation comprises the "Book of Tristram" and "The Tale of the Sankgreal," and it is these tales which have given critics and readers the greatest trouble, for Malory is writing without a coherent metaphysical framework to subsume and explain each detail. But we can understand the tales, if we consider what the knights involved actually do when they arrive at a point of self-analysis and culture-analysis which is no longer synthetic but truly analytic.

The decision to negate an ideology arises from feelings of failure--meaninglessness--the opposite of the feeling of the numinous and a feeling that suggests disintegration rather than wholeness. One becomes aware of failure--meaninglessness--only when he perceives that the source of his identity is against what he knows himself to be; that is, he perceives the institution as an inhibition to becoming what he should be, even by institutional standards. At this point emerges a sensitivity to the "I"; one becomes aware of acts that are not called out by the conversation with the generalized other and are therefore socially meaningless but, nonetheless, his own acts. His failures teach him to see something in himself that cannot be seen in the generalized other (the center) and, therefore, cannot be called out by the other or legitimated by it. This is the purely unique, the random, and perhaps even the mistake.

The case of Palomides has been discussed already, and it is well to mention here Lancelot's feelings of failure in the healing of Sir Urry. Lancelot, however, will never admit failure; his orientation does not include it. The discovery of a disparity between oneself and the real world that is presented to a person leads inevitably to a choice, one which involves the destruction of the self or of the society. If the self is chosen, as Tristram does, some rather aggressive and self-assertive behavior is likely to follow. Erik Erikson sees this perception of disparity and the refusal to ignore it, as Lancelot and Arthur do, as the origin of Martin Luther's negation and cultural transcendence. His comment applies well to Malory's analytic knight, Tristram:

> Millions of boys face these problems and solve them in some way or another--they live as Captain Ahab says, with half their heart and with only one of their lungs, and the world is worse for it [social identification]. Now and again, however, an individual is called upon (called by whom, only the theologians claim to know, and by what only bad psychologists) to lift his individual patienthood to the level of a universal one and try to solve for all what he could not solve for himself alone. (Young Man Luther, 67)

The feeling of failure also results from the perception of incoherence in culture and the inability to cover it up or explain it away. Sir Sadok and Sir Denis the Seneschal, for example, are caught between Tristram as champion and Mark as king. They believe fully in the validity of both institutions, but the tension between the two becomes so glaring that they must choose to repudiate one or the other: "But whan sir Sadock had tolde sir Dynas of all the treson of kynge Marke, than he defyed suche a kynge and seyde that he wolde gyff up all his londis that [he] hylde of hym" (412). Previously Denis and Sadok had maintained harmony between Mark and Tristram, but finally the tension becomes insurmountable and they, importantly, shift their orientation from harmony to disharmony. Though a full discussion of this shift will have to wait until Chapter Three, it must be noted that the shift is not made possible by Mark's duplicity (that is legitimately--if lamentably--permitted for all social rulers and was certainly Malory's own experience) but rather by Tristram's ceasing to use his force to cover up incoherence in what Mark does and what he should be. The same insight explains Kayhedin's death for the love of Isode. Rather than use the systems of Knighthood and Governance to legitimate his love as a culturally convergent act, as Meleagant does, Kayhedins is forced into the open by Tristram's discovery of his love-letters to Isode. The result is a broken relationship with both Tristram and Isode; although the letters amounted to nothing, no attempt is made to resolve the conflict. The usefulness of the model in orienting the knights toward order and harmony by explaining and promoting relationships between individuals is simply foregone. Even for Bors, the emphasis is upon his inability to achieve fully the quest for the Holy Grail because of his experience in Love. Percival is just the opposite. Because of his radical purity he is not able to perform well at all in the political sphere.

The ideological model as represented by the diagrams exists as an internalized world view (Weltanschauung). For the knights, therefore, ideology is a personal experience, but one which is acquired only by undergoing the social process of interaction. As mentioned at the outset of section 2.2, the problem in approaching the Round Table is that we must see it in two stages of development. We are now able to discern the import of the second stage. In the second stage, the society has become fixed and well defined as a reified institution to which the knights belong if they are able to repress enough of their individuality to conform to the tenets of the society. In the second stage as opposed to the first, "why-concerns" become as important as actions because all actions need now to be subsumed by some ideological category. Gareth embarks on his quest because he desires to beome one of the best knights; he desires that because such a status confers upon the individual worship sufficient to transform him from a valueless entity to a man of renown and reputation. He has, moreover, Lancelot and Gawain as role models. As a result of Merlin's work, the emphasis of the second stage is on the end, the telos, or the pay-off. Acts come to be performed solely for the sake of producing the ends that they are reputed to be capable of. The war is replaced by the tournament or the "batayle for love"--as

Dynadan sarcastically but truly calls it. It is love because it is performed only for the worship of the members of the insitution. The result is that the social process, now tournament, produces its own new social order; it creates new selves which are not the same as those who experienced the original social process of war.

These second generation knights are a class of capitalists who, unlike Arthur, know exactly what they want and will go to any length, even cheating and exploiting their own values, to acquire the most worship. Palomides is initially of this sort: "I woll nat juste, for I am sure at justynge I gete no pryce" (370). Even more serious is the disorder which results from behavior designed to acquire and manipulate worship as capital. It places one knight in competition with another for the most highly sought after quantity. For example, "sir Trystram enchevyd many grete batayles, wherethorow all the noyse and brewte felle to sir Trystram, and the name ceased of sir Launcelot. And therefore sir Launcelottis bretherne and his kynnysmen wolde have slayne sir Trystram bycause of his fame" (476). Although this murder never takes place, the notion that in a hierarchy of social order and social value the position of one knight undercuts the position of another knight forms, certainly, a large part of the motivation of King Mark, the Orkneys, the Meleagant; and it accounts for the deaths of Lamerok, Alexander the Orphan, and Amant, to name only a few of the very many. As worship replaces the fundamental erotic energy that Arthur is, the social product is finally competition and incohesion as opposed to the tensionlessness that the roundness and non-hierarchical arrangement of seats that the Round Table officially denotes.

The term worship has been used all along without giving it the special treatment it deserves; perhaps this is the proper place. P. E. Tucker, among other critics of Malory, has noticed that worship is Malory's special term for a complex of meanings involving chivalry, glory, prowess, nobility, and, in short, the highest praise accorded to the most excellent of men ("Chivalry in the Morte," 65-68). Worship, moreover, seems to be a term of Malory's invention in order to suggest a secular equivalent to the theological grace. Grace is the measure of the Christian's value and his means to perfection just as worship is the means and measure of a knight. But worship also inculcates the phenomenon of hero-worship in the sense that worship is exactly the reward which a society gives to the hero for being its savior. Worship, therefore, goes beyond grace and represents adulation proper to the creator or the redeemer of the world, just the proper term for the first generation knights who established the Round Table as symbolic universe. The role-model for the knight-hero is Christ the redeemer who is also worshipped for his actions. The notion that Christ should be the model knight is as old as the Anglo-Saxon "Dream of the Rood," and it is apparent that the Round Table considers its knights as redeemers, imitating on a secular level the spiritual redemption. The hero releases mankind from the bonds and sufferings of living in the fallen world.

Malory's term worship makes the imitation obvious, but it also does something else just as important. A knight's identity is defined in terms of his worship; that is, the praise a society gives to him for his deeds becomes his estimation of himself. Earlier on, it was mentioned that institutions arise as individuals attain common goals by habitualizing their actions; institutions such as the Church or the Round Table, moreover, ascribe value or to members who are most proficient in limiting themselves to behaviors that maintain the institution. The number of acts, therefore, which can be done to attain identity is limited to what sustains ideology. What this means is that the deeds of the hero have been habituated or conventionalized and now comprise the function of universe maintenance or stabilizing response to stimuli to preserve the institution as truth and prevent innovative responses. Worship is accorded for policing a definition of reality. As we know from studies such as Joseph Campbell's The Hero with a Thousand Faces, in the monomyth of the hero, the hero always must come from outside the society or at least spend enough time outside of it to establish himself as different from the group (30-46 and 337). The reason for this is that the hero is the redeemer of the sick society, and therefore he must transcend the sickness in order to bring a new life to the members of the society. The hero is a phenomenon of the first stage of civilization because he brings a new life. But in Malory, worship holds all of the heroes tightly within the institution. The true hero must be free from the value rituals because these rituals and this socially constructed reality are the sickness or loss of meaning.

Malory's knights, however, cannot break free from the worship which lies at the heart of what they are as knights. Arthur refuses to admit any sickness within his realm and thus denies any need for a hero.   His "all holé togydirs" speech presented in an effort to forestall the potentially redemptive Quest for the Holy Grail makes it clear that he has settled for the conventional role of the hero and would prefer to see the knights performing artificial acts devised both to demonstrate and elicit worship, but not to redeem or to change the social structure and its basic behavioral patterns in any way.   In the second stage of the Round Table, preserving the stability of the truth of the ideology is foremost.   In the entire Morte, only two knights are heroic in the mythic and redemptive sense: Tristram for repudiating his society and dying rather than being re-integrated with it and Palomides for losing all his battles for Christ and then being Baptized anyway.   They each refuse finally to play the social role of the hero, even if it means their own deaths and the deconstruction of their civilization.   Even the model Christ knew he would have to tear down the Temple in Jerusalem before he could rebuild it again and that the stone rejected by the present builders (insiders) would become the corner stone of the new construction (Matthew, 21 and 24).

In the usual sense in the Morte, the acquisition of worship looks very much like a game; the tournament and initiation quest imitate the battle and quest for order (identity equals personal order) but without producing any real redemptive consequences in the sense of further developing that order and determining man's environment.   The knight cannot become heroic in the meaningful way by defeating a pretended enemy, someone he really loves.   The battle for love preserves the outer shell of the knight's mode of life, but it takes away the openness of the meaningful quest for the numen.   And yet the imitation attempts to give the same value-feeling for essentially unproductive and worthless acts.   What is wrong with Malory's heroes (and I think this would answer Bloomfield's questions about the problem of the hero in the later Middle Ages, cited in Chapter One) is that in both Cornwall, Camelot, and the late Middle Ages they are simply not wanted; at the second stage of all civilizations, redemption or radical (root) innovation has been a crime, as the story of Christ, again, makes clear.   After the event of Gareth's triumph on the Feast of the Assumption, no one wants to change the society or its ideology. The tournament is a ritual designed to preserve the status quo by subverting the hero's genuine inventiveness. No one at the Round Table believes that it is any longer necessary to do what they did prior to Gareth's coming of age; after all, Arthur has succeeded in conquering all of his enemies. The society feels itself to have come of age and innovation is so openly condemned that it is only through madness--the condition of being separated totally from one's value institutions--that Tristram is able to transcend the meaninglessness of the status quo. As Campbell writes, "The effect of the successful adventure of the hero is the unlocking and release again of the flow of life into the body of the world" (Hero, 40). And yet as Arthur believes the "flow of life" is the status quo of the Round Table:

> And so aftir uppon that to sowper, and every knyght şette in hys owne place as they were toforehonde.
>   Than anone they harde crakynge and cryynge of thundir, that hem thought the palyse shoulde all to-dryve. So in the myddys of the blast entyrde a sonnebeame, more clerer by seven tymys than ever they saw day, and all they were alyghted of the grace of the Holy Goste. Than began every knyght to beholde other, and eyther say other, by their semyng, faryer than ever they were before. . . .
>   'Sertes,' seyde the kynge, 'we ought to thanke oure Lorde Jesu Cryste gretly that he hath shewed us thys day at the reverence of thys hyghe feste of Pentecoste.' (521-22)

Just following this passage, Arthur opposes the Grail Quest, knowing that it will mean a radical change in the nature of his Round Table. In the speech of the Queen of the West Lands to Percival, when she tells him that the members of the Round Table feel more blessed and more worshipped than if they owned half the world, the words "blessed" and "worship" do not appear in the French Queste del Saint Graal, Malory's source for this episode; rather the French writer includes a long discussion about the transition from the table of the Last Supper to the Round Table. The point is the same; the institution feels itself to have been redeemed and that redemption is a one-time act which establishes a permanent society.

Worship in the sense that it implies the end of the quest for meaning becomes the origin of a crisis in culture which grows slowly but steadily from within the Round Table. Arthur's society represents an attempt on a secular level to establish a potentially perfect world by including those who behave properly --that is, succeed in earning worship--and excluding those who fail to prove worthy. The roundness of the table symbolizes perfection and selective inclusiveness. By definition, therefore, those who are included cannot be less than moral and tending toward perfection. A knight's moral character is validated by institutional membership. Here again the Round Table imitates the structure of the Chruch as a value giving institution. Those who have been baptized and who frequent the sacraments obtain a special status not available to non-members. The rituals determine the elect; goodness or morality is defined by performance of authorized good works. No external grounds for the goodness of an act can theoretically exist. If ideology which lies behind the rituals were perfectly comprehensive and, in fact, did resolve all the problems of existence, then a perfect society could not fail to result. If incoherent, however, and totally beside the point of resolving human problems, as sacraments and indulgences generally were and continue to be, the individual must still live the doctrine to the full and tragic end. The important point in the structure of both the Church and the Round Table is that salvation--in a secular sense, the meaningful--is available only through the institution, and one may attain it by doing things, such as repeating a senseless prayer or fighting a tournament, that address only problems made up to fit the need of the institution for solidifying the allegiance of its members and socializing new ones. The difference between the Round Table and the Church is that as secular institution the Round Table must present immediate and tangible evidence of salvation. This evidence is worship or the feeling of value. The knights, therefore, because they are worshipped have proof that their society has resolved all tensions--at least in potential--and that their own lives are exemplifications of the highest good.

Such tangible proof actually prevents the institution from discerning good acts from bad acts; that is, prevents it from identifying real cultural problems in any other than conventional terms, which, of course, only mask the true nature of the problem and call out for conventional responses. Ultimately the social condition allows for inconsistent acts to be validated, as in the case of Lancelot's dual loyalty to his lady and his king. The incoherence results from a tension between the private and the public roles, a tension which Lancelot and everyone else always believed was thoroughly resolved. To the very end, he maintains loyalty to both Guinevere and Arthur, never perceiving the inherent impossibility. After he has been taken in Guinevere's chamber by Aggravain and Mordred, for example, Lancelot comments: "I woll feyght for the quene, that she ys a trew lady untyll her lorde. But the kynge in hys hete, I drede, woll nat take me as I ought to be takyn" (680). One can look at the doctrine, as Lancelot does, which specifies that the knight must radically devote himself to the highest lady, or one can look at the phenomenon of Lancelot's acts. The different modes of analysis lead to vastly different conclusions about what Lancelot does. As an ideological institution, the Round Table claims the authority of universal Truth, and as long as the knight's acts are done in its name and he uses the doctrines to explain those acts, his value and worship increase. Lancelot thinks that he should be understood in this manner. He thinks that Arthur ought to take or consider him in terms of the code, that is, as Guinevere's defender. He goes on to explain how often he has defended Guinevere on other occasions and has been worshipped for it. Why not now? Are moral judgments really situational?

Le Morte Darthur depicts the increasing inability of the knights to do anything truly good--from an empirical or personal point of view--in the name of worship, Knighthood or the Round Table. Arthur's famous "all holé togydirs" speech is his final plea for the stability of the Round Table, but at the same time Malory sets up the speech so that we can not fail to feel the impending tragedy in following conventions too long. P. J. C. Field has observed that Malory's basic technique for making suggestions to the reader is a clustering or a repeating of key terms ("Description and Narration in Malory," 43). In Arthur's speech, Malory repeats in order to vary the connotations and suggest a new meaning. Just thirty lines above this speech, Galahad uses the word hole (a near homophone) in a sense very close to Arthur's holē (wholly), but with a different reference: "kynge Pelles, the whych ys nat yett hole, nor naught shall be tyll that I hele hym" (520). The maimed king and his wasteland ostensibly contrast with Arthur's whole or unified and therefore healthy Round Table. But beginning forty lines after the speech, Malory uses the term Holy Grayle five of the eight times that it appears in the entire romance (Malory's usual term is Sankgreal). Malory is capable of a great deal more subtlety than is generally acknowledged. While overtly inculcating wholeness and health, Malory, through Arthur's speech, aligns the Round Table with the wounding of King Pelles (by Balin, of course) and with the failure of the Round Table knights to heal Pelles and bring back the Grail. His use of the term hole in this context cannot help connoting health and holiness, qualities which the Round Table is becoming increasingly less able to insure, and yet qualities which the Round Table was designed to secure. Arthur desperately wants to keep his knights "all holē togydirs," and yet doing so is exactly why Truth through Arthur and the Round Table becomes the destroyer of the knights, for those qualities at the second stage depend upon transcending the sickness of the institution just as Arthur transcended the social contract of the Eleven Kings.

While the Church offers intangible sanctifying grace and the promise of heaven as signs of value and the threat of eternal punishment as a de-ascription of value, the secular institution has no such recourse to realms outside of the world in order to bond its members to its doctrine. Instead the secular institution offers social rank. The tendency is, therefore, to use rank as a way of pre-judging the moral value of any act. Officially the knights renew the same vows at a tournament each Pentecost, but something very strange has happened to the ceremonies and rituals. The Church insists upon the absolute reality of its sacramental rituals, as apparent in the Doctrine of Transubstantiation, adopted at the Fourth Lateran Council of 1215. The real body and blood of Christ are present in the bread and wine of the Mass. The Christian's identity, on the other hand, is ephemeral; the believer continues in a process of becoming until his death. The secular institution turns this relationship on its head. The identity of the knight is considered real and the rituals remain simply metaphoric of the original initiation which once completed cannot be repeated except in a metaphoric manner. When a knight earns identity and rank in the hierarchy of value, he can only live it--or, as in the case of Palomides and Tristram, live to deny it.

The Round Table begins to be interested only in representations, names, and symbolic social health. The character of Arthur's aboriginal acts is that they are directed toward interaction with the phenomenal world, but now the knights' orientation is toward the abstract, toward the category of the mind which validates the act, just as St. Thomas directs his philosophy toward wisdom. Dynadan asks a knight whether he wants to joust for love or hate; a father forgives the murder of his two sons because it was done for the sake of knighthood. Thus the Round Table knights are increasingly unable to control empirically real events in their society and are increasingly more unsuccessful in any real productive acts, even though they are ascribed value for their deeds. They cannot contain Brewnes Sans Pité or reduce the mounting hatred between the Orkneys and Lamerok, and it is suggested that the knights feel defeating Brewnes would be, in fact, less worthwhile than winning the "gre" at some tournament. A knight's name and rank may actually make acts which are immoral and productive of inter-personal discord seem worthy and ethical.

Such is the case with Lancelot. His name works as a shield and therefore validates acts which should be condemned. It is not merely Lancelot's might that makes whatever he does right, but rather the structure of the society which has accepted its ideology as truth and lost, therefore, the ability to modify it by analyzing it from the point of view of the "real" world. This is not to say that men know reality in itself, but rather that the "real" world becomes simply an alternative construct or an a-cultural point of view from which to analyze ideology. Reality becomes the "outside" from which the genuine hero or redeemer must come, for only on the outside can one become free from the sickness of the "inside." The phenomenal world is above all a strategy for cultural transcendence and recovery of the world openness, since reality is just as "wholly other" as the original numen. But the Round Table, since it has aligned itself with Truth, perceives no need for self-analysis.

St. Augustine's concept of evil is at work in the structure of the Round Table. St. Augustine argues that evil is a privation of the good and hence a privation of being. The only evil knights in Malory's romance, therefore, are those who have no worship, such as Mordred or Brewnes, whose epithet "sans pité" (i.e., without pity) is more properly recorded in the Tavola Ritonda where it appears as without "pieta"--piety, dutifulness, or faith. Brewnes is always unorthodox in the way he fights, and that is why he is evil. Arthur frequently uses the threat of evil to control his subjects; he, for example, summons King Angwish "uppon payne of forfeture of kynge Arthurs good grace" (252). Thus the categorizing of good and evil depends upon the ideology--the moral conditions of nationalism or fascism. Lancelot never loses his good grace (except for a brief period in the eyes of Guinevere, who doesn't matter anyway), and therefore whatever he does is by definition moral. Condemning Brewnes or Mordred is easy, but doing so would produce only a very small gain to the civilization. What is needed is a condemnation of Lancelot and Arthur, and yet the social structure makes that sort of judgment impossible, as Meleagant much to his own loss discovers.

The symbiotic relationship between the knights and their institution (in which the knights create the institution as the institution confirms (i.e. creates) their selves) includes the potential for the unending quest, but, as it comes to be in the Morte, the knight's career looks more like indoctrination than creative participation. The two are structurally very similar, but quite different in final purpose: indoctrination aims at a stable social structure through the production of radically overdetermined individuals, while creative participation always results in flexible institutions and unstable individuals who are in a process of becoming. Briefly, indoctrination involves the following: a separation of the individual from others and his customary environment in order to reduce sensory intake; a disengagement from traditional values, beliefs, and aspirations by isolation from the signs of those convictions; induced feelings of anxiety, depression, and self-worthlessness; simultaneous intensification of new behavioral and cognitive patterns through repetitious exposure to a carefully constructed stimulus field; and finally an emphasis on comradeship and constituency as preparation for entry into the new group. In other words, indoctrination induces and aggravates an identity crisis by placing the individual in circumstances where he can find no symbols or rituals for practicing and confirming his identity; Gareth's role as kitchen-boy for one year induces this sort of identity crisis or confusion of inner attitudes. Then indoctrination remedies the identity crisis by providing a new identity.

The difference between the indoctrinated and the self-created human, therefore, lies not in the structure but in the careful control of the content of experience which an individual has in the social process. Indoctrination can produce stable societies--at least in the short run--because it trains individuals to stabilize their identities and behavior by limiting the field of perception to a coherent matrix of signs. In the Middle Ages, the preponderance of signs to which a conventional response was appropriate can be seen in the ever increasing number of relics, devotions, sacred objects, prayers, and so forth that the Church offered to the faithful who were eager to perform the conventional response. The attempt is to produce a unified stimulus field calling out a narrow pattern of responses.

Readers of Malory, and the French prose romances, who have thought the style overly repetitious have not considered that the field cognition mode of the indoctrinated knights enables them to perceive only a very limited range of sensory detail. They just do not have a very broad world view. They are, in a sense, mental aphasiacs who carry with them the crippling predisposition to acknowledge only a certain class of stimuli: that class which will call out behaviors which will be rewarded with worship. We must always remember that romance literature is written in the way individuals see their world, an important point brought out by Robert Hanning in his The Individual in Twelfth Century Romance. And because the knights are driven to move up in the social ranking by acquiring ever more worship, they are inclined to reduce even more sharply the stimulus field as they limit the kind of responsive behaviors they are interested in performing to only optimal strategies for maximizing worship. Everything else that may exist in the "real" world is simply not of interest to them. In the end, however, indoctrination, as a result of its inherently narrowing inertia, produces a class of psychotics from which a rebel will emerge who will not be content until the old model is thoroughly dismantled. This tragic pattern underlies the careers of the four best knights whose repressed individuality leads to such acts as loving the king's wife, fighting their best friends (optimal means of securing worship) or the madness in which they alienate themselves from the society that depends upon them for its security. The general condition of psychosis implies that the "me" or the culturally determined component so totally dominates the "I" component that the "I" cannot find expression except in violent and destructive acts (i.e., marginal behavior), whether against itself or the outside world.

Creative participation, on the other hand, can never lead to such stability because in normal circumstances (that is, without artificial intensification of certain signs) habituated stimulus-response patterns decay rapidly. Small variations in response (technological improvements, mistakes, personal style, boredom, competition, or influence of distracting stimuli) accumulate to produce an overall drift in the meaning or response to the sign. The ideology which claims to represent truth cannot tolerate such semantic drift. Without truth, however, the individual and his institutions are in a process of permanent drifting and evolving rather than a fixed condition. Thus one's identity is continually modified by his experiences. In Malory, Lancelot does not change throughout the romance; he only attempts to cover up more and more of his identity as the romance progresses. Dynadan, who claims "Though I be nat of worship myself" (381), does change and grow, and he undercuts the conventional response by introducing into the rigidly controlled stimulus field distractions--often humorous, as his title "the japer" suggests. While much more will have to be said about Dynadan later on, here it is enough to point out the origin of Dynadan's non-conformity. We are never told anything about Dynadan's socialization. When he first joins company with Tristram, he opposes Knighthood principally because at this point Tristram responds to every situation as an ideal knight should.   For example,

And whan they were unarmed and thought to be myry and in good reste, there cam in at the yatis sir Palomydes and sir Gaherys, requyryng to have the custum of the castle.

`What aray ys thys?´ seyde sir Dynadan, `I wolde
fayne have my reste.´
`That may nat be,´ syde sir Trystram. `Now
muste we nedis defende the custum of thys castell
insomuch as we have the bettir of this lordes of thys
castell. And therefore,´ seyde sir Trystram, `nedis
must ye make you redy.´
`In the devyls name,´ syde sir Dynadan, `cam I
unto youre company!´ (312-13)

Dynadan will, however, at this point in time, fight for ladies
because Tristram is now separated from Isode and angry with
her for her sympathetic response to Kayhedin´s love letters:
"`Lat hym com!´ seyde sir Dynadan. `And bycause of honoure of
all women I woll do my parte´" (339). But when Tristram gives
up Knighthood and exiles himself with Isode at the Joyous
Garde, we find Dynadan reversing himself and calling Tristram
to battle:

Sir Dynadan rayled wyth sir Trystram and sayde,
`What the devyll ys uppon the this day? For sir
Palomydes strengthe fyeblede never this day, but
every he doubled. And sir Trystram fared all this
day as he had bene on slepe, and therefore I call
hym a cowarde.´
`Well, sir Dynadan,´ syde sir Trystram, `I was
never called cowarde or now of eartheley knyght in
my lyff.´ (450)

And of course, at this point, "Dynadan hylde ayenste all lovers"
(423). Dynadan joins Tristram at the moment he is exiled from
Cornwall by Mark and becomes Tristram´s model for randomizing
his response to cultural signs, for Dynadan always responds in a
manner opposite from what is appropriate or conventional.
Dynadan is always unable to restrict adequately the contents of
his stimulus field. As a knight charges him, he is just as likely
to notice the hardness of the spear or of the ground awaiting
his probable fall as he is to notice the identity of the knight
from whom he may win some worship.
  The related notions of the essentially healthy nature of
unstable individuals, of the unstable contents which men ascribe

to the category of the numen for legitimizing their institutions, and of the openness of the world as stimulus field are perhaps Malory's most important discoveries. The Middle Ages had always believed the world to be unstable, but instability was defined as evil, corruption, and the mistake of taking inferior goods before higher goods. The orientation was always upon the immutable even when that orientation implicitly condemned the present life. In asserting the health of instability, Malory follows the pattern established by the twelfth and thirteenth century writers of courtly love in making the greatest of traditional sins a new virtue (see, Hanning, The Individual in Twelfth-Century Romance). Courtly love raised cupidity to the level of the highest good. Malory, however, looks forward to Michel de Montaigne (1533-1592) who in describing himself, in his Essais can never come to a consistent self-concept; rather he emphasizes the self as a history of momentary responses to situations, subject always to changes of the next moment. Montaigne, in the opinion of John Middleton Murry, was the first to discover that man could love himself as a mutable being, but already in Malory, Lancelot's self-hatred is being transcended by essential health and self-love of Dynadan, Tristram, and Palomides. In "Of the Inconsistency of Our Actions," Montaigne describes the kind of program that Dynadan presents to Tristram:

> There is some justification for basing a judgment of man on the most ordinary [i.e., marginal] acts of his life; but in view of the natural instability of our conduct and opinions, it has often seemed to me that even good authors are wrong to insist on fashioning a consistent and solid fabric out of us. They choose one general characteristic, and go and arrange and interpret all a man's actions to fit their picture; and if they cannot twist them enough, they go and set them down to dissimulation. Augustus has escaped them; for there is in this man throughout the course of his life such an obvious, abrupt, and continual variety of actions that even the boldest judges have had to let him go, intact and unsolved. (238)

The last comment about letting someone be, intact and unsolved, is exactly the way Dynadan treats his fellow knights, but no institution can emerge from this perspectiveless relationship.   As Malory says, "for hit was his maner to be prevy with all good knyghtes" (381); Dynadan knows their ordinary and private acts, not merely their reputations and social rank.   Dynadan loves them for their private acts, and he shows them how to love themselves in the same manner.

The emergence of individualism as a revolt against truth--not necessarily any particular truths, but rather the orientation toward universals and immutability as Montaigne suggests--and the social system which precipitated from it is best seen in Malory's, and indeed Montaigne's, interest in the individual as a responder to the created reality of his culture. The emphasis shifts from the narrowly controlled stimulus field to the inconsistency of response.   The "I" component of the individual sometimes feels the embarrassment of seeing himself respond conventionally when that response conflicts with other responses the "I" is aware of.   The self sees itself acting with the attitude of the group and yet feels the failure and inadequacy of the response in the present circumstances. Although examples of this feeling are numerous in the Morte and will be discussed more fully in the next chapter, here it might be useful to cite one case in which the term "abaysshed"--meaning ashamed or disconcerted as a loss of ideological perspective--represents feelings precisely opposite to what "worship" suggests.   One can feel abashed as well as worshipped for his conventionally moral behavior.   The great example is, of course, Lancelot's feelings after healing Sir Urry, but just as instructive is Sir Bors' experience with a lady who tells him that unless he makes love to her she will kill herself.   Bors refuses because such love is sinful; he did it once and he knows the painful wages.   But in this case, he does not feel worship for making the moral decision:

> Than he had of hem grete pite; natforthat he was
> nat uncounceyled in hymselff that levir he had they
> all had loste their soules than he hys soule.   And
> with that they felle all at onys unto the erthe, and
> whan he saw that, he was all abaysshed and had
> thereof grete mervayle.   And with that he blyssed
> hys body and hys vysayge.   (571)

The individual whose self-conception is a process appeals, as it were, to a higher authority. Such a demand is for freedom from a world so small that men, like Bors, can only lose no matter what they choose to do. Freedom is nothing in itself, only an authority one step higher than or just different from that which now terminates the explanatory regress, as Montaigne appeals to "ordinary acts" as the basis for judging a man. The field of sensory perception is opened up as the search or quest for signs of variations in behavior begins. As the individual responds to the new and various signs, his behavior appears chaotic, he has trouble interacting with others in his community, and eventually he repudiates the group and the ideology of the group because their universe is simply too small for the man he has now become. The ideology represents for the culturally transcendent individual the utopia of the past or of the future, and yet what men demand is meaning in the present life.

This is the moment of the heroic "I will not serve"-- words which recognize the institution's control of the ground of reality--stimulus and response--and, therefore, control of actions, aspirations, and selfhood. In Malory, this new raising of the level of self-consciousness one step higher is, again, structured identically to the development of the self-consciousness which enabled Arthur and his original knights to assert themselves against the Eleven Kings, Emperor Lucius, and the Five Kings. But for the second generation of knights, rising to a new level involves asserting oneself against a new enemy: the Round Table itself. Failure to do so produces the tragedy of Arthur and Lancelot who because they would never acknowledge their enmity become the greatest enemies of all. For the rebel knights, of whom Tristram is foremost, the new self-consciousness grows out of an attempt to again resolve the condition of meaninglessness that Arthur and Lancelot will not recognize. It finds its energy in the feeling of failure and abashment, its occasion in madness and self-imposed exile, and its attainment in love of self and of other. It is to these conditions which Malory presents so forcefully in his "Book of Tristram de Lyones" that we now must turn.

The call of conscience in the natural man is an attempt on the part of the ego to justify itself in its knowledge of good and evil before God, before men, and before itself, and to secure its own continuance in this self-justification. Finding no firm support in its own contingent individuality the ego traces its own derivation back to a universal law of good and seeks to achieve unity with itself in conformity with this law. Thus the call of conscience has its origin and its goal in the autonomy of a man's own ego. A man's purpose in obeying this call is on each occasion anew that he should himself once more realize this autonomy which has its origin beyond his own will and knowledge 'in Adam'. Thus in his conscience he continues to be bound by a law of his finding, a law which may assume different concrete forms but which he can transgress only at the price of losing his own self.

We can now understand that the great change takes place at the moment when the unity of human experience ceases to consist in its autonomy and is found, through the miracle of faith, beyond the man's own ego and its law, in Jesus Christ. The form of this change in the point of unity has an exact analogy in the secular sphere. When the national socialist says 'My conscience is Adolf Hitler' that, too, is an attempt to find a foundation for the unity of his own ego somewhere beyond himself. The consequence of this is the surrender of one's autonomy for the sake of an unconditional heteronomy, and this in turn is possible only if the other man, the man to whom I look for the unity of my life, fulfills the function of a redeemer for me.

--Dietrich Bonhoeffer, Ethics

3.

The King and the Knight
or the End of the Quest

3.1 Tristram as Thematic Center

The interpretation of <u>Le Morte Darthur</u> advanced in the previous pages suggests that Malory sees in the history of Arthur and the knights of the Round Table a condensation of the highest efforts of the Christian world to embody its truths in a political structure, and yet he regards these efforts as inherently tragic because in the final stages the structure cuts men off from their creative source and destroys their ability to contribute to the constructed reality of their social universe. Humans must have, above all else, meaning in life, and this realization leads us to Malory's "Book of Sir Tristram de Lyones" where he turns away from the growing tragedy of the Round Table to look closely at the irresolvable tensions in human existence, particularly that between the individual and his institutions, as those are manifest in the king, laws, and the explanatory synthesis. He turns, in the sections dealing with Tristram, Isode, Palomides, Dynadan, Galahad, and Percival, to the meaninglessness of the acts that men and women perform in the service of cultural ideals, and to what Morse Peckham calls in <u>Romanticism and Behavior</u> the "analytic dismantlement" of culture. Malory's "Tale of Tristram" follows the traditional <u>Tristan</u> of Gottfried von Strassburg and Thomas of Britain whose <u>Tristan</u> finds himself ardently wanting only those things which are forbidden, against the law, or in violation of his socially determined self: "If the good thing that he has were not his, he would not be averse to it; but in his heart he cannot like what he perforce must own. If he could not have had what he possesses, he would have longed to acquire it" (304-05).

Every medieval political tract I know of assumes that individuals and society orientate themselves toward the good; this is the quest for the center. In a primitive sense, good and evil are no more than pleasure and pain, and although a good act may involve some pain or a delay of pleasure, the gain in pleasure always outweighs the pain in the end or something is not called good. St. Thomas Aquinas is representative: "The end is that wherein the appetite of that agent or mover is at rest, as also the appetite of that which is moved. Now it is the very notion of good to be the term of appetite, since good is the object of every appetite. Therefore all action and movement is for a good. . . . All admit that happiness is a perfect good: else it would not bring rest to the appetite" (Summa Contra Gentiles, III). For Sigmund Freud the same orientation is fundamental: "The dominating tendency of mental life, and perhaps of nervous life in general, is the effort to reduce, to keep constant or to remove internal tension due to stumuli (the Nirvana principle, to borrow a term from Barbara Low)--a tendency which finds its expression in the pleasure principle" (Beyond the Pleasure Principle, 49-50). But Tristram seeks suffering and tension. In section 1.2, I indicated Gottfried's interest in tension by citing his prologue which dedicates his Tristan to those who are able to endure sorrow and tension:

> What I have to say does not concern that world and such a way of life [bliss and tension reduction]; their way and mine diverge sharply. I have another world in mind which together in one heart bears its bitter-sweet, its dear sorrow, its heart's joy, its love's pain, its dear life, its sorrowful death, its dear death, its sorrowful life. (42)

What we are confronted with in the Morte is the strange fact that immediately following the "Tale of Gareth" and the institutionalization of the quest for the highest good at the center, when as Malory remarks, "In Arthurs dayes, when he helde the Rounde Table moste plenoure" (177), the narrative abruptly turns to Tristram and his quest for suffering and tension. Malory injects the "Tale of Tristram" at the fullness of the Round Table. While he omits almost everything else, Malory is careful to preserve the legendary birth of Tristram as the man of sorrows: "`A, my lytyll son, thou haste murtherd thy modir! And therfore I suppose thou that arte a murtherer so yonge, thow arte full lykly to be a manly man in thyne ayge." Just before she dies, Elizabeth charges her maid to "calle hym Trystrams, that is as much to say as a sorowfull byrth" (230).

The romance of Tristram, then, is traditionally, a tale of tension and paradox. For the medieval mind it was a tale of sin, the source of worldly sorrow. St. Augustine's conception of cupiditas underlies the orientation of Tristram's life toward the margins of being. God is the creator of all good in the world, St. Augustine argues, and yet He gave men free will in order that they might freely choose to direct their lives toward Him. When they do not, he writes in On Free Choice of the Will, they commit sin, and tensions or unhappiness result: "All sins are included under this one class: when someone is turned away from divine things that are truly everlasting, toward things that change and are uncertain" (33). Tristram's orientation toward the mutable, the ordinary, and tension may, indeed, look like sin, and his tale has very often been interpreted this way; but it can just as well be read, as Robert Hanning's study of twelfth century romance shows, as the origin of culturally transcendent innovations that would move Western civilization from medievalism to modernism: "Inevitably, these two impulses collided within twelfth-century culture. Tensions between private freedoms or desires and the structures on which a complex society depends for its functioning can be called endemic to Western society from this period right down to our own day" (The Individual in Twelfth Century Romance, 21). The orientations of Lancelot and Arthur toward the center must in this new perspective be regarded not as a universal predicate of human nature, but only as one half of a cultural dialectic, the thesis, the mere existence of which calls out a confrontation with the antithetical movement of Tristram and the Grail Quest. Synthetic thinkers who write that all men desire happiness are only covering up fully one half of life--

motivated certainly as St. Augustine was by an abnormal need for unity and order.   The true genius of Malory lies in his abandonment of cyclic or linear notions of history and in his refutation of the single orientation of St. Augustine toward the good. The structure of his work is finally an historical dialectic.

Most every reader perceives a great difference between the sections of Le Morte Darthur dealing with Tristram and the Quest for the Holy Grail and the sections dealing with the rise and fall of the Round Table, but they are at a loss to describe or account for the difference since most critics look for a thematic continuity between Malory and the French prose Arthurian Romances in which Tristram and the Grail Quest are narratively and thematically subsumed by the Arthurian material.   The usual explanation of the difference is that Malory's art failed him in the "middle."   But the point of this chapter is to show that the difference is precisely that between analysis and synthesis.   Perhaps the ultimate model for Malory's structuring of his romance is the dialectic of scholastic philosophy, not the neat thesis-antithesis and resolution of St. Thomas, but the simple tension and conflict of Peter Abelard's Sic et Non which presented contradictory statements from doctrine without any resolution.   In the sections leading up to the "Tristram," what has often been called the "Rise" of the Round Table, a synthetic approach to culture dominates.   In the "Tristram" or in what has never been called until now the "Flowering" of the Round Table, an analytic and deconstructive approach to culture dominates.   Malory analyzes his culture; that is, he becomes interested not in the whole but in the components and enhances the tension and incoherence in order to expose the nature of the parts.   We might also understand the difference in terms of perspective.   In the middle, Malory focuses on the knights as individuals trying to respond to the demands of cultural ideals.   In the beginning and the end, he focuses on the ideal itself. The familiar theorem that a whole is greater than the sum of its parts gets reversed in the middle sections of the romance.   Earlier we saw that institutions arise only through the destruction of a great deal of information of private experience.   In the middle, Malory presents that information as if to show that the sum of experience far exceeds any whole.

We see the dialectic clearly in the difference between Lancelot and Tristram. Lancelot always uses his force to cover up tensions and incoherencies; he avoids situations that will make tensions apparent. His habit of answering questions equivocally, fighting in disguise, refusing to give his name, and insisting on the faithfulness of himself and Guinevere suggests an attempt to keep the present or the concrete ill-defined and flexible so that it might conform smoothly to the truth of the explanation if anyone were to stop and analyze it. We are almost never really sure that Lancelot does anything wrong because his life is designed to support the thesis of his culture. When Lancelot is caught in Guinevere's chambers, Malory speaks equivocally: "And whether they were abed other at other maner of disportis, me lyste nat thereof make no mencion, for love that tyme was nat as love ys nowadayes" (676). Tristram's case, on the other hand, is blunt and open: "And there sir Trystrames was takyn nakyd a-bed with La Beale Isode" (271). Tristram himself aggravates tensions as can clearly be seen in his treatment of Palomides. Near the end of Tristram's tale, when Palomides' identity and self-value are so low that he contemplates suicide, Tristram meets him in a forest and insists upon doing battle even though Tristram is unarmed. For Palomides this is the last straw; to fight the defenseless Tristram would destroy the last shred of his honor, and yet Tristram exhorts: "Thou cowarde knyght, what castyste thou to do? And why wolt thou nat do batayle wyth me? For have thou no doute I shall endure the and all thy malyce" (507).

The orientation toward the mutable, toward tension, toward reality and what St. Augustine defines as sin eventually means the dismantlement and modification of the medieval synthesis. As this chapter will demonstrate, there is no tragic end to Malory's tale of Tristram because without truth and the orientation toward the immutable, tragedy is simply impossible. Malory, in the flowering of his romance, arrives at the same conclusion as Friedrich Nietzsche in the Birth of Tragedy and especially in The Gay Science where he writes, "Charitably interpreted, such a resolve might perhaps be a quixotism, a minor slightly mad enthusiasm; but it might also be something more serious, namely, a principle that is hostile to life and destructive--'Will to Truth'--that might be a concealed will to death" (282). The two artists were looking at the same kind of cultural phenomenon, a socially constructed symbolic universe (metaphysics) and reality that has in the present begun to deny the lives of individuals. Galahad who demonstrates more than anyone else a "will to truth" in the full Augustinian sense leaves the romance with a will to die:

> sir Galahad felle on hys kneys and prayde longe tyme
> to oure Lorde, that at what tyme that he asked, he
> myght passe oute of this worlde.   (605)

Ultimately Malory is suggesting that the orientation toward immutable and everlasting perfection produces a syndrome that Freud has termed the "Death Instinct."   But before we can examine the theme of the "Death Instinct" in the Tristram and Grail sections (see section 4.1), it is necessary to consider the more traditional approaches to these sections and elucidate in them certain problems that make this new approach necessary.

The efforts of such scholars as Rumble, Benson, Scheuler, Mahoney, Fries, Vinaver, Moorman, Lumiansky, and Knight to explain the role and meaning of "The Book of Sir Tristram" have not been able to assert that the middle of the romance is as artistically successful as the other sections.   To be sure they have offered valid themes and structural principles, but in general the beginning assumption of such studies is D. S. Brewer's conclusion in "`the hoole book'" that Malory "was simply not up to the problem he had perhaps unwittingly set himself" (55).   Even so, it seems rather strange that Malory would allow such an anomaly to occupy about one-half (if we include the Grail section) of the entire romance. The argument that none of the Morte shows signs of revision and the "Tristram" would have benefited from thorough revision (i.e., cutting) is silly for it is wishful thinking, and the wishes are those of a truth-oriented reader who is looking for an intelligible explanatory center which controls every detail on the narrative periphery.   The logic of consistency in structure is a feature of synthetic thinking and the orientation towards order, and if the analytic and deconstructive Malory had revised his manuscript there is little chance he would have made it more like a nineteenth century novel.

T. C. Rumble is typical of those who are devoted to order and synthesis above all art:

It is a long and rambling section, and revision would almost surely have reduced it considerably and made its relation to the rest of the work more evident and emphatic [i.e., cover up the tensions]. But its length and its great multitude of episodes and themes ought not to prevent entirely our separating essentials from incidentals and seeing as clearly as possible, at least, what seems to have been Malory's intent.   ("Development by Analogy," 121)

Rumble proceeds to select out those essential episodes which demonstrate an analogy or likeness of values between the "Tristram" and the Round Table sections.   But every reader senses a great difference; why cover it up merely to satisfy the critic's desire for a coherent narrative?   So far every study of the Morte has presumed an analogical (Rumble), parallel (Mahoney), or mirror (Fries) relationship between the middle sections and the beginning and end, but if we look carefully at the Morte, it appears that either Malory did, in fact, revise to suit his intentions or he selected and arranged the episodes with an original plan that can make a great deal of sense once we abandon the rage for order. In Chatper One, I argued that explanatory incoherence lies at the heart of Le Morte Darthur, and if we are to understand the romance we must no longer explain away the tension between what the knights actually do and the ideological structure which is losing its ability to make the knights understand their own careers from the standpoint of a tensionless center of being.   A little later than Malory, Francis Bacon, the ideologue of the emerging modern world, would urge philosophers to follow Machiavelli who "write[s] what men do, and not what they ought to do" (cited in Bush, 8). Niccolo Machiavelli was born in 1469, the year during which Malory was almost certainly writing Le Morte Darthur.   Though they were separated by a thousand miles, it is certain that Malory perceived the same reality of pluralism and the coerciveness of order that was to inspire not only Machiavelli but also Wycliff, Marsilius, John Hus, Luther, Montaigne, and Bacon.   This was not merely a recognition of man's inability to live up to the ideals which were set before him in philosophy and theology; his perception was something much more profound: that the institution itself which had arisen as a strategy for resolving human problems had now itself become the central human problem and the environmental source of tension.

It seems to me, as it has seemed to Larry Benson, though for different reasons, that something about Tristram's career especially appealed to Malory. I alluded to this point in Chapter One, but this is finally the place to examine it in more detail. If we pay careful attention to the tone of Malory's narration, there can be little doubt that it is Tristram and not Lancelot or Arthur with whom Malory shares a deep and unconscious identity. Only for Tristram is Malory so emphatic as to write: "And to telle the joyes that were betwyxte La Beall Isode and sir Trystramys, there ys no maker [poet] can make hit, nothir no harte can thynke hit, nother no penne can wryte hit, nother no mowth can speke hit" (302). The reason is simply that Tristram, like Malory himself, is an exile and a wanted man wherever he travels. He is more at home with Mark than he is with Arthur, and yet Mark is for Tristram the greatest source of danger, suffering, and meaninglessness. Malory likens this being at home with suffering to the prisoner or fugitive. Tristram's career, for example, like Malory's own, is composed of a pattern of imprisonment and release followed by imprisonment again:

> And so when sir Trystram was let into that castell he had good chere all that nyght. And so upon the morne, whan he woulde have departed, the quene [Morgan le Fay] seyde,
> 'Wyte you well ye shall nat departe lyghtly, for ye ar here as a presonere'
> 'Jesu deffende me!' seyde sir Trystram, 'for I was but late a presonere.' (339)

Morgan le Fay eventually releases Tristram but not without extracting from him a promise to carry a certain shield at the Tournament of the Castle of the Harde Roche. We know from "Alexander the Orphan" the true import of such promises: "for now I stonde as a presonere by my promyse" (395). What makes both Tristram and Malory prisoners and exiles wherever they go is the service they owe to not only their social superiors but especially to the ideology that claims to explain their actions and thus control the feelings of the meaningful. This service causes Tristram a great deal of suffering, for the force of duty, tradition, and morality demands that he serve Mark and yet serving Mark means his own death. While he could easily escape and reduce the tensions of his life by living at the Round Table, he returns over and over to Cornwall to face the problem he cannot solve; but only by suffering Mark, in the way Althusser notes that men suffer ideology, can Tristram elucidate the cultural crisis and find a way of transcendence, a path that takes the hero through the jaws of death. Tristram has to endure the incoherence of culture in order to know that it is incoherent. His name means sorrow, and the ideology, the orientation toward truth that he must maintain, causes his sorrow. No life at all is possible outside of the institution: Pope Innocent III meant it when he said that outside of the church there is absolutely no salvation. But for Tristram, the institution is now also death. The requirement that one focus his life upon the immutable means, in Malory's view, an inescapable disparagement of oneself and of the present life; although institutions arise in autonomy, as Dietrich Bonhoeffer writes, they end in heteronomy and an unconditional surrender of the self. While institutions initially fulfill the function of a redeemer for men, they inevitably end only in condemnation of life (Ethics, 243).

The explanatory synthesis, the state, and the king hold in relation to the knight the role of the father and the knight, therefore, the position of son. St. Augustine makes this clear in On Free Choice of the Will where he includes among things that must be loved "the state itself, which is usually held to have the place of a parent" (31). The parent-child relationship is a central structural assumption of most important sociological works of the Middle Ages from St. Augustine onward. I will have more to say about this relationship in section 3.3; here the concern is cultural transcendence as the unconscious indentification of Malory with Tristram and as the thematic center of the Morte itself. The son cannot transcend his father-culture as long as his self-conception remains that of a son, but medieval ideology and theology demanded that the individual play the role of the son throughout his life. To deviate from the orientations of sonhood was to commit sin, specifically heresy and pride. Erik Erikson sees a similar restraint as the central force behind the rebellion of Martin Luther. Anyone familiar with Luther's writings will recall the trauma of his first mass: Luther's terror, his attempt to flee the altar, and his father's angry denunciations at the concluding ceremonial dinner. This trauma has been interpreted in various ways; Roland Bainton emphasizes "the terror of the Holy, the horror of Infinitude" (Here I Stand, 30), but most useful is Erikson's recognition that the Mass was performed in an environment of fathers:

> In this moment he had the presence of the Eucharist in front of him--and the presence of the father behind him. He had not yet learned to speak to God `without embarrassment´ and he had not seen his father since the visit home before the thunderstorm. At this moment, then, when he was to mediate between the father and the Father he still felt torn in his obedience to both. (Young Man Luther, 139)

This first mass was also overseen by Staupitz, Luther's superior and whom he always referred to as "Father." About that mass, Luther himself has written that he felt like fleeing the world as a Judas and that he actually made an attempt to escape. He could not face an authority on any level which only condemned him, and yet he knew of no justification for an independent self. The quest for selfhood, what Bainton calls "The Way of Self Help," became the core of Luther's rebellion. As Erikson generalizes, "at this late date, Martin was thrown back into the infantile struggle, not only over his obedience towards, but also over his identification with, his father [on all levels]. This regression and the personalization of his conflicts cost him that belief in the monastic way and in his superiors which during the first year had been of such `godly´ support. He was alone in the monastery, too, and soon showed it in a behavior that became increasingly un-understandable even to those who believed in him. To be justified became his stumbling block as a believer, his obsession as a neurotic sufferer, and his pre-occupation as a theologian" (145).

Tristram as well as Malory himself, if we accept the accounts of his biographers, exhibits increasingly incomprehensible behavior which, however, can be understood in terms of an Oedipal relationship with a father: a need to be justified, to be a man, in front of a father who will only condemn the son. At the very center of Malory's cultural analysis is the experience of facing the father, full of the tensions and differences necessitated by the inherently different needs of a son and a father. The quest for the center promises justification and tensionlessness, just as the church promises salvation to those whose whole lives are dedicated to charity (the orientation of the father). What Tristram and indeed Luther find at the center is, however, a father who only condemns his sons by requiring that the son permanently renounce his own orientation and adopt the orientation of the father toward himself--thus the permanent condition of sonhood. As Tristram is first exiled from Cornwall, he complains of the absence of justification, even after he has sacrificed himself as a dutiful son to Mark. Instead of a unity of father and son at the center of culture, he discovers enmity:

> Grete well kyng Marke and all myne enemyes, and sey to hem I woll com agayne when I may. And sey hym well am I rewarded for the fyghtyng with sir Marhalt, and delyverd all hys countrey frome servayge. And well I am rewarded for the fecchynge and costis of quene Isode oute off Irelonde and the daunger that I was in firste and laste. And by the way commynge home what daunger I had to brynge agayne quene Isode frome the Castell Pleure! And well am I rewarded whan I fought with sir Bleoberys for sir Segwarydes wyff. (310)

Tristram goes on and on citing instances that should justify him and make him fully acceptable to his father, King Mark. In this, his orientations are clearly those of a son. To be a son means to do the work of the father for the father's sake, and yet to acknowledge the suffering of such a role is to reveal the injustice of the father. Although Tristram is happy while at the Joyous Garde, he is always drawn back to Cornwall and to the demands of Mark. But, in contrast to the Round Table sections, the overall progression, as we shall see in the course of this Chapter, in Malory's "Tristram" is toward joy and liberation from the father. Like the life of Martin

Luther, Tristram's career is often absurd, violent, and filled with hatred; but at other times tranquil and filled with deep love. For Tristram, although it is painful, the tension of Cornwall is superior to the official and enforced meaning and order that obtains at the Round Table and which draws inexorably toward tragedy. In the end, it is true to say that Tristram is happier than Lancelot, although this is not the traditional conclusion of their tales. Tristram's happiness, while it is momentary, is not the result of a moral life and an orientation toward the father, but rather it is the result of his rebellion and insight.

The best analogy to Malory's Tristram is Albert Camus' Sisyphus, the man who revealed the secrets of Zeus and for that was condemned by Zeus to death. But Sisyphus outwitted even death and chained him so that no mortal need any longer die. Eventually betrayed by Ares, Sisyphus was again condemned to the absurd life of pushing a huge rock up a hill only to slip and have the rock descend again to the bottom of hell. Tristram's service to Mark and, indeed, the service all knights owe to their cultural ideals are just such futile labors, and yet in this meaningless labor resides hope. Tristram, like Sisyphus, ends a happy man; their happiness derives from, as Camus puts it, a recognition of the conditions of life, not dreams of immortality. I quote Camus at length because understanding the absurd hero is prerequisite to understanding the middle of Malory's romance, and I do not want this absurd life mistaken for the madness presented in the French fragments about the "folie" of Tristan nor the "wisdom of fools" illustrated in Hieronymus Bosch's "Ship of Fools." These works simply support wisdom by showing the horrible conditions it transforms (see Foucault, Madness and Civilization, "Stultifera Navis"). Camus has something entirely different in mind:

> You have already grasped that Sisyphus is the absurd hero. He is, as much through his passions as through his torture. His scorn for the gods, his hatred of death, and his passion for life won him that unspeakable penalty in which the whole being is exerted toward accomplishing nothing. . . .
> If the descent is thus sometimes performed in sorrow, it can also take place in joy. This word is

not too much. Again I fancy Sisyphus returning toward his rock, and the sorrow was in the beginning. When the images of earth cling too tightly to memory, when the call of happiness becomes too insistent, it happens that melancholy rises in man's heart; this is the rock's victory, this is the rock itself . . . our nights of Gethsemane. But crushing truths perish from being acknowledged. . . .
   All Sisyphus' silent joy is contained therein. His fate belongs to him. His rock is his thing. Likewise, the absurd man, when he contemplates his torment, silences all the idols. In the universe suddenly restored to its silence, the myriad wondering little voices of the earth rise up. . . . At that subtle moment when man glances backward over his life, Sisyphus returning toward his rock, in that slight pivoting he contemplates that series of unrelated actions which becomes his fate, created by him, combined under his memory's eye and soon sealed by his death. Thus convinced of the wholly human origin of all that is human, a blind man eager to see who knows that night has no end, he is still on the go. The rock is still rolling.
   I leave Sisyphus at the foot of the mountain. One always finds one's burden again. But Sisyphus teaches the higher fidelity that negates the gods and raises rocks. He too concludes that all is well. The universe henceforth without a master seems to him neither sterile nor futile. Each atom of that stone, each mineral flake of that night-filled mountain, in itself forms a world. The struggle itself toward the heights is enough to fill a man's heart. One must imagine Sisyphus happy. (89-91)

What finally unifies Malory, Tristram and, indeed, Sisyphus is the abandonment of the quest to be justified before a father and a turning toward contemplation of torment and human struggles; he becomes sensitive to human problems on the empirical level--the only level on which they can ever be resolved. The emphasis upon the son's sorrow silences the father, and without such a master from whom justification could never have been wrenched anyway, the son discovers the paradoxical happiness of "love's pain" which Camus knows and to which Gottfried dedicated his tale of Tristan.   One transcends the father by facing him and forcing into the center of culture the oppositional stance of son against father, man against world.   Thus Tristram always returns to Cornwall.

In contrast to the sections which deal with the rise and fall of the Round Table, all of which are controlled by an orientation to the Round Table, a creative source and thus a father, the "Tristram" section lacks such a unified orientation and explanatory center.   It is a search in the full sense of the word involving high levels of frustration, randomness, violence, hope and despair.   Nothing could better describe Malory's own life, for it appears from the records that he was a terrorist, or in the more descriptive phrase of Morse Peckham, a "symbolic or cultural vandal."   Peckham argues in Romanticism and Behavior that innovation and cultural transcendence require cultural vandalism: "Symbolic vandalism is no less real for being symbolic.   I call it symbolic because vandalism is performed under circumstances from which the possibilities of retaliation by others is absent.   Empty houses are splendid targets for adolescent vandalism. What vandalism produces in the individual is a powerful sense of selfhood, of being a man; it is that sense of sudden glory which Hobbes called the result of the aggressive act of laughter. `I´ is opposed to `they,´ and not the `I´ but the `they´ are the victims. . . .   [The Romantics] were not vandalizing empty houses but rather the behavior-validating and instructing rhetorical modes of European high culture, and the Romantics were cultural vandals without exception" (23-24). The nature of Malory's crimes do not suggest that he was concerned simply with profit but rather with rebellion, destruction, and vengeance against an authority that he hated. Attacking someone's property is simply the most effective way of expressing hatred for that person because property is, among other things, a sign of the value of the owner.   We must understand about terrorism or cultural vandalism that it has no articulated conception of a better system or a replacement for the ideology being attacked--in spite of the fact that terrorists often claim certain ideologies of their own.   Rather the purpose is simply to destroy what prevails, for the existence of what prevails is the source of the terrorist's feeling of repression and meaninglessness.

Edward P. Cheyney arrives at a similar conclusion in writing about the rise of heresy and dissent in the fifteenth century: "Viewing the long procession of these rebellious spirits as they appear in the contemporary chronicles, as they pass through the pages of Foxe or as their trials and beliefs are more critically discussed in the pages of modern writers, one is struct with the hunger of a multitude of souls for something which the church was not giving them. . . . The period was one of restlessness, of criticism, of insurgency against fixed conditions" (Dawn of a New Era, 226). The real motivation is self-assertion on a level of aggression equal to the perceived aggression and violence of the institution against the individual. Terrorists always evoke further repression and more stringent security measures on the part of the authority, but this is a sure way of demonstrating even more openly the injustice and the self-centeredness of the authority. It is well to remember how Nietzsche explains nihilism as a constructive philosophy; not that it offers a better system but rather that it effectively clears the ground of that which prevents new growth.

I am suggesting that the "Tristram" is absurd art, and by absurd is meant only that the world in which the characters live is meaningless; that is, actions cannot be traced to a coherent explanatory system, a benevolent God, or a predictable nature. It is a world in which fathers have abandoned their sons, the institutional reality has begun to deny man. In the words of Jean-Paul Sartre, "when we speak of abandonment . . . we mean only to say that God does not exist, and that it is necessary to draw the consequences of this absence right to the end . . . there disappears with Him all possibility of finding values in an intelligible heaven. There can no longer be any good a priori, since there is no infinite and perfect consciousness to think it" (Existentialism and Humanism, 32-33). The surface or the literal level of such works, like the "Tristram," appears absurd, illogical, and chaotic because its theme is to vandalize institutionalized sign-response systems of meaning by acknowledging the merely coercive nature of any stable response to a sign. No natural reason exists for Tristram to love Mark as king; he is held to it by the force of culture. This does not imply, however, that absurd works are themselves meaningless. The contrary is in fact true. The behavior of any terrorist or vandal is quite sensible and significant in the dynamic of cultural evolution, but we must drop the centrist orientation that unconditionally condemns innovative behavior carried on outside of institutional directives if we are to grasp its import.

If we are to assert, therefore, that the "Tristram" is as aesthetically successful as the remainder of the Morte and, in fact, Malory's real center of interest, then it will be necessary to do what other critics have not done: dispute with Vinaver's rather definitive objections. The only way to do this is to take the "Tristram" out of the realm of synthetic art which is designed to exemplify ideologies and to place it within a model for cultural evolution, an historical dialectic. The problem is mainly structural, for Malory vandalizes even his own literary structure because of the overwhelming value a structured narrative has always had for intellectuals. St. Augustine's interest in rhetorical unity, as noted in 2.3, is a case in point. Toward the end of his career, Eugène Vinaver was beginning to recognize the similarity between medieval romance and modern existential and absurd literature. In an article, published in 1980, "The Questing Knight," he writes that

> You may wonder how this kind of structure [of romance] can be fitted into what we normally regard as the right sort of pattern of dramatic or narrative composition. The answer is that it cannot be so fitted because it is different from anything that we are familiar with, unless we happen to have more than a superficial acquaintance with the literature and art of our own time. (131)

Vinaver also notes that the interest in the structure itself became more and more prominent as romance literature developed, but still he refuses to relate literary structures to larger cultural issues. In the case of Chrétien de Troyes, for example, Vinaver points out that "the motive for the creation of knight-errantry is to be found within the works in which it appears and no where else. . . . Chrétien wrote two romances after the Lancelot, and in both he placed more emphasis than he ever did before on the itinerant aspect of knighthood" (130). Although he sees that itinerancy of knighthood--wandering, random encounters, and dissolution of unity and structure--

increases over time, Vinaver continues to believe that the revolutionary structure of romance is a literary phenomenon only, just as D. W. Robertson believes that courtly love had nothing to do with a cultural crisis in the Middle Ages. Vinaver cannot admit that innovations in literary style, theme, and narrative structure correspond to institutional and ideological upheavals all of which grow out of the discovery of a new point of view from which to observe the world, but he does, somewhat paradoxically, admit that these books had a revolutionary effect. In writing of Don Quixote's housekeeper, he does grasp the central issue:

> What in her simplicity she did not and could not know was that it was not the enchanters from these books, but the books themselves that had fired Don Quixote's imagination and made him into an out-of-date knight-errant--and not so much the stories told in those books, but the way they were told, the way the characters were made to behave in order to enact the stories. The fire that the curate and the barber lit in the courtyard of Don Quixote's house was not meant to destroy the enchanters or even the enchantments; it was meant to destroy--at least symbolically--a particular brand of imagination that, they thought, was contrary to orderly human life. The books, they felt, were dangerous because they had no beginning, no middle, and no end, because they were a living negation of what by that time had become the 'madness of the many'--the belief in rational organization in any form of art. (127-28, emphasis mine)

Vinaver's point is somewhat misleading, for the romances clearly have beginnings, middles, and ends both structurally and thematically in the sense of the whole work. What he means to say is that there is no proper cohesion and unity between the structural parts and that any single adventure seems to begin and end nowhere. Later on he points out, as I have been saying all along, "we shall have great difficulty in understanding the romances of chivalry, for they are a negation of everything that we have been brought up to regard as essential in any art, visual or literary" (131). And finally the importance of this structural principle is that "two events will interact in such a way as to bring forth, as no other device could have done, the meaning of both: form will generate a new meaning" (138). It has taken Vinaver almost an entire career to reach this understanding of romance, although the seeds of it were already present in his insistence upon dividing Malory's romance into eight separate romances. He could not find in Malory a single unity or purpose, and, therefore, he saw no reason, as Caxton had, to insist upon unity of form. But by separating the tales, he had, in effect, preserved as much unity as was possible; each separate tale preserves a coherence between purpose and form within its own narrative boundaries. His latest position only extends the earlier one; Vinaver now sees romance as polycentric, a useful concept if Vinaver had only resisted the urge to subsume polycentrism under a larger cohesion:

> .The classical doctrine assumes that there can be no proper cohesion, or integrity, in a work of art without singleness of purpose; that is what we call the doctrine of unity. . . . But once we realize that there are in fact several centers instead of one, we can just as easily call it a positive feature. Instead of seeing the absence of a center we would then see a polycentric design of correspondingly greater complexity. . . . [W]hat we see is a very careful working out of two basic patterns of ornamentation, both polycentric and both highly cohesive. (132-37)

But Vinaver's original and rather definitive objections to the "Tristram" have stuck, and his recent ideas about form and meaning have not received the attention that they should have. Briefly Vinaver's original objections to the "Book of Sir Tristram" are that

> Malory failed to give it a meaning, a sen, capable of supporting its complex and delicate narrative frame. He failed above all to grasp and bring out the tragic theme, essential to any coherent form of the Tristan legend and still discernable in its prose version. . . .

In all essentials, then, Malory's "Tristram" is but another example of a medieval romance in which the author's sen fails to harmonize with the matière. (Works, I, lxxxviii)

Scholars since this remark in 1947 have generally tried to show how the "Tristram" could be subsumed within the general "sen" of the Round Table ideology and how Malory did, in fact, grasp the tragic implications of Tristram's tale.   This is to miss the point entirely.   Vinaver's formula is that good works of art must illustrate coherence in form and content.   These assumptions or aesthetic criteria are shared even by those who have tried to dispute with Vinaver and show the unity of all the tales and the artistic success of the "Tristram."   But neither is that the issue.   Of course, the "Tristram" lacks coherence if it is read with the expectation that Malory's fundamental outlook upon life, culture, and explanation remains consistent throughout the work.   But it does not.   Consistency, structural coherence, and logic are aesthetic criteria for only those who believe in and need universal truths.   For Malory truth and the institutional center are the causes of tragedy, and Tristram moves away from these.

Psychoanalysts hold that imagery and behavior are major outlets for the unconscious; imagery and behavior comprise the matière of romance.   What sort of sen can we, therefore, infer from Tristram's adventures?   The critics who have sought unity have made the "Tristram" into a dumping ground for all the events too sordid to be mentioned in direct connection with the Round Table: "The `Tristram' section, then, seems designed to complement Malory's Arthurian story and to throw into sharper relief than would otherwise have been possible not only the tragic fall of an almost perfect world but the reasons for that fall" ("Analogy," 147).   Or even worse, Rumble goes on, "he had to make clearer than ever before the causes of that tragedy . . . it is just this sense of causality that is underscored, though implicitly rather than explicitly, by the addition of the `Tristram' material" (145).   But it would require little argument to show that events even more sordid take place in the Round Table sections than in the "Tristram" section.   One needs only to point out Arthur's Mayday massacre, Balin, Lancelot's murder of Meleagant (to my mind the most sordid event in the entire romance), and the rebellion of Mordred. And besides, are we to believe that because an event is narrated within the context of the "Tale of Tristram" it is only a cause and not part and parcel of the Round Table. Following this principle, what is to be said of the report of Mark's murder of Tristram which is not reported and does not happen until the final sections of the fall of the Round Table? What sort of causality is at work here? Something else beside logic and causality is at work; Malory shows no interest in supporting orthodox or moral explanations of life--as he did not in his own life--for the reason that he sees these explanations as the cause of the tragedy. The cause is Lancelot and Arthur and the fact that they use all of their force to demonstrate that their culture is tensionless, congruent with reality, and, therefore, the fulfillment of human nature. What the ideology fulfills is exactly death for everyone.

Tristram, on the other hand, perceives culture as a control, a repressive and destructive force. Instead of assimilating the dominant Weltanschauung and developing a super-ego which would make the culture a part of him, Tristram tries as hard as he can to randomize his behavior. He spends as much time as possible outside of the courts of Mark and Arthur. His book appears to lack a sen because it cannot be related point for point to the medieval explanatory structure as can the adventures of Gareth, for example. The critic can select out certain passages, the "essentials" as Rumble calls them, but this is to miss the fact that Tristram moves away from the explanatory center. Such critics can never account for the inconclusive nature of the "Tristram"; we are never able to say finally what he accomplishes or what he stands for. Some readers look back to St. Augustine's definition of sin and condemn Tristram and his actions as evil. It is more accurate to say, however, that the "Tristram" looks forward to the anti-medievalism of the Renaissance and Reformation, especially Luther, Machiavelli, Montaigne, Bacon, and the rise of the individual (for better or worse) as the quintessential unit of existence.

If, as the last section noted, the movement toward the center of the mature institution has the characteristics of indoctrination, then we need to understand something about the opposite process of deprograming or dedoctrination. Within any institution or culture--since one is always already accultura ted--deprograming has the same form as cultural transcendence. The stages of deprograming reverse the process of indoctrination. In the sections following this one, I plan to examine the process of deprograming in some detail; here my concern is simply to grasp the kind of theme Malory presents in the "Tristram." Briefly, the individual must significantly experience the feeling of the failure of the explanatory synthesis to produce the feeling of value in himself; abashment and Tristram's acknowledgment of Mark's failure to reward him for all his service to Cornwall have already been noted. "Abaysshed" is also the word Malory uses for Lamerok's response to Gaheris' murder of Morgause, his own mother and at the time Lamerok's lover. The feeling is a profound loss of faith. Morse Peckham, my authority for much of this discussion, very aptly calls this experience "explanatory collapse." The power of culture to make life meaningful by resolving incoherence in experience suddenly collapses. Culture itself now becomes the great source of tension and anxiety in an individual's life. I shall return to this important point in section 3.3, "The Father and the Son."

The second stage is cultural alienation, a withdrawal from tension causing situations and experimentation with different, or a-cultural experiences. Alienation opens up the stimulus field; one begins to respond to stimuli and situations that simply do not relate to the interests of the institution which formerly were held to be identical to the individual's interest. Behavior becomes irrelevant, random, trivial, incomprehensible, or even criminal, as the individual develops interests that are wholly his own and his attitude toward cultural ideals becomes ambivalent: a wish to do two contradictory things, as Palomides always seems to wish. Just prior to his quest for the Red City, Palomides exclaims, "I hate sir Trystram moste to deth, for and I may mete wyth hym the tone of us shall dye," but almost immediately he understands his words and goes on to say that "ye [Tristram] ar a good knyght; and that ony other knyght that namyth hymself a good knyght sholde hate you, me sore mervaylyth" (426). The net effect of alienation and ambivalence is a loosening of control and an increase in the aggressive self-assertion of the individual. The next step is cultural vandalization, attacking institutional symbols of value; vandalism makes one feel a sense of self power. At this point the individual has arrived at an oppositional stance with regard to the center of the institution, a relationship which gives birth again to a self but one which is now independent of the institution and which has little interest in or interaction with the members of the institution. At this point also, the individual gathers around him his own group, as Tristram, Dynadan, and Isode do at the Joyous Garde. The emergent counter-culture becomes the origin from which a new institution will develop over time, if the behavioral habituations upon which it is being built actually resolve the problems a significant number of people are experiencing in the dominant culture.

None of this can be made to cohere with the theme of the Round Table section. There is no tragic theme in the "Tristram" not because Malory failed to grasp it but because Tristram repudiates truths of the Round Table, and without such universal human forms there can be no tragedy, no sudden eye-gouging discovery, like Oedipus, that all one's life has been wrong. In the two movements, Malory presents a much more complete picture of culture than most artists are capable of. He attains the level of a Shakespeare in presenting culture as a dialectic, a site of forces for innovation and transcendence constantly conflicting with forces of tradition and stability. In "The Questing Knight," Vinaver concludes his discussion of polycentric narratives by saying that "the form of romance as a whole generates a new mode of feeling and a new way of life that otherwise would not have been" (138). Vinaver himself never quite comprehends the new feeling or a new way of life; he refers continually what is old in the values of knighthood and love. For the new feeling and life, we must look toward the cultural transcendence of the absurd hero, a consciousness which emerges only out of the perception of incoherence in culture.

The movement of the "Tristram" section suggests somewhat of a salvation and an increase in happiness through a separation from the ideals that lead only to oppression and meaninglessness. Tristram's death while harping before Isode is not tragic but rather is a transcendence of the meaninglessness of the Round Table and of Cornwall. Malory is not so naive as to hope that Tristram could resolve the fundamental tension between the individual and the group, but his portrayal of

Tristram as happy or peaceful at the end is certainly a revision of the traditional ending of the Tristram legend, and it contrasts profoundly with the growing sense of doom and hatred of the Round Table. Tristram is content because he has come to accept and love the world with all of its mutability and injustice; the necessary complement of this love is a hatred for the centering orientation which denies being to the margins of life. Tristram returns home to Cornwall to do the thing he loves most but also the thing that will make him most vulnerable to death.

The imperfect world of Cornwall--as opposed to the enforced perfection of the Round Table--is his home, and he harps before Isode in full view of King Mark because Isode is now his personal adventure; he has made her his source of value and has abandoned the illusion that meaning must transform the suffering world into a tensionless paradise. Tristram harps before Isode in Cornwall because again like Sisyphus the tension and the absurdity of life are most explicit in Cornwall. Malory shows us that man is most human not in perfection and order but in strife and tension. This position is indeed a transcendence of the desperate longing for peace and stability that had begun with St. Augustine and had driven the Middle Ages to the most vicious level of meaninglessness, repression, exploitation, and torture that the world has ever seen short of the twentieth century. As Joseph Henderson points out, certain types of death are symbols of transcendence:

> These godlike figures are in fact symbolic representations of the whole psyche, the larger and more comprehensive identity that supplies the strength that the personal ego lacks [i.e., Malory himself]. Their special role suggests that the essential function of the heroic myth is the development of the individual's ego-consciousness-- his awareness of his own strengths and weaknesses-- in a manner that will equip him for the arduous tasks with which life confronts him. Once the individual has passed his initial test and can enter the mature phase of life, the hero myth loses its relevance. The hero's symbolic death becomes, as it were, the achievement of that maturity. (Man and His Symbols, 101-103)

As strange as this analysis may seem, it is what critics have always missed in Malory's "Tristram." Malory, it seems to me, inserted the tale of Tristram into the rise, flowering, and fall of the Round Table to symbolize his own coming to maturity, his own alienation and oppositional stance to the Round-Table-like culture of fifteenth century England. The ability to perceive within one's symbolic universe the forces Tristram represents signals a level of intellectual astuteness attained by no more than a few hundred individuals in the entire history of Western civilization.

3.2 Narrative Structure
and Deconstruction

The principles by which Le Morte Darthur is arranged are usually called entrelacement, polycentric, polyphonic or retrospective narrative. Malory has presented a complex chronology of events in order that the parts of the narrative that are thematically related would fall together. In general, he has simplified his French sources, for he seems to have wanted to write the complete story of Arthur and his most famous knights, and it was necessary to abbreviate a good deal in order to do so. It seems also that Malory is not primarily interested in portrayal of knight-errantry, as Vinaver thinks he was, but rather in being comprehensive, in presenting the whole history from the beginning to the end in the simplest and clearest form. Thus in ordering the tales, Malory places Arthur's wars with Emperor Lucius in Book II, at the outset of the romance when the Round Table is in its period of expansion. This episode in the sources was considered to be one of Arthur's last adventures. The report of Tristram's death also shows Malory's organizational strategy. We do not hear of the murder until the main story line is well within the movement toward tragedy and the subject of a king's treacherous murder of his best knight is an immediate problem for Lancelot to consider. Moreover, Malory radically condenses the long discussion of Tristram's parentage and omits all of his training because the sections leading up to the "Tristram" have said all that needs to be said about a knight's socialization; Gareth is the archetype, and we can apply what happens to him to any other major knight. What this organizational strategy amounts to, then, is nothing more than juxtaposition; Malory narrates an episode at the moment that his overall theme or plan calls for it, not necessarily when it falls chronologically. We can establish that Malory is thinking thematically, not logically or chronologically, as when, for example, he has Tristram finish second best at the Michaelmas Tournament before we are even aware that Tristram has been born or will play a part in the romance.

   In Chapter One it was pointed out that Malory pushes the method of philosophic Realism to the extreme by diminishing the attributional or literal qualities of the foreground in order to emphasize the background--the Form or ideology behind the events. In like manner, he diminishes the account of the relationships between the various actions of the narrative; he reduces what medieval logicians and grammarians called "syncategoremata": the words such as prepositions, conjuctions, copulatives, and some adjectives that make clear the relationship between "categorematic" terms or nouns and verbs standing for the categories of the mind. "Syncategoremata" should be distinguished from the retrospective and prospective "links" that serve principally a narrative rather than a logical or heuristic function; although Murry Evans in his recent "Ordinatio and Narrative Links: The Impact of Malory's Tales as a `hoole book'" argues convincingly how these two functions necessarily work together. The question Evans addresses and also my concern here is the problem of the cause of a reader's judgment or a knight's judgment that a series of events is related or that two distinct events can be interpreted as forms of the same thing; readers feel the unity of the narrative just as the knights feel the ideological unity of the Round Table, but we cannot, as the knights cannot, put a finger on exactly what makes it unified.

   The problem of syncategoremata was of great interest to the nominalist William of Ockham (1285-1349), and it can provide us with a clear way of understanding the constructive/deconstructive dialectic in Malory's romance. Ockham argued that universals and truths--where unity is found--were properties of language, signs, and the mind, not of the physical world. Reified universals and institutions are in Ockham's view not naturally possible. The relationship or meaning of things and actions in the physical world, then, might very well not be the same as the relationship depicted in the symbolic universe. Ockham is pointing to an ambiguity or a discontinuity between universals and particulars and, thus, to a potential for the separate development of thought and action.

The interest in syncategoremata signals the emergence of cultural analysis. One of the founders of modern symbolic logic, William of Sherwood (1210-1271)), begins his <u>Treatise on Syncategorematic Words</u> from the analytic position:

> In order to understand anything one must understand its parts; thus in order that the statement (<u>enuntiatio</u>) may be understood one must understand the parts of it. Its parts are of two kinds: principal and secondary. The principal parts are the substantival name and the verb, for they are necessary for an understanding of the statement. The secondary parts are the adjectival name, the adverb, and conjuctions, and prepositions, for they are not necessary for the statement's being.

William goes on to define the principal parts as categorial terms and then defines the relationship between the two kinds of parts:

> Other [secondary parts] are determinations of principal parts insofar as they [principal parts] are subjects and predicates. For example, when I say 'every man is running' the word 'every,' which is a universal sign, does not signify that some thing belonging to 'man' is universal, but rather that 'man' is a universal subject. [Secondary parts] of this kind are called syncategorematic words. They cause a great deal of difficulty in discourse, and for that reason they are to be investigated.
>
> The name <u>syncategoremata</u> comes from <u>sin</u>--i.e., 'con'--and <u>categoreuma</u>--i.e., 'significative' or

`predicative´--as if to say `conpredicative,´ for a
syncategorematic word is always joined with
something else in discourse. (13-16)

Syncategorematic terms determine, therefore, the extent
to which a universal applies to a particular or the nature of the
relationship between two universals or two particulars. "Every"
in William´s example means that "man" is universal with respect
to the predicate "running." In terms of the romance, for
example, syncategorematic terms explain to us the relationship
between categorematic terms such as Knighthood or Governance
and the individuals. Or the syncategorematic term may provide
an explanation of the relationship between two or several
actions. Malory´s interest lies in the basis for judgments of
unity and compliance; he seems to be following the penchant of
such nominalists as Ockham who began to understand that "The
problem of individuation is a logical problem of showing how
general terms are used in propositions to refer to individuals
signified by them; this problem is resolved in terms of the
quantifying prefixes and other syncategorematic determinants of
the referential use of terms in propositions" (Moody, 8, 308).
Logic and social stability are, of course, intimately related.
Logic is the set of rules about how to produce and interpret
verbal propositions; verbal propositions determine acceptable
(moral) behavior; social stability, therefore, depends upon
inducing individuals to think and verbalize logically.
    An interest in syncategoremata, however, implies a
recognition of the problem of individuation and signals a shift in
orientation from universals to particulars. Ockham began to
recognize that fallacies of ambiguity often did not reside in
universals but in syncategoremata. If, for example, Knighthood
is predicated of men, is it of all men, some men, necessarily of
men, contingently, if and only if, and. so on and on. The
romance shows Malory´s supreme awareness of ambiguity in the
relation of universals to particulars; in general, he suppresses
or diminishes syncategoremata to allow the reader to supply
them of himself, proving, in a way, that the order one finds in
the world is a mental rather than a natural phenomenon.
Ideology which is replete with syncategoremata allows thinkers
to provide the proper quantifying determinants. This is what
Lancelot does when a lady tells him of "a knyght that dystressis

all ladyes and jantylwomen, and at the leste he robbyth them other lyeth by them." The lady is saying that the universal "Knighthood" is distributed affirmatively among all particulars: "men." Lancelot's reply suggests that "Knighthood" is distributed exceptively and exclusively; that is, "What . . . is he a theff and a knyght? And a ravyssher of women? He doth shame unto the Order of Knyghthode" (160). While the lady conjoins "thief" and "knight" Lancelot disjoins them: "thief" or "knight." In Lancelot's mind no ambiguity is suggested in the universal; the categories "thief," "ravisher," and "knight" simply share no attributes. Ambiguity enters, however, in the way the categories are applied to a particular. Is a man sometimes a knight and sometimes not? What syncategorematic terms will relate Knighthood to this man who will not stop pestering this woman but who nonetheless exhibits some attributes of Knighthood? At what point does he cease being a knight and become simply a thief or a rapist? Malory, just as the nominalists, raises the question of the relationship between actions and universals because he was able to perceive that the actions of a knight such as Tristram are inconsistent and therefore we have a great deal of trouble in applying to him the universal of knighthood in order to legitimate what he does. If our orientation is toward the coherence of universal categories and logic, as it is for Lancelot, then we end up condemning Tristram. The question finally raised by the interest in syncategoremata is whether or not there exists a logical, necessary, and natural relationship between the categories of the mind and the phenomenon of the world. Clearly for Malory there is not.

Now it is true that no medieval philosopher expected the physical world to be consistent and stable; that is not the point. Political thought, particularly that of the "glossators" and commentators on canon law, had generally developed precise methods for articulating and valuing stability and consistency but almost no method for comprehending instability in any terms other than sin or crime. As Malory's romance progresses, logical determinations of the relationship between universals and particulars, and therefore the value of any act, become increasingly difficult as the situational components of the act become more complex. Universals are constantly invoked, but their application becomes less and less secure.

Malory allows ambiguity to develop about whether an act is knightly or not, and he leaves it to the reader to posit the syncategoremata. Evans' study of narrative links leads to this same conclusion: "Malory's narrative links illuminate his method. In a narrative whose fabric is often understatement, Malory's links function as dropped analogies which invite the reader to complete structuring the story, discerning its <u>significatio</u>. What is more, Malory's own comments in the 'virtuous love' digression suggest some guidelines for our interpretation" (45). Ultimately, as Evans does not see, however, this method deconstructs universal interpretations, for the reader's logical judgments, as they certainly do in the "virtuous love" digression, prove to be insupportable later on. Increasingly, Malory forces the reader to find fault with either the universal or with the individual knight. Any reader who categorizes Lancelot's decision to rescue Guinevere from her final trial by ordeal, as Sir Bors does, with Knighthood will face the problem of a knightly act causing an unknightly act; that is, a good causing an evil, something illogical and impossible to the medieval mind, unless, of course, the original good were not truly good in the first place. If we categorize Guinevere as a "true lover" then we face the necessary conclusion that all the tragedy results from "true love."

In the "Tristram" section, the problem of syncategorematic terms becomes particularly acute because of the discontinuity between what happens in one episode and what occurs in the succeeding one. The kind of relationships that can exist between two or more juxtaposed episodes is quite various, but Malory's strategy remains consistent. Malory simply does not tell us why "Now leve we of sir Lamerok and speke we of sir Gawayne and his bretherne, sir Aggravayne and sir Mordred" (378), for example; or why "now turne we to another mater." Malory simply narrates his episodes allowing the actions to stand symbolic of the world of the medieval explanatory synthesis. He allows the reader predisposed to order and coherence to include and exclude each action as it comes along and thereby construct the mental model of the world. For the Middle Ages, this process of including all the good and excluding all the evil should lead inexorably to an orderly and consistent explanation of the world, but in Malory it simply will not work out and leads to tragedy. The

"Tristram" section contains a higher density of episode shifts which are not sufficiently explained than any of the other sections and the frequency of these shifts increases as the tale progresses. This narrative strategy accounts for the failure of the reader who is looking for a well-made plot to find much sense in the "Tristram"; he simply cannot find sufficient motivation and preparation for each episode.

With respect to book divisions, we see the problem of insufficient motivation and syncategoremata at work in the expected but inappropriate continuity between "The Book of Sir Gareth" and "The Book of Sir Tristram" which follows it. Gareth undergoes an exemplary initiation process in which success in one battle qualifies him to seek a higher and more difficult test of fitness. So the pattern goes until he wins the utlimate honor, "the gre," at a major tournament on the Feast of the Assumption and is therefore proved worthy to be married to dame Lyones. Then Malory turns to Sir Tristram and there is suddenly no initiation within the social process. Malory goes to considerable length to emphasize that Tristram is unproven and therefore should not be able to respond with the culturally prescribed behaviors. In the fight with Marhalt, Tristram emphasizes his lack of experience by repeating three times "for never yett was I proved with a good knyght" (236). Gareth's quest establishes the paradigm in the mind of the reader who, when he sees Tristram defeat Marhalt, the second best knight in the world, judges that Tristram has somewhere acquired all of the values and doctrines that Gareth learned in his initiation quest. We expect Tristram to be a noble knight not because of what he has learned or has done but rather because of our knowledge of Knighthood and the mere fact that he has killed Marhalt. We are judging Tristram not by what he actually does but rather by what he ought to do and by our expectations of the universal applicability of Knighthood.

One act, however, does not make the man, and in fact the behavioral requirements of Knighthood are always a problem for Tristram. Innovation originates in improper or incomplete socialization; to some extent, Tristram is bound to do things differently. The same inappropriate continuity holds for Cornwall and King Mark. Mark's regime begins fully developed, as it were, at the condition to which the Round Table aspires-- the perfect symbiosis of the King and Champion. We expect therefore the same political ideals to hold for Cornwall and the Round Table, but as we see more of the situation at Cornwall we begin to believe that Cornwall is different from the Round Table. Bors makes this incorrect judgment in his attempt to reassure Lancelot that he need not fear treachery from Arthur: "`All thys ys trouthe,´ seyde sir Bors, `but there ys one thyng shall corrayge you and us all: ye know well that kynge Arthur and kynge Marke were never of lyke condycions´" (681). We know, of course, how deeply Bors has been indoctrinated. What else could he think? Edward Kennedy in "Malory´s King Mark and King Arthur" has articulated very fully the distinction pointed out by Bors. The two kings belong to different categories of kingship: Mark to the kingship of bonum privatum and Arthur to the kingship of bonum commune.

My own analysis reveals, however, that Arthur is not different from Mark. In the sections leading up to the "Tristram," we get the rise of the Round Table and the building or synthesis of a civilization; then in the "Tristram" we get the analysis or tearing apart of the same kind of civilization. The correct syncategoremata for Cornwall and the Round Table is consecutive conjunction; one represents the early stage of a civilization, while the other represents the high point or the flowering stage. And yet this continuity seems inappropriate to the reader whose behavior and judgments are controlled by the ideology of Governance and Knighthood, for he sees only contrast or disjunction between Mark and Arthur. Such a judgment originates, as we shall see in a moment, in an ambiguity in the operational meaning of "common good."

The concept of syncategoremata, then, provides a key for understanding the order and meaning of the episodes in, especially, the "Tristram," for Tristram has many problems in being the ideal knight that the reader expects him to be. The source of these problems is the lack of experience in the social process of knighthood; Tristram is often unable to provide the culturally determined link between two acts, and therefore he is unable to derive the benefit of the culturally accepted resolution of whatever tensions or incoherencies he experiences when several categoremata come into play. In the "Tristram," Malory focuses upon those very instances of tension and incoherence which the culture, as it exists in Tristram, cannot cover over or explain away by the process of applying universals to particular actions. Sometimes the universals just do not apply, which means, of course, that they are not very universal: "Here men may undirstonde that bene men of worshyp that man was never fourmed that all tymes myght attayne, but somtyme he was put to the worse by malefortune and at som tyme the wayker knyght put the byggar knyght to a rebuke" (296).

The logic of William of Sherwood provides a set of rules about how to interpret categorematic words; that is, he explains precisely how these words direct a person in understanding the existent world from the point of view of the universals. Ideology, the totality of the knowledge of an institution, possesses, of course, its own logic, its own prescriptions about what kind of relationships are acceptable and what are not. Normally speaking it is not possible to get outside of logic; meta-logic is initially not possible since logic applies to the totality of the real and symbolic universe. Whatever lies outside of logic is merely error, "malefortune," or non-being. Cultural innovation, therefore, begins in the syncategoremata for negation: no, not, and non. New ideologies cannot possibly begin fully formed; they must be behaviorally constructed just as the dominant ideology was. Thus dissent from the dominant ideology is the first innovative and culturally transcendent act. In explaining the heuristic function of negative syncategoremata, William writes, "When, on the one hand, the mind consents to the composition, it asserts, and there is an affirmation; when, on the other hand, the mind dissents, it disasserts (deasserit), and there is a negation. Therefore the composition belonging to the verb `is´ is , as it were, a subject for affirmation and for negation, and the negation belonging to `not´ is opposed to affirmation and not to the composition" (94). One cannot logically create new compositions or ideologies by merely negating compositions that presently exist; one can only dissent from the socially constructed reality he knows.

The experience of Tristram must be seen, then, as largely a negation of the universal explanations of the Round Table. Tristram´s experience acknowledges that sometimes the universals do not apply; he has no idea what else might exist, only that he cannot assent to the terms of Knighthood or Governance that are presented to him. Negation or dissent is, however, a very strange action for it obliquely suggests the existence of nonexistents. William goes to great lengths to deny that negations give rise to suppositions for nonexistents because if that were the case all logic would dissolve into nothing more than an arbitrary control of verbal behavior based upon one conception of reality and excluding other realities: "There is a doubt whether the word `no´ makes a term attached to it stand for nonexistents.  And it seems that it does so, for, as matters stand, this now follows: `no man is running; therefore Caesar is not running.´ Proof: Grant the opposite, that Caesar is running, and it follows that some man is running, since he cannot run unless he is and is also a man. But if one can infer thus, then `man´ supposits for nonentities, as it seems.  But this is contrary to the rule of suppositions, since `man´ has sufficient appellata" (52).   The problem of alternative realities or pluralistic truths will not go away by merely invoking another rule of logic. To suggest that a universal, such as Knighthood, does not apply to a particular action that Tristram or anyone does inevitably opens the door to suppositions about what the nature of that action might be.

As I pointed out in the last section, an innovator such as Merlin or a cultural vandal cannot know what he will invent until after he has done it.   Innovators never really have a developed conception of a replacement for the institution they attack; rather they are motivated by the possibility and the dream of another kind of social structure, the understanding of which grows only as the innovator acts out his dissent. This is utopic thinking, the ability to believe in something which is presently not part of the social reality, and it works powerfully to undermine an individual's willingness to affirm the accepted reality. Logic, as William's treatise itself claims, passes itself off as the necessary, natural, and true rules for determining the existence and value of every experience, but dissent establishes the possibility of a counter logic or counter-reality, the mere possibility of which refutes or deconstructs the claim of the dominant logic to be natural, necessary and absolute. In the "Tristram," Dynadan initially thinks with a counter logic. Logic is a collection of laws governing mental behavior in the same manner that Knighthood regulates fight behavior. Dynadan asks constantly whether a fight should be interpreted as an act of love or of hate. The same fight cannot be both love and hate simultaneously; the knights simply know as a matter of natural law that fights occur because of love.

Dynadan's dissent raises an issue of increasing importance in the late Middle Ages, and that is the basis of law itself. Marsilius of Padua, one of the great political theorists of the fourteenth century, held that the ultimate determination of law is merely the coercive power of the state; there is no natural basis of law just as Ockham argued that no natural basis for universals exists. Universals are, in fact, laws themselves. To grasp how revolutionary Marsilius' legal conceptions were, we need to compare them to the more orthodox St. Thomas who writes that all laws are derived from nature: "As Augustine says `that which is not just seems to be no law at all'; therefore the force of a law depends upon the extent of its justice. Now in human affairs a thing is said to be just from being right according to the rule of reason. But the first rule of reason is the law of nature. . . . Consequently every human law has just so much of the character of law as it is derived from the law of nature. But if in any point it differs from the law of nature, it is no longer a law but a corruption of law" (Summa Theologica, II, i, q. 95, a. 2). Marsilius' discovery that laws are not a manifestation of the natural order of God's creation but are rather the coercive prescriptions of the present monarch is well exemplified in the Defensor Pacis, his refutation of papal plenitudo potestatis. Marsilius, who it should be noted was excommunicated for saying this, writes:

> In one way, it [law] may be considered in itself, as it only shows what is just or unjust, beneficial or harmful; and as such it is called the science or doctrine of right (juris). In another way it may be considered according as with regard to its observance there is a given command coercive through punishment or reward to be distributed in the present world, or according as it is handed down by way of such a command; and considered in this way it most properly is called, and is, a law. . . . Law, then, is a discourse or statement emerging from prudence and political understanding, that is, it is an ordinance made by political prudence, concerning matters of justice and benefit and their

opposites, and having coercive force, that is,
concerning whose observance there is given a
command which one is compelled to observe, or
which is made by way of such command.

For Marsilius, law is conventional, the sum of behavioral
habituations validated by the institution; what makes it law is
the coercive power of the papacy or state to distribute it in
the present world. Individuals can certainly have interests
outside of the law, which in itself is neither just nor unjust.
Theories of the natural basis of law only represent the fact that
all institutions ground themselves in some transcendental or
numinal realm which, of course, prevents anyone from
questioning the legitimacy of the institution itself.

As for the meaning of "political prudence," Marsilius
writes a little later:

The principal end [of law] is civil justice and the
common benefit; the secondary end is the security of
the rulers, especially those with heredity succession,
and the long duration of governments.

At the Round Table, the assertion is clearly that the primary
and secondary ends of law are in complete harmony, although
increasing amounts of energy are required to cover up the
tension. In Cornwall, the opposition of the primary and the
secondary goals are made explicit. As long as the ends are in
harmony, law is not perceived to be coercive and repressive,
but when tension arises, as it does in Cornwall, the king has
but one choice in the service of his own security and that is
the repression of the individual. In the chapter "Slander and
Strife," the fundamental coerciveness of even Arthur's law rises
to the surface: "me sore repentith that ever sir Launcelot
should be ayenste me. . . . [B]ut I woll nat that way worke
with sir Launcelot [judicial battle], for he trustyth so much
uppon hys hondis and hys myght that he doutyth no man. And
therefore for my quene he shall nevermore fyght, for she shall
have the law. And if I may gete sir Launcelot, wyte you well
he shall have as shamefull a death" (682-83).

Logic or the means of arriving at ideologically valid
conclusions has also, therefore, its ground in the political

authority as Malory demonstrates in his use of the theme of disguise. The episode at the end of "The Tournament of Surluse" presents very clearly the way in which institutional order is maintained by the covert force of rational thought. This is the episode in which Lancelot dresses as a woman in order, it appears, to have some fun with Dynadan:

> And as he [Dynadan] was departed, sir Launcelot disgysed hymselff and put uppon his armour a maydyns garmente freysshely attyred. Than sir Launcelot made sir Galyhodyn to lede hym thorow the raunge, and all men had wondir what damsell was that. And so as sir Dynadan cam into the raunge, sir Launcelot, that was in the damesels aray, gate sir Galyhodyns speare and ran unto sir Dynadan.
> And allwayes he loked up thereas sir Launcelot was, and than he sawe one sytte in the stede of sir Launcelot armed. But whan sir Dynadan saw a maner of a damesell, he dradde perellys lest hit sholde be sir Launcelot disgysed. But sir Launcelot cam on hym so faste that he smote sir Dynadan over his horse croupe. (410)

The knights all laugh at Lancelot's prank, Guinevere so hard that as Malory says "she fell downe," but Dynadan who is renowned for his sense of humor does not laugh at all; rather he returns a comment the angry tone of which unmasks Lancelot's true intentions:

> 'Well,' seyde sir Dynadan, 'sir Launcelot, thou arte so false that I can never beware of the.' (410)

This reply is not in any French version that I have been able to find; rather the probable source tale says only that Dynadan "se deffendoit de tout moult bien" (deffended himself very well from all). It is likely that Dynadan's comment is Malory's small addition that changes the tone and intention of the passage radically. By comparison with Malory's sources, critics are constrained to take Dynadan's comment ironically and interpret it as a humorous rejoinder in character with

Dynadan's traditional role of the fool. The overall context of the joke, however, makes that interpretation naive, and in fact, misguided, for immediately following Dynadan's comment Malory mentions the feud between Lamerok and the Orkneys. Lamerok's problem here is that he cannot bring the feud into open discussion: "and hit were nat for my lorde kynge Arthurs sake, I shuld macche sir Gawayne and his bretherne well inowghe" (410). Lamerok, as it were, must disguise his real feelings and fears in order to preserve the harmony within the Round Table. And immediately following the remarks about Lamerok, Malory includes the narrative link: "AND HERE BEGYNNYTH THE TRESON OF KYNGE MARKE THAT HE ORDAYNED AGAYNE SIR TRISTRAM" (411). Again, the motif is disguise:

> Than kynge Marke unbethought hym that he wolde have sir Trystram unto the turnemente disgysed, that no man sholde knowe hym, to that entente that the Haute Prynce sholde wene that sir Trystram were sir Launcelot. (411)

Mark wants Tristram disguised as Sir Lancelot because "sir Galahalt the Haute Prynce and kynge Bagdemagus [called the tournament] to the entente to sle syr Launcelot other ellys uttirly to destroy hym and shame hym, bycause sir Launcelot had evermore the hygher degre" (411). Now clearly, the disguise represents treachery and murder.

The important point is the identity of the concealed intentions of each instance of disguise. Disguise is a means of achieving goals no one will publically acknowledge. In the first case, Lancelot had promised not to fight with Dynadan personally so that Dynadan might gain some honor for himself at the tournament. But lest Dynadan win too much honor and upset the hierarchy among the knights, Lancelot disguises himself in a woman's dress and destroys Dynadan's moment of glory, insuring thereby that

> by all the assente they gaff sir Launcelot the pryce; the next was sir Lameroke de Galys, and the thirde was sir Palomydes; the fourth was kynge Bagdemagus. So these four knyghtes had the pryce.

And there was grete joy and grete nobley in all the courte. (410)

In the second instance, Lamerok suppresses his urge to confront Gawain openly in order that the peace, great joy, and nobility of the Round Table might continue to appear actual. The pattern here is personal sacrifice for the good of the social order. In the third episode, Tristram covers up his real identity in order that he might please King Mark and thus perform his duty as the champion of Cornwall. In all three cases, the will of the individual is subjugated to the needs of universal concord. While Tristram believes that Mark simply asks a harmless disguise, we see that Mark's real demand is nothing less than the death of Tristram. As Freud has pointed out in Civilization and its Discontents, the civilization demands the selective repression of certain traits and impulses in the individual for the maintenance of the common social order. The principle is, of course, very old and medieval political theory defined justice in terms of suppression of lower or lesser important goods in favor of higher goods. Justice has always been seen in terms of the maintenance of the created order of the universe. But how does Malory see that this order is maintained:

GOALS	MEANS
1. Hierarchy of prowess	1. Disguise; shaming of Dynadan
2. Concord among knights	2. Repressed feeling; personal risk
3. Primacy of king	3. Death of the individual

For Malory, the maintenance of the social reality always involves the forceful destruction of the individual. Dynadan is serious when he calls Lancelot a false knight, for to disguise oneself means, finally, to be false to oneself, even if one is being true to a higher order. Logic, just as disguise, allows the column of GOALS to appear necessary and natural in the action and discourse of men while keeping the MEANS concealed.   A great deal more could be said about the sequence of episodes here, for when Mark's plan to murder Tristram fails he goes on to deceive Tristram with kindness and "grete tokenynge of love" in order only to imprison him.   We should not read an episode of disguise without recalling the story of Balin and Balan and the tragic consequences of submitting oneself to an adventure which requires a degree of self-subjection so intense that the individual is no longer recognizable even to a brother.

Another of the traditional donnees in the Tristan legends shows in Malory's handling even more clearly the coercive, if covert, power of logic.   Vinaver suggests that the theme of the weakness of Cornish knights is "quite common in the early Tristan romances" and it emphasizes the "absence of any material obstacle to Tristram's freedom."   He goes on to point out that "both [Malory] and the French prose-writer would probably be at a loss to explain them [references to weakness]" (Works, III, 1460).   Vinaver suggests that obstacles to Tristram's freedom are not sufficient to warrant the amount of suffering and labor that Tristram undergoes.   The absence, however, of a material obstacle (i.e., knights allied with Mark and powerful enough to control Tristram) suggests--since Tristram is, in fact, not free--an immaterial obstacle to his freedom.   There can be no strong knights in Cornwall, except for a single champion, and he only intermittently, because the Governance is designed to perpetuate and enhance the king as the head of the polity or as the manifestation of the center of the explanatory synthesis.   In Cornwall, the common good (that of the knights or the people) is identical to the good of the state.   The presence of strong knights when there is no immediate enemy to be vanquished implicitly diminshes and undermines the strength of the king, for it demonstrates the disunity of the king's power and his person.   The knight as an individual is different from the knight as champion.   The champion is an extension of the king and hence his actions are under strict control, but as an individual the knight's actions are uncontrollable and unpredictable.   The dire result of having strong knights in a polity when no immediate enemy threatens can be seen in the feuds that develop at the Round Table or in the episode involving Sir Segwarde's wife.

The immaterial obstacle to Tristram's freedom, then, is the ideological control that requires the knight to support his king over and above his own personal concerns. The immaterial obstacle is medieval law in all its forms--civil law, laws of logic, canon law, natural law--and these laws are internalized in the knights as super-ego or conscience. We must always remember that Tristram's desire to be the champion of Cornwall is his foremost moral duty and amounts to his orientating his life toward the immutable and the highest good. Rejecting this duty is tantamount to denying the existence of God and the order or creation. Although John of Salisbury, as early as the twelfth century, could advocate tyrannicide, it is not likely that a member of the knightly class could possess such independence from the ideological explanations of the relationship between the king and the knight. The traditional explanation demands that the knight orientate his life toward the king and the society, as Salisbury writes,

> We indeed but follow nature, the best guide of life; for nature has gathered together all the senses of her microcosm or little world, which is man, into the head, and has subjected all the members in obedience to it in such a wise that they will all function properly so long as they follow the guidance of the head, and the head remains sane. Therefore the prince stands on a pinnacle which is exalted and made splendid with all the great and high privileges which he deems necessary for himself. And rightly so, because nothing is more advantageous to the people than that the needs of the prince should be fully satisfied, since it is impossible that his will should be found opposed to justice. (Policraticus, IV. 1)

The mere existence of the knight, moreover, in a time of peace suggests the awkward condition of vain or superfluous existence. The knight without an immediate function, from the point of view of metaphysics, loses his being: "a proper functioning does not exist for the sake of the being which functions, but rather the being exists for the sake of its function" (Dante, De Monarchia, 5). Thus the fact that there are no strong knights in Cornwall is a necessary consequence of Governance; a knight's being is contingent upon his function as champion or defender of the polity.   And yet Tristram, through Isode's love and Dynadan's dissent, gradually becomes aware that he does indeed have an existence of his own.

Malory's "blackening" of King Mark suggests only his own view that the authority of the state derives from repression and exploitation of the citizenry of knights.   The same assumption of Governance obtains in Camelot only it is disguised in such terms as "concord," "justice," and the "common good" and the syncategoremata which posit these qualities of all worshipful men.   The immaterial sen which accounts for Tristram's lack of freedom and which accounts for the weakness of not only the knights of Cornwall but of the Round Table as well is the political structure articulated by Dante in De Monarchia; Dante is both explicit and thoroughly orthodox about this point and for that reason worth quoting at length:

> Now I must explain that 'being' 'unity,' and 'good' have an order of precedence in the fifth sense of 'precedence,' namely, priority.   For by its nature being is prior to unity and unity prior to the good, because whatever is in the fullest sense a being is most unified, and when most unified it is most good. . . .   It is therefore certain that whatever is good is good because it is unified.   And since concord is essentially a good, it is clear that at its root there must be some kind of unity; what this root is will become evident if we examine the nature and ground of concord. . . .   So we speak of a number of men as being in concord when in moving together toward a single goal their wills are formally united, that is, the form of unity is in their wills. . . .
>
> All concord depends on a unity of wills; the best state of mankind is a kind of concord, for as a man is in excellent health when he enjoys concord in soul and body, and similarly a family, a city, or a state, so mankind as a whole.   Therefore the well-being of mankind depends upon the unity of wills.   But this is possible only if there is a single, dominant will which directs all others toward unity, for the wills

of mortals need direction because they are subject
to the captivating delights of youth (so teaches the
philosopher at the end of his Nicomachean Ethics).
And this will cannot be if there be not a single
governor of all whose will can be dominant and
directive of all others. (21)

What Dante describes is precisely the obstacle to the freedom
of all knights, for as long as they direct their lives toward the
highest good they cannot possibly conceive of a will and a
rational process outside of the dominant ideology. We see
Governance at work in the many times when Tristram overrules
his own will and desires in order to fulfill the will of Mark.
When Mark is challenged by Helias, for example, it is Tristram's
duty by logic and reason to defend Mark, even though Tristram
knows full well that Mark will try to have him killed when the
battle is over:

> `Sir,´ seyde sir Trystram, `now I undirstonde ye
> wolde have my succour, and reson wolde that I
> sholde do all that lyyth in me to do, savynge my
> worshyp and my lyff, howbehit that I am sore brused
> and hurte. And sytthyn sir Elyas proferyth so
> largely, I shall fyght with hym. Other ellys I woll
> be slayne in the fylde, other ellys delyver Cornwayle
> of the olde trewage.´ (386, emphasis mine)

Tristram speaks of "reson wolde" and his thought here
shows us that he is confronted with a conflict of goods; his own
injuries which need healing and Mark who needs defending. The
will, in medieval philosophy, is always directed toward the
good, but the reason operating according to logical principles
determines the hierarchy of goods and therefore which good the
will should seek. As St. Thomas explains, "In this way the
intellect moves the will, because the good understood is the
object of the will" (I, q. 82, a. 4). A little later in the Summa,
St. Thomas describes a decision such as Tristram's as the
proper exercise of free choice: "man acts from judgment
because by his knowing power he judges that something should
be avoided or sought. But because this judgment, in the case
of some particular act, is not from instinct, but from some act

of comparison in the reason, therefore he acts from free judgment" (I, q. 83, a. 1). Malory, however, constructs the situation so that Tristram's own good is precisely the opposite of the good which is rational. Tristram, of course, at this point chooses the good that is in his reason. Logic, we see finally, is nothing more than the dominant rational procedure, and it maintains dominance only because of the force (deceit, fraud, arms, money, prison, and so on) of those who are dominant.

Because of the "form of unity" that lies in Tristram's as well as everyone else's will, it takes a long time before Tristram discovers that his own will is different from that of the state. The origin of Tristram's feeling of alienation lies in his unconscious awareness that the service he owes to Mark inhibits his erotic impulses for the woman he loves. For the most part of his early career, Tristram has nothing of what we might call a life of his own. A life of one's own was simply not provided for in orthodox medieval institutions--or, for that matter, any institution. And yet the frustration of Tristram's erotic impulses leads him to discovers that he does, in fact, have an existence outside of his role as champion of Cornwall. St. Augustine bases his definition of sin upon the discovery of and attention to one's own individual concerns: radix malorum est cupiditas. The origin of sin and human unhappiness is, according to St. Augustine, "a motion of the soul toward the enjoyment of one's self, one's neighbor, or any corporeal thing for the sake of something other than God" (On Christian Doctrine, 88). In orthodox theory, too, it was always argued that an orientation toward the center of the institution actually makes the individual happy and free, as, for example, St. Augustine writes in On Free Choice of the Will (although the point is ubiquitous): "when the highest good has been pursued and obtained, each man becomes happy--which beyond a doubt is what we all wish. . . . No man is happy except through the highest good, which is to be found and included in that truth which we call wisdom." And wisdom is simply "the truth in which the highest good is discerned and grasped" (58-59).

The immaterial obstacle to Tristram's freedom, then, is much more powerful than any material obstacle could ever be, for it has Tristram himself to defend and enforce it. Were Tristram to follow his own impulses, his own eros, and marry Isode--and there is no material obstacle to prevent his doing so--he would lose his sense of value and identity; in theological terms, he would be guilty of mortal sin and no longer pleasing in the sight of God; and in metaphysical terms he would simply cease to exist, at least as champion of Cornwall which is the most important form of existence. Tristram's essence or identity is that of defender of the peace and concord in Cornwall. If he were to marry Isode, he would cease to defend Cornwall or Mark and hence cease to be at all. Although most critics have argued that Malory "blackens" the traditional character of Mark, if we look at Mark without modern sentiment (whose formula is private interest for public good, the opposite of the medieval notion) and approach from him the perspective of the political writings of St. Augustine, Dante, St. Thomas, Salisbury, Innocent III and a whole host of others whose theme is public concord for private good, we discover that Mark is well justified in all that he does. Beginning with St. Augustine, the first assumption of medieval political theorists was that without concord and peace centered in an authority whose prestige and power were unquestionable and derived from God, no personal good was at all possible. St. Augustine insists upon political order and stability because only when a polity is in peace can men devote their energies to the more important task of saving their souls (see "Philosophy and Christianity on Man's End," The City of God, XIX). The political institution, therefore, has no more important function than the maintenance of peace and order, the sort of concord that Dante wrote of as cited a moment ago.

Mark appears evil only from the standpoint of modern individualism and the rejection of the world order as truth, the very position that Malory and the analytic tradition helped establish. To be sure, Malory sees Mark as evil, but Malory was a revolutionary, and his calling Mark evil is a great deal like Martin Luther's or William of Ockham's calling the pope an anti-christ. From an orthodox or a Realist's point of view, there is little difference between Mark and, for example, William the Conqueror who held his son Robert in prison for years and held captive his half-brother, Odo of Bayeaux, in order to insure the absolute authority of his commands. William as much as Mark or Arthur or any pope simply followed the political theory that saw the stability and peace of the state as a manifestation of the order of creation; such order was to be maintained at all costs. It was just this sort of dilemma that heresy presented to defenders of the faith. The consolamentum of the Cathars, for example, suggested a direct communication between the individual and God and thus challenged the hierarchical order of creation and the position of the church at the pinnacle of that order. The debate between the Cathars and the Catholics ended with Innocent III's famous letter of 1205, "Actions rank higher than contemplation," and in his later calls for the "extermination" of the heretics (Heer, 213-214). In this, Innocent III overtly reasons logically. At the Council of Constance in 1414, John Hus was condemned to be burned at the stake for refusing to swear an oath of obedience to the church hierarchy, an institution and officials he charged with corruptions so rife as to be unfit even to call him to judgment.

Malory does not blacken Mark; rather he presents Mark as overtly and unsentimentally concerned with what monarchs of the period (of all periods) were concerned with. We must not think of common good in terms of individual rights and perquisites--that sort of thinking is modern and the result of rebels such as Malory, Ockham, and Luther. Both William of Ockham and Marsilius of Padua were excommunicated for championing the rights of the individual and suggesting that common good meant the good of the plurality. Marsilius even argued for the election of monarchs by a majority vote of the people. The orthodox position is that the common good is the continuity of the office of the king, even if it means the suppression of individual interests and deviations. As Dante points out, "Whoever is mindful of the good of the commonwealth is ipso facto mindful of the purpose of right. The truth of the proposition is proved as follows: the definition of right given in the Digest of Laws, namely, 'Right is a real and personal bond between man and man whose preservation preserves society and whose corruption corrupts society'" (De Monarchia, 32).

The emphasis of Dante's analysis is not upon man and man as it eventually comes to be in Malory's romance between Tristram and Isode or Tristram and Palomides, but rather the emphasis is upon the bond itself or the syncategoremata of ideology. Sustaining the explanatory bond or law, whether behavioral or rational, is always more important than sustaining the individual; Dante earlier points out that "Pythagoras in his system of relations places unity on the side of good and plurality on the side of evil. Thus we can see what sin is: it is to scorn unity and hence to proceed toward plurality" (21). Unity, of course, is a hierarchy which terminates in God, but no individual has direct access to God. The pope is, for all practical purposes, the termination of the hierarchy on earth (although many such as Ockham and Marsilius argued for the primacy of the secular authority), and he therefore possesses a plenitude of power which should be used, actively, to sustain the unity and the hierarchy. Sustaining the hierarchy means exactly sustaining God's created order in the universe: Egidius of Rome writes that "no men are under the rule of Christ unless they are under the supreme pontiff, who is Christ's general vicar." This means that in the words of Augustus Triumphus "the sentence of the pope and the sentence of God are one sentence" (cited by Gewirth, 15-16).

Sustaining the preeminence of the pope becomes, therefore, the same act as sustaining the authority of the word of God. Malory's portrait of King Mark, then, from the standpoint of orthodox medieval metaphysics and political theory, is that of a good king. Tristram as a deviant and insubordinate knight is in Mark's judgment evil. Mark is orientated toward unity, and he is quite correct in his judgment of Tristram as a force for plurality and disorder. At the Round Table, the problem of plurality and concord is handled in a slightly different manner, but the issue remains the same. While Mark relies upon overt coercion, treachery, disguise, and so forth to control plurality, Arthur relies upon the more subtle and ultimately more powerful form of social control which is directed to the individual's mind. Arthur's knights are thoroughly socialized or indoctrinated with the orientation toward the center. This point was developed in Chapter Two. Arthur, moreover, does not need to use the deceptive means that Mark uses because he has Lancelot to enforce the unity, and Lancelot has no identity or being other than his social self- -except for his brief period of madness. It is Lancelot who uses the deception, fraud, treachery, coercion, and force to sustain the unity of the Round Table. The tragedy of the Round Table, however, grows out of Arthur's failure to recognize Lancelot as his worst enemy, a realization that Mark has made of Tristram and one that Mark tries to point out to Arthur:

"And to begyn, the kyngis lettirs [Mark's] spake wondirly shorte unto kynge Arthur, and bade hym entermete with hymself and wyth hys wyff, and of his kynghtes, for he [Mark] was able to rule his wyff and his knights" (381).

Malory's attitude toward Mark, what amounts to hatred, reveals his own dissent from the medieval synthesis. The Round Table is not a counter-reality that Tristram aspires to but merely the coercive nature of an institution as it normally appears--with its repressive measures well disguised as logic, law, and the common good. All Malory does to Mark is make the motivations for his actions overt and personal, but Mark does no worse to Tristram than any number of kings, popes, and overlords had done to their subjects and than was done to Malory himself. And yet many of these kings were given the title of "saint" by subsequent generations. The title does not represent a sentimental concern for fellow men, as the histories of such persons (even Arthur) would have us believe, but rather it derives from their success making institution dominant and therefore making dominant the illusion that the interests of the dominant class are the interests of all men and women.

If someone wanted to say that the "Tristram" section contains the sins or the causes which undermine the Round Table, we had better be clear about just what those sins are. They are not the adulterous affairs of Tristram, Isode, or Lamerok, the treachery of Mark, or the feuding of the Orkneys. There can be little doubt that Malory's purpose was just the opposite; his purpose in including the "Tristram" was not to expose the sins of the knights as individuals but to expose the repressive nature of all institutions and social order. The great sin in Le Morte Darthur is the Round Table's seizure of the knight's means for finding value and meaning in his life and its demand that the knight submit himself to the ideology of the institution in order to achieve any identity and feeling of value. The petty immoralities of the knights are in actuality their rather feeble attempts to find a unique outlet for personal energies or, in other cases, the simple recognition that the set of ideologically validated acts is inadequate for occupying all a knight's time and interests and inadequate for all the situations the individual might face. In the face of overweening ideological control, the individual may have to resort to perverse and destructive actions in order to assert his own eros; this is either the bullying of social inferiors by what Nietzsche calls men of resentment or the masochism of the severely erotically repressed.

Certainly the motivation underlying Lamerok's love for Queen Morgause is the anxiety he experiences in performance of cultural ideals. We must wonder why Lamerok would be willing to fight Meleagant to the point of death for love of "quene Morgause of Orkeney, modir unto sir Gawayne, for she ys the fayryst lady that beryth the lyff" (298). Considering the hatred that the Orkneys have for Lamerok resulting from their belief that Pellinore killed King Lot, Morgause is precisely the wrong woman for Lamerok to love. The affair can lead only to social disruption. Tony Tanner is his study, Adultery in the Novel recognizes this overt pursuit of self-destruction as the major theme of medieval romance literature. Commenting upon the Tristan he writes: "But in his endless compulsive return to the gravitational center of his desire, he is continually reapproaching the point of his own destruction. 'Madman, will you forever be seeking death?' asks a loyal friend. The answer is yes, because it is inseparable from forever seeking Iseult" (32).

Tanner, however, never adequately answers the question why so many of the greatest heroes of the later Middle Ages or of the nineteenth century should seek their own destruction in precisely this manner. The cause is the dominant explanation which demands an orientation toward the highest good and the highest beauty and makes impossible, therefore, the simple, but pluralistic, impulse of the individual to express his eros or to feel that "every man thynkith hys own lady fayryste, and thoughe I prayse the lady I love most, ye [Lancelot] sholde nat be wrothe. For thoughe my lady quene Gwenyver be fayryst in your eye, wyte you well quene Morgause of Orkney ys fayryste in myne eye, and so every knyght thynkith hys owne lady fayryste" (298). To the orthodox mind, such pluralism is unthinkable, sinful, insane, and a source of pain and death--as it certainly turns out to be for Lamerok. But Malory as an advocate of the emerging individualism would not call this orientation a sin at all. Lamerok's expression of his own point of view is destructive because his society holds that point of view to be sinful and exerts all its power to crush such deviants.

As the romance progresses comments about the genuinely good and moral (not in a orthodox sense) character of Tristram increase in number and seriousness. Palomides is the chief knight to recognize the humanly healthy nature of Tristram. Although Tristram remains for Palomides the greatest obstacle to his own career in social climbing and although Tristram causes Palomides a great deal of suffering, Palomides recognizes a special love between himself and Tristram: "My lorde, sir Trystram, muche am I beholdynge unto you of youre grete goodnes, that wolde proffir youre noble body to rescow me undeserved, for I have greatly offended you" (472). Although at the Tournament of the Castle of Maidens Tristram frustrates Palomides' eros for worship to the point that Palomides remarks that if he could meet Tristram alone in the forest "I would fyght with hym . . . and ease my harte uppon hym," Palomides can overcome his institutionally mandated hatred and see deeper into Tristram, acknowledging that "to say the sothe, sir Trystram ys the jantytllyste knyght in thys worlde lyvynge" (325). The context and tone of such passages, moreover, suggests that Malory is sympathetic and sincere. While for Lancelot, who never abandons his orientation toward Arthur and the explanatory center, comments about his moral character increasingly appear in an ironic context so that a pathetic distrust grows around the name of Lancelot. One needs only to examine the events involving the Maid of Astolat or Meleagant to see that the acts which should exemplify Lancelot's moral character are not very humanly healthy. They rather maintain only ideological cohesion. No one criticizes Lancelot because of the institutional costs of doing so: "the kynge was full lothe that such a noyse shulde be uppon sir Launcelot and his quene; for the kynge had a demyng of hit, but he wold nat here thereoff, for sir Launcelot had done so much for hym and for the quene so many tymes that wyte you well the kynge loved hym passyngly well" (674).

These late adventures of Lancelot should be compared with the late adventures of Tristram with Dynadan, Gareth, and Palomides, for it becomes readily apparent that the tone of the passages tells Malory's intentions. Vinaver thinks that Tristram's apparent happiness during his late period results from Malory's disinterest in the traditional tragedy: "he [Malory] insists on making his heroes uniformly happy" (750). But in fact

Tristram is not really very happy at all; he seems so only to the reader who instinctively compares him with Lancelot. When the two are taken side by side, Tristram for all his overt problems is the more happy.

It is remarkable that Malory's critics have discounted his interest in the psychological conditions of the characters. Lancelot's unhappiness--"But, madame, ever I muste suffir you, but what sorow that I endure, ye take no forse" (642)--is the manifestation of an extreme and advanced psychosis. There is no organic cause for this trauma; rather its origin is cultural and religious. The premise of Freud's Civilization and Its Discontents is that "What we call our civilization is largely responsible for our misery, and that we should be much happier if we gave up and returned to primitive conditions" (33). But it is, in fact, impossible to give up civilization, for what one is, his identity, is a product of his experience within society and therefore to escape civilization would mean to escape oneself, an impossible act except through suicide. Only Palomides degenerates this far. While there is no escape from civilization, cultural innovation and transcendence remain possible. Freud goes on to point out that "It was discovered that a person becomes neurotic because he cannot tolerate the amount of frustration which society imposes on him in the service of its cultural ideals" (34). Lancelot's psychosis appears whenever he is in a position that demonstrates to him that as the flower of knighthood he embodies the explanatory synthesis; it appears because at these moments he understands that in submitting himself totally to the quest for the explanatory center he has relinquished everything that might be uniquely his. In short Lancelot realizes that as an individual he has ceased to exist; he is no more than a function or an extension of the institution.

In the very cogent tale of the "Fair Maid of Astolat," Lancelot is offered the opportunity to dissent from the ideology in the love of a woman who loves him "oute of measure"; that is, who loves him in an irrational and anti-explanatory or un-orthodox manner. This is Lancelot's chance to repudiate the control of Arthur and the Round Table by taking a lover who is suited to him as an individual. But of course Lancelot refuses her saying that "I love nat to be constrayned to love, for love muste only aryse of the harte selff, and nat by none constraynte" (641). The opposite is, however, the truth;

Lancelot is constrained by his orientation toward the center to love Guinevere, the highest lady, and no other lady. What his love for Guinevere amounts to, since it can never be openly expressed, is a renunciation of love altogether. Institutions require such renunciations on the part of individuals; as Freud remarks, "it is impossible to overlook the extent to which civilization is built up upon a renunciation of instinct, how much it presupposes precisely the non-satisfaction (by suppression, repression, or some other means?) of powerful instincts. This `cultural frustration´ dominates the large field of social relationships between human beings" (44).

Our awareness of the constraints upon Lancelot comes in the perception of Lancelot´s unconscious wish to be against Arthur. This is, as Freud writes, "The urge for freedom [which], therefore, is directed against particular forms and demands of civilization or against civilization altogether" (43). At the tournament of Winchester, Lancelot wears Elaine´s red sleeve and vows "at that justys I woll be ayenste the kynge and ayenste all his felyship" (622). Lancelot´s subtle rebellion against Arthur represents his moment of freedom from the oppressiveness of culture, as is recognized by the hermit who cares for the wounded Lancelot after the tournament:

> `On whose party was he?´ seyde the ermyte.
> `Sir,´ seyde sir Lavayne, `he was thys day ayenste kynge Arthure, and there he wanne the pryce of all the knyghtis of the Rounde Table.´
> `I have seyne the day,´ seyde the ermyte, `I wolde have loved hym the worse bycause he was ayenste my lorde kynge Arthure, for sometyme I was one of the felyship, but now I thanke God I am othirwyse disposed. But where ys he? Lat me se hym.´ (628)

The hermit provides the model for Lancelot´s negation of civilization and release from suffering and psychosis. But as soon as Lancelot comes again to the Round Table and sees Guinevere, his freedom vanishes and his suffering returns. He falls again under the constraints of culture.

Tristram suffers the same psychosis or meaninglessness as does Lancelot, but he, unlike Lancelot, is able to do something about it. He becomes consciously aware of the emptiness of the explanatory center which claims to provide the direction for his life and he brings out into the open the incoherencies of the center. Tristram accepts that there exists a plurality of views about any issue and comes to recognize his own personal view as it appears in opposition to the official view of Mark. Tristram discovers his personal identity in opposition to his role as Mark's champion, and he abandons his allegiance to Mark because there is nothing else he can do if he is to stay alive. He abandons the set of explanations which are his culture and identity because they now demand his death.

The sins, therefore, which undermine the Round Table and lead to the tragedy are not to be associated with Tristram, for it is he who eventually comes to terms with his own sins while Lancelot is destroyed by his. But by these sins, Malory does not mean the petty immoralities we so often hear literary critics trot out, but rather the one large sin of submitting oneself whole-heartedly to the ideology. Such submission or orientation toward the universal concord of wills controls both Cornwall and Camelot, but only at Cornwall does it become an open topic of dispute. Sublimation of the personal erotic energy into the social goals or quests, it will be recalled, forms the basis of the tales of Gareth and Balin; both lives end in the tragic situation in which one member of the society kills another believing that he is doing the right thing and is carrying out his socially validated quest. There is no such tragic end to the "Tristram" because the issue of social repression is resolved before it can reach its logical consequence.

3.3 The Father and the Son

The current discussion of the political structure in both Cornwall and Camelot is meant to bring to light the two central features of institutional life which Malory regards as the inherent tragedy of political life: the necessity of the weakness or submissiveness of the knight and the overwhelming power of the king as the embodiement of the institution itself. In the structure of any institution, the "bonum privatum" is perforce the "bonum commune," no matter how much rhetoric exists to explain it in another way. As John Morrall in Political Thought in Medieval Times points out, no other issue more than this problem of the plenitude of power occupied the thoughts of the great politicians, ecclesiastics, philosophers, and poets of the thirteenth, fourteenth, and fifteenth century. In his depiction, Malory represents newly emerged and growing contemporary conceptions of the state, church, or body-politic as corporation; Morrall writes, "Some thirteenth-century thinkers, notably Pope Innocent IV (1243-1245), himself a distinguished canonist, thought it perfectly possible to reconcile the idea of the whole church as a corporation with papal plenitudo potestatis. They did so by arguing that all the powers of a corporation were vested in its head, in this case the Papacy. Here again we meet an echo of the absolutist interpretation of Roman Law"

(57). The metaphysical implications of the issue were vast, for
if power were not centralized in the head as microcosm of the
corporation and if the plurality of wills were not oriented
toward concord, how could one claim unity and order for the
created world itself?   But how does Malory see it?   The chief
characteristics of both Mark and Arthur are these needs of
making themselves supreme in their own land and securing the
stability of their own positions as corporate microcosm.   The
means of doing that require necessarily repression of plurality.
No one will be surprised by this interpretation of Mark; after
all, he openly murders his own brother, Baldwin, because

> Whan kynge Marke wyste this [that Baldwin defeated
> the Saracens] he was wondirly wrothe that his
> brother sholde wynne suche worship and honour.
> And bycause this prynce was bettir beloved than he
> in all that contrey, and also this prynce Bodwyne
> lovid well sir Trystram, and therefore he thought to
> sle hym.   (388)

Mark invites Baldwin to Cornwall with the intent to
murder him, and what he says to Baldwin reveals why.   This is
not petty jealousy, but rather Malory's open description of the
responsibilities of the king as institutional center:

> `Brothir, how sped you whan the myscreauntes
> aryved by you?   Mesemyth hit had bene your parte
> to have sente me worde, that I myght have bene at
> that journey; for hit had bene reson that I had had
> the honoure and nat you.´   (389)

The reason that Mark kills Baldwin is to maintain the
hierarchical order of the devotion of the people and to maintain
the image of unity and centrality of power.   The unity is
maintained through the symbiosis of the king and the champion;
Mark would have sent Tristram to fight with the Saracens, but
Tristram as champion of Cornwall would demonstrate that Mark
holds the seat of power.
    These concerns are of utmost importance to Mark, and the
situation for Arthur is no different.   The fact that a power
exists which is not under the total control of the king implies

that the king is weak and that his society in being a plurality is evil and weak.   When Arthur finally understands that Lancelot might direct his energies toward goals other than Arthur's power, he understands also that the institution will collapse: "'Jesu mercy!' seyde the kynge, 'he ys a mervaylous knyght of proues.   And alas,' seyde the kynge, 'me sore repentith that ever sir Launcelot sholde be ayenste me, for now I am sure the noble felyshyp of the Rounde Table ys brokyn for ever'" (682).   When Arthur first sees Tristram at the Tournament of the Castle of Maidens, moreover, he thinks of Tristram as a free force capable of upsetting the hierarchy of his knights and thus a threat to himself.   Tristram's allegiance to Arthur must be acquired.   Lancelot is Arthur's means of subduing Tristram.   At the Tournament, Tristram defeats all of Arthur's knights while Lancelot looks on from the sidelines:

> Than sir Trystram rode here and there and ded hys grete payne, that a twelve of the good knyghtes of the bloode of kynge Ban that were of sir Launcelottis kyn that day sir Trystram smote downe, that all the estatis mervayled of their great dedis, and all people cryede uppon the knyght with the blacke shylde.   (326)

Lancelot is aware that the hierarchy and social order are about to be overthrown:

> So thys cry was so large that sir Launcelot harde hit, and than he gate a grete speare in hys honde and cam towardis the cry.   (326)

In the fight that ensues, Lancelot seriously wounds Tristram in the side, and Tristram rides off into the forest not to be seen again by the knights of the Round Table until his fight with Lancelot at the great stone of Camelot.   In the defeat of Tristram, Lancelot insures that he remains the top-rated knight and secures, thereby, Arthur's position as top-rated king: "Sir Launcelot hath wonne the filde thys day!" (328).   Pretending modesty Lancelot replies, "Sir Trystram hath won the fylde, for he began firste, and lengyst hylde on, and so hathe he done the firste day, the secunde, and the thirde day!" (328).   But the people for whom the social hierarchy is the foundation of their own self-conception will not accept Lancelot's denial. Malory emphasizes their hierarchical identifications:

> Than all the astatis and degrees, hyghe and lowe, seyde of sir Launcelot grete worship for the honoure that he ded to sir Trystram, and for the honoure of doying by sir. Launcelot he was at that tyme more praysed and renowmed than and he had overthrowyn fyve hondred knyghtes. And all the peple hole for hys jantilnes, firste the astatis, hyghe and lowe, and after the comynalte, at onys cryed
> 'Sir Launcelot hath won the gre, whosoever sayth nay!' (328)

The most important point, however, is Arthur's response; he wants to acquire Tristram and to do so he manipulates Lancelot by withholding his own ascription of "worship" that Lancelot should receive for his act as Arthur's champion and by instilling in Lancelot feelings of guilt for not completing Arthur's wishes.

> 'So God me helpe,' seyde kynge Arthur, 'I am more hevy that I can nat mete with hym [Tristram] than I am for all the hurtys that all my knyghtes have had at the turnement.' (329)

Arthur's lack of concern for his own knights is typical and indicates that he is more concerned with assimilating an unregulated power into his own circle. He goes on to praise Tristram so much that Lancelot begins to feel that in defeating Tristram he has offended Arthur. But the real motive of Arthur's praise for Tristram is to get Lancelot to bring him back to the Round Table. Lancelot's response to Arthur's praise of Tristram is very interesting for it shows the kind of control that Arthur exerts upon Lancelot and the kind of means that Lancelot must use to support Arthur:

> 'for all the londys that ever my fadir leffte I wolde nat have hurt sir Trystram and I had knowyn hym at that tyme that I hurte hym: for I saw not hys

shylde. For <u>and I had seyne hys blacke shylde</u>, I
wolde nat have medled with hym for many causis.'
(329, emphasis mine)

Lancelot's excuses are outright lies; he challenged
Tristram with the words: "Knyght with the blacke shylde, make
ye redy to just with me!" (326). But Arthur has forced him to
lie by changing his will and, of course, Lancelot must support
Arthur's will. Lancelot, as Arthur's champion, always follows
what he perceives to be the will of Arthur, and this orientation
means that many times Lancelot will have to perform
contradictory actions or repudiate one act in favor of another
which supports better the will of Arthur. This kind of
frustration accounts for Lancelot's psychosis and for the fact
that whenever he can Lancelot disguises himself so that he will
not have to perform the will of Arthur.

In the passage at hand, Arthur goes on to blame Lancelot
directly for the loss of Tristram. We should compare Mark's
accusations against his brother Baldwin with Arthur's
accusations against Lancelot. In both cases, the knight's
impulsiveness is taken as the cause of the king's displeasure, in
spite of the fact that the knights only acted to protect their
kings from an immediate and serious threat. Arthur tells
Lancelot that "Had nat ye bene, we had nat loste sir Trystram,
for he was here dayly unto the tyme ye mette with hym. And
in an evyll tyme . . . ye encountred with hym." And finally by
the power of guilt and of suggestion, Arthur prompts Lancelot
to vow to bring Tristram in, dead or alive, to the court of the
Round Table. It is important that the king does not demand
performance from his champion; rather the will of the king and
the will of the champion are held to be one so that the wishes
of the king are the thoughts of the other. Arthur never tells
Lancelot what to do, but the social structure makes clear what
is expected of him. The concord of wills was held by the
Middle Ages to be a symbiosis in which the king benefitted only
as much as the individual. But a close reading of Malory's
portrayal of the king-champion relationship suggests that the
individual will is dominated totally by the king's will. Lancelot
has to change his will or position three times in order to
conform to Arthur's needs. Lancelot never wanted to fight with
Tristram in the first place, but he did so to protect the

hierarchy of the Round Table. Lancelot's final response to Arthur shows that he is a man so totally frustrated by the demands society imposes upon him that he will carry out the next duty without regard for its inherent goodness or evil. He has toally submitted his own judgment and his own will to the common will:

> 'My lorde Arthure,' seyde sir Launcelot, 'ye shall undirstonde the cause. Ye put now uppon me that I sholde be causer of hys departicion; God knoweth hit was ayenste my wyll! But whan men bene hote in dedis of armys, oftyn hit ys seyne they hurte their frendis as well as their foys. And, my lorde,' seyde sir Launcelot, 'ye shall undirstonde that sir Trystram ys a man that I am ryght lothe to offende to, for he hath done more for me than ever y ded for hym as yet.'
> '. . . And as for me,' seyde sir Launcelot, 'I promyse you uppon thys booke that, and I may mete with hym, other with fayrenes othir with fowlnes, I shall brynge hym to this courte other elles I shall dye therefore.' (330-31)

Lancelot is a man who has been manipulated by the system to the point that he cannot respond to any influences upon his actions except the will of Arthur. Arthur has become his conscience. In the repudiation of other demands such as Lancelot's personal interest in the "fayrness othir fowlness" of his own position, his debt of friendship to Tristram, and his instinct to self-preservation, we see the self-centeredness of the king and the institution. We also see that the demands of the institution often leave the individual ashamed and embarrassed that he has succeeded so well in something that he cannot personally assent to. After defeating Tristram and receiving the "gre"--that is, after insuring that all is ordered by degree, as cited above--Malory tells us that "Than was sir Launcelot wrothe and ashamed" (328).

This sort of manipulation and self-centeredness which produces such negative feelings in individuals is precisely the character of both Mark and Arthur. On a later occasion, for example, when Arthur suddenly desires to get a close look at

Isode, he overrules Lancelot's advice that such a visit would be an insult to Tristram: "sir, I pray you, be nat to hasty; for peradventure there woll be some knyghtes that woll be displeased and we come suddenly uppon them." Arthur's only reply is characteristic: "`As for that,´ seyde kynge Arthure, `I woll se her, for I take no forse whom I gryeve" (451-52). And again in calling the Tournament of Surluse, Arthur demonstrates his concern for enhancing institutional order and his carelessness for the labor and suffering of his men:

> `Sir,´ seyde sir Launcelot, `by this cry that ye have made ye woll put us that bene aboute you in grete jouparte, for there be many knyghtes that hath envy to us. Therefore whan we shall mete at the day of justis there woll be harde skyffte for us.´
> `As for that,´ seyde kynge Arthure, `I care nat. There shall we preve whoo shall be beste of his hondis.´ (416)

Although it is only Mark who is called "the destroyer of all good knyghtes" and although Bors tells Lancelot that "there ys one thyng shall corrayge you and us all: ye know that kynge Arthur and kynge Marke were never of lyke condycions" (681), it seems rather that Mark and Arthur are identical in what they demand from their knights. The king never understands very well the intra-structure of the knights for he is outside of the community of knights and above them; in general terms, institutions never intend to serve personal interests of members, except for those personal interests that the institution has induced members to hold. Tristram and Lancelot understand each other perfectly well, and naturally Mark and Arthur understand each other very well. What separates them is the difference between Tristram and Lancelot. Had Lancelot openly challenged Arthur as Tristram eventually does, Arthur would certainly have sought Lancelot's destruction. While Lancelot remains absolutely faithful to Arthur, some intuition that will not break onto the surface of consciousness keeps nagging at him that Arthur is, in fact, his greatest enemy and destroyer. On numerous occasions, he wonders what reason there is to fight for Arthur. For example, after Arthur has insisted upon invading Isode's privacy, a fight develops in which Palomides gives Arthur a great fall; Lancelot, knowing that Arthur was in the wrong and that he received only what he deserved, also knows that he must avenge his lord:

> `As for to juste wyth me,´ seyde sir Launcelot, `I woll nat fayle you for no drede that I have of you [Tristram]. But I am lothe to have ado wyth you and I myght chose, for I woll that ye wyte that I muste revenge my speciall lorde and my moste bedrad frynde that was unhorsed unwarely and unknyghtly. And therefore, sir, thoughe I revenge that falle, take ye no displesure, for he is to me such a frynde that I may nat se hym shamed´ (452, emphasis mine)

Lancelot´s words (including more lies) enable Tristram to recognize him and Tristram declines to fight; the words are important because they show us what Lancelot thinks of Arthur and how Tristram recognizes both Lancelot and Arthur: "`But I shall nat forgete,´ seyde sir Trystram, `the wordys of sir Launcelot when he called hym a man of grete worshyp, and thereby I wyste that hit was kynge Arthure´" (453, emphasis mine). Nowhere does Lancelot call him a man of great worship; rather, he called him a "special friend," a "dreaded" friend and "such a friend" that, as he mumbles to himself immediately prior to confronting Tristram, "whethir I lyve or dye, nedys muste I revenge my lorde Arthure, and so I woll, whatsomever befalle me" (452). Lancelot´s words are much more equivocal than what Tristram repeats to Palomides, and they suggest that the image of Arthur Lancelot holds in his mind is of a far different sort of king than the institutional conceptions of Arthur denote. Lancelot regards Arthur as something to which he has wholly submitted himself for better or for worse; he has no ability of his own to choose. Lancelot´s devotion to Arthur is precisely the submission described by Dante in De Monarchia to the good of the whole community, as described in the last section. Arthur, then, in the imagination of Lancelot holds the position of the institution itself. Chapter Two of this study argued that the explanatory synthesis reified in the institution holds the position of creative source of a knight´s identity. Malory depicts a father-son relationship between the king and his champion or the institution and the individual.   John of Paris (1250-1306) in his On Royal and Papal Power explains why the king must be the focal point of all individuals in a community: "A society in which everyone seeks only his own advantage will collapse and disintegrate unless it is ordered to the good of all by some one ruler who has charge of the common good, just as a man's body would collapse if there were not in it some general force directing the common good of the members as a whole" (77).   We should recall that in discussing things which men must love St. Augustine includes "the state itself, which is usually held to have the place of a parent" (On Free Choice of the Will, 31).   Medieval political tracts are replete with similar analogies; St. Thomas' On Kingship is typical of the arguments: "Hence the man ruling a perfect community, i.e., a city or a province, is antonomastically called the king.   The ruler of a household is called father, not king, although he bears a certain resemblance to the king, for which reason kings are sometimes called the fathers of their peoples" (I, i, 14).

Le Morte Darthur depicts a father-son relationship fraught with problems, what Freud has called the Oedipus Complex.   Freud always felt that more has been known about the Oedipus Complex and its related Castration Complex in myths and literature than psychoanalysis could ever hope to elucidate, and it seems to me that the writers of Arthurian Romance and Courtly Love literature have been particularly acute in perceiving the tensions, neuroses, and cultural crises that the Oedipus Complex is a name for.   They tell of the adventures of knights who for reasons they are unable to analyze must love the wives of men who hold for them a father-position.   Malory, as well as medieval thought in general, asserts an identity along a hierarchical scale among the father, the king, the state, and God.   In Freudian terms these are fathers in that they create out of the individual who is a no-man a social self and identity with value, in the same sense that St. Thomas argues that all kings are in essence founders of their cities or nations.   They become the source of the son's super-ego and his ability to analyze and reflect upon himself as a being with certain characteristics.   But this is a father who, as we discover, demands the absolute submission of the son. The Oedipus Complex arises only as the son begins to assert his own independence and begins to respond to emerging impulses of psychic or erotic energy which demand fulfillment that the father cannot accept. To resolve this tension was the central cultural crisis of the late Middle Ages for which conceptions of "plenitudo potestatis" were designed, and it was also the crisis that gave rise to Martin Luther's tormented career. He begins his Treatise on Christian Liberty with the basic tension of the Oedipus Complex between duty and freedom:

> I shall set down the following two propositions concerning the freedom and bondage of the spirit:
> A Christian is a perfectly free lord of all, subject to none.
> A Christian man is a perfectly dutiful servant of all, subject to all.
> These two theses seem to contradict each other. If, however, they should be found to fit together they would serve our purpose beautifully. (277)

At an earlier period in the Middle Ages, the time of St. Thomas, John of Salisbury, Alanus, or Dante, for example, the tension between the individual and the institution was resolved at least in political theories favoring duty, but later writers-- Malory, Marsilius, Wycliff, or Luther--who asserted pluralism never found the harmony. Malory openly makes this condition the theme of his version of the "Tristram" and the "Quest of the Holy Grail." Early in the Grail Quest, for example, Galahad comes upon Nacien the hermit who tells him of the great sin of the world:

> `Sir, I shall telle you what betokenyth of that ye saw in the tombe. Sir, that that coverede the body, hit betokenyth the duras of the worlde, and the grete synne that oure Lorde founde in the worlde. For there was suche wrecchydnesse that the fadir loved nat the sonne, nother the sonne loved nat the fadir. And that was one of the causys that oure Lorde toke fleysh and bloode of a clene maydyn; for oure synnes were so grete at that tyme that well-nyghe all was wyckednesse.´ (528)

When this passage is compared with its French source, it becomes quite clear how much peripheral matter Malory omitted in order to focus simply on the hatred between the father and the son. The focus is the same in the "Tristram":

> Than Kynge Marke had grete dispyte at sir Trystram. And whan he chaced hym oute of Cornwayle (yette was he nevew unto kynge Marke, but he had grete suspeccion unto sir Trystram bycause of his quene, La Beall Isode, for hym semed that there was muche love betwene them twayne), so whan Trystram was departed oute of Cornwayle into Ingelonde, kynge Marke harde of the grete proues that sir Trystram ded there, wyth the whyche he greved. (353)

We must always be aware that "sir Trystrams was nat so behated as was sir Launcelot, nat wythin the realme of Ingelonde" (411, but the comment is frequently made). This hatred is that of the state and all those who identify with it for the individual. Malory concerns himself with all levels of the Oedipus Complex; and this concern may underlie his desire to write the whole book of King Arthur. The father embodies all the social and religious restrictions and requirements placed upon an individual and against which the individual's own psychic energy strives for fulfillment. In short, the father is, as Freud sees him, the force of frustrations of the erotic impulses and the pleasure principle. I shall return to this erotic or psychic energy, but first it is necessary to examine a little more the nature of the father.

This father-figure Freud describes in terms of a hypothetical primal horde. The point is not to suggest that such a primal horde and primal father ever existed but rather to assert that the social or corporate relations illustrated in the primitive situation are abstracted from present social situations just as the one that Malory presents. Freud describes the primal father as a terrifying figure whose self-interest, jealousy, violent power, suspicions of his sons, and seeming immortality (the son never experiences the origin of the father) led to the murder, maiming (often castration), or banishment of the sons--just what Mark attempts to do to Tristram in the passage cited above. The son carries with him overwhelming fantasies of the tremendous power of the father. To the boy or young knight, the father appears mysterious and god-like because he has driven out, maimed, or rendered subordinate all other males of a competing stature with the father. We should recall Arthur's wars with the Eleven Kings, the Five Kings, and Emperor Lucius and Malory's frequent comments at this time that "kynge Arthure dud so mervaylesly in armys that all men had wondir" (19). As the sons reach maturity, the father requires of them complete submission in the form of identification with him and renunciation of erotic impulses. The father keeps all the females and property for himself, and thus in frustrating the son's erotic impulses insures a class of sons who are weak and inferior to the father.

It is always well to remember, as Matthew Erdelyi reminds us, that psychoanalysis is a metaphoric science; it describes the contents of inaccessible mental regions in analogies and images that make sense to the conscious mind. The point is that symptoms and behaviors have meanings in the same way that images and metaphors do (see Psychoanalysis: Freud's Cognitive Psychology, 24 and 109-115). The image of a primal father is exactly how Lancelot sees God in a dream. The dream, of course, expresses more clearly the real feelings that Lancelot has about God and Arthur because only in a dream can Lancelot's thoughts be free from the controls of reason and dogma which require Lancelot's repression of his own independent impulses. Lancelot sees God as an old man who demands submission of his sons and banishes those, like Lancelot, who will not submit:

> And anone as he was on slepe hit befyll hym there a vision; that there com a man afore hym all bycompast with sterris, and that man had a crowne of golde on hys hede. And that man lad in hys felyship seven kynges and two knyghtes, and all thes worshipt the crosse, knelyng uppon their kneys, holdyng up their hondys towarde the hevyn, and all they seyde:
>
> `Swete Fadir of Hevyn, com and visite us, and yelde unto everych of us as we have deserved.´
>
> Than loked sir Launcelot up to the hevyn and hym semed the clowdis ded opyn, and an old man

com downe with a company of angels and alyghte amonge them and gaff unto everych hys blyssynge and called them hys servauntes and hys good and trew knyghtes. And whan thys olde man had seyde thus he com to one of the kynghtes and seyde,

`I have loste all that I have besette in the, for thou hast ruled the ayenste me as a warryoure and used wronge warris with vayneglory for the pleasure of the worlde more than to please me, therefore thou shalt be confounded withoute thou yelde me my tresoure.´ (553-54)

The sons´ identification with the father causes them to see the father´s cruelty in the way the father himself sees it: as blessings and bounty toward his true sons. What God objects to is Lancelot´s vayneglory which is in Freudian terms eros and the pleasure principle. Because Lancelot would not renounce these forms of individualism and self-love, God banishes him from the society of Celestial Knights. God alludes to St. Augustine´s doctrine that no man ought to love himself or any thing of the world for its own sake but rather for the sake of God. This orientation toward the father amounts to a renunciation of eros, for eros is always an inherent threat to the position of God or of the king. The kings Malory presents are always aware of what all fathers fear and what is so well expressed in an unpublished study of Finnegan´s Wake by Nathan Halper:

And when he looks at Shaun, the Father sees himself. He sees himself--unmarred by time, by guilt, by defeat. He sees himself--unshamed by Shem.

In the Future, Shaun--unshamed by Shem--he will do all the things that the Father did not do.

In him he will live again.

And yet--he himself replaced his own Father. Knowing this, the Father knows that his son will replace him.

He knows that this son will wear the face of Shaun. . . .

He, who was Tristan once, sees himself as Mark.

Shaun is Tristan now.

Shaun is Edipus. He will be king.

He is the Edipus who will take the Father's wife.
Who will take the Father's life.

And yet--the Father knows he himself was
Edipus. He himself was Tristan once.

His anxieties mingle with a sense of guilt. (cited
by Mullahy, 112-13)

Malory's Le Morte Darthur tells two tales simultaneously:
the tale of the death of the sons at the hands of the father and
the tale of the death of the father's position of authority. The
final meaning of his version of the "Tristram" and the "Quest of
the Holy Grail" is the revolt of the disinherited; it is the tale of
a son who "shold passe hys fadir as much as the lyon passith
the lybarde, both of strength and of hardines" (542), and the
tale about "tho dayes [when] the sonne spared nat the fadir no
more than a stranger" (546). Here again Malory looks like a
cultural vandal. He wants to attack the culture, but he knows
one can never get outside of culture in order to make a direct
confrontation; the entire being of a son, moreover, is composed
of internalized orientations of the father. The attack,
therefore, is a concealed one; in the father's ruthless repression
of his sons we ultimately see the injustice of the father's
demands. The Morte is tragedy because there is no
transcendent life for the sons who, like Galahad, surpass their
father's greatness. Malory's attack works through the reader's
recognition of the injustice of the son's death, and in this sense
the Grail Quest serves as the transition between the tale of
Tristram and "The most Piteous Tale of the Morte Arthur Saunz
Guerdon." In the "Tristram" and "Grail" the father is successful
in driving out the son and finally killing him, whereas in the
"Morte Arthur" the son succeeds in killing the father--Mordred
and Arthur. The death of Arthur means the destruction of the
larger father which is the civilization and its explanatory
system as the source of the repression of individuals.

In this final fight, Mordred is also killed, and it seems
that neither Malory nor the other writers of Arthurian Romance
were able to conceive of the existence of individuals without a
civilization, for, as they perceived, identity and self are social
constructs and the individual, therefore, depends upon the

society for his life. As revolutionary as much of Arthurian Romance is, it still needs the orthodox institution against which to rebell. In Gottfried's Tristan, complete freedom exists for Tristan and Isolde in the cave of lovers, but they return to Cornwall and are far happier for, as Gottfried tells us, the sake of God and for their place in society. Malory's Tristram does not remain forever at the Joyous Garde but returns to Cornwall to harp in front of Isode in Mark's castle where such an act will clearly be rebellious. Erich Fromm has pointed out in his Escape From Freedom that in repressive societies sin and disobedience of authorities are the first acts of freedom and are the first acts of assertion of the individual will. Deprived of the authority which maintains the definitions of what is sinful, the repressed individual cannot find freedom at all. Tristram and Isode, therefore, feel less free in isolation than they do in Cornwall because at this first stage of rebellion they can only conceive of their freedom and individuality over against or in opposition to some authority. Fromm calls this first stage of revolt against the father "freedom from"; the later stage of development which Arthurian Romance anticipates but does not achieve is the "freedom to" (24-39). It remained for later thinkers of the Reformation and Renaissance to establish the independence of the individual or at least establish a new institution and explanation to which the individual could become attached. Arthur and Mordred simply kill each other because the writers of Arthurian Romance could never conceive of life in which the two, the father and the son, were separate.

On this highly abstracted and symbolic level, the desire of all kings, fathers, gods, and the inertia of institutions toward stability is ultimately the death of male babies because of the inherent threat of replacement and disunity that the male child poses. Arthur, like Herod, heard the prophecy that a son had been born who would grow up to destroy the king and all his land. Arthur's only salvation lay in the order to kill all male babies born on May day. For Tristram, the theme becomes explicit while on his way from Ireland to Cornwall bringing Isode to King Mark in his adventure at the Castle Plewre (the weeping castle) where he encounters an evil custom held by Sir Brewnor. This episode suggests that the custom itself or the civilization, as Freud maintains, is the source of the frustrations and unhappiness in individual lives. Malory has already established that Tristram should have married Isode himself; they have drunk the love potion and have consumated their love, but Tristram's duty to Mark prohibits his loving anyone outside of Mark. Loving someone other than Mark would mean obtaining his own creative source and a life of his own. His obligations to Mark also prevent him from seeking Lancelot and increasing his fame in an area not related to the championship of Cornwall: "Alas . . . and I had nat this messayge in hande with this fayre lady, truly I wolde never stynte or I had founde sir Launcelot" (263).

The custom of the Castle Plewre and, indeed, civilization in general "was suche that who that rode by that castell and brought ony lady wyth hym he must nedys fyght with the lorde that hyght Brewnour" (258). The implications of the custom are that knights must not have ladies, that Brewnor wishes to kill all knights with ladies, and that all ladies belong to Brewnor. After the fight, Brewnor compares the knight's lady with his own, keeping the fairer one and killing the fouler. This custom--because Brewnor has always won in the past-- insures the maintenance of the hierarchical explanation of society; the highest man will be matched with the most beautiful lady. The metaphoric value of the episode at the Castle Plewre is that it represents Tristram's acquiescence to Mark's scheme (or evil usage) for getting the beautiful Isode as his wife and getting Tristram killed in the process. Mark and Sir Brewnor in their regard for Tristram are identical:

> So whan this was done kynge Mark caste all the the wayes that he myght to dystroy sir Trystrames, and than imagened in hymselff to sende sir Trystramys into Irelonde for La Beale Isode. For sir Trystrames had so preysed her for hir beaute and hir goodnesse that kynge Marke seyde he wolde wedde hir; whereuppon he prayde sir Trystramys to take his way into Irelonde for hym on message. And all this was done to the entente to sle sir Trystramys. Natwithstondynge he wolde nat refuse the messayge for no daunger nother perell that myght falle, for the pleasure of his uncle. (251)

Mark seeks Tristram's death; Brewnor desires Tristram's lady: "for of all women I sawe never none so fayre. And therefore . . . I doute nat I shall sle the and have thy lady" (259). To deprive a knight of his lady, however, means to kill him, as, of course, the adventure at the Castle Plewre proves. To deprive a knight of his lady is to deprive him of, in Freudian terms, the aim and object of his erotic impulses. This has almost nothing to do with sex; sex is in both Freud and Malory and similar works on eros all the way back to Plato's Symposium a metaphor for psychic energy, as Jung was to call eros in a revision of Freud's theory. Rather, all this has to do with self-assertion and identity formation. Eros is questing love, seeking the resolution of internal tensions in private ways that are not authorized by one's culture but in a manner parallel and competing, and therefore threatening, to the dominant culture. Morse Peckham's discussion of eroticism in "Romanticism and Behavior" makes this point especially succinct: "by eroticism I mean, not sexual behavior, but that peculiar cognition of a woman, a man, or an old shoe that invests that object with the power to elicit from the individual a total resolution of tensions, a paradisiacal state of being. Now explanation [and culture] itself is a resolution of judgmental incoherence, and of the tension that judgmental incoherence elicits. I do not mean that explanation and eroticization of experience are identical, but that they are similar in their tension resolving capacity" (17).

The lady provides the aim for the fulfillment of the individual's impulses to drive himself out against the environment and unify or organize it. It should be recalled that Arthur represents this sort of energy at the founding of the Round Table. The difference between questing out against a lady or a land marks one important difference between romance and epic. Romance is the literature of repressive cultures, for the lady becomes the individual's own and secret adventure through which he can create his own identity. The structure of each experience is, however, identical. The lady or the environment responds to the impulses of the questing lover and becomes for him a creative source in the symbiotic sense as discussed in Chapter Two. The principle is that one creates himself through the goals he has chosen. There is hardly a more familiar scene in romance literature than that of a knight doing battle with some enemy while his lady looks down upon him from her tower. It is she that the knight fights to obtain, for loving her symbolizes the attainment of the state of tensions resolved or battles won. Only through her can this energy be finally and completely satisfied and brought to a dynamic equilibrium and rest beyond what the knight was originally. In obtaining her, he becomes a great knight and fighter.

"Woman," as Joseph Campbell writes in The Hero with a Thousand Faces, "in the picture language of mythology, represents the totality of what can be known. The hero is the one who comes to know. As he progresses in the slow initiation which is life, the form of the goddess undergoes for him a series of transfigurations; she can never be greater than himself, though she can always promise more than he is yet capable of comprehending. She lures, she guides, she bids him burst his fetters. And if he can match her import, the two, knower and known, will be released from every limitation" (116). Release from every limitation or "freedom from" is, of course, exactly what the father has achieved and exactly what he fears most in his sons. This point the Hebrew Old Testament makes especially clear: "And the Lord God said, Behold the man is become as one of us, to know good and evil; and now, lest he put forth his hand, and take also of the tree of life, and eat, and live forever, therefore, the Lord God sent him forth from the garden of Eden, to till the ground from whence he was taken" (Genesis, 3: 22-23).

Various names have been given to the energy which impels the man in his quest for the woman; for Freud it is libido or eros, for Adler it is the desire for life fulfillment, and for Jung it is psychic energy. Although the names carry with them different connotations, ultimately they refer to the same unconscious impulse which as Jung points out in his final revisions of his theory underlies and is required for all human action. In On Psychic Energy, he writes:

> The energic point of view on the other hand is in essence final; the event is traced back from cause to effect on the assumption that some kind of energy underlies the changes in phenomena, that it maintains itself as a constant throughout these changes and finally leads to entropy, a condition of

general equilibrium. The flow of energy has a
definite direction (goal) in that it follows the
gradient of potential in a way that cannot be
reversed. (8. 4)

Malory sees this energy as the very basis of all human action,
but it is an energy which can be directed to the resolution of
any tension which the knight experiences and thus is an energy
for pluralism and change. The problem facing Mark, Arthur, Sir
Brewnor, or any father is to preserve their civilization or
customs as status quo. To do this they must control the
psychic energy of the knights by sublimation, substitution, or
repression. Sublimation and substitution channel the energy
into orthodox goals; that is, the civilization provides socially
validated means or made-up personal and social crises through
which or against which the knight may carry out his aggressive
energy and thus engage in the experience of creating his
identity through his own actions. The Round Table offers
tournaments to sublimate the eros of its knights who might
otherwise direct their energies to pluralistic and socially
disruptive ends. The tournament presents a conventional
personal problem which anyone can spend a great deal of
energy resolving. The great knights, of course, whose eros is
much too large to ever be satisfied by a tournament find aims
such as Lamerok's love for Morgause which cannot be controlled
by the society and thus becomes destructive of the peace of the
community.
        Lancelot is a difficult case. His psychic energy is super-
abundant, but he has so thoroughly submitted himself to Arthur
and the explanatory synthesis that he denies its existence in a
form of self-repression or self-policing; he actually, as we shall
see, has learned to turn his psychic energy against himself in
acts of self-control. When asked, for example, by a lady why
"ye woll nat love som mayden other jantylwoman," his answer
suggests that his orientation toward the explanatory center
leaves him no opportunity for personal and pluralistic ends:

    `I may nat warne peple to speke of me what hit
    pleasyth hem. But for to be a weddyd man, I thynke
    hit nat, for than I muste couche with hir and leve
    armys and turnamentis, batellys and adventures.

> And as for to sey to take my pleasaunce with
> peramours, that woll I refuse: in prencipall for drede
> of God, for knyghtes that bene adventures shoulde
> nat be advoutrers nothir lecherous, for than they be
> nat happy nothir fortunate unto the werrys; for
> other they shall be overcom with a sympler knyght
> than they be hemself, other ellys they shall sle by
> unhappe and hir cursednesse bettir men than they be
> hemself. An so who that usyth peramours shall be
> unhappy, and all thynge unhappy that is about them.'
> (161)

Lancelot is saying that the expenditure of one's energy in a
direction which does not support the civilization is sinful and
leads to unhappiness. Pluralistic aims lead to the sort of chaos
in which a weaker knight can actually defeat a stronger, higher
knight--something that actually happens during the "Tale of
Tristram" and a proposition that Tristram eventually assents to.
But again Lancelot is lying; his affair with Guinevere has
already been suggested and he is either expressing the truth of
his own unhappiness or the falseness of the doctrine that only
the righteous are happy. Civilization demands, as Lancelot's
case repeatedly shows, that individuals be unfaithful to
themselves and others on a personal level, and the tragedy of
Lancelot's case is far worse than the trivial hierarchical
disruptions he imagines.

In a sense, Arthur's control of Lancelot's eros amounts to
a psychic castration. Although more will have to be said about
his problem later on, it should be recalled here that during the
war with Emperor Lucius, when Arthur first meets Lancelot and
first acquires his complete submission, a very strange event
occurs. Arthur fights a horrible glutton--one whose eros for
food is excessive and out of control--and the conclusion of the
fight is thus:

> The kynge coverede hym with his shylde and rechis
> a boxe evyn infourmede in the myddis of his
> forehede, that the slypped blade unto the braune
> rechis. Yet he shappis at sir Arthure, but the kynge
> shuntys a lytyll and rechis hym a dynte hyghe uppon
> the haunche, and ther he swappis his genytrottys in
> sondir. (121)

Arthur goes on to dismember the giant, cutting off other sinful parts such as his belly. Sir Brewnor wants Tristram's lady, and in a sense, therefore, seeks a castration of Tristram. If eros is taken as a life force, as Plato sees it, "the mortal nature is seeking as far as is possible to be everlasting and immortal," and as Diotoma concludes, "in this way, Socrates, the mortal body, or mortal anything, partakes of immortality" (Symposium, 48-49), then to demand submission of eros to culturally determined goals is to deprive the individual of his means of self-generation and ability to reduce internal tensions, which is what, of course, "immortal" really only means. What the repression of eros makes immortal is the culture and the roles it offers to individuals; thus it makes permanent mal-adaptive roles and tension causing situations. Sir Brewnor wants Tristram's lady. To control psychic energy is finally to control the individual's life. Mark wants Tristram's life. If eros is the energy individuals expend in reducing tensions arising from interaction with external stimuli, then what Malory presents is the case in which the institution has become the greatest source of tension and psychosis in the lives of individuals.

In terms of the metaphor, the king feels the necessity for killing the son, but in reality he needs only to control the son's eros. This fact suggests that the civilization or the king becomes the set of controls upon the individual's eros, the set of regulations for the expenditure of his psychic energy. These controls are seen by Freud to hold the position of a father when considered externally and when considered internally a conscience or super-ego. Thus the individual who submits his eros to the controls of his civilization internalizes his father and begins, as Lancelot does, to carry out of his own choice the father's aggressions against himself:

What happens in him to render his desire for aggression innocuous? Something very remarkable, which we should never have guessed and which is nevertheless quite obvious. His aggressiveness is introjected, internalized; it is, in point of fact, sent back to where it came from--that is, it is directed toward his own ego. There it is taken over by a portion of the ego, which sets itself over against the rest of the ego as super-ego, and which now, in the

form of 'conscience', is ready to put into action
against the ego the same harsh aggressiveness that
the ego would have liked to satisfy upon other,
extraneous individuals.   The tension between the
harsh super-ego and the ego that is subjected to it,
is called the sense of guilt; it expresses itself as a
need for punishment.   Civilization, therefore, obtains
mastery over the individual's dangerous desire for
aggression by weakening and disarming it and by
setting up an agency within him to watch over it,
like a garrison in a conquered city.   (70-71)

This process works smoothly in the case of Gareth and La
Cote Male Tayle; in these tales Malory exemplifies the
synthetic process in which the two forces, the one of personal
assertion and the other of the culture, meet and create the
concord of wills or the community of the present.   Lancelot,
however, whose aggressions are super-abundant, develops an
overwhelming sense of guilt about his own life as he
internalizes more and more of the restrictions of his culture.
Malory's tale of "La Cote de Male Tayle" occurs as an allegory
of psychic energy and the control of psychic energy.   It occurs
in the "Tristram" just after the initial tales of "Isode the Fair"
and "Lamerok de Galys" in which Tristram's own aggressive
energy has been severely repressed by Mark's authority and just
before the tales dealing with Tristram's madness and exile in
which his energy reaches levels of self-assertion and violence
unmatched elsewhere in the romance.   The tale of La Cote
establishes the theoretical explanation for Tristram's surreal
adventures on the island of Nabon Le Noir and in the Perilous
forest.   Thus in "La Cote Male Tayle" Malory addresses directly
the nature of the controls upon psychic energy, and we need
the allegory in order to understand the delayed reactions and
explosions of Tristram's repressed energy later on.

As the tale itself opens, Malory tells us that "To the
courte of kynge Arthure there cam a younge man bygly made,
and he was rychely beseyne, and he desyred to be made a
knyght of the kynges" (282).   This knight is identified initially
by only his body size and his misshapen coat; no one pays any
attention at all to his name.   As Mead emphasizes, "The body is
not a self, as such; it becomes a self only when it has

developed a mind within the context of social experience" (Mind, Self, and Society, 50). This condition of mere bodily existence is the way all young men--Gareth, Percival, Torre, Gawain--appear before their self-creating quests. In Gareth's case, Malory emphasizes the bigness of his hands. But with Brewnor, Malory adds a new dimension. Brewnor wears an "Evyll-Shapyn Cote" which he says he cannot take off until he has avenged the murder of his father. The coat was his father's coat, and it becomes the metaphor for the general father as Brewnor is now related to him. Brewnor carries his father as an external authority, reminiscent of the Trojan Aeneas who carried upon his shoulders his father, Anchises, as he leaves burning Troy seeking to establish the new civilization at Rome. The responsibilities which the son owes to the father and which are represented by the coat constitute the controls on the son's behavior and suggest that in seeking to become "a knyght of the kynges" Brewnor seeks to internalize his own father, that is, free himself from the external control of the coat by taking the coat over into his consciousness. Malory is at this point emphasizing the progression of moral development, to use Kohlberg's terms, from the external authority to an internal, self-motivated morality. Malory's attitude, however, suggests that this is hardly a positive progression; his tale of La Cote depicts the way in which civilizations demand that individuals direct the expression of their own eros against themselves.

The quest which Brewnor undertakes is the quest of the Black Shield. Malory describes the shield as being "a grete blacke shylde with a whyghte honde in the myddis holdynge a swerde, and other pyctoure was there none in that shylde" (283). The damsel who brings the shield explains that it was once owned by a knight who fought a tremendous battle which ended in a draw and in the owner's death. The subsequent owner must continue the original owner's quest, but the damsel will not disclose the nature of that quest. The shield, in itself, however, allegorizes the quest clearly enough. The white hand with the sword represents personal aggression or the emerging erotic energy of the individual, while the black background symbolizes just the opposite: renunciation, energy repressed, and control. Later on in the quest, Mordred explains this dialectic in terms of a knight's growth to maturity. Young knights, he says, can be recognized by their mighty strong arms:

But as yette he may nat sytte sure on horsebacke, for he that muste be a good horseman hit muste com of usage and excercise. But whan he commyth to the strokis of his swerde he is than noble and myghty. And that saw sir Bleoberys and sir Palomydes; for wete you well they were wyly men of warre, for they wolde know anon, whan they sye a yonge knyght, by his rydynge, how they were sure to gyffe hym a falle frome his horse othir a grete buffett. But for the moste party they wyll nat lyght on foote with yonge knyghtes, for they are myghtyly and strongely armed. (287)

The quest of the shield involves the process described by Mordred; that is, La Cote will enter his own psychic energy into the give and take of the social process and acquire thereby a role and identity which the society has available for him.

The quest itself follows the pattern established by Gareth. The name "La Cote Male Tayle" is taken to be a derogatory appellation, and he begins the adventure in the company of a female who denigrates his every action. To be socialized into a stable institution, one must first learn to hold very negative opinions of himself; he must learn that autonomous existence is a form of inferiority and failure. Malory makes the allegorical nature of the quest apparent by naming the woman the "Damesell Maledysaunte," the evil speaking woman, but she comes as a result of La Cote's actions to be transformed herself into a woman of beautiful thoughts, "the Damesell Byeau-Pansaunte" (290), as she begins to see prowess and valor in La Cote. Eventually she and La Cote marry and she achieves the name "the Lady Byeaue-Vyvante" (294). Thus the hostile woman is transformed into a loving woman, and it appears that Brewnor's quest is simultaneously a quest for Knighthood and Love, two of the categories in which a knight must excel and the two components of the whole life with which Tristram is, at this moment in the narrative, having the greatest problems. Malory reminds the reader that the action in "La Cote Male Tayle" applies allegorically to Tristram's career by mentioning a letter Tristram had sent to Lancelot "excusynge hym [Tristram] of the weddynge of Isod Le Blaunche Maynes, and seyde in the lettir, as he was a true knyght, he had never had ado fleyshly with Isode Le Blaunche Maynys" (288). Tristram is having a great deal of trouble achieving the sort of inner controls that will enable him to love Isode and be Mark's knight within a social context. He cannot develop a proper conscience which will guide his actions and moderate his aggressions.

La Cote's first adventure is at the Castle Orgulus where the custom obtains "that there myght com no knyght by the castell but other he muste juste othir be presonere, othir at the leste to lose his horse and harneyse" (285). The evil custon is soon shown to be a false choice since one hundred knights attack La Cote. The result is that the knight must be a prisoner; the odds are simply overwhelming. With the aid of a lady, La Cote escapes only to be taken prisoner again shortly at the Castle Pendragon. We should recall at this point the problems that Tristram is having in expressing his eros; he, too, is taken prisoner after many of his encounters. The young knight seeking a place in society faces an unassailable authority which simply denies his interest in making his own place in society; one must adopt the roles offered to him which are also required to maintain the social order. La Cote's quest is going badly, and it is likely that he will perish in prison. But Lancelot has heard that La Cote has undertaken the Quest of the Black Shield, and knowing that "suche a yonge knyghte to take so hyghe adventure on hym [is] hys distruccion" (287), Lancelot has set out to oversee the quest. Lancelot rescues La Cote and directs him to two knights who will offer him a suitable social experience.

La Cote meets a pair of brothers named "sir Playne de Fors" and "sir Playne de Amoris." Force (i.e., knighthood) and Love are just exactly what La Cote seeks to get under his control. He easily defeats these knights which indicates that in the fights he assimilates enough of the behavioral modes of Love and Knighthood to be considered competent in both areas. The competence represents a newly acquired selfhood, but it is the result of his experience with an unassailable authority; that is, his experience of defeat at the hands of the more powerful knights earlier on has caused him to internalize the authority as a conscience, the content of which is the behavioral codes of Knighthood and Love. When he fights the appropriate enemy, he wins. Addressing the appropriate adversary, whether in love or in battle, is of course a great part of the codes of

Knighthood and Love and a great part of what it means to be civilized. This is the point at which the damsel Maledysaunte becomes the damsel Beau-Pansaunte: "for now I woll sey unto you and to hym bothe, I rebuked hym never for none hate that I hated hym, but for grete love that I had to hym" (290). She now, of course, as the impending defeat of Playne de Fors and Playne de Amoris shows and as she did not have before, has someone to love, a knight whose force and love are under his control, which is the same as to say that they are under cultural control.

What makes La Cote different from Gareth and the reason Malory had to redevelop the theme of initiation is that La Cote achieves identity and ultimately fulfillment of eros through a process of renunciation and denial--the black shield--for to bring one's force and love under one's control in the process of playing a social role means to accept the restrictions of the Round Table's codes of Love and Knighthood and simply to forget about or repress whatever other interests one might have. In his notes for this tale, Vinaver points out that the French source contains no parallel to Malory's descriptions of knightly "usages and exercises"--the codes. These now become La Cote's own interests, no longer external as the coat initially was. While a lesser knight such as La Cote may achieve mature independence or selfhood by taking over into himself the cultural restrictions on force and love, the great knight, such as Lancelot, Tristram, Lamerok, or Palomides, can never totally replace his own unconscious desires with a social role. After the fight with Playne de Fors and Playne de Amoris, a third brother appears whose name, Sir Plenoryus, suggests activity beyond the limits and a superabundant expenditure of eros. This third brother defeats La Cote but praises the young knight for his "noble dedys of armys" and promises "I shall shew to you kyndenes and jantilnes all that I may" (292).

These events suggest what Freud has called the Reality Principle in which moderate defeats or privations of gratification are positively helpful in developing active mastery of the self and environment or in encouraging the developing individual to hold more realistic and less vainglorious conceptions of his own social attainment. One learns to curtail dreams and aggressions and to fit in. Identity in any mature and stable institution is more the result of institutional needs than it is of individual choice. Shortly after the defeat La Cote marries the lady whose name now is changed to Byeau-Vyvante. La Cote finds happiness and fulfillment within the limits imposed upon him by external authorities because he is not able even to exhaust that limited range of activity. The limits do not feel repressive to the knight who cannot see beyond them--who cannot defeat sir Plenoryus. The great silent majority of any society is always quite content with the repressions of their own society; that, the contentedness and the repression, is why they are silent.

Malory understands, however, that while the rank and file knight finds comfort in the security of the controls placed upon his psychic energy, the great knight must go beyond those controls in order to feel that same sense of fulfillment. Lancelot defeats easily Sir Plenoryus and the allegory suggests that he, therefore, exhausts the behavioral range of Knighthood and Love as it is defined by the codes. If Plenoryus subsumes his two lesser brothers, Playne de Fors and Playne de Amoris, then Lancelot's demand for total surrender of Plenoryus has the effect of deconstructing the customs that helped internalize the regulations on La Cote's psychic energy:

> Than sir Plenoryus yelded hym and hys towre and all
> his presoners at hys wylle. Than sir Launcelot
> receyved hym and toke hys trowthe. (293)

Lancelot has no shred of an intention to deconstruct knighthood, but the mere fact of his ability to exhaust its behavioral range and the fact that he has desires over and above those validated by the institution inevitably demonstrate how narrow and provincial a behavioral control it is. Lancelot becomes so dangerous to the Round Table because with his eros and psychic needs the individual cannot long be held a prisoner of culture. By defeating Plenoryus, Lancelot makes himself the hero who will destroy his own society because his psychic energy is so large and so out of control that he becomes the master of the authority which limits the actions of the regular knights. Lancelot's transcendence will re-define Knighthood and Love in terms of his own behavior, and the society to which he has pledged his fidelity will become too small for his desires and impulses. He will attempt gratifications not possible within the limits of the Round Table and thus will break the Round Table apart at the seams as the regular knights attempt either to retain him within the Round Table or to punish him for obvious transgressions.

As Freud maintains, a civilization insures its stability by seeing that its behavioral codes and ideology are internalized by each member; that is, "there is an extraneous influence at work, and it is this that decides what is to be called good or bad. Since a person's own feelings would not have led him along this path, he must have had a motive for submitting to this extraneous influence. Such a motive is easily discovered in his helplessness and his dependence on other people, and it can best be designated as fear of loss of love. . . . Above all, he is exposed to the danger that this stronger person [father or civilization] will show his superiority in the form of punishment" (Civilization and Its Discontents, (71). While this is certainly the case for the regular knights, for Lancelot and Tristram there. is no stronger person; the knights are larger than their civilizations which seek to control them. Later on, during the Quest for the Holy Grail, Lancelot will meet an authority whose power does destroy him, but in this context Lancelot's aggressiveness is meant to reflect upon the problems Tristram is having in Cornwall. Both Tristram and Lancelot gradually learn that their performance reverses the repressions of the external authority. To Lancelot this is tragedy; to Tristram it is transcendence.

This reversal is confirmed and allegorically expanded by Malory in Lancelot's ensuing fight with three more brothers: Sir Pyllownes, Sir Pellogres, and Sir Pelaundris. Lancelot aggressively attacks and smites down the final brothers. These names, original with Malory, suggest the ultimate direction of the great knight's expression of psychic energy. "La Cote Male Tayle" is a tale in which Malory plays with names and these names are fabricated from the noun pel plus the nouns lounes, logres, and laundris. In the fourteenth century, a pel was "a stake at which swordsmanship was practiced" (OED). Thus as the allegory implies, Lancelot goes far beyond La Cote and makes his society a practice stake for his swordsmanship, the expression of his aggressive psychic energy. If the stability of the civilization relies upon the repression and control of the individual's psychic energy, then what Lancelot practices in defeating Pyllownes, Pellogres, and Pelaundris is violating those controls; he is "the knyght that hath trespassed" (501) in more meanings than the context of "Lancelot and Elaine" is usually held to suggest. The meaning of the nouns is specifically what he attacks:

> **lounes:** Fact or condition of not projecting upward; humility, meekness; also obedience (OED).

> **logres:** The realm of the Round Table; the explanatory synthesis.

> **laundris:** Land (OED, "laund").

La Cote has entered the quest of the Black Shield in order to learn "lowness" or the humility and control that makes the knight obedient to the codes of Knighthood; Lancelot violates it. "Lounes" can also have the meaning of quiet, calm, and peace which is, of course, the result of the condition of each individual bringing his force and love under ideological control. After the final battle between Arthur and Mordred, Lancelot knows that his love for Guinevere is what destroyed the "realme [that] was evir in quyet and reste" (698). La Cote and knights like him make for stable societies because they come under the dominance of culture. "Dominance" is an extremely important word and concept for medieval sociological discussions of civil tranquility. One who internalizes the dominant ideology and behaviors, as La Cote does, does not feel the domination of an external authority. Malory, however, means for us to see dominance as the negative, tension producing control that institutions exert upon individuals. The nonchalance of Lancelot's final fight with the Pel-brothers suggests practice and ease but reinforces the growing antipathy between the knight as individual and his civilization: "At first uppon horsebacke sir Launcelot smote hem doune, and aftirwarde he bete them on foote and made them to yelde them unto hym" (293).

Lancelot, of course, does not challenge Arthur or Logres overtly; rather here Lancelot is himself an allegorical figure that indicates the direction in which Tristram's psychic energy is being molded. In the allegory, we also see something very interesting which, of course, should have been apparent all along. Carl Jung believes that one of the chief values of studying human behavior from the energic point of view is that "it enables us to recognize just those quantitative relations whose existence in the psyche cannot possibly be denied but which are easily overlooked from a purely qualitative standpoint" (On Psychic Energy, 8, 16). The qualitative aspects of the psychic process are the goals or aims toward which the purely quantitative element of energy may be directed. These goals include pleasure, sensation, attitude and identity acquisition on the psychic level and Love, Knighthood, Governance, and Christianity on the level of institutional ideology. The combination of the qualitative and the quantitative aspects appears as wishing, instinct, willing, capacity for work, attentiveness, striving--all of which amount to motivation. We have already seen that culture controls the goals toward which an individual's life ought to be directed-- Knighthood, Love, Governance, and Christianity--and the tale of La Cote now indicates that culture also seeks to regulate the amount of energy which may be expended in seeking such goals.

What is taking place in the psyche of Tristram at this point in the narrative is a tremendous quantitative increase in the level of his psychic energy. Critics who have problems understanding Tristram's behavior in the sections of "Madness and Exile," "The Castle of Maidens," and "The Round Table" are looking at the qualitative aspects of his behavior, and they cannot be quite sure just what is wrong with Tristram since, indeed, he pursues the goals provided by his societly. If we follow the lead established in "La Cote Male Tayle," however, it becomes clear that Malory's emphasis is upon the quantitative aspects of human behavior, the level of energy expenditure which makes Tristram fight "so rowghly and so bygly that there was none myght withstonde hym." One knight thinks that Tristram "ys a devyll and no man" (324). At the Tournament of the Castle of Maidens, we can see clearly the personal origin of Tristram's excessive violence in the way he fights Palomides. Here is Arthur's description of it:

'For full harde I sye hym bestad,' seyde kynge
Arthure, 'whan he smote sir Palomydes upon the

helme thryse, that he abaysshed hys helme with hys
strokis.   And also he sedye "here ys a stroke for sir
Trystram", and thus he seyde thryse.´   (328)

Tristram´s rather unusual battle cry, "have thys for sir
Trystramys sake!" (326), points to an internal, psychic goal for
the expression of energy rather than an external, ideological
one.   The goal is simply to sustain his autonomy, as he tells
Dynadan who has become concerned about the severity of this
wounds: "´Nay, nay,´ seyde sir Trystram, ´never drede you, sir
Dynadan, for I am harte-hole, and of thys wounde I shall sone
be hole, by the mercy of God!´" (327).   In a repressive culture,
personal autonomy can only be maintained by extreme and
violent expenditures of energy, aggressions equal to the
aggressive dominance of the culture itself.

In an attempt to simplify his concept of psychic energy,
Jung generalizes the psychic process as simply a life process:
"In this way we enlarge the narrower concept of psychic energy
to a broader one of life-energy, which includes ´psychic energy´
as a specific part" (8, 19).   This life-energy is expended in
order to maintain individual autonomy at the least possible
level of tension and frustration, that is, the greatest possible
harmony with his environment.   Constant energy expenditures
are required to make the changes and adaptations to the
unstable social and natural worlds.   The tremendous
quantitative increase in Tristram´s energy, therefore, suggests
the tremendous difficulty Tristram is having in living at all.   In
the face of Mark´s demands and repressions--those of the father
and the civilization which at least symbolically require the
death of the son--Tristram must exert an incredible amount of
energy in order to attain some equilibrium and remain alive as
an autonomous being.   A lesser knight such as La Cote would
have to compromise with the external authority by surrendering
autonomy, but Tristram´s energy, like Lancelot´s appears
limitless.   The direction of Lancelot´s attack upon the Pel-
brothers indicates the impulse toward autonomy and "freedom
from," while the high level of energy expenditure makes such an
act unacceptable to the authority.

It is important to see the tale of La Cote in the context
of Cornwall where Malory is analytic; he enhances the tension
and the struggle between the culture and the individual because

in his own life he felt the repressive nature of culture. If the lady represents for the knight the aim of his erotic impulses, then the king represents the control of eros and, in extreme cases such as Mark´s, the repression of eros. From the point of view of psychoanalysis, the king as the civilization and as the regulator of the knight´s eros is exactly a father who demands the death of the son and the possession of his lady. The original dispute between Mark and Tristram arose over their competing love for the wife of Sir Segwarde. The episode, because it is open, blunt, and somewhat distasteful, has given Malory´s critics a great deal of trouble; its importance, however, cannot be overstated, and failure to understand it aright makes understanding any further animosities nearly impossible.

Prior to the struggle over Sir Segwarde´s wife, Mark and Tristram exist as a perfect symbiosis of king and champion; that is, all Tristram´s psychic energy is directed into behaviors which support Mark as king and Cornwall as symbolic universe, and all Mark´s energy is devoted to rewarding and valuing Tristram for his service. This is the time during which Tristram defeats Marhalt and brings security and prosperity to Cornwall: "I dud the batayle for the love of myne uncle kynge Marke and for the love of the countrey of Cornwayle, and for to encrece myne honoure" (243). And Mark responds with a father´s love: "And whan he was commyn unto the londe knyge Mark toke hym in hys armys, and he and sir Dynas the Senescyall lad sir Tristrames into the castell of Tyntagyll . . . `So God me helpe,´ seyde kynge Marke, `I wolde nat for all my londys that my nevew dyed´" (238). Malory tells us that this king-champion symbiosis lasted for a long time; what makes it last is the identity of sonhood. Tristram´s own consciousness contains nothing outside of the orientations of the father which cause him to see himself in the role of a son.

> And there he lyved longe in grete joy longe
> tyme, untyll at the laste there befelle a jolesy and
> an unkyndenesse betwyxte kynge Marke and sir
> Trystrames . . . (244)

The nature of the dispute suggests precisely what Freud has illustrated in his primal horde, and it demonstrates the kind of problems eros poses for a civilization. Explanations and behavioral models such as Knighthood and Governance provide resolutions for experiential tensions, but other tensions may emerge from areas of life that the present culture simply did not take into account and therefore has no way of resolving. In this case, the culture now becomes the source of tension in a knight's life, and no institutional way of dealing with that sort of frustration exists. Tristram's emerging sexual impulses have nothing to do with Knighthood or Governance, and they direct him toward a lady who has no connection, at least in herself, with the defense of Cornwall. Eros always arises from a deficiency or an unsatisfied appetite, and its mere exercise in a-cultural areas overtly threatens the king or father in that it means the son's identity will no longer be constituted entirely of the father's orientations. Institutions in general, moreover, so often condemn eros because it points to inadequacies in them as adaptive strategies; there are simply more desires and more things for humans to do than any ideology can subsume into a coherent system. In the case at hand, what disturbs Mark is Tristram's directing his eros to an aim other than his social role as champion: "they loved bothe one lady, and she was an erlys wyff that hyght sir Segwarydes. And this lady loved sir Trystrames passyngly well, and he loved hir agayne, for she was a passynge fayre lady and that aspyed sir Trystrames well. Than Kynge Marke undirstode that and was jeluse, for kynge Marke loved hir passynge welle. (244)

Malory's purpose in telling the episode of Sir Segwarde's wife is to ground the dispute between Tristram and Mark in the control of the knight's eros. We should compare this situation with Freud's description in Totem and Taboo of the origin of taboos on sexual promiscuity, that is, controls upon the satisfaction of erotic impulses outside of the culturally authorized goals:

> The attempt [to explain the origin] is associated with a hypothesis of Charles Darwin about the primal social state of man. From the habits of the higher apes Darwin concluded that men, too, originally lived in small hordes in which the jealousy of the oldest and strongest male prevented sexual promiscuity. We may indeed conclude from what we

know of the jealousy of all male quadrupeds, armed,
as many of them are, with special weapons for
battling with their rivals, that promiscious
intercourse in a state of nature is extremely
improbable. . . . Judging from the social habits of
man as he now exists, the most probable view is
that he originally lived in small communities, each
with a single wife, or if powerful with several, whom
he jealousy defended against all other men. Or he
may not have been a social animal and yet have
lived with several wives. . . . When the young male
grows up a contest takes place for mastery, and the
strongest, by killing and driving out the others,
establishes himself as the head of the community.
(162-63)

The hypothesis of Freud and Darwin was a common explanation
for the origin of the state in medieval political theory, invoked
both to substantiate social cohesion and to demonstrate the
primacy of kingly power. We find it in John of Salisbury, St.
Thomas, or Marsilius of Padua who writes, "For the first and
smallest combination of human beings, wherefrom the other
combinations emerged, was that of male and female, as the
foremost of the philosophers says in the Politics. . . . From this
combination were generated other humans. . . . So long as men
were in a single household, all their actions, especially those
we shall henceforth call `civil,´ were regulated by the elder
among them as being more discerning, but apart from laws or
customs, because these could not yet have been discovered.
Not only were the men of a single household ruled in this way,
but so too was the first community, called the village . . . the
head of a single household might have been allowed to pardon
or to punish domestic injuries entirely according to his own will
and pleasure" (10).
 Mark, of course, has no wife at this point, but his position
as lord (dominus) entitles him to ownership of all property and
even women in the realm. Marsilius´ discussion of dominium or
"lordship" is, again, especially revealing: "In its strict sense,
this term means the principal power to lay claim to something
rightfully acquired in accordance with right taken in its first
sense; that is, the power of a person . . . who wants to allow

no one else to handle that thing without his, the owner's, express consent, while he owns it. This power is none other than the actual or habitual will thus to have the rightfully acquired thing" (192). Mark's interests are the same as those Freud describes; he must as king-father-civilization have or possess all females only in order to prevent other males from handling them and to impose, thereby, controls upon the exercise of the son's erotic energy. Thus his jealousy about Tristram's affair with the wife of Sir Segwarde is nothing more than his exercise of dominium, lordship, or ownership of Tristram himself. Mark's interest in the woman is only a concealed desire to remain lord in Cornwall, and he must frustrate or prevent Tristram's love of other objects outside of Cornwall and himself. The same lordship motivates him to marry Isode and send Tristram to Ireland bring her.

To frustrate Tristram's eros, Mark sets up an ambush as Tristram makes his way to the house of Sir Segwarde's wife. This ambush fails to stop Tristram, but he receives from Mark the wound which "bledde bothe the over-shete, and the neyther-sheete, and the pylowes and the hede-shete" (245). Many readers have been displeased with Malory's explicit and sometimes gory description of the eros and aggression, but it is clear that Malory intends to demonstrate the high level of aggressiveness and energy which Tristram exhibits at this moment when the aggressions of the dominant culture are themselves most violent. Malory's interest here is in the quantity of eros required on the part of an individual in order to remain "owner" or, in Luther's term, "lord" of himself; Malory shows a wild and violent Tristram, who, when Sir Segwarde rebukes him for the violation of his wife and marriage, flaunts his power saying that he cares nothing for "the wrongys that I have done you" and that he would like nothing better than to beat-up Segwarde also: "and thorow the waste of the body he smote sir Segwarydes, that he felle to the erthe in sowne" (246).

In section 3.2, I mentioned that an inappropriate continuity exists between the tales of Gareth and of Tristram. We saw that Gareth's psychic energy is carefully brought under the control of an internalized explanatory synthesis (super-ego), and we, therefore, expect that the same sort of super-ego to exist in Tristram. But it does not and cannot because a super-ego or conscience is the result of experience within the social process. What has been taken over into Tristram's super-ego is merely the cognitive and behavioral values of the king-champion relationship in which the champion's actions include the violent assertion of personal energy for the benefit of the state. John of Salisbury in the Polycraticus understands the knight this way: "The armed hand is that which performs the soldiering of camps and blood . . . those who do military service for the commonwealth who, protected by helmets and cuirasses, ply their swords or what other weapons you please against the foe" (6. 1). But in a different context--one not related in any way to the king or the state--all Tristram knows is violent assertion. He does not know that it was Mark who attempted to restrain him and that Mark gave him his wound. Rather Tristram only knows that it was an enemy and that enemies are to be vanquished; in war frustrations are to be overcome with all the aggressive violence one is able to muster. His fight with Marhalt taught him this.

Because his socialization has identified him with Mark, it takes Tristram a long time, indeed, to discover that Mark is the origin of the frustrations. Mark's actions on the following day indicate his continuing concern for controlling the psychological growth of Tristram, and Malory's phrasing suggests his own belief that such controls are in reality repressive, hateful, and representative of a desire to destroy the individual:

> Also knyge Marke wolde nat be a-knowyn of that he had done unto sir Trystramys whan he mette that nyght; and so for sir Trystramys, he knew nat that kynge Marke had mette with hym. And so the kynge com ascawnce to sir Trystrames to comforte hym as he lay syke in his bedde. But as longe as kynge Marke lyved he loved never aftir sir Trystramys. So aftir that, thoughe there were fayre speche, love was there none. (246)

In this manner, Tristram cannot perceive his king and his civilization as the controls which demand his renunciation of eros and hence demand a death of self. This is, of course, the problem Lancelot never surmounts and the reason why cultural transcendence is so difficult. But for Tristram, Malory makes the theme clear to his readers. While it is usually argued, as Benson and Mahoney do, that the principal theme of the "Tristram" is Tristram's attainment of knighthood as one of the four best knights in the world, it now seems rather that he achieves full knighthood in the stroke that fatally wounds Marhalt and therefore allows Tristram to take Marhalt's place as one of the four best knights (he later takes Marhalt's seat at the Round Table); the principal theme is rather Tristram's growth toward the discovery of the origin of the force which creates the meaninglessness and death in his life. In short, he must discover the demands of the father and upon that discovery kill his father. The first step in this discovery is his adventure at the Castle Plewre where, as in Mark's case, the authority figure attempts to deprive Tristram of his lady. The result of this battle is that "So anone sir Trystrames thruste sir Brewnor down grovelyng, and than he unlaced his helme and strake of his hede" (260). Malory goes further to show the meaning of such a killing of a father; the son who kills the father, as in Oedipus' case, replaces the father: "And than all they that longed to the castell com to hym and dud hym homage and feaute, praying hym that he wolde abyde stylle there a lytyll whyle to fordo that foule custom. So this sir Trystrames graunted thereto" (260). The great theme of the "Tristram" is, therefore, the undoing of culture, the deconstruction of such father-son relationships.

The adventure at the Castle Plewre provides an analog for the situation Tristram faces at Cornwall and, for that matter, Lancelot at the Round Table. Its structure suggests the Oedipus Complex and the necessity of the individual to transcend cultural controls in order to grow into his full potential as an individual and assume a position of his own similar to that of the powerful authority which he has replaced. In Chapter Two it was pointed out that the meaningful life depends upon the individual's ability to contribute personally to the creation of his own world and god, and to do so inescapably means replacing the ones he inherits. As long as Tristram's orientations remain those of a son, he will remain the weak knight that everyone expects to come from Cornwall. In fighting everyone except Mark, however, Tristram's strength is unparalleled, as we so frequently hear: "Than was sir Trystrames called the strengyst knyght of the worlde, for he was called bygger than sir Launcelotte, but sir Launcelot was bettir brethid" (261).   And yet Tristram cannot until the very end of the tale openly confront and challenge Mark with any means that might effectively damage Mark.

Sometime after the event at the Castle Plewre, after Mark has been married to Isode, Sir Andred reports to Mark that "Trystram talked with La Beale Isode in a wyndowe" (267).   Believing that Tristram continues to attempt to steal his wife (symbolically, to replace him), Mark attacks Tristram, as before, with the intent of subduing his psychic energy.   The passage is as follows:

> Than kynge Marke toke a swerde in his honde and cam to sir Trystrames and called hym `false traytowre´, and wolde have stryken hym, but sir Trystrames was nyghe hym and ran undir his swerde and toke hit oute of his honde.   (267)

Indeed, from the king's point of view, Tristram has betrayed Mark.   Mark calls for his men to restrain Tristram and protect their king, but of course no one wants to fight Tristram and no one ever needs to, for Malory makes it clear that Tristram at this point cannot harm Mark.   Malory continues:

> [Tristram] shoke hys swerde to the kynge and made countenaunce as he wolde have strykyn hym.   And than kynge Marke fledde, and sir Trystrames folowed hym and smote hym fyve or six strokys flatlynge in the necke, and that he made hym falle on the nose. (268)

To be sure such treatment is embarrassing to Mark, as falling on one's nose suggests, but Mark never fears for his life, and even afterward he instinctively thinks of Tristram as the military extension of himself.   As long as Tristram remains conscious and rational, he will pose no serious threat to Mark because of the conscience or super-ego of Tristram which explains that his relationship to Mark is always that of an inferior and that of Mark's champion or defender.   Tristram's own feelings and actions are always regulated by the rational and ideological super-ego.   George Herbert Mead tells us: "This is what you are doing when you act in a rational fashion: you are indicating to yourself what the stimuli are that will call out a complex response, and by the order of the stimuli you are determining what the whole response will be. . . . Man is distinguished by that power of analysis of the field of stimulation which enables him to pick out one stimulus rather than another and so to hold on to the response that belongs to that stimulus" (Mind, Self, and Society, 94). The stimulus which would call out a fight response for Tristram is the aggressive posture of an enemy, and his rational response would, of course, be to kill the enemy, something he physically could do with the greatest of ease. As Salisbury writes in the Policraticus, "The armed hand is employed only against the enemy" (6. 1), but Tristram right now can isolate no such stimuli: "Tristram sawe that there was none that wolde be ayenste hym" (267), and he has, most importantly, not yet learned to see Mark in the position of enemy. He cannot yet perceive Mark as a repressive control which demands the renunciation of his eros; he rather sees Mark from Mark's perspective, exactly what has been induced in him and exactly what a champion should rationally do.

The next passage, however, shows us how the event is taken by the unconscious. His next acts are delayed reactions, explosive displacements, and energic transfers of behavior that would have been appropriate for Mark and, indeed, the reactions that Tristram himself most deeply wants. The passage shows Malory's remarkable understanding of the issues in the psychoanalytic approach to social behavior:

> And than sir Trystrames yode his way and armed hym and toke his horse and his men, and so he rode into the foreste. And there uppon a day sir Trystrames mette with two bretherne that were wyth kynge Marke knyghtes, and there he strake of the hede of the tone brother and wounded that other to the deth, and he made hym to bere the hede in his helme. And thirty mo he there wounded. And whan that knyght com before the kynge to say hys message he dyed there before the kynge and quene. (268)

Malory indicates that Tristram has some small awareness of the source of his frustration by having Tristram send the dead and wounded knights back to Cornwall, but Mark understands completely: "Than Kynge Marke called his counceyle unto hym and asked avyce of his barownes, what we're beste to do with sir Trystrames" (268). Tristram's violence increases throughout his section of the <u>Morte</u> until the point of his denial of Mark. Tristram's behavior becomes increasingly what the sociologist Orin E. Klapp has called "ego screaming--behavior which says ʽlook at me,ʼ ʽplease pay attention to me.ʼ This shows the need for recognition. It indicates that such people feel ego deprivation" ("Style Rebellion and Identity Crisis," 71). Later when Mark banishes Tristram from Cornwall, Tristram will recount all of the heroic services he has performed for Mark as if to say, again, "pay attention to me," "your social system is not satisfying sincere desires I cannot help feeling," "why don't you understand me and who I am."

Tristram's is a case of severe ego repression, and he reacts with a tremendous increase in the quantitative level of his psychic energy. We must not think merely of sexual frustration; the stakes are far too serious and culturally pervasive for that, and, as argued earlier, the lady represents not merely a sexual object but rather the means by which the knight can establish himself, through fulfillment of psychic energy, as a complete and independent being. It might be useful at this point to return to one of Malory's own experiences which exhibits the very same pattern. At the outset of Chapter One, the event of Malory's raid upon Caludon was presented and after Malory's arrest and subsequent escape he seems to have acted out the same sort of energic transfer when he rifled and vandalized the Abbey of the Blessed Mary at Combe. He and his men smashed down the doors to the monks' cells and shouted insults and profanities at them. This was an abbey affiliated with Warwick, the man who had incarcerated Malory just two days earlier. The experience Tristram has with Mark as father and lord must have reminded Malory of his own social experience. Too many of Malory's reported crimes bear the the stamp of vengeance, violent self-assertion, and ego-screaming.

3.4 The Son as Redeemer

Mark and Arthur represent forces of unmeasurable strength and immovable stability for Tristram and Lancelot, and the knights have no means, as did Oedipus, of asserting themselves against this authority. Unlike Oedipus whose father abandoned him on the mountainside in Kithairon and who grew up in Corinth, they cannot get outside of the explanatory superstructure which they have taken over as a super-ego, and thus they cannot see their kings-fathers-civilizations as forces different from themselves and the cause of their suffering. Tristram's ambivalence toward Cornwall suggests the supreme need both to remain in Cornwall and to get outside of it. Certainly Tristram is violent enough to have killed Mark, but he exhibits a remarkable self-control in striking Mark with only the flat side of his sword.

Larry Benson in his discussion of the "Tristram" in Malory's Morte Darthur remarks that "Tristram's obligation to Mark seems to depend more upon Mark's good conduct than on any inviolable feudal bond, and, like many in the fifteenth century, Tristram easily serves two lords at once, Mark and Arthur," (144), but it would be difficult to discover even a single passage in which Tristram actually serves Arthur in the way that he serves Mark. True enough, Tristram acknowledges

Arthur's greatness on several occasions, and once he rescues Arthur from two knights who had beaten him down and were about to cut off his head (301), but Tristram never shows more than a distant and casual interest in Arthur and the Round Table; his real center of concern is Mark and Cornwall.

Just prior to the dramatic rescue of Arthur, Sir Brandeles tells Tristram that he ought to join the Round Table: "And wyte you well that we be ryght glad that we have founde you, and we be of a felyship that wolde be ryght glad of youre company, for ye ar the knyght in the worlde that the felyship of the Rounde Table desyryth moste to have the company off" (300). Tristram's response is simply that he feels he is not yet of the stature to join such a fellowship. At this point, we can take Tristram at his word, but after his rescue of Arthur when Arthur repeats the membership offer Tristram again refuses. Even after his climactic fight with Lancelot at the perron of Camelot, Tristram still remains aloof from the Round Table. To Arthur's request that "ye shall abyde in my courte," Tristram replies simply "thereto me is lothe, for I have to do in many contreys" (352). Although he hesitates to name Cornwall, that is precisely where he returns, demonstrating that the psychological bond between Mark and Tristram continues to be the most dominant influence on Tristram's life to the very end. After many years in exile and apparent happiness with Isode at the Joyous Garde, Tristram still returns to Mark and Cornwall.

This relationship is the bond between a king and a champion or, as the argument being presented here explains it, between a father and a son or an individual and his institution. Patriotism is not at all an inappropriate name for this bond, provided we understand it as the secular equivalent of religious faith, a faith and a father for which individuals are just as willing to die as any godhead. Arthur, as great as he may be, never assumes the position of father to Tristram in the way that Mark does. Arthur is father to Lancelot, and the distinction is important to grasp because contrasting Mark and Arthur in this way is part of Malory's demonstration that social relationships are habituations and do not have any basis in nature. Mark's coercive commands and Tristram's experiences in defending Cornwall are the creative sources of his identity in the same way that Gareth's experiences were. But whereas the structure of Gareth's identity quest ends in the synthesis of the four branches of the explanatory model, Knighthood, Governance, Love, and Christianity, so that Gareth becomes the sort of responsible and rational nobleman that the fifteenth century knight was supposed to be, Tristram's identity ends up much differently. Gareth is born into a growing and vital institution which, indeed, offers him an enhanced way of life. Tristram, born into a society already psychically dead becomes the son who is a redeemer.

Malory condenses radically the matter of Tristram's parentage and enfance, but what he does include emphasizes Tristram's origin as a redeemer--the son who must suffer and die so that other sons and daughters may live beyond the father. Malory focuses upon the paired episodes of the death of Tristram's natural mother, Elizabeth, and the redemption of his adoptive mother. The story of Elizabeth's death at Tristram's birth is well known, and Elizabeth's last words, according to Malory, set up the son's life long quest to overcome the death (on all levels) into which he was born:

> `A, my lytyll son, thou haste murtherd thy modir!
> And therefore I suppose thou that arte a murtherer
> so yonge, thow arte full lykly to be a manly man in
> thyne ayge; and bycause I shall dye of the byrth of
> the, I charge my jantyllwoman that she pray my
> lorde, the kynge Melyodas, that whan he is
> crystened let calle hym Trystrams, that is as muche
> to say as a sorowfull byrth. (230)

Immediately after this, Malory shifts to the scene in which King Melyodas' second wife has become jealous of the superior nature of Tristram in comparison with her own children by Melyodas and has, therefore, set out poison to kill Tristram. This step-mother's love for her own children leads her to seek the death of other children who might compete favorably with her own objects of love. This sort of motherly-love is the counterpart in ideology to the father's wish to destroy his male children. Its aim of securing one's position by destroying the opposition is just as institutionally orthodox. Her plot, however, is discovered by Melyodas who immediately condemns her to be burnt. Tristram, quite remarkably and inexplicably, intercedes with the father to save the life of the mother: "Geff

me the lyff of your quene, my step-modir" (231).   His argument
to Melyodas demonstrates a very high form of love; neither the
self-love of the father and mother nor the questing or
acquisitive love, eros, but rather the unmotivated, God-like
love--agape.   He invokes the godly love over against the
judgment of "the lawe."   Tristram becomes the man who
transcends the law, and in doing so reveals the deathly nature
of the law:

> `Sir,´ seyde Trystrams, `as for that, I besech you
> of your mercy that ye woll forgyff hir.   As for my
> parte, God forgyff her and I do.   And hit lyked so
> muche your hyghenesse to graunte me my boone, for
> Goddis love I requyre you holde your promyse.
> (231)

The personal cost of Tristram´s restoring his mother to life is
the death of his own sonhood and the loss of his own father´s
love.   In transcending the laws of the father, he also transcends
the father and loses thereby his position as son.   After this
episode, Melyodas abandons Tristram: "but than the kynge wolde
nat suffir yonge Trystrams to abyde but lytyll in his courte"
(231).   These brief episodes establish Malory´s overall concerns
with the mythic pattern of the redeemer who must give up his
own life or social position in order to restore life to men in
general.   The forces of institutional stability, counter-
revolution, and patriotism are simply always too strong and too
unrelenting for any possibility that the culturally transcending
hero might live long enough to understand and enjoy what his
sufferings have bought.   By the end of this book we will see
that Palomides is the symbolic recipient of the new life
Tristram purchases at the cost of his own.

Joseph Campbell calls the events of Tristram´s life the
"monomyth of the hero" and writes that "The effect of the
successful adventure of the hero is the unlocking and release
again of the flow of life into the body of the world.   The
miracle of this flow may be represented in physical terms as a
circulation of food substance, dynamically as a streaming of
energy, or spiritually as a manifestation of grace" (The Hero
with a Thousand Faces, 40).   This task is from the very outset
Tristram´s personal adventure; the deep structure and source of

his psychic energy is the undeniable need to insure, as Campbell phrases it, the "continuous circulation of spiritual energy into the world" (36). This is the energy which, as we saw in the last section, the father seeks to control, just in the way that Melyodas banishes Tristram at the instant he asserts his own psychic energy; the bursting forth of energy from a source free from the father's control is what he cannot tolerate in his sons because through it the sons will attain the same godlike stature that the father now alone possesses. Campbell goes on to say, "for the hero as the incarnation of God is himself the navel of the world, the umbilical point through which the energies of eternity break into time. Thus the World Navel is the symbol of continuous creation [the quest without end]: the mystery of the maintenance of the world through that continuous miracle of vivification which wells within all things" (41).

While it is fruitless to speculate about why Tristram in particular should be so chosen, it is clear that the son who is born into a dead world must in his own way become the bearer of new life; faced with a father who only condemns and a mother who can no longer supply him with life and love, Tristram must raise his own failing sonhood to the universal level and solve for all mankind what he could not resolve for himself alone. This is, of course, precisely what Arthur accomplished at the outset of the Round Table; he was initially the son who transcended his failed sonhood and became, himself, the father of a new people. Tristram remains in Cornwall because it is the world of his failing sonhood, and it is the world which he is born to transcend and to which he can bring new life. Tristram's quest becomes, more than anything else, an attempt as son to be justified in front of his father. When that fails, as it certainly does, he will seek to destroy the father who deprives him of life.

The failed son of Melyodas comes to Cornwall in order to perfect the role of sonhood by becoming Mark's son. When Tristram arrives at the court of his uncle, he comes as Cornwall's defender, and he continues to see himself in this capacity until the final break with Mark in the section called "Joyous Garde." Even late in the romance, when Cornwall is beseiged by Saracens under the leadership of Elyas, Tristram understands his social function as service and self-sacrifice:

"Other ellys I woll be slayne in the fylde, othir ellys delyver Cornwayle of the old trewage" (386). In the initial event, the fight with Marhalt, he comes "for none other cause" (234) than to release Cornwall from the old bondage of Ireland. It is important for us to understand Cornwall in the way Tristram experiences it--as a society always in bondage. Tristram's personal life as dutiful son exemplifies that bondage, and yet he comes to Cornwall to free people from their bonds--the restraint of the son by the father. As before, Malory greatly condenses the fight with Marhalt in order to focus upon the basic theme of the hero's quest for redemption and the new life:

> `A, fayre knyght and well proved,´ seyde sir Trystrams, `thou shalt well wete I may nat forsake the in this quarell. For I am for thy sake made knyght, and thou shalt well wete that <u>I am a kynges sonne, borne and gotyn uppon a quene.</u> And suche promyse I have made at my nevewys [Mark's] requeste and myne owne sekynge that I shall fyght with the unto the uttirmuste and delyvir Cornwayle frome the olde trewage.´ (236, emphasis mine)

Some controversy has arisen among critics about the meaning and purpose of the scene of Tristram's arrival at Cornwall and his proposal to Mark that he will fight with Marhalt. Vinaver's original notes suggest that Malory became confused in the narration and repeated himself needlessly. Vinaver's position has been challenged in "Tristram's First Interview with Mark in Malory's <u>Morte Darthur</u>" by R. M. Lumiansky who sees no confusion but rather a gradual revelation of Tristram's origin, identity, and purpose. While the literal meaning is now established, Malory's purpose and theme is as yet undisclosed. What is important is that Tristram has to tell Mark three times <u>who he is</u> and <u>where he comes from</u>: "`What ar ye?´ seyde the kynge, ´and frome whens be ye com?´ `Sir,´ seyde Trystrames, `I com frome kynge Melyodas that wedded your systir, and a jantylman, wete you welle, I am´" (234). This exchange is repeated three times. In every case, Mark understands clearly that Tristram offers to fight Marhalt but does not understand <u>who he is</u>. Malory's emphasis here is on Mark's failure to grasp the full significance of the man who has offered to rescue Cornwall from its bondage. Mark, like Arthur, is aware only of what should be called "the social role of the hero"; Mark expects a champion who redeems only in the sense that he sustains the life of the king as he presently rules. By repeating Tristram's origin three times, Malory emphasizes that Tristram is, as Joseph Campbell defines, the hero who comes from outside of the society and is therefore free from the sickness and psychic bondage that troubles those within the society. Mark recognizes in Tristram only his connection with Cornwall--"welcom, fayre nevew"--not his dissociation from Cornwall. For Tristram, the major quest of his entire career is to discover and assert who he is.

Joseph Campbell writes, "The cosmogonic cycle is presented with astonishing consistency in the sacred writings of all the continents, and it gives to the adventure of the hero a new and interesting turn; for now it appears that the perilous journey was a labor not of attainment but of reattainment, not of discovery but of rediscovery. The godly powers sought and dangerously won are revealed to have been within the heart of the hero all the time. He is 'the king's son' who has come to know who he is and therewith has entered into the exercise of his proper power-- 'God's son,' who has learned to know how much that title means. From this point of view the hero is symbolical of that divine creative and redemptive image that is hidden within us all, only waiting to be known and rendered into life" (Hero, 39, emphasis mine).

Mark's misconception of the hero is tantamount to seeing in Christ only his manhood and expecting him to take a place within the institution among the scribes and teachers at the temple of Jerusalem. It does not recognize his divinity and what transcends the institution. A connection between the hero and the spiritually sick land always exists, but without the element of the new or the radically different and transcendental no new life could be brought by the hero. And this is the point. Mark and Arthur are not interested in new life and change; they seek the social role of the hero who will maintain them as dominant or dominus, and not change the society. But the very nature of redemption is change; we see this in Galahad's coming to the Round Table when Malory again emphasizes redemption and Arthur's acknowledgment that the old order is threatened by the new: "Wherefore hit [Galahad's quest] shall greve me ryght sore, the departicion of thys felyship, for I have had an olde custom to have hem in my felyship" (522). This divergence between the true redeemer and the social role of the hero becomes, then, the second source of the dispute and hatred between Mark and Tristram.

The cultural crisis which Malory's romance depicts concerns the role of the hero in a society or, more generally, the role of innovation in an institution. In his The Discarded Image, C. S. Lewis traces the conception of the medieval champion to Cicero's Somnium Scipionis in which Scipio dreams of how Africanus Major explains to Africanus Minor that "all who have been saviors or champions of their native land or have increased its dominions have their appointed place in heaven" (24). And Morton Bloomfield in writing about the position of the hero in medieval society also traces the hero's classical origins in which the name itself meant "protector" or "helper" and the role was that of semi-divine or super-human being "whose special powers were put forth to save or help all mankind" ("The Problem of the Hero," 27). He notes that the term hero did not come into common English usage until the sixteenth century. For Malory, the term is always "champyon" which is the French cognate of the old English "cempa." The concept of the hero is fully explicit in English literature as far back as Beowulf whom the poet calls "maere cempa." Bloomfield goes on to suggest that "the fact is that after Roland and some of the heroes of the Norse sagas and of early romances, no hero of any note from the later Middle Ages leaps to mind" and that "there is something powerfully wrong with these later medieval heroes which seriously compromises their heroism. This self-destructive heroism, or more precisely unheroic heroism, dominates all later medieval and early Renaissance literature until Tasso and Shakespeare. The drastic ambiguity of the hero in the later Middle Ages is perfectly revealed in Gawain and the Green Knight where the problem of the hero becomes acute. Scholars simply cannot agree on whether Gawain is to be admired or condemned" (33). While Bloomfield does think Beowulf is a true hero, I have always felt that the Beowulf-poet perceives something intrinsically tragic and fundamentally wrong, ineffective, and unjust with the hero in his role as the defender of his native land.

Bloomfield's basic observation is correct and it applies not only to Gawain but to Chaucer's Knight, Tristram, Lancelot, Lamerok, Percival, Galahad, and many more. Although less obvious ambiguity exists about the actions of heroes like Beowulf or Roland, the authors of those tales plant openly in the reader's mind the question of just what good the hero's death accomplished. The late Middle Ages were flatly anti-heroic and skepticism about heroism continued to mount throughout the Middle Ages, even in the midst of a body of literature that has traditionally been interpreted as consumately "heroic"; plainly speaking, much of this literature is just misinterpreted. Bloomfield poses the basic problem: "why do we have this retreat from heroism in the later Middle Ages?" Bloomfield confesses an inability to answer his own question, and goes on simply to describe some of the contexts in which we see the non-heroic such as a boredom with the heroic literature of the early Middle Ages, an interest in elaboration, decoration, or Gothicism, and finally a suspicion of earthly achievements. I am not so sure that the spirit of "contemptu mundi" restricted heroism; it certainly did not for John of Salisbury who in the Polycraticus explains unwittingly precisely why late medieval heroes are so unheroic:

But what is the office of the duly ordained soldiery? To defend the Church, to assail infidelity, to venerate the priesthood, to protect the poor from injuries, to pacify the province, to pour out their blood for their brothers, and, if need be, to lay down their lives. The high praises of God are in their throats, and the two-edged swords are in their hands to execute punishment on the [enemy] nations and rebuke upon the peoples, and to bind their kings in chains and their nobles in links of iron. But to what end? To the end that they may serve madness, vanity, avarice, or their own private self-will? By no means. Rather to the end that they may execute the judgment that is committed to them to execute; wherein each follows not his own will but the deliberate decision of God, the angels, and men, in accordance with equity and the public utility. (VI, 8)

Malory's portrayal of the adventures of Tristram in the middle of his romance demonstrates precisely why significant heroism could not exist in the late Middle Ages. The problem with these late medieval heroes is the ideal or the explanatory synthesis which they are bound to protect and serve, just as Salisbury explains. These heroes are committed to the Augustinian principle that man knows himself by the ideal he resembles and serves, and yet this ideal leads the knights to self-denial and death-in-life. It is an ideal which has become repressive and meaningless and, therefore, far too small for the men who desperately need to transcend it.

In order to answer, therefore, Bloomfield's question about why there should exist a retreat from heroism in the late Middle Ages, we need to examine the nature of Mark's demands upon Tristram or, in other words, the social role he offers Tristram at their first interview. Hero, as we now should be able to see, can have two meanings: the redeemer which Tristram is born to be and who innovates a new social reality and the champion who performs the social role of the soldier or warrior to maintain the social reality of the father. The difference is profound, for the redeemer brings new life and new laws that make the old law obsolete, while the champion or soldier sustains the old law. It is important to understand that soldiers are never heroic in the full and redemptive sense of the term. They are, rather, only more victims of the institution's increasingly paranoid desire to enhance its stability and security by symbolically, or as Salisbury defines, literally, killing all those who threaten it, especially its own deviant or heretical sons. Victimhood seems to be Malory's view of the role of the soldier: "And whan kynge Marke and his barownes of Cornwayle behelde how yonge sir Trystrams departed with such a caryage to feyght for the ryght of Cornwayle, there was nother man nother woman of worshyp but they wepte to se and undirstonde so yonge a knyght to jouparte hymself for theire ryght" (235). They do, nonetheless, let him go to the battlefield; it seems that most people on the social level of "barownes" simply come to accept the death of soldiers as the price of social stability and the security of "their rights." As mentioned before, Mark demands that Tristram preserve only the old law--the peace, stability, and justice of Cornwall.

Malory repeats the first interview of Mark and Tristram three times because of the complete mis-match of minds that begins at this crucial point. Mark offers Tristram the social role of soldier, but Tristram understands his mission to Cornwall as redemption and cultural transcendence. Mark wants Tristram to defend him, but Tristram as king's son wants to replace him as king.

The hero has become such a problem because of certain inherent limitations in the way any institution develops. The institutional reality, the symbolic universe, is the father's reality; he created it and maintaining it is his primary interest. To the father, his reality is simply all that exists; it is truth. This fact, as Peter Berger and Thomas Luckmann point out, means that the inertia or the inherent direction of development of an institution stands in opposition to the outside forces of innovation that the redemptive hero represents: "Traditional definitions of reality inhibit social change" (122) because "Institutions tend to persist unless they become `problematic.´ Ultimate legitimations inevitably strengthen this tendency. The more abstract the legitimations are, the less likely they are to be modified in accordance with changing pragmatic exigencies. . . . This means that institutions may persist even when, to an outside observer, they have lost their original functionality or practicality. One does certain things not because they work but because they are right--right, that is, in terms of the ultimate definitions of reality promulgated by the universal experts" (117-18). The definition of the hero, therefore, could for the Middle Ages not be conceived in any terms other than those of defending what all of the socially acknowledged experts, such as Salisbury himself, knew was right. Who would listen to the words of an upstart Tristram? The same conception is prominent today.

Now identity in a mature and stable institution is not something an individual constructs himself, not a result of "his private self-will"; rather it is a role the institution offers to the pre-social individual. Such roles exist because the institution has need for them; the role always exists because, as Salisbury says, of its "public utility." The sociologists point out a little later in The Social Construction of Reality that

> Since every individual is confronted with essentially
> the same institutional program for his life in the
> society, the total force of the institutional order is
> brought to bear with more or less equal weight on
> each individual, producing a compelling massivity for
> the objective reality to be internalized. Identity
> then is highly profiled in the sense of representing
> fully the objective reality within which it is located.
> Put simply, everyone pretty much _is_ what he is
> supposed to be. In such a society identities are
> easily recognizable, objectively and subjectively.
> Everybody knows who everybody else is and who he
> is himself. A knight _is_ a knight and a peasant _is_ a
> peasant. (164)

We might add, a hero is a hero. In the eyes of the father, who
is, of course, satisfied with himself and therefore with the
social reality grounded in his view of the world, the society
itself is not sick, not psychically unhealthy. Identity is not a
problem for the father to contemplate because he has attained
it and it is grounded in objective reality; he knows who
everyone is in precisely the manner Mark recognized Tristram
at their first interview. Mark appears not to be paying
attention to Tristram's explanations of "who he is" because he
already knows all that he is interested in. He needs a soldier,
not some energetic and idealistic young man who might want to
have things too much his own way. For Mark it is just as easy
to recognize a traitor or a heretic as it is the soldier. Berger
and Luckmann arrive at this important conclusion:

> There is, therefore, no _problem_ of identity. The
> question 'who am I?' is unlikely to arise in
> consciousness, since the socially predefined answer
> is massively real subjectively and consistently
> confirmed in all significant social interaction. (164)

Tristram is, however, an outsider, one who has not
already been socialized into the world of Cornwall and Mark,
and he comes to Cornwall deeply troubled by questions about
his sonhood: who he is and what it should mean to be the son of
a king and a queen. Identity for him will become a real

problem as he begins to ask himself "who he is" in terms that
implicitly threaten the stability of Mark's conceptions of what
sort of social roles are to be made available to young knights.
Berger and Luckmann point to this "outsider" status as the
starting point for cultural transcendence: "The possibility of
'individualism' . . . is directly linked to the possibility of
unsuccessful socialization. We have argued that unsuccessful
socialization opens up the question of 'Who I am?'" Such a
question is so dangerous to any institution because it breeds
questions of identity in others and it supposits heretofore
nonexistent points of view one might hold in regard to himself.
It opens the way for pluralism and deconstructs the dominant
point of view. We should recall how Tristram raises just these
questions in Sir Baldwin, Sir Dynas, and Sir Sadock--all of
whom begin to see themselves as lovers or followers of Tristram
rather than Mark. Berger and Luckmann continue, "In the
social-context in which unsuccessful socialization becomes so
recognized, the same question arises for the successfully
socialized individual by virtue of his reflection about the
unsuccessfully socialized. He will sooner or later encounter
those with 'hidden selves,' the 'traitors,' those who have
alternated or are alternating between discrepant worlds" (171).
I need hardly mention Tristram's alternations which include the
Round Table, Isode, and Dynadan and which Mark feels as
threatening.

Malory's tragic romance illustrates the way in which
institutions are unable to redeem themselves or, more
accurately, unable to resolve the social problems that their own
existence and own truths create, the cultural crisis that they
themselves have become. The tragedy inherent in political life
can only be avoided by a redeeming hero, and yet everything
that is central to the institution opposes such a hero, precisely
as the medieval Catholic Church opposed reformers as heretics
and has never been able to carry out its own basic reforms. In
terms of the political theory and practices of the late Middle
Ages, we are referring to the importance of the continuity and
preservation of justice in the world because from justice follows
peace and the proper life for men. But justice and peace, the
great social goals, exclude redemption and innovation because
of the amount of pluralism and disorder these initially introduce
into the social sphere. All redeemers or cultural innovators

present different social structures and different behavioral programs legitimized by what the redeemer himself claims is an authority higher than the present termination of the institution's explanatory regress. We might recall, for example, the many times that Jesus Christ legitimated his actions by invoking his father in heaven, while the defenders of the present dominant ideology, the pharasees, traced their legitimations only to Mosaic law: "And then he said unto them, Ye are from beneath: I am from above; ye are of this world; I am not of this world . . . I speak that which I have seen with my Father; and ye do that which ye have seen with your father [Abraham]" (John 8: 23 and 41).

The chaos of having two or even a plurality of legitimating terminations simply cannot be tolerated by the well-socialized, for it refutes the ultimate truth upon which their world is based. Ultimate legitimations, logic, and the personal identities of the already-socialized function in relation to institutional development in the way a railroad track determines the movement of a train. One cannot simply turn to the left or right without ultimate consequences. Even the mere suggestion of alternate routes, as one might take in an automobile, strikes panic in the hearts and minds of the vast majority of riders. As Dante puts it in **De Monarchia**, "Things hate to be in disorder, but a plurality of authorities is disorder; therefore, authority is single," and later "justice is by its nature a kind of rightness or straight rule without deviation . . . Therefore, justice is the most powerful in the world when it resides solely in the world-govenor" (12-14). St. Thomas Aquinas holds the same view: "Now the welfare and safety of a multitude formed into a society lies in the preservation of its unity, which is called peace. . . . The chief concern of the ruler of a multitude, therefore, is to procure the unity of peace" (On Kingship, 11). Those in power, therefore, tend to exert all their effort to keep the train, so to speak, on the track. Of this peace, Dante concludes:

> I have now made clear enough that the proper work of mankind taken as a whole is to exercise continually its entire capacity for intellectual growth, first, in theoretical matters, and secondarily, in an extension of theory in practice.

And since the part is a sample of the whole, and since individual men find that they grow in prudence and wisdom when they can sit quietly, it is evident that mankind, too, is most free and easy to carry on its work when it enjoys the quiet and tranquility of peace. Man's work is almost divine . . . and it is clear that of all things that have been ordained for our happiness, the greatest is universal peace. (7)

This political theory is all-pervasive in the Middle Ages, from the Civitas Dei of St. Augustine to John of Salisbury's Polycraticus where the polity is compared to the human body, one body with various members, or to a hive of bees. Malory's contemporary, the fifteenth-century Sir John Fortesque, sees the continuity of the king's office as the most fundamental political issue of the times. This emphasis is, in fact, perennial in synthetic philosophy and social science as John of Salisbury writes in the Polycraticus: "Run through all the authors who have written of the commonwealth, turn over all the histories of commonwealths, and you will find no truer or more appropriate description of life in a civil society. And without doubt states would be happy if indeed they prescribed this form of life for themselves ['the pattern of civil life from the bees']" (VI, 21).

While this corporatistic theory remains perennial, the problems in the meaning of the people's work continue to grow steadily. The philosophers imply that the quest of any person's life should simply fulfill a social role in the same way that bees do or that parts of one's body do. Joseph Campbell has observed, as noted above, that the monomyth of the hero found in all cultures turns out to be a myth of self-fulfillment and self-creation: "the hero is symbolical of that divine creative and redemptive image which is hidden within us all, only waiting to be known and rendered into life." The crisis in heroism should now be obvious; heroism is absolutely not possible within the framework of any institution grounded in stability, nor is it possible to make redemptive heroes out of soldiers.

Universal peace is maintained by the performance of specified behaviors, people's work, that have been identified by the ideology as contributing to the unity of the institution and thus universal peace. At the outset of the institution these behaviors must have been effective in creating human dominance of a particular environment or no institution would have grown around them. We should recall that institutions emerge when a number of individuals decide to give up behaving in a random fashion and all adopt a single, now social, goal and agree to limit their behaviors to the most effective means of achieving that goal. Individuals make such agreements because the goals and behaviors associated with emerging institutions are truly more effective than the random behavior that previously existed. Initially, institutions offer marked advantages over individual effort. The direction of development of any institution is to repeat and to devise legitimations (philosophy and Merlin's task) for optimal behaviors; complementary to this inertia is a tendency gradually to forget through lack of practice less optimal behaviors. This is all very practical and profitable. Who would be interested in less efficient means of attaining goals that the society year by year was proving to be more and more central to life itself?

Thus the range of behavior in any institution narrows over time. Fewer and fewer acts are judged to be truly praiseworthy, while more and more individuals seek to practice the same act in order to gain the social rewards in worship or wealth. Fighting among the knights works this way. Inevitably, however, this inertia of institutions creates imbalances within the relation of humans to the natural world and within the relations of humans in the institution itself. Imbalances become the preoccupation and the social problem that the redeeming hero seeks to resolve, while everyone else continues to want to do the things that will pay off the most. As a whole, the institution really does not need so many people concentrating on one kind of activity, especially when such concentration prevents attention to other, marginal areas of life. The concentration, as we see in modern times and not really in medieval romance, overloads the natural environment to the point of resource depletion or pathogenic pollution.

In the romance, the social problem caused directly by the institution itself is simply the lack of peace or social cohesion which results from a disproportionate number of knights devoting themselves to the maintenance of peace. So many knights fighting for peace just get in each other's way, and soon they begin fighting each other to prove who is the better fighter for peace. To the outsider, the social situation no longer looks peaceful, as it clearly does not at the Tournament of Lonzep, but to the insider all this feuding and fighting can be explained as peace. No one can break out of this vicious spiral toward tragedy because of the powerful legitimations for participation; that is, the powerful training that demands that each knight view his own actions from the point of view of the needs of the institution itself. To get outside of it, one would have to posit a different termination of the explanatory regress, a different ground of reality, or different God. Meanwhile, other areas of life are ignored; there exists no institutionally legitimate way of defining one's own problem as a central problem to spend one's energy on resolving, and, if someone were to suggest his own problem, the vicious defenders of the peace would be ready and duty-bound, as the philosphers write, to execute the judgment and punishment on the deviant and heretical individual.

What Mark demands is that Tristram, as well, view every situation from the king's point of view; Mark is simply enforcing the notion of a concord of wills in opposition to a plurality of wills. Malory makes these demands very clear in the episode of Tristram's first fight with Lamerok. The situation is briefly that Mark and Tristram are watching a tournament at which Lamerok has overthrown thirty knights. Mark marvels at the knight's prowess, and Tristram informs him that the knight is Lamerok de Galis. Then Mark replies, "Hit were shame . . . that he sholde go thus away onles that he were manne-handled" (268). The only sense in which Lamerok's victorious departure could be shameful is that of the ego-centric point of view of the king who knows that a plurality of power implicitly undermines the legitimation of his own authority. The case of Sir Baldwin was discussed earlier, and we now see that the jealousy of a king-father who knows of the warrior-son's potential for replacing him is always with Mark. We see it again when, after Mark has banished Tristram, Gaheris comes to Cornwall to tell Mark of Tristram's victories at the Castle of Maidens. Mark's response here defines the sort of shame he feels in seeing Lamerok's victories:

And therewithall he smote downe hys hede, and
in hys harte he feyrd sore that sir Trystram sholde
gete hym such worship in the realme of Logrys
wherethorow hymself shuld nat be able to withstonde
hym. (333-34)

Tristram, of course, feels no jealousy toward Lamerok, his
brother, and sees shame in something different. He replies to
Mark's request for the fight, "mesemyth hit were no worshyp for
a nobleman to have ado with hym, and for this cause: for at
this tyme he hath done overmuche for ony meane knyght
lyvynge. And as me semyth . . . hit were shame to tempte hym
ony more" (269). Malory presents two distinct explanatory
regresses from the observation of Lamerok's prowess: one
terminates in kingship and the other in brotherhood. And yet if
the champion is to be the protector and sustainer of the peace
of the state, he cannot maintain a point of view contrary to
that of the king. As Dante so clearly puts it, "Therefore the
well-being of mankind depends upon the unity of wills. But this
is possible only if there is a single, dominant will which directs
all others toward unity, for the wills of mortals need direction
because they are subject to the captivating delights of youth"
(De Monarchia, 22). While John of Salisbury could advocate
tyrannicide for a king who deviated from the higher justice and
from God's will, the more traditional view is St. Thomas'
assertion that "this opinion [tyrannicide] is not in accord with
apostolic teaching. For Peter admonishes us to be reverently
subject to our masters, not only the good and the gentle but
also the froward: 'For if one who suffers unjustly bears his
troubles for conscience' sake, this is grace'" (On Kingship, 26).
Thus Tristram--the potential redeemer--becomes the
sufferer, and grace--the spiritual and psychic energy of the
world--becomes the hero's reward for accepting the social role
offered by the institution and denying his own spiritual
potential. St. Thomas' conception of grace is not life but
rather a meaningless death-in-life, exactly what worship comes
to be in the Morte. Mark counters Tristram's self-assertive
point of view with a demand which carries with it the authority
of the highest good and beauty in the world--one's love for the
king and the lady:

> `As for that,´ seyde kynge Marke, `I requyre you,
> as ye love me and my lady the quene La Beale
> Isode, take youre armys and juste with sir Lameroke
> de Galis.´   (269)

Tristram can only acquiesce and adopt Mark´s point of view
over and above his own: "ye bydde me do a thynge that is
ayenste knyghthode. . . . But bycause I woll nat displase, as
ye requyre me so muste I do and obey youre commaundemente"
(269). The stakes are too high. To enforce his own point of
view would mean to overthrow Mark, the father, in favor of
Lamerok, the brother, and chaos would ensue. Tristram would,
in addition at this early point in his life, be destroying his own
self-conception in sonhood since he would lose the core of his
own identity as knight and champion of Cornwall; his ability to
internalize Mark´s point of view created his identity as
champion in the first place. Although he desperately needs this
death of self that will bring new life, he is at this stage not
ready for it.   Certainly the greatest insight of Arthurian
Romance and Courtly Love is that there not only exists various
points of view about any issue but also that the single point of
view is destructive of the very persons it created and thus
ultimately destructive of society. St. Augustine, St. Thomas,
and Dante could never perceive this point and fought pluralism
with all the repressive force they could muster. For Malory,
the unified point of view becomes the sin while the diversity of
opinions becomes the way of salvation.

   Mark´s demands create for Tristram the role of champion
and negate his redemptive potential which would require
Tristram to see Mark and his society in the position of enemy
and direct, therefore, his energy and hatred against the
institution.   In the Polycraticus, John of Salisbury articulates
the way champions act in an institutional or corporate context;
they have no autonomous existence, but are merely the "armed
hand of the commonwealth." He considers the soldier class as
an integral or organic part of the commonwealth--"mutual
cohesion of head and members"--to be used "only against the
enemy" of the commonwealth. Continuing the metaphor of the
body politic, Salisbury writes, "the way in which the hands are
used bears witness to the character of the head. . . . The hand
of each militia, to wit both the armed and the unarmed [the

judicial function], is the hand of the prince himself" (VI, 1).
Salisbury goes on to describe the social necessity for the
champion to deny his individual will and eros. The champion in
his social role is no more than an extension of the king and is,
therefore, without a life of his own. This situation, in fact, was
the political ideal--if only theoretical--of the Middle Ages.
When Palomides comes to Cornwall, for example, returning the
abducted Brangwain and hoping thereby to win Isode's love,
Malory shows us that Mark's only defense, even of his queen, is
Tristram. Palomides demands as fulfillment of his boon that "I
woll that ye wete that I woll have youre quene to lede hir and
to governe her whereas me lyste" (264). Mark is not at all
disturbed by the request for, as Malory puts it,

> Therewyth the kynge stoode stylle and
> unbethought hym of sir Trystrames and demed that
> he wolde rescowe her. And than hastely the kynge
> answered and seyde,
> `Take hir to the and the adventures withall that
> woll falle of hit, for, as I suppose, thou wolt nat
> enjoy her no whyle' (264).

The episode of Brangwain's abduction is one that Malory
has altered radically from his sources. Principally he has
removed all suggestions of duplicity about Isode--remarks that
hold a central position in the traditional telling of the episode.
Critics have been quick to notice the change in the
characterization of Isode, but they have not adequately
recognized the significance of what Malory retains and enhances
in his version. Malory focuses upon Tristram's championhood
and upon the naturalness with which Mark relies upon Tristram
as a military extension. What interests Malory at this point are
the possibilities inherent in the king-champion symbiosis. As it
happens here, Tristram is out hunting and cannot be found.
Malory's interest is not in Isode but in Mark's response and his
concern only for the king-champion unity: "Alas . . . now am I
shamed forever, that be myne owne assente my lady and my
quene shall be devoured" (264). This remark must be
considered in relation to the discussion above about Lamerok
and the shame that he potentially presents to Mark. The king's
shame or honor and the authority of his assents and assertions

depend upon the presence and fidelity of his champion, that is, the unity of wills in the commonwealth. The unity of the commonwealth, Malory shows us, is not a unity by nature, but rather a synthesis which serves only the interests of the king or the institution itself.

Tristram finally arrives, is apprised of the abduction of Isode, and rescues her. The emphasis is, again, upon Mark's response: "sir Trystrames toke the quene and brought her agayne unto kynge Marke. And than was there made grete joy of hir home-commynge. Than who was cheryshed but sir Trystrames!" (267). This remark puzzles Vinaver who writes "M[alory] seems to imply that the king was genuinely glad to welcome Tristram back to the court." He points out further that in the French version, Mark's joy is clearly a deception: "le roi monstre a Tristan moult bel semblant pour le decepvoir" ("Mark shows Tristram a very kind countenance in order to deceive him," Works, III, 1464). Malory's version, however, cannot be understood by reference to the French at this point. Mark is sincere in his joy for he knows how much his position as king depends upon the champion who can sustain him.

The origin of Mark's relationship with Tristram in the fight with Marhalt exhibits the same point. Mark sends messengers to King Angwysh with words that he will not pay the truage and that Angwysh should send his knight to fight with a knight of Cornwall. When his bluff fails and Marhalt appears, Mark is left in the embarrassing and helpless position of having no champion: "And when kynge Marke undirstood that he was there aryved for to fyght for Irelonde, than made kynge Marke grete sorow, whan he undirstood that the good knyght sir Marhalt was com; for they knew no knyght that durste have ado with hym, for at that tyme sir Marhalte was called one of the famuste knyghtes of the worlde" (233). Malory dwells to a considerable extent upon the helplessness of Mark at this point. It is apparent that his attempt to free Cornwall from its bondage--symbolically to restore its freedom and life--will fail. Malory's point is that institutions cannot resolve their own problems, cannot save themselves. In every case Mark's motives are to enhance the prestige of Cornwall or to insure the peace of Cornwall, but nothing that is already inside of the institution can accomplish these goals. As a ruler, Mark is bound to promote the higher or universal law of justice, peace, and freedom, but he cannot of himself bring these to Cornwall, for these qualities of a polity mean, from an analytical standpoint, only that the institution is aggressively socializing more and more individuals into its order.

Institutions are inevitably imperialistic with regard to individual autonomy. Marsilius of Padua in developing a distinction between the way in which Christ rules mankind according to love for individuals and the governance of secular princes cites Origen's remark that "You know that the princes of the Gentiles lord it over them, that is they are not content merely to rule their subjects, but try to exercise violent lordship over them." Marsilius adds, "that is, by coercive force if necessary," and he goes on to quote at length from St. John Chrysostom: "The rulers of the world exist in order to lord it over their subjects, to cast them into slavery and to despoil them [namely, if they deserve it] and to use them even unto death for their [that is, the rulers'] own advantage and glory" (124-25). Mark's position as lord requires a champion, and he recognizes in Tristram the potential for redeeming Cornwall. The people themselves, symbolized by Tristram, carry out Mark's directions and restore to Cornwall the justice, peace, and freedom by identifying with Mark or by acting like patriots. But Malory's interest in the "Book of Tristram" is analytic; he wants to show the inherent separateness of ideology and individuals or, in Salisbury's terms, of justice and force. Though they are impotent by themselves, Malory is concerned with showing that when justice and force do unite it is only at a great cost to the individuals who must submit themselves to the ostensibly higher unity.

Mark's joy in seeing Tristram return with Isode is sincere, and it, the father's love, is the source of the champion's feeling of worship and self-value. Hero worship is the debt that any society owes to the individuals who makes the existence of the society a reality. But Mark's attitude toward Tristram vacillates from love to hatred; there is, however, a consistency in the vascillation. He loves and rewards Tristram when Tristram submits himself to the social role of the champion, and he hates Tristram whenever Tristram asserts an individual will. This consistency remains to the very end of their relationship; Malory tells us that Mark kills Tristram as Tristram is harping before Isode, a clear deviation from the champion's role. The consistency shows us that the only possible social role that will produce feelings of value and meaning in the individual is the role of champion, that of submitting oneself to the institution's needs. No other behavioral options are available for the knight. Mark's love for Tristram, offered as it is at certain strategic times, means that the actions which are meaningful in identity formation are those in which the knight practices submission to the society's point of view.   In other words, the institution requires that Tristram come to know "who he is" in terms of Mark's interests; within an institution this is the only possible way of attaining what Erik Erikson calls "An optimal sense of identity . . . [which] is experienced as a sense of psychological well being. Its most obvious concomitants are a feeling of being at home in one's body, a sense of 'knowing where one is going,' and an inner assuredness of anticipated recognition from those who count" (Identity: Youth and Crisis, 165). After all of the trouble and negative value feelings he encountered in the experience with the wife of Sir Segwarde, Tristram resolves to control more carefully the expression of his erotic impulses: "I thanke you . . . but for her sake I shall beware what maner of lady I shall love or truste" (251). This over-determined and culturally conditioned orientation is the reason that he does not consider marrying Isode when he meets her and clearly loves her in Ireland.   Marriage has no part in his social role, as it does not in the role of Lancelot.   Malory points out very clearly that to gain a socially recognizable identity means inevitably to lose autonomy.

Over and over again in the "Book of Tristram" Tristram sees himself only as someone's champion, but the central theme of his tale is the gradual awakening of his need to negate and transcend that identity and follow a life that is his own adventure, to restore to man as individual the peace, justice, and freedom that at the outset he had given to Cornwall but which in the hands of his king have become his bonds. For Tristram to come to know himself only in the light of the interests of Cornwall and Mark--that is, for him to follow on a secular level St. Augustine's admonition that all men must orientate themselves totally toward the highest good--means that he must submit his own desires and impulses to the demands of the state and the father. Malory constructs the "Tristram" so that this inescapable tension between the father and the son lies at the center of everything that Tristram does. In freeing Cornwall from its bondage, Tristram takes upon himself the bondage of all mankind, and his quest is to work out and finally achieve a release from this bondage and a freedom on a level beyond Mark's legitimations. Cultural innovation always initially emerges as an antithesis to the dominant culture, especially to its ultimate legitimations.

Throughout the "Tristram" we see two sides of Tristram: the champion and the redeemer. For example, when Arthur charges that "ye ought nat to beare none armys but yf ye wyste what ye bare" (343) and demands an explanation of Morgan le Fay's shield which depicts a knight standing above another knight and a lady, Tristram sees his own role as merely a servant who "as for me I can nat dyscryve this armys, for hit is no poynte of my charge, and yet I truste to God to beare hit with worship" (343). The central theme of Chapter Two was to assert that life becomes meaningful only when an individual is able to feel that he is actively participating in creating his God, his society, and himself; but the sort of service Tristram owes to his superiors makes it clear that he has no influence upon them and that he has no idea of the meaning of the tasks required of him, only that he will perform well.

The condition of this service produces the neurosis, violence, eroticism, madness, and other anti-social behaviors in which originates the other side of Tristram and his function as redeemer. They lead to his final position at the Tournament of Lonzep where he has adopted Isode as the legitimating center of his own little world at the Joyous Garde, he knows himself now as the lover of Isode, and he repudiates allegiance to anyone else. At the Tournament, Malory emphasizes the problem of allegiance and Governance:

> And all thes drewe them to a counceyle to undirstonde what governance they shall be of. But the kynge of Irelonde his name was sir Marhalte . . . had the speache, that sir Trystram myght hyre:
> 'Now, lordis and felowis, lat us loke to oureselff.
> . . . Therefore, by my rede, lat every knyght have a standarde and a cognyssaunce by hymselff, that every knyght may draw to his naturall lorde. And than may every kynge and captayne helpe his knyght yf he have nede" (442, emphasis mine).

Malory sets up very concisely the terms of the king-champion symbiosis, especially its oft-promoted illusion about common good, but Tristram's response shows how far he has gone in rejecting that explanatory model. To Arthur's question "Well, uppon what party woll ye holde?" Tristram responds flatly, "Truly . . . I wote nat yet on what party I woll be on untyll I com to the fylde. And thereas my harte gyvyth me, there woll I holde me. But to-morow ye shall se and preve on what party I shall come" (445). Tristram has come a long way from the young man who was made a knight to fight for the well-being of Cornwall and his natural lord. Now clearly his only "natural lord" is his own heart which he follows as surely as Palomides will soon, again, follow the Questing Beast.

The theme of allegiance is indeed important in Malory; the passage about the "greate defaughte of us Englysshemen, for there may no thynge us please no terme" (708) has been quoted so often by those who consider the Morte moralistic and revivalistic that it becomes difficult to accept the real fact that Malory's romance depicts the inevitable tragedy of allegiance and the ultimate beauty of revolt. In trying to make a lack of allegiance the central flaw of the romance, Stephen Miko asserts that "His [Lancelot's] tragic flaw, if he has one, is mainly symbolic; he represents the principle of fidelity, and that principle is finally not enough" ("Malory and the Chivalric Order," 224). Not only is fidelity not enough, but even perfect fidelity to an explanatory system which on the highest level demands the death of the individual is the direct cause of the tragedy. What Tristram, Lancelot, and men of the late Middle Ages needed for psychic survival was revolt and transcendence; they needed a new conception of faith that would empower them to create anew their god, their society, and themselves. John Wyclif understood very well this new sort of faith grounded again in individual eros and pluralism:

> but feith may be taken in manye maneres. Sum tyme feith is clepid the truthe that men trowen, and so ther is a comune feith to alle cristen men. Sum tyme feith is clepid vertu that maken trewe men, and so eche trewe man hath diverse feith. And sum tyme feith is clepid oure trowynge in werkys. (English Works, 347, spelling slightly modernized)

This theme expresses the cultural problems of Malory's time. Changing economic and social conditions in England from about 1300 onward had produced a class of rather wealthy and independent merchants, laborers, knights, and professionals--the sort of folk Chaucer presents in his Canterbury Tales. These are people whose interests are intensely self-directed, and, as Chaucer perceives, they have acquired an acute sense of personal identity and have lost the unconditional orientation toward the unity of the commonwealth. More and more throughout the late Middle Ages, the relationship among the members of the commonwealth was growing away from the hierarchical and submissive bond of the body politic toward pluralism and money ties. Serious shortages of labor caused by the Black Death of the middle fourteenth century made laws against high wages for labor necessary in order to prevent the increase in independence of peasants who were beginning to discover that they could leave a natural lord and move to employment that would offer them higher wages.

As Jean Froissart in the Chronicles tells us, a "crack-brained" priest from Kent named John Ball used to assemble the common people after mass on Sundays to tell them:

> Good people, things cannot go right in England and never will, until goods are held in common and there are no more villeins and gentlefolk, but we are all one and the same. In what way are those whom we call lords greater masters than ourselves? How have they deserved it? Why do they hold us in bondage? If we all spring from a single father and mother, Adam and Eve, how can they claim or prove that they are lords more than us, except by making us produce and grow the wealth which they spend. (212)

The manifesto presented by John Ball, Wat Tyler, Jack Straw and the peasants who revolted in 1381 demanded the abolition of villeinage, the establishment of labor service based upon free contracts, equality for all men, confiscation of church estates, and no more lordships except for the king. These were indeed radical demands; so radical even by today's standards that the historian Edward Cheney writes, "An equalitarian, almost a communistic thread ran through the popular revolts, as indeed it did through the heresies of the period. They were both rebellions of the common man against the powers of this world, economic, political and ecclesiastical" (Dawn of a New Era, 132). In June of 1381, King Richard II finally met the mob of peasants and asked them what they wanted. Froissart reports that their reply was "we want you to make us free for ever and ever, we and our heirs and our lands, so that we shall never again be called serfs or bondsmen" (221). These peasants were demanding for themselves what Mark demands for Cornwall from Ireland. Freedom is also what Tristram demands from Mark at a point a little later on when Mark himself has assumed the role of the father demanding truage from the son. Richard, like Mark, seeing the difficulty of his position as he was surrounded by sixty thousand drunk and angry peasants and artisans readily assented, answering "that I grant you. Now go back home in your village companies as you came here" (221). Such are the deceits to which the king is permitted.

But the crowds did not disperse and later with their anger increased they met at the horse market in Smithfield intent upon sacking London and carrying off as much wealth as they could find. Led by Wat Tyler, the mob demanded a confrontation with the king. In front of the king, Tyler was insulting and rude; he demanded that the king's sword bearer give him the sword he was carrying. "Never," we are told the squire replied to Tyler, "it's the King's sword. It's not for such as you, you're only a boor." As the two men in the presence of Richard himself fought over the King's sword, the Lord Mayor of London, one Sir William Walworth, arrived fully armed and challenged Wat Tyler, saying, "Fellow, how dare you say such things in the King's presence. . . . You talk like that in the presence of the King, my natural lord? I'll be hanged if you don't pay for it." With that, he drew a cutlass and hewed Tyler to death in full view of the mob of peasants.

What is important about this confrontation is that it reveals the real power of the king and why cultural evolution or redemption is so traumatic. After Tyler is killed by Walworth, the mob, seeing the murder, resolves to kill Richard who was accompanied by a mere seventy-two men. Although the peasants out-number the king tremendously, their violence is stopped by the mere presence and eminence of the king's person. They cannot continue their revolt face to face with the king. Richard is said to have ridden forward to meet the mob saying "Sirs, what more do you want? You have no other captain but me. I am your king, behave peaceably" (Froissart, 225-27). Edward Cheyney doubts "whether a boy of fourteen, even if endowed with the precocity and duplicity of Richard, could have so easily made his peace with a mob long out of hand. But whatever the cause"--and this is the important point--"the morale of the rebels was lost. London was soon abandoned" (135-36).

We should not, however, even for a moment doubt the power of the king's presence or, more generally, the state to intimidate a mob of revolutionaries. As the peasants melt before the king, we see same sort of rational self-restraint that governs Tristram in his confrontations with Mark. They cannot, even now, hold the king as enemy because, after all, Tyler was murdered by the Mayor of London. These peasants have been, as everyone else, socialized within the political ideology of England so that the king represents in the super-ego of any peasant a force of immeasurable and unassailable strength, one that the individual with his own life must protect and a strength which no individual judges himself to possess. Richard III in Shakespeare's play understands this clearly: "the King's name is a tower of strength, which they upon the adverse faction want" (V. iii, 12). The king's presence stands as a concrete symbol for the ultimate legitimation; no revolution can go forward until the revolutionaries have first learned to alienate themselves from the culture's ultimate explanations and legitimations. Very interestingly, Paulo Freire, in his The Pedagogy of the Oppressed, reports that even today peasants who in South America rebelled against their landowners and had even taken some landowners captive refused to stand guard over them, so terrifying was their mere presence. After a day or so of rebellion, the landowners simply walked free. The Anonimalle Chronicle tells us that after the confrontation in Smithfield, on the same day Richard II made knights of those who had defended him, giving them also forty pounds in land; to Sir William Walworth, the killer of Wat Tyler, he gave one hundred pounds in land.

Malory was certainly a part of this popular drive for independence and individualism, and while the revolt of 1381 melted before the person of the king, Malory makes this sort of internal control upon the individual--the dominant super-ego--the theme and greatest problem of his romance. The headnote for this chapter from Dietrich Bonhoeffer's Ethics exemplifies the transition from the healthy and meaningful society and individuals to the repressive society and psychotic individuals that I am arguing is the theme of Malory's attempt to write the whole book of king Arthur. Bonhoeffer recognizes the human inability to exist merely upon one's "own contingent individuality" and the concomitant quest to unify oneself with a Christ who in becoming both origin and goal empowers the individual to create his own identity and self-value. Jesus Christ as redeemer releases mankind from the limitations of his contingent individuality by fulfilling the position of a trans-personal legitimation which makes possible a new and ever more autonomous life for the individual. The quest for identity originates in a desire for autonomy, and Jesus Christ is man's freedom. Marsilius recognized this sort of governance in Christ.

But what happens we may ask, as Bonhoeffer does and as Malory does, when the Christ and the Redeemer turn out to be an Adolf Hitler, a Mark, an Arthur, or, more generally, a reified institution committed to its own stability? Suddenly the miracles of faith and redemption retain the exact structure as before but the effect is to deprive the individual of his autonomy and demand of the individual total renunciation of his heretofore unceasing quest for his own origin in Christ and in freedom. The knight who says my conscience is Mark, Arthur, or the doctrines of the church just as the man who says "my conscious is Adolf Hitler" loses the ability to continue the circulation of spiritual energy in the world (as Campbell says) and spreads only death and destruction across the earth, creating, as Balin was the first to do, a wasteland in his wake.

The difference between what Jesus Christ offered men and what the late medieval Church as official representative of Christ offered men is most profound. The character of Jesus Christ cannot be fully developed here, but it is enough to point out that Christ's position can never be solidly pinned down; he is always indefinite. His message is of an explanatory regress that transcends the laws and ideology of the present social reality and, therefore, of forgiveness which means that every action can always be undone and reversed and that every son can find justification in front of a father.   There is no corporate and doctrinal stability in Jesus Christ; his religion is one of ever developing identity.   This is essentially Luther's view of Christ, as we shall see toward the end of Chapter Four.   But the Church, on the other hand, hardened Christ's words into teachings, laws, obligatory rituals; it was the perception of the writers of Courtly Love and Arthurian Romance that this definition of religion was in reality the annihilation of the existence of the individual.   In Chapter Two, the point was made that the Roman Church had by the twelfth century assumed a position as mediator between man and God and therefore had made itself, in effect, man's redeemer or Christ. It was shortly after this time that revolutionary thinkers such as Ockham, Wyclif, or Marsilius began to think of the pope as an "anti-christ" in recognition that in demanding obedience and submission the pope had ended the possibility of the individual's finding freedom and release from the isolation of biological existence in redemption or in Christ and instituted repression in the form of social identification in its place.   The true and redemptive hero must also learn to see his father, his state, and his inherited explanations of the world as "anti-christs" so that he can continue to modify and build human institutions that serve ever-changing human needs.

Galahad's and Percival's overpowering interest in the life after death represents the great shift from what Bonhoeffer calls <u>autonomy</u> to <u>heteronomy</u> and from what I have been calling mythic association to social identification.   It represents also the transition from the first stage of civilization in which the society <u>is</u> the actions of the knights to the second stage in which the knights must repeat the rituals as performances which have no ability to continue creating healthy selves and societies.   The tournament is not something within the knight as the quest is; rather it is something held in a place "out there" to which the knight must travel in a very specified direction.   This transition is also the movement from a meaningful society to a repressive one that ends only in the sort of tragedy in which the knights simply kill each other off because their minds are focused on codes and gods which are "out there" rather than the ones that exist within and the problems they immediately face. The ineffable and infinite quest for the numen through which Sir Gareth created both himself and the Round Table has become heteronomous because the indeterminacy of the quest for the numen, which enabled autonomous participation, has been replaced by fixed and absolute doctrines and laws. As the Grail Quest begins, Malory tells us

> And so on the morne they were all accorded that they sholde departe everych from othir. And on the morne they departed with wepying chere, and than every knyght toke the way that hym lyked beste. (524)

Every real quest begins as an autonomous adventure of each knight following the path of life that he likes best, the path that best suits his eros; at the beginning of the Round Table, they follow the unfolding of their own fates in the form of a questing beast, a white stag, a black shield, a beautiful woman, or whatever, for the quest is the natural impulse of eros to fulfill psychic and physical needs arising from contact with the outside world. But as the romance progresses just as the medieval world progressed, the quest has come to have only one end. Though it began in pluralism, it must end in unity. In writing Le Morte Darthur, Malory traces the development of the mythic understructure of the medieval world as it progresses toward the point of tragedy. This point, as Anders Nygren has written of the individual in relation to medieval theology, is the point at which "His ego must be killed and annihilated only so he can pass into God and become one" (Agape and Eros, 649). How in a world like this can the redemptive hero come through the quest of his life to learn who he is?

A realization of the catastrophic implications for theology of the idea of "transcendence" was first delivered to Christian Europe through that "Invincible Doctor," as he was called, the nominalist William of Occam (c. 1300-1349), after whose quick keen slash across the whole great big balloon, scholastic "philosophy" collapsed of its own dead weight. Already in the writings of Thomas Aquinas, in whose vast **Summa Theologica** the art of inflating revelation with reason came to culmination, there is at least one great word in recognition of the ineffable as just that, ineffable; namely, in the **Summa Contra Gentiles,** the phrase: "For then alone do we know God truly, when we believe that He is far above all that man can possibly think of God." However, the Angelic Doctor went on then to expatiate in his **Summa Theologica** on God as Being, First Cause, A Personality, Immutable, et cetera, refuting heresies right and left (other people's concepts of the inconceivable), as far as to the beginning of an exposition of the sacraments--when saying Mass one morning in the chapel of Saint Nicholas at Naples, he experienced a sort of thunderclap from aloft, a raptus mentis.

In Aquinas' case, the moment of supreme rapture had apparently so diminished his respect for the long, sober, "healthy" labor of his life, that his energies could not return to it. They had passed to another sphere: the same at sight of which Galahad, trembling right hard, as when flesh begins to behold spiritual things, held up his hands to heaven and gave thanks and asked to die. It was ineffable, beyond words, beyond signs: transcendent.

--Joseph Campbell, The Masks of God:
Creative Mythology

4.
Evolution in Culture

4.1 The Triumph of the Father

When Malory turns to the "Quest of the Holy Grail," he raises to a metaphysical and mythical level the failure that Tristram discovers in seeking to redeem himself by seeking a redeeming king. Malory has greatly reduced the French Queste del Saint Graal, but what he eliminates is mostly the explanatory sections which justify submission to God by explaining submission in terms of freedom and release. Vinaver, among others, thinks that this tendency to suppress the dogmatic parts of the "Grail Quest" represents Malory's interest in displaying the feats of knight-errantry, but it also, and perhaps more significantly, allows actions to stand on their own merit. This strategy becomes a subtle way of denying the heteronomous God because it allows the demands of this God for the death of the son to stand without regress to ultimate legitimations: "Sir Galahad, thou shalt have thy requeste, and whan thou askyst the deth of thy body thou shalt have hit, and than thou shalt have the lyff of thy soule" (605). This is a God who requires the death of the body in return for the freedom or redemption of the soul. In historical terms, this demand means the renunciation of the present in favor of the future or of the past. In social terms, it means the renunciation of individual or personal interests in favor of the interests of the state or the king.

As Malory's version of the Grail Quest develops, this submission becomes exactly what Freud has defined as Thanatos or the Death Instinct. In Beyond the Pleasure Principle, Freud recognizes that in addition to the pleasure principle which is the instinct to exercise eros or psychic energy toward the goal of tension reduction there exists in human beings the instinct or wish simply to stop striving, to become inert, and to be subsumed back into the elements of nature where the energy for maintaining individuality and life will no longer have to be expended. The imagery associated with the death instinct frequently suggests a return to the womb or a Nirvana, a tensionless place not of this world where the individual becomes lost in his creative source and does not have to exert himself to be happy. Freud hesitates to call the death instinct a contrastive impulse to the pleasure principle and psychic energy because it might actually be a continuation of the pleasure principle to a gratification even higher and more stable than the object of the psychic energy. It is "beyond the pleasure principle," but it is also the end of the pleasure principle and the end of psychic energy and thus of life itself (32-42).

Galahad and Percival come to represent the death instinct, an impulse that Lancelot and Tristram never submit to for it means in Malory's terms an end to the world of striving and questing. Galahad sees the direction of his life as moving toward death and the loss of his individual existence:

> `Sir, that shall I telle you,` seyde sir Galahad,
> `Thys othir day, when we sawe a parte of the
> adventures of the Sangreall, I was in such joy of
> herte that I trow never man was that was erthely.
> And therefore I wote well, when my body ys dede,
> my soule, shall be in grete joy to se the Blyssed
> Trinite every day and the majeste of oure Lorde
> Jesu Cryste` (605).

Thus the Grail Quest ends in another kind of redemption, the highest meaning of which is a reconciliation between the father and the son. In terms of the conflicts central to the last chapter, this redemption now means removal of the tensions between the individual and culture or the perfection of sonhood that Tristram could not attain. The quest begins with a very

clear statement of the need of the land for redemption.
Galahad is revealed by a hermit to be a Christ-figure who
comes to release men from the bondage of their present lives:

> Also I may sey you that the Castell of Maydyns
> betokenyth the good soulys that were in preson
> before the Incarnacion of oure Lorde Jesu Cryste.
> And the seven knyghtes betokenyth the seven dedly
> synnes that regned that time in the worlde. And I
> may lycken the good knyght Galahad unto the Sonne
> of the Hyghe Fadir that lyght within a maydyn and
> bought all the soules oute of thralle: so ded sir
> Galahad delyver all the maydyns oute of the woofull
> castell. (535)

The meaning of redemption for both Tristram and Galahad is
release from bonds, and it is accomplished only when an
individual has, as Joseph of Aramathea advises, "leffte hys
beleve of the olde law and beleeve uppon the new law" (520).
Just what is old and what in new in law is the issue which this
chapter undertakes.

The conditions of the wasteland to which Galahad comes
are those of the meaningless, repressive society that I have
been describing as prevailing in Cornwall in an open manner
and at the Round Table in a covert manner. At the outset of
the Grail Quest, Malory makes these conditions very explicit.
Although he shortens the French version of the Queste, he
retains and enhances the references to the nature of the
meaninglessness. He first emphasizes the isolation and
contingent individuality of men: "And ye have sene that they
have loste hir fadirs and hir modirs and all hir kynne, and hir
wyves and hir chyldren, for to be of youre felyship" (541).
Such a condition prompts one to unify oneself with a Christ or
a redeeming institution, but inevitably strife emerges within the
institution between the jealous father and a restless son. For
Malory, institutions are inherently inadequate adaptations; an
abbot tells Galahad that the great sin in the world is that "the
fadir loved nat the sonne, nother the sonne loved nat the fadir.
And that was one of the causys that oure Lorde toke fleysh and
blood of a clene maydyn" (528).

The condition of enmity between the father and the son reproduces anew in the son the sensation of alienation and contingent individuality that he originally sought to remedy. It also leads to the obvious conclusion of the Oedipal situation in which "the sonne spared nat the fadir no more than a straunger" (546). The general condition, as Malory so clearly perceives, is that of being dispossessed or disinherited. Each of the great Grail Knights--Percival, Bors, and Galahad--faces at least one major adventure involving someone who has been disinherited or cut off from the happiness and well-being from which he came and toward which he is uncontrollably and unconsciously directed. Malory's Grail Quest pushes social concerns to their ultimate level, just as Sigmund Freud does in Beyond the Pleasure Principle, where he searches for an understanding of human impulses toward the paradisiacal state of tensionlessness on a basis much deeper than the instinct for sex; in the new theory he seeks to account for the compulsion to repeat tension reductive acts in far broader areas than sex might encompass. Freud alights upon a myth of Plato which suggests an unconscious impulse to return to an earlier state of being from which the individual has been expelled but whose memory lingers in the unconscious. It seems to me, Freud's discovery is especially instructive in our investigation of Malory's Grail Quest:

> Science has so little to tell us about the origin of sexuality that we can liken the problem to a darkness into which not so much as a ray of a hypothesis has penetrated. In quite a different region, it is true, we do meet with such a hypothesis; but it is of so fantastic a kind--a myth rather than a scientific explanation--that I should not venture to produce it here, were it not that it fulfills precisely the one condition whose fulfillment we desire. For it traces the origin of an instinct to a need to restore an earlier state of things.
> What I have in mind is, of course, the theory which Plato put into the mouth of Aristophanes in the Symposium, and which deals not only with the origin of the sexual instinct but also with the most important of its variations in relation to its object.

`The original human nature was not like the present, but different. In the first place, the sexes were originally three in number, not two as they are now; there was man, woman, and the union of the two. . .

Everything about these primaeval men was double: they had four hands and four feet, two faces, two privy parts, and so on. Eventually Zeus decided to cut these men in two, `like a sorb-apple which is halved for pickling`. After the division had been made, `the two parts of man, each desiring the other half, came together, and threw their arms about one another eager to grow into one`. (51-51)

This theme of being disinherited or being cut off from what one originally was is of utmost importance because, as we shall see at the end of the Grail Quest, God decides finally and once and for all to disinherit the Round Table as He withdraws the Grail from the realm of men. Being cut off from one's other half or being expelled from one's true home in heaven signifies the human condition of alienation and contingent individuality for which redemption is the remedy. As just mentioned, each major Grail-knight encounters someone who has been disinherited. Percival's adventure will suffice for an example; while the obvious archetype is the fall of Lucifer, we should also read what follows as an allegory of birth, as the soul pre-existing in heaven is consigned to a period of earthly existence in a mortal and mutable body. We should also recall Tristram and Melyodas.

`Sir,` she said, `I dwelled with the grettist man of the worlde, and he made me so fayre and so clere that there was none lyke me. And of that grete beawte I had a litill pryde, more than I oughte to have had. Also I sayde a worde that plesed hym nat, and than he wolde nat suffir me to be no lenger in his company. And so he drove me frome myne herytayge and disheryted me for ever, and he had never pite of me nother of none of my counceyle nother of my courte. And sitthyn, sir kynght, hit hath befallyn me to be so overthrowyn and all myne, yet I have benomme hym of som of hys men and

made hem to becom my men, for they aske never
nothynge of me but I gyff hem that and much more.
Thus I and my servauntes werre ayenste hym nyght
and day, therefore I know no good knyght nor no
good man but I gete hem on my syde and I may.
And for that I know that ye are a good knyght I
beseche you to helpe me, and for ye be a felowe of
the Rounde Table, wherefore ye ought nat to fayle
no jantillwoman which ys disherite and she besought
you of helpe.´   (549)

The terms upon which this woman's story is built are
important.   She speaks of a golden age, an Eden, or paradise
which was destroyed by her own pride or transgression and the
resulting war between herself and the ruler.   We should see in
this story an exact parallel to what has happened at Cornwall
and the Round Table in the relationships between Mark and
Arthur and their great knights.   We should also see in this
situation a neurosis of the sort which Alfred Adler claims is the
human condition--a feeling of anxiety, abandonment, or
inferiority in the face of stimuli coming from the environment.
The recognition that disinheritance is a neurotic condition
directs us to look for its causes and for strategies for relief
since, as was mentioned before, the orientation of psychic life
is toward removal of these internal tensions.   In the case at
hand, the cause is "a litill pryde" which clearly suggests an
impulse of psychic energy to assert oneself in ways not
legitimated in ideology.   The remedy for which the woman seeks
Percival's help is the Oedipus Complex, war against the father,
or even greater pride and self-assertion.   But the remedy which
the Grail Quest as a whole offers is precisely the opposite;
neuroses of this sort are remedied by redemption as penance
and submission.   These episodes raise, perhaps, the ultimate
question asked by writers of Arthurian Romance: on what terms
are peace and harmony between the individual and the state
possible?   Or, what means does man have for returning to the
original paradisiacal state of being?   These terms are precisely
the meaning of redemption.
    The adventure of Percival makes the entire process clear.
Percival begins at the point of anxiety and isolation; he has
departed from his mother and a world of innocence which he

will never see again. He enters immediately into the realm of
the knights of the Round Table because it replaces the security
and family-feeling that his mother had offered. The Queen of
the West Lands makes all this clear to him: "Hit ys well seyne
be you, for synes ye departed from your modir ye wolde never
se her, ye founde such felyship at the Table Rounde" (541).
Joining an institution or moving from one small institution
whose behavioral range the individual has outgrown into a
larger one satisfies the impulse to recover the earlier state of
tensionlessness, but on another level it means that Percival
retains the orientations of a son; he does not suffer the
repression of the Round Table since as a son he has not yet
experienced impulses to progress on to a yet higher level of
being and maturity. The disinherited woman asks him to wage
war upon a father, and Malory makes it clear that Percival
knows nothing yet of the Oedipus Complex:

> Than was sir Percivale alone. And as the tale
> tellith, he was at that tyme, one of the men of the
> worlde whych moste beleved in oure Lorde Jesu
> Cryste, for in tho dayes there was but fewe folkes
> at that tyme that beleved perfitely; for in tho days
> the sonne spared nat the fadir no more than a
> straunger.
>   And so sir Percivale comforted hymselff in oure
> Lorde Jesu and besought Hym that no temptacion
> sholde brynge hym oute of Goddys servys, but to
> endure as His trew champyon. (546)

We have already seen in the case of Tristram that to be a
champion is to submit one's autonomous point of view to the
point of view of the authority; thus to be a champion is to be a
son. As Percival's adventure develops, the temptation which
confronts him will ask him to give up his sonhood and
championhood.

Carl Jung tells us that one of the essential roles of
psychic energy is to fund the progression of the individual with
energy to advance daily in the process of psychological and
physiological adaptation or growth. Progression is a continuous
process; Jung stresses that "Adaptation is not something that is
achieved once and for all, though there is a tendency to believe

the contrary." Psychological progress springs from the confrontation of environmental conditions the infinite variety of which presents, of course, "a vital need for such adaptation" (Psychic Energy, 32-39). Thus progression is life itself seen as growth and change. When the woman approaches Percival with her story of disinheritance, she presents to Percival an environmental confrontation. The woman is a temptress and she asks Percival to join her in a war against her father. In psychoanalytic terms she awakens in Percival the Oedipus Complex, as all environmental confrontations potentially do in the sense that they present opportunities for behavioral and psychological growth. If growth occurs, Percival will nullify his previously held orientations of a son; he will come to regard the father as a stranger.

That Malory and his French source-writer are aware of the psychoanalytic implications of Percival's progress or growth is clear from what ensues. There is no overt battle with a father; rather the trauma is completely within Percival. He removes his armor and drinks enough wine so that he begins to forget the restrictions of the father's laws and to have amorous desires for the lady. The awakening of sexual impulses images forth the potential that a son could become a father himself and, therefore, at least psychically, equal to the father. The son seeks to replace his father in the sense that he will no longer retain the orientations of a son and no longer renounce the impulses that kept him a son; he will learn to see the world as a father sees it. At this point the father loses control of the son.

The description of Percival at this point indicates a quantitative increase in the level of his psychic energy. Passion and ardor are frequently images for an otherwise ineffable psychic energy, but the point is that we see an individual who is stimulated, aggressive and culturally dangerous:

> therewith he was chaffett a lityll more than he oughte to be. With that he behylde that jantilwoman, and hym thought she was the fayryst creature that ever he saw.
> And than sir Percivale profird her love and prayde hir that she woulde be hys. Than she refused

hym in a maner whan he requyred her, for cause he
sholde be the more ardente on hir. And ever he
sesed nat to pray hir of love. And whan she saw
hym well enchaffed. . . . (549)

In return for her acquiesence, the woman asks that Percival
pledge his faith to her:

`Sir Percivale, wyte you well I shall nat fulfylle
youre wylle but if ye swere frome henseforthe ye
shall by my trew servaunte, and to do nothynge but
that I shall commaunde you. Woll ye ensure me thys
as ye be a trew knyght?´ (550)

Psychologically and culturally, this demand represents the
change in orientations from those of a son to those of a lover
and potentially a father. At the very least, it represents
freedom from the demands of the father and freedom from
ultimate legitimations and the logic which controls Percival's
ability to choose rationally his actions. Percival has already
been warned in a dream that "to-morne thou muste fyght with
the strongest champion of the worlde. And if thou be overcom
thou shalt nat be quytte for losyng of ony of thy membrys, but
thou shalt be shamed for ever to the worldis ende" (546). What
can this dream mean? If Percival submits to the temptation,
loses the fight, he will not lose any of his members but he will
lose his soul. If, on the contrary, he defeats the temptation, he
will save his soul but lose one of his members. As a son
Percival responded to the controls of a heteronomous authority-
-"I serve the beste man of the worlde, and in Hys servyse He
woll nat suffir me to dye" (548)--but now he begins to respond
to impulses arising from within him; in the father's eyes eros is
the "strongest champion of the worlde." The woman or
temptress will not become his master; she is, as argued before,
his aim and occasion. Percival's master will be his own psychic
energy or eros, as he learns by the end of the episode: "Sitthyn
my fleyssh woll be my mayster I shall punyssh hit" (550).
    As Malory so clearly sees, the war against the father--
"Thus I and my servauntes werre ayenste hym nyght and day"--
actually takes place within the individual as the struggle for
freedom of impulses of psychic energy from the controls of the

super-ego. Psychic energy is the origin of progress, adaptation, and change against which the rational and legitimating function of the super-ego stands. Before, of course, Percival can consumate his sin by adopting an orientation other than toward God, he is saved by the over-powering stimulus of a father-symbol. I want to emphasize that the symbol does nothing itself, it is inert; but Percival's cognition fixes upon this one stimuli and its culturally determined response to the exculsion of all others:

> And by adventure and grace he saw hys swerde ly on the erthe naked, where in the pomell was a rede crosse and the synge of the crucifixe therin, and bethought hym on hys knyghthode and hys promyse made unto the good man tofornehande, and than he made a synge in the forehed of hys. (550)

Immediately he re-adopts the son's orientations and views his aborted self-expression in the way the father would regard it: "Fayre swete Lorde Jesu Cryste, ne lette me nat be shamed, which was nyghe loste had nat Thy good grace bene!" His next act is to punish himself; to carry out on his own the aggression which the father would have used to prevent the son's rebellion: "And therewith he rooff hymselff thorow the thygh, that the blood sterte aboute hym, and seyde, `A, good Lord, take thys in recompensacion of that I have myssedone ayenste The, Lorde!" (550). We must view this act as a self-castration, the loss of the member prophesied in Percival's dream, and symbolizing both the son's renunciation of psychic energic impulses and the aggressive destruction of those impulses by the father. Freud holds that castration or some symbolic form of it--shame, submissiveness, guilty conscience, mental or physical debilitation--is the father's defense against the emergence of the Oedipus Complex in the son, and the process of socialization or identification with the father induces in the son a willingness to carry out these measures against himself, even in the absence of the father. Freud also maintains that castration or its symbolic forms are necessary in order for the child to remain in the father's home.

On a larger level, an institution or a civilization is the home for each human being. We see in Percival's adventure that in order to avoid suffering the anxiety and isolation of disinheritance which the woman's temptations were designed to lead Percival into, the individual must renounce his impulses toward progress and growth in favor of the laws or behavioral programs of the institution. Any organism is always initially less emotionally secure in the new and higher role it has moved into, and initially there is always a strong impulse to return, let's say, from adulthood to childhood where life was not fraught with such tensions and complications. This is just what Mark demands of Tristram. In order to remain in Cornwall, Tristram must retain totally the role of the dutiful son. For Percival, in order to remain a Christian he must continue to "serve the beste man of the worlde, [because] in Hys servyce He woll nat suffir me to dye" (548).

What Malory's version of the Grail Quest implicitly asks is what happens when the father does ask the servant to die, either in literal death or in death as a renunciation of autonomy and psychic energy. And these are, finally, the terms, Malory suggests, upon which peace and harmony between the individual and the authority are possible. Redemption, the reconciliation of the father and the son and the attainment of the earlier state of tensionlessness, occurs only as the sons fail to progress to a level of maturity beyond what they now hold and choose, as Percival does, to move backward into earlier states. In the course of his quest for the Grail, Percival even returns to his childhood home and mother whom, of course, he finds has died of a broken heart after he left her. This discovery only makes Percival feel more guilt, more psychic castration.

None of this is to suggest that Malory is writing a Freudian romance but rather that both Freud and Malory faced in their own times a highly similar set of cultural problems. The late Middle Ages and the late Modern Age (nineteenth and early twentieth centuries) are sometimes compared, and the most obvious point of comparison is the revolutions which stemmed from the perception that the present powers (whether ecclesiastical or industrial) were so tyrannical as to have no right to rule an essentially free and noble populace. Both Malory and Freud see happiness in the unhindered expression of psychic or erotic impulses and they see the frustration of eros as the source of evil and unhappiness in the world. For the late Middle Ages, the oppressive authority was the Church, and the revolution was the reformation which had the effect of fragmenting the unity of the ultimate legitimating authority and transferring authority to disparate locations. The nineteenth century revolted against secular authorities, but it completes the reformation in the sense that it further fragments the location of authority by discovering it within the unconscious of each individual. I discussed at some length the problem of revivalism and historicism in Chapter One; now I believe that we are able to see that any attempt to look backward in history for a justification of the present life would simply, in Malory's mind, represent a cultural regression amounting to psychic death.

Writers of these periods perceive, more than writers of other periods, the dominant institutions of their own times as especially inadequate adaptations to the environments they are facing. The adult who dreams of returning to childhood as a happier time of life forgets that the behavioral and cognitive programs of childhood would be quite inadequate for the situations he now finds himself in. For Malory, the dominant institutions of the late Middle Ages simply were not addressing what he had come to believe were the real problems of life. At times like these, we recognize an increased interest in sex or what is popularly called a sexual revolution within a culture, and it signifies an awareness of the regressiveness of that culture's explanatory synthesis and behavioral programs. Sex provides an escape route and a private life in which one can experiment with innovations beyond the control of ideology; because of the easily attainable sense of physical arousal, the great amounts of psychic energy necessary for negating cultural controls are available almost on demand. The convenient structural relation between and cultural revolution and both the phsyical and emotional sexual act is why writers such as Andreas Capellanus emphasize the necessity of keeping the love affair secret. The lover shifts the explanatory regress of his own actions from the termination in the state to the termination in the lady.

Our interest here, therefore, is not specifically in the sexual act; rather I raise the issue because specific sexual acts play--oddly enough--an even greater role in the Grail Quest than elsewhere in Arthurian Romance. The Grail is, of course, in many accounts a sexual symbol or a symbol of ultimate gratification of desire and appetite: "for thys day the Sankegreall appered in thy house and fedde the and all thy felyship" (520). Sexual impulses for both Freud and Malory are symbolic of the expression of psychic energy and personal authority in the direction of gratification or tension reduction. One is free only when he can exercise his psychic energy without frustration and restraint. Sexual restrictions and taboos only symbolize the terms of cultural controls on freedom to perform an almost infinite number of other acts. Sex in itself is not an act of freedom except in the rather trivial sense of a revolt against some specific moral code; rather the heightened interest in sex and the ascription to sex of the most basic impulse and concern in human behavior symbolize a feeling or a psychic stance that is cultivated by such persons who have become aware (though perhaps not consciously) of the regressiveness of culture. Sex of the sort that interests Lancelot, Tristram, Lamerok, or Meleagant offers the promise of living without restraint and frustration; they are aroused and seeking gratifications that the behavioral programs of the institution cannot provide. Their attempts actually to do it demonstrate just how repressive and unfree one's culture really is. Sex has the unique distinction of being able to raise all the religious and cultural issues that are involved in the conflict of regressive and progressive movements within culture. Sex is the vortex born of the collision of personal progress and regress. Sex is the world-wide and timeless metaphor for cultural evolution.

The sexual impulse, then, which Percival experiences in the woman's temptation is the impulse to return to the tensionless state by means of personal growth or progress forward into forms of existence and identity which Percival has not previously known. In the sense that it is directed toward what Percival has not yet experienced, it is an adaptive impulse and an impulse for change. It is also a paradoxical impulse since it can never be fully realized and rapidly becomes the source of further frustrations. These subsequent frustrations, of course, prompt further strivings toward resolutions so that the living, I might say sexually active, man or woman is forever on the go, adapting and adjusting himself or herself to the constant ebb and flow of both internal and external stimuli. In the terms developed in Chapter Two, expression of psychic energy and its adaptive function are the quest without end: Palomides' Questing Beast or Tristram's Isode. And this finally is the freedom sought by the revolutionary thinkers of late Middle Ages and the late Modern Age. They sought freedom from a narrow and limited explanatory structure and the freedom to become mythically identified with a new authority whose indefinite and infinite aspect would insure the autonomy of the individual's life and the ability to modify himself and his institutions.

The father, on the other hand, demands a renunciation of such impulses; that is, the father takes away growth and adaptability; in its place he offers a program of personal regression or movement back to stasis and complete fulfillment in a prior form of existence, ultimately, of course, heaven which symbolizes in orthodox anagogy the final goal which is also the home from which one originally came. The metaphor in the Grail Quest for such a program of cultural regression is virginity, and in the sense that virginity represents a renunciation of the impulse of psychic energy, it is identical to the Castration Complex. As a redeemer, Galahad like Tristram is also a son who surpasses his father, but he does so by moving backward toward the womb rather than forward toward fatherhood. I will return to Galahad's case in section 4.2; here it is necessary to consider Lancelot and the problem of personal and cultural regression.

The means through which an individual achieves some measure of identity and psychic health shift radically as Malory turns from the realm of the Round Table to the Grail Quest. Success at the Round Table is achieved by mastering an opponent with better strokes, better breathing, longer endurance, or a stronger spear --all of which suggest the ability to expend a greater amount of energy both physical and mental than the opponent. But on the Grail Quest, the conditions are reversed: "for hit may nat be encheved but by vertuous lyvynge" (531) which turns out, as we see, to be pure virginity. It is patently untrue when a Hermit tells Gawain that "therefore was the Rounde Table founden, and the shevalry hath ben at all tymes so hyghe by the fraternite which was there that she myght nat be overcom: for men seyde she was founded in paciens and in humilite" (561). Chapter Two of this book demonstrated that Arthur was never patient or humble. The Grail Quest is conducted in patience and humility; the Round Table was founded upon aggression and vanity.

The same Hermit also explains to Gawain the meaning of the white and black bulls which he has seen in a dream. The white bulls are the Grail knights in opposition to the black bulls which are the Round Table knights. The Hermit explains:

> The too whyght [bulls] betokenythe sir Galahad and sir Percivale, for they be maydyns and clene withoute spotte, and the thirde, that had a spotte, signifieth sir Bors de Gaynes, which trespassed but onys in hys virginite. But sithyn he kepyth hymselff so wel in chastite that all ys forgyffyn hym and hys myssededys. And why tho three were tyed by the neckes, they be three knyghtes in virginite and chastite, and there ys no pryde symtten in them" (560-61).

The parable of the bulls makes it clear that virginity is the proper means for identity formation and environmental adaptation on the Grail Quest, and it symbolizes the repression of psychic energy or eros--another name for which is, of course, pride or self-assertion. The French Queste makes the allegory of the ropes quite clear: "The three bulls were yoked together at the neck, which is to say that virginity is so engrafted in these knights that they are powerless to lift their heads: meaning they are secure against the assaults of pride" (170, trans., Matarasso). Malory is just as emphatic about the ropes; the initial description of Gawain's dream mentions the ropes which restrain the bulls: "And thes three bullis which were so fayre were tyed with two stronge cordis" (559). The other bulls, the black ones, are free to wander and graze where they wish: "Go we hens to seke betir pasture," the black bulls say among themselves.

A bull, by its very nature, is a metaphor for energy, power, and eros; and yet the white bulls are restrained by the command that only the virginal shall be successful in the Quest of the Holy Grail. The French Queste does not recognize the awkardness of the condition of the white bulls, but in Malory, Lancelot, who could have been a white bull but is not, has the problem that he can never renounce his power as a knight and individual. Lancelot's pride and self-assertion become the central issue between him and God in the adventure at the Castle of Corbenic. Lancelot's refusal to be a virgin or at least chaste means that he will not suppress his psychic energy; in the Castle of Corbenic adventure the issue is portrayed directly in terms of strength and power: the power of Lancelot <u>versus</u> the power of the father. As Lancelot approaches the castle, Malory tells us

> Thenne sette he hand to his suerd and drew hit. So ther cam a dwerf sodenly and smote hym the arme so sore that the suerd felle oute of his hand. Then herde he a voice say,
>   'O, man of evylle feyth and poure byleve! Wherefore trustist thou more on thy harneyse than in thy Maker? For He myght more avayle the than thyne armour, in what servyse that thou arte sette in.' (595-96).

Lancelot's dilemma is that he has to pass between two lions in order to enter the castle. The castle, of course, holds the Sankgreal and is the goal of tension reduction and the lions are frustrations or obstacles. God demands that Lancelot relinquish the expression of his own aggressive energy against the environment and submit his personal fate to the care of God. The same pattern can be observed as Lancelot approaches the castle door: "And at laste he founde a chambir wherof the doore was shutte, and he sett hys honde thereto have opened hit, but he myght nat. <u>Than he enforced hym myckyll</u> to undo the doore" (596, emphasis mine). At the Round Table, the force of Lancelot's hand had been invincible, and it accounted for, to a large extent, the success of the Round Table as a civilization: "as longe as ye were knyght of erthly knyghthode ye were the moste mervayloust man of the worlde, and most adventurest" (557). And yet here God demands that Lancelot repudiate that force; no amount of force will budge the door. It opens only after Lancelot releases his grip and goes down upon his knees to ask God for forgiveness.

    Lancelot's instinctively aggressive (L. ad + gradus: to step toward) and, therefore, psychically progressive response to all environmental stimuli is repeated again when he sees beyond the door a priest elevating a chalice. Above the priest two men place a younger man in the hands of the priest. Lancelot thinks that "the pryste was so gretly charged of the vygoure [God's power] that hym semed that he shoulde falle to the erth" (597). His spontaneous response is to enter the chamber and aid the priest; the moral lesson, however, of this adventure is such an aggressive response to stimuli is sin: "Fayre Fadir, Jesu Cryste, ne take hit for no synne if I helpe the good man whych hath grete nede of helpe" (596) God does indeed take it as sin and strikes down Lancelot into the unconscious state in which he remains "four-and-twenty dayes and also many nyghtis, that ever he lay stylle as a dede man" (597).

What leads Lancelot to this symbolic death is clearly his interest in helping himself, his concern for active mastery of environmental tensions, and his willingness to respond to impulses arising as psychic energy; he does not exhibit a sufficient level of internal control over his personal impulses and therefore the father strikes him down in a display of external authority. On an earlier occasion, the issue of Lancelot's refusal to allow his neck to become bound with a rope, as Galahad's, was also the subject of a dispute between God and Lancelot. What we see is that God as the father cannot accept the son's individuation and self-love, for if He could then the son through his own resolution of the problems of sonhood would inevitably progress to the position of a god himself. Out of self-defense, the father must seek to repress the son through some means of punishment or fear: "Now have I warned the of thy vayneglory and of thy pryde, that thou haste many tyme arred ayenste thy Maker. Beware of everlastyng payne, for of all erthly knyghtes I have moste pite of the, for I know well thou haste nat thy pere of ony erthy synfull man" (557). A moment earlier, Lancelot is told that his vainglory is "nat worth a peare" (557).

What we should also see in this adventure at the Castle of Corbenic is the aggressiveness of the father toward the son and the resultant feelings in the son. One of the greatest problems in understanding Lancelot is Lancelot's ambivalence toward himself. Unlike Tristram, he can never hate his father-figures and come to regard them as strangers because he can never breakdown the logic and the legitimations which sustain their "godly" image, but rather he imitates the father's aggressiveness and his hatred of vainglory in a son toward himself. Lancelot's incredible unhappiness and self-hatred becomes understandable in terms of the father's point of view toward the son or the father's aggressiveness taken over as guilt into the son's psyche. Early in the Grail Quest when Lancelot attempts to enter a chapel, a voice rejects him saying "Sir Launcelot, more harder than ys the stone, and more bitter than ys the woode, and more naked and barer than ys the lyeff of the fyggetre! Therefore go thou from hens, and withdraw the from thys holy places!" (537). This voice expresses the hatred for Lancelot that he, too, learns to express toward himself.

The aggressiveness of the father becomes the central theme of the chapter entitled "Sir Lancelot"; it is here that Lancelot dreams of God as the ogre-father, the "olde man" who rewards his subservient sons and punishes his rebellious sons. In addition to his dream, this chapter is built upon two adventures: Lancelot's attempt to recover a horse and armor which were stolen from him earlier on, and his attempt to aid a weaker group of knights in a tournament. Lancelot enters the tournament out of self-love: "in incresyng of hys shevalry" (556). As it turns out he is defeated, and a recluse later explains to him that his opponent was God. In a manner similar to what we discovered in the adventures of La Cote Male Tayle, Lancelot's defeat produces in him feelings of self-denigration and self-hatred: "For never or now was I never at turnemente nor at justes but I had the beste. And now I am shamed, and am sure that I am more synfuller than ever I was" (556).

But it is the episode involving the horse and armor which gives us the meaning of the whole chapter. Lancelot's horse is stolen at precisely the moment when he most violently accuses himself and despairs of ever again attaining worship. The mysterious voice has just told him to withdraw from holy places and that he is harder than a stone. He leaves the chapel: "Than sir Launcelot wente to the crosse and founde hys helme, hys swerde, and hys horse away. And than he called hymselff a verry wrecch and most unhappy of all knyghtes, and there he seyde, `My synne and my wyckednes hath brought me unto grete dishonoure" (538). The important point about Lancelot's horse and armor, as Malory emphasizes when they are recovered, is

Lancelot's ownership of them.   The horse is Lancelot's property and the following passage indicates Lancelot's attitude toward the ownership of property:

> And there by adventure he mette the same knyght that toke hys horse, helme and hys swerde whan he slepte, whan the Sankgreall appered afore the crosse.   So whan sir Launcelot saw hym he salewede hym nat fayre, but cryed on hyght,
> `Knyght, kepe the, for thou deddist me grete unkyndnes.´
> And than they put afore them their spearis, and sir Launcelot com so fyersely that he smote hym and hys horse downe to the erthe, that he had nyghe brokyn hys neck.   Than sir Launcelot toke the knyghtes horse that was hys owne beforehonde, and descended frome the horse he sate uppon, and mownted uppon hys horse, and tyed the knyghtes owne horse to a tre, that he myght fynde that horse whan he was rysen.   (554)

Ownership of property makes possible, as G. W. F. Hegel in The Philosophy of the Right points out, the objectification of the self.   The woman was discussed earlier as the aim or object of the expression of psychic energy and so too is property an aim of psychic energy.   A knight's sword is a symbol for his energy and to deprive him of his sword is to castrate him, but a knight's property is the objectification or concrètization of who he is, and to steal his property is to deprive him of his being. Lancelot's violence here in defending his property must be read as self-defense in the context of the aggressions which God is mounting against his vainglory.   This is a very old principle as it underlies the importance of gift giving in epic literature from Homer onward.   Wealth and the abilty to give rich gifts define the being of the giver in objective or concrete terms.   In the famous passage, for example, in the Odyssey when Telemachos receives gifts from Menelaos, Homer makes clear the role of property: "And then I will give you a lovely libation cup, so that you may pour to the immortal gods, remembering me all your days."   In the Middle Ages, John of Paris (1250-1310) described the way in which ownership of property makes each man a lord: "it must be remembered that lay property as a whole is not granted to the community as a whole as is ecclesiastical property, but is acquired by individual people through their own skill, labour, and diligence, and individuals, as individuals, have right and power over it and valid lordship; each person may order his own and dispose, administer, hold or alienate it as he wishes, so long as he causes no injury to anyone else, since he is lord" (On Papal and Royal Power, 103).

On the opposite side of the scale, vows of poverty taken by religious orders and even the Teutonic Knights serve the purpose of deflating the ego by denying its lordship and preventing its objective and external manifestation. Ownership of property was no minor issue in the Middle Ages. The whole concept of dominium or lordship is actually a theory of ownership, whose most radical expression forms the treatise De Potestate Ecclesiastica by Giles of Rome (1246-1316). Giles argues that no one can legitimatly own any property unless he is in the state of grace. What this means, as John Morrall puts it in Political Thought in Medieval Times, is that "any ownership of property (dominium) depends, not upon natural inheritance or acquisition but on loyal membership of the church. . . . Giles himself sums up the consequences of his argument in this striking phrase: `The Church is more the owner of thy property that thou thyself art´" (87).

Thus ownership of property becomes, just as pride, an inherent threat to the father whose own position depends upon his success in preventing the sons now from owning things and becominmg lords in the way he alone is. It is no coincidence that individual ownership of property became one of the cornerstones of modern ideology and the institutionalization of individualism. At the end of the chapter as Lancelot rides away from the recluse who has explained to him that all his actions only serve to make God his adversary, Lancelot comes to a river through which he must pass:

> And aftir dyner he toke hys horse and commaunde her to God, and so rode into depe valey. And there he saw a ryver that hyght Mortays. And thorow the watir he muste nedis passe, the whych was hedyous. And than in the name of God he toke hit with good herte. (557)

The river seems to be the sort of frustration that Lancelot encounters in asserting his will against the will of God. Initially he seems to be successful, as crossing the river is difficult but Lancelot is strong. But once over the river, a very strange event occurs:

> And whan he com over he saw an armed knyght, horse and man all black as a bere. Withoute ony worde he smote sir Launcelottis horse to the dethe. And so he paste on and wyst nat where he was becom 558).

Lancelot, the man who guided La Cote in his quest for the Black Shield and who in that adventure transgressed the limitations of the Black Shield by defeating Sir Plenoryus, now meets himself a force of renunciation he cannot overcome. Lancelot encounters now the aggressive violence of the father, this time directed toward his property.

In Civilization and Its Discontents, Freud asks "What means does civilization employ in order to inhibit the aggressiveness [of individuals] which opposes it, to make it harmless, to get rid of it, perhaps?" One way, of course, is the overt aggression of the social authority, as in the case just cited or as Mark attempts, but, more powerfully, the father attempts to induce in the sons regressive psychic impulses to replace those of aggression; of his own, the well-socialized son who pursues the state of grace will turn his ego-aggressions backwards upon himself. Freud terms this process the development of the super-ego in which the external aggressions of the father are taken over into the son in the form of a guilty conscience or aggressive super-ego; this is precisely what happens to all the knights on the Quest for the Holy Grail. In the words of Freud,

> The effect of instinctual renunciation [denial of eros] on the conscience then is that every piece of aggression whose satisfaction the subject gives up is taken over by the super-ego and increases the latter's aggressiveness against the ego. . . aggressiveness of conscience is a continuence of the

severity of the external authority. . . . By means of identification he takes the unattackable authority into himself. The authority now turns into his super-ego and enters into possession of all the aggressiveness which a child would have liked to exercise against it [i.e., Oedipus Complex]. The child's ego has to content itself with the unhappy role of the authority--the father--who has been thus degraded. . . . If this is correct, we may assert truly that in the beginning conscience arises through the suppression of an aggressive impulse, and that it is subsequently reinforced by fresh suppressions of the same kind. (76-77)

A little earlier, Freud explains the process which Lancelot and Percival, when he wounds himself in the thigh, undergo in terms of a chronological sequence; this sequence matches precisely the structure of each adventure on the Grail Quest: "First comes renunciation of instinct owing to fear of aggression by the external authority. (This is, of course, what fear of the loss of love amounts to, for love is a protection against punitive aggression.)" We should recall Percival's comment that "in Hys servyse He woll nat suffir me to dye" (548). Freud goes on: "After that comes the erection of an internal authority, and renunciation of instinct owing to fear of it--owing to fear of conscience. In the second situation bad intentions are equated with bad actions, and hence a sense of guilt and a need for punishment. The aggressiveness of conscience keeps up the aggressiveness of authority" (75).

After he leaves the chapel and just before his horse is stolen, Lancelot confesses to a Hermit that "Ye, forsoth, sir, and my name is sir Launcelot du Lake, that hath been ryght well seyde off. And now my good fortune ys chonged, for I am the moste wrecch of the worlde" (538). The father's aggressiveness toward the son is taken over as self-hatred and self-denigration; at this point the son himself begins to carry out and continue the father's aggressiveness and repressions as if those acts were the son's own judgments and wishes. Malory's and the French Grail-writer's perceptions about the formation of a conscience or super-ego are incredibly acute. After being banished from the Grail Chapel, Lancelot completes

the process of internalizing the aggressiveness of the external
authority as he rides away condemning himself: "And so [he]
departed sore wepynge and cursed the tyme that he was borne,
for than he demed never to have worship more" (537-38).

There is no doubt that the original writers of the French
Queste saw such a process as positive and productive of healthy
and moral individuals. The archetype which the original writers
represent and which is the major theme of the traditional Grail
Quest is the sacrament of Penance. The behavioral and
cognitive program of the romance is precisely the same as the
chronological process that Freud describes. One first must
confess and renounce his sins knowing, of course, of the threat
of damnation by the external authority. Sin means the loss of
God's love, for sin is the result of orientations other than those
of the father, and the father's love is all that sinners have to
protect them from eternal suffering and damnation. After
renunciation, one must perform the penance given him by the
confessor. Lancelot wears a hair shirt and promises not to
sleep in the same place two nights in a row until he has found
the Grail. The taking on of such sufferings symbolizes the
aggressions of the external authority and gives further and
continual reasons for renouncing the sin. The final step is the
promise to sin no more. This promise can only be kept if the
individual has internalized the authority, that is, only if he has
replaced his erotic impulses with the orientations and the
behavioral codes of the authority. Thus arises a conscience or
super-ego devoted to the retreat from progressive solutions of
personal problems into moral laws and the demands of the
father.

The remarkable discovery of Courtly and Arthurian
Romanace, however, is that civilizations arise from the
successful confrontation and overthrow of the external
authority. Gareth has his Dame Lyonet whose denigrating and
aggressive attitude toward Gareth might have produced feelings
of guilt and inferiority had he not been able to muster sufficient
energy to defeat whatever frustrations he encountered and
eventually overcome the aggressiveness of Lyonet toward him.
The same pattern is true for La Cote Male Talye and, though
on a much more difficult level, Tristram. Arthurian Romance
sees the origin of civilization and healthy individuals in the
Oedipus Complex and in the wishes of the son to replace his

father and become himself the authority in the land. This is precisely what Arthur and Merlin accomplished at the outset of the Round Table civilization. Arthurian Romance discovers that civilizations are moved by psychic energy or eros and not by the renunciation of it, for only through ego expression can individuals rise to the level of selfhood and independence that the term father denotes. Civilizations, at least healthy ones, are composed of fathers. This point is also Freud's: "I may now add that civilization is a process in the service of Eros, whose purpose is to combine single human individuals, and after that families, then races, peoples and nations into one great unity, the unity of mankind. Why this has to happen we do not know; the work of Eros is precisely this. These collections of men are to be libidinally bound to one another" (69).

Given this fundamental insight of Arthurian Romance, the Quest for the Holy Grail within the context of Malory's whole book of King Arthur and the desperate needs of the Round Table to modify its ideology in order to resolve the growing competition among the knights for reward in the performance of a too narrow range of behavior, becomes a destructive quest, a quest which inhibits the growth of the civilization by destroying the ability of individuals to innovate new behavioral resolutions to institutionally caused tensions. The Quest simply ends anyone's, especially Lancelot's, interest in continuous adaptation and progress. This is finally Arthur's understanding of the Quest when he says "I am sure at this quest of Sankegreall shall all ye of the Rownde Table departe, and nevyr shall I se you agayne hole togydirs" (520). Following the Quest, Arthur is left with a group of knights who are convinced that "wyte you welle there shall none attayne hit but by clennes, that ys pure confession" (564). In the last days of the Round Table, their only interest will be in exposing and punishing the sins of fellow members of the Round Table.

4.2 Law and Beyond Law

The ideal condition of human existence would not be a
state of pure and unbounded energy expression. This state
would not produce psychically healthy individuals at all; it is
rather simply the theoretical opposite of the condition of
absolute control of energy expression and a strategy for
vandalizing the dominant culture by elevating the highly
abstract notion of psychic energy to a position on the
explanatory regress one step higher than the dominant culture's
own termination. The ideal is rather the dialectic in which
identity is formed of both a creative source and an individual.
The key is that the authority must be a creative source and not
an absolute authority, for it must itself grow and develop in the
process in which identities are growing and developing; that is,
members of an institution must have the ability to make
fundamental, radical, or root modifications of the institution
itself. Unfortunately, as we see from history, such changes
have never occurred without violent revolution; the forces of
counter-revolution have simply always been unrelenting. What
we see in the culture of Malory's time is the break-up of the
symbiosis and a polarization of those who in romance, for
example, claim absolute primacy of eros and those who in
theology, for example, claim the absolute necessity of ego-

renunciation.   In the late Middle Ages, the poles became more and more difficult to harmonize and prepared for all out war. Malory takes his position against the authorities.

If we consider his presentation of the Grail Quest in relation to the issues raised throughout the sections dealing with Arthur, Merlin, Gareth, and in general the rise of the Round Table, it becomes clear that renunciation of eros in favor of laws which are the demands of the external authority is destructive in that it denies the precise qualities which gave rise to the civilization.   I have been suggesting all along that Malory's themes look forward to the theology of Martin Luther in the sense that Luther's primary concern was with external authority and internal grace or health.   Luther succeeded in establishing individual freedom in faith as an ultimate legitimation, while in Malory's romance it is only anticipated as the polar opposite of the direction of development of the Round Table civilization.   Luther's works illustrate a search for the meaning of righteousness and justification; that is, he is searching for the grounds upon which the individual can base the judgment that his life is holy, healthy, and, in short, meaningful.   We have just seen the miserable failure of Lancelot to arrive at such a judgment.   In the opposition between the doctrine, law, and the pope of the external authority and faith as the internal authority arising only from within the human heart, Luther rediscovers the world openness of the numen.   He discovers, as orthodox theologians could not, the true place for illogical, anarchic, and pluralistic expressions of the individual's desire to resolve the tension of his disconnected individuality. Faith goes beyond laws, and, for Luther, faith is the same sort of individual psychic energic expression that drives Malory's great knights.   Its opposition is the law and the father.   In, for example, his Lectures on the Epistle of St. Paul to the Galatians, Luther writes:

> I am willing to kiss your feet, pope, and to acknowledge you as the supreme pontiff, if you adore my Christ and grant that we have the forgiveness of sins and eternal life through His death and resurrection and not through observance of your traditions.   If you yield here, I shall not take away your crown and power.   But if you do not, I shall

constantly cry out that you are the Antichrist.
(Works, 26, 224)

The aggressiveness of Luther's language is important to
understand. Such boldness corresponds to the violence that we
see in Tristram's murder and thrashing of thirty-two knights
who belong to King Mark or in his wildness at the Tournament
of the Castle of Maidens. The aggressiveness is, of course, eros
rising to the level of energy required to match an
overwhelmingly powerful father, as Luther clearly understands
in the passage cited below. Luther goes on to indicate the
destructiveness of laws and external authorities, and we should
see that Luther is concerned, just as are Freud or Malory, with
the aggressive and repressive control of the individual by the
external authority which rather than really having the growth
and health of the civilization in mind places only its own
security and power foremost:

> I am gladly willing to bear the laws of the pope,
> provided that he leaves them free and does not bind
> consciences to them so that men think that they are
> justified for observing them and damned for not
> observing them. But he does not do this; for if he
> did not bind consciences to his laws, where would
> his power be? Therefore he is concerned above all
> to hold consciences bound and captive by his laws.
> That is the basis of the statement: 'Unless you obey
> the Roman see, you cannot be saved.' That is also
> the basis of this thunder and lightning in his bulls:
> 'Let anyone who dares resist in bold temerity know
> that he must bear the wrath of Almighty God.' Here
> he denies salvation to all who do not obey his laws,
> and he promises eternal life to all who observe
> them. Thus he drives us into the net of the
> righteousness of works, as if no one could be
> justified and saved without obeying his laws. In
> short, not with one word does he mention faith; but
> he teaches only his own ideas. (26, 225)

The external authority cannot mention faith because faith
is free to all, and it arises from within the individual. Although

the point under examination here is the destructiveness of law in the sense that law brings an end to the quest for selfhood, civilization, and meaning; it might be well to go on for a moment with what Luther sees as the human potential beyond law. Luther conceives of faith in the symbiotic sense of the meaningful as was constructed in Chapter Two. Faith is an unceasing quest which simultaneously creates God as it creates the Christian believer. In On Christian Liberty, Luther asserts that faith is the supreme freedom. Why that should be so becomes most clear in the discussion of the power of faith in the Lectures on Galatians:

> Whoever is an orator, let him develop his topic. He will see that faith is something omnipotent, and that its power is inestimable and infinite; for it attributes glory to God, which is the highest thing that can be attributed to Him. To attribute glory to God is to believe in Him, to regard Him as truthful, wise, righteous, merciful, and almighty, in short, to acknowledge Him as the Author and Donor of every good. Reason does not do this, but faith does. It consummates the Deity; and, if I may put it this way, it is the creator of the Deity, not in the substance of God but in us. For without faith God loses His glory, wisdom, righteousness, truthfulness, mercy, etc., in us; in short, God has none of His majesty or divinity where faith is absent. Nor does God require anything greater of man than that he attribute to Him His glory and His divinity; that is . . . He has whatever a believing heart is able to attribute to Him. To be able to attribute such glory to God is wisdom beyond wisdom, righteousness beyond righteousness, religion beyond religion, and sacrifice beyond sacrifice. (Works, 26, 226-27, emphasis mine)

Luther is saying that what God, the real termination of one's self-explanation, demands is that men create God in the autonomous impulses of their hearts to create or fulfill themselves as individuals. Man creates God in himself and thus creates the image of what his nature ought to imitate. Only in this way does God not demand the death of the sons, but rather he wishes them to have more and more abundant lives. In this sense also, man can be justified; that is, he can arrive at the judgment that his life is valuable and healthy, a judgment that is impossible for the knights on the Quest for the Holy Grail except through their own deaths. Luther continues:

> Therefore faith justifies because it renders to God what is due Him; whoever does this is righteous. The laws also define what it means to be righteous in this way: to render to each what is his. For faith speaks as follows: 'I believe Thee, God, when Thou dost speak.' What does God say? Things that are impossible, untrue, foolish, weak, absurd, abominable, heretical, and diabolical--if you consult reason. For what is more ridiculous, foolish, and impossible than when God says to Abraham that he is to get a son from the body of Sarah, which is barren and already dead?
>
> Thus when God proposes the doctrines of faith, He always proposes things that are simply impossible and absurd--if, that is, you want to follow the judgment of reason. (26, 227)

What Luther calls impossible and absurd is the indefinite nature of the quest for both God and selfhood; in other words, the unending quest for civilization or the world openness of the numen. Reason and law bring that quest to an end, for they prohibit pluralistic, innovative, and adaptive responses to environmental stimuli (revelation), and they command that all individuals import the social reality into their own private experience and interpret that experience in ways that serve institutional rather than private goals. This means that an inherently absurd and paradoxical situation must not be the occasion for innovation and self-assertion on the part of the individual but rather the occasion of resignation and endurance. Faith, however, which is in theology frequently called the content of Hope, empowers individuals to resolve the problems they face. For the authorities--Mark, Arthur, and the Pope-- faith cannot be creative in this manner but rather is a debt of allegiance owed to the authority and his particular articulation of reality.   In the theology of St. Thomas, for example, these two conceptions are given different names: <u>fides</u> for the autonomous expression of desire to be identified with God, and <u>fiducia</u> for the debt of trust and allegiance that men owe to God, the church authority, and the civil power.

The experiences of Sir Bors on the Grail Quest demonstrate the way in which laws and codes which precede experience and are internalized as a super-ego prohibit the individual from responding in a manner called for by the unique demands of the situation and contribute only to the eminence of the explanatory superstructure.   This is not to say that laws are entirely useless but rather to indicate Malory's and Luther's perception that when law replaces faith the individual loses his ability to control his life and therefore the possibility of feeling happy about his life.   Law enables one to see only what is common and already known in experience; faith enables an individual to attribute his own needs, values, and interests--in short, what is unique--to a situation and therefore devise his own response which makes the situation his own personal adventure.   Law permits no such personal adventures, as the experience of Sir Bors indicates, and it therefore makes individuals unable to solve their own problems.   If we think about law and its coercive commands, we readily see that the desire to make all individuals behave in the same way has very little to do with the real benefit of the individuals concerned; enforced laws, rather, operationalize and therefore demonstrate the validity of a particular conception of reality.   One can always remark, everyone is doing it and so it must be valid.

Briefly, Bors is confronted with the dilemma of having to choose between rescuing his brother, Lyonell, who is bound to a cart and is being beaten by two knights who apparently will kill him and rescuing a lady who had been abducted and is about to be raped by a knight.   The lady appeals to Bors' debt to the law.   The French <u>Queste</u> mentions only God's laws at this point, but Malory adds in the secular laws to emphasize the role of law in any individual's interpretation of his own experience:

> And anone as she syghe sir Bors she demed hym
> a knyght of the Rounde Table, whereof she hoped to
> have some comforte.   Than she conjoured hym, by
> the faythe that he ought unto Hym 'in whos servyse

thou arte entred and for the feythe ye owe to the
hyghe Ordre of Knyghthode, and for kynge Arthures
sake, which I suppose made the knyght, that thou
helpe me and suffir me nat to be shamed of this
knyght´. (568)

The response to this situation demands that Bors choose
between saving life or preventing sin. A priest (who turns out
later on to be a devil in disguise) makes clear the direction of
the choice: "Now loke thou whether hit had been gretter harme
of thy brothirs dethe, othir ellis to have suffirde her to have
loste hir maydynhede" (570). Bors dilemma reveals incoherence
within the body of laws; in this case, no legitimate response
will leave Bors satisfied because in choosing one legitimate act
he violates another. Malory shows us that the well-socialized
man is rendered helpless by the experience of explanatory
incoherence; the usual response is to condemn oneself and pass
the decision on to someone higher-up in the social hierarchy:
"Whan sir Bors herde hir say thus, he had so much sorow that
he wyst nat what to do. . . . Than lyffte he up hys yghen and
seyde wepynge, `Fayre swete Lorde Jesu Cryst, whos creature I
am, kepe me sir Lyonell, my brothir, that thes knyghtes sle hym
nat, and for pite of you and for mylde Maryes sake, I shall
succour thys mayde´" (568). His decision to save the maiden
indicates that he prefers to prevent sin rather than to preserve
life; that is, he chooses what is symbolic and moral over life
itself. On a broader level, Bors exhibits a preference for law
over the complexities of real life. It is also important to note
that he ascribes to Christ the authority in the decision saying
that he himself is merely a creature.

Later Bors is confronted in a dream with the same
dilemma, only the stakes are increased. He meets a lady who
tells him that she loves him and that unless he lies by her that
night she will kill herself and her death will be the cause of the
deaths of many people of her castle. The direction of Bors´
decision is the same: "in no wyse he wolde breke his chastite"
(570). The people of the castle plead with Bors saying, "Have
mercy on us all, and suffir my lady to have hir wyll; and if ye
do nat, we muste suffir dethe with oure lady for to falle downe
of this hyghe towre. And if ye suffir us thus to dye for so litill
a thynge all ladys and jantillwomen woll sey you dishonoure"

(571). Bors' two dilemmas are constructed by the devil to tempt him, but even so Bors makes real decisions which reveal the content of his conscience. Virginity and chastity represent renunciations of eros which is the psychic component of the faith he owes to law and the external authority. What Bors loses, however, in submitting himself to law is the ability to interpret his experiences in any terms other than the institutionally valid ones, and he loses, therefore, his ability to progress in the quest of self-creation by resolving problems that institutional knowledge has no good way of even defining.

While these first two experiences involve death for others, Lyonell, the lady, and the townspeople, Bors' third encounter illustrates how submission to the law actually destroys the civilization: it leaves the individual not knowing what to do in situations where the law itself is inadequate or incoherent. As it turns out, Lyonell is not murdered and escapes from his captors. In front of a chapel, he meets his brother who reproves him for his betrayal. Lyonell vows to fight his brother to death. Bors' dilemma now is "that he must fyght with his brothir othir ellis to dye" (574). Malory again emphasizes: "he wyst nat what to do" (574). Bors attempts to reason it out: "so hys herte counceyled hym nat therto inasmuch as sir Lyonell was hys elder brother, wherefore he ought to bere hym reverence. Yette kneled he adowne agayne tofore sir Lyonelles horse feet" (574). We are told at this point that Lyonell is possessed by a devil which had brought "hym in such a wylle that he sholde slay hym." Because of his feeling of guilt for having betrayed his brother and because of the faith he owes to an older brother, Bors is willing to submit himself to death. Unwittingly, he cooperates with the devil, and we must remember that the Round Table desperately needs Bors because he is one of the knights who will achieve the Grail Quest. A hermit understands this, throws himself in front of Bors, and is immediately killed by Lyonell. Then Collgrevance steps in to fight Lyonell. Now Bors is confronted with a new problem. What if Collgrevance should kill Lyonell? Will Bors then have to fight with Collgrevance to avenge his brother's death? Or what if Lyonell kills Collgrevance? Will Bors then have to fight Lyonell for the killing of Collgrevance in addition to his own self-defense.

Equipped only with institutional knowledge, problems and impossible situations continue to compound themselves until every knight of the Round Table becomes involved and is faced-off with another knight who is duty-bound to kill him. But they are impossible only because Bors has been trained to select only certain attributes from the almost infinite number of attributes of any situation; the ideological hierarchy Bors sees is taken as the only reality and the true interpretation of the event. There are, in fact, many ways to respond to the situation confronting Bors, but to do that Bors would have to innovate without ultimate legitimation (see the discussion of Tristram and Palomides below). This situation clearly looks forward to the final battle between Lancelot and Gawain in which Gawain's vow to kill Lancelot and Lancelot's vow not to kill Gawain result only in the daily slaughter of lesser knights allied to each side. Gawain and Lancelot, just as much as Bors, let the world die and the civilization fall apart in order to maintain their absolute fidelity to right. Bors, Gawain, and Lancelot illustrate perfect explanatory order and yet as heroes and saviors of their society they fail miserably. This situation also looks back to Balan and Balin who as a result of their differing experiences and allegiances could no longer recognize themselves as brothers. Laws, moral codes, and fixed doctrine--in short, the social construction of reality--preempt the essential brotherhood of all men by supplanting it with brotherhood in the institution. As Luther would point out fifty years after Malory's death, God conceived as a giver of laws can only condemn: "If here we cannot distinguish between these two kinds of righteousness [faith and works] . . . then we are under the law and not under grace, and Christ is no longer a Savior. Then He is a lawgiver. Then there can be no salvation left, but sure despair and eternal death will follow" (Works, 26, 11).

Bors thinks only in terms of works which are specified and regulated by the laws of the father. The entire institution of Knighthood seems to be based upon the Christian concept of the efficacy of good works. In 1095 when Pope Urban III called the first Crusade and made knights soldiers for Christ, he elevated the codes and laws of Knighthood to the level of other Christian works of charity and mercy--works by which an individual can justify himself before God. John of Salisbury makes the connection explicit: "For soldiers that do these things are `saints,´ and are the more loyal to their prince in proportion as they more zealousy keep faith in God" (Polycraticus, VI, 8). Good works themselves do not originate from within, for then they would necessarily be pluralistic and adaptive and not therefore tending toward a priori institutional conceptions of unity and good; rather good works originate in the demands of the external authority. We must recall that what the father desires above all else is the total submission of his sons, even if it means the death of the son. The increasing complexity of Bors´ dilemmas indicates that the orientations of sonhood make men increasingly unable to solve the problems they face. Sonhood suggests a refusal to be responsible for the content of one´s conscience and a reliance upon the father to get the sons out of trouble. This is finally the sense in which law destroys civilization, for when individual responsibilities are deferred to law, man has given up his ability to adapt which is the quest of the meaningful and the quest to create both himself and his law. When the problems one faces are the laws themselves or one´s institution, it can hardly be effective to leave the resolution in the hands of the law.

Orthodox thinkers, such as St. Augustine, St. Thomas, Salisbury, or Dante, consider the origin of law to be in human nature or in Divine Providence, and thus see it as an external authority whose fulfillment would mean perfection for men. The implications of this are that the law and civilization (by definition a group of individuals sharing common laws) are not the result of eros and a self-creative quest but rather are something eternal and universal, beyond the reach of human creativity. St. Thomas, for example, in his discussion in the Summa Theologica of eternal law, natural law, and human law, points out the essential sameness of all three--differentiated only by decreasing levels of perfection. The direction or ends of all kinds of law remain the same:

> As stated above, a law is nothing else but a dictate of practical reason emanating from the ruler who governs a perfect community. Now it is evident, granted that the world is ruled by Divine Providence, as was stated in the First Part, that the whole community of the universe is governed by

Divine Reason.   Therefore the very Idea of the
government of things in God, the Ruler of the
universe, has the nature of a law. . . .
  Law implies order to the end actively, in so far,
that is, as it directs certain things to the end; but
not passively--that is to say, the law itself is not
ordered to the end, except accidentally, in a
governor whose end is extrinsic to him, and to which
end his law must needs be ordered. (II, i, q. 91, a.
1).

Bors' decisions illustrate St. Thomas' principle.   The end to
which his decisions are directed is extrinsic to himself and is
the maintenance of explanatory order.   The law itself has no
interest in whether or not Bors lives, only that the law is
obeyed.   In this way, the romance shows that such an
orientation results in increasing problems on the behavioral or
personal level.   Law gives men only one way of defining the
conflicts which are presented to them daily, but such conflicts
often involve contradictory goods and necessary bad choices.
Moreover, what concerns the pious individual at this point is
not the terms of the situation in which he finds himself but
rather the law itself.   He must rehearse in his own mind just
how such a situation would be interpreted by the father.   In
such a case the law only condemns.
  Malory belongs to the movement in the late Middle Ages
which was beginning to see with increasing clarity that such an
understanding of law and civilization was making life
increasingly more difficult to live.   When a civilization's or an
individual's ends are extrinsic to himself, he cannot call upon
his resources of psychic energy because psychic energy comes
into play only when personal tensions are felt.   That, of course,
would mean to comprehend the problem in personal rather than
universal terms.   Ideology addresses the reason or super-ego
and demands that man see only what is universal even in his
own personal problems, and he can only hope, therefore, as Bors
does, for some external redeemer, some deus ex machina, to
remove him from conditions which will inevitably grow worse
and worse.   Bors' adventure comes to an end with such a
miracle:

And so with that sir Bors lyffte up hys honde and wolde have smyttyn hys brothir. And with that he harde a voice whych seyde,
`Fle, sir Bors, and towche hym nat, othir ellis thou shalt sle hym!´
Ryght so alyght a clowde betwyxte them in lykenes of a fayre and a mervaylous flame, that bothe hir two shyldis brente. Than were they sore aferde and felle both to the erthe and lay there a grete whyle in a swone. (576)

From the cloud Bors hears a voice telling him to leave his brother and seek Sir Percival. While he gets out of this dilemma, he leaves the larger problem unresolved. The same can be said for the growing feuds at the Round Table; ultimately, we know, that running away from a problem is not much of a solution. What is needed is a new concept of law and civilization that would originate in the eros or psychic energy of the individual as the guiding principle and which would begin again the continual quest for the fulfillment of eros in the resolution of tension and better adaptation to situations. The origin and end of law must be within man, and civilization must be the quest of individuals to be fulfilled. Such a notion of law is implicit in Malory´s tale of Arthur and the rise of the Round Table, and it is explicit in the Defensor Pacis of Marsilius of Padua. St. Thomas is emphatic in asserting that "all laws proceed from the eternal law," but Marsilius perceives that laws grow out of psychic energy and the desire of men for the sufficient life. We should see in Marsilius´ emphasis on the present life the very same issues that interest Freud in his discussion of civilization:

That practical matter whose proper establishment is of greatest importance for the common sufficiency of the citizens in this life, and whose poor establishment threatens harm for the community, must be established only by the whole body of citizens. But such a matter is the law. Therefore, the establishment of the law pertains only to the whole body of citizens. . . . For in the laws being rightly made consists a large part of the whole

common sufficiency of men, while under bad laws
there arise unbearable slavery, oppression, and
misery of the citizens, the final result of which is
that the polity is destroyed.   (48)

St. Augustine or St. Thomas would object to Marsilius'
claim that law originates in the need of the majority of citizens
to resolve the problems of their lives and reply that the
common people are far too undiscerning and uneducated to be
the source of law.   The very purpose of law, moreover, in the
orthodox view is to compel such people to proper behavior and
ends.   How can those people who need such compulsion be the
origin of coercive laws?   St. Augustine regards governance and
law as the consequences of sin and which exist to turn men to
ends which they do not innately possess: "[law] maintains order
through fear, twisting and turning to what it wants the minds of
those unhappy men whom it has been adapted to rule" (On Free
Choice of the Will, 32).   On another occasion St. Augustine says
that law trains and tames men the way that men train and tame
animals.   But Marsilius argues that law is the expressions of an
individual's desire for a fulfilled life.   Law resolves the tension
and anxiety of, in Bonhoeffer's terms, the contingent
individuality because it becomes the relationship or the unity
between individuals.   Marsilius' basic assumption in all his
writings is that a principle akin to psychic energy underlies the
creation of law and thus civilization:

From what we assumed above as the principle of
all things to be demonstrated in this book, namely,
that all men desire sufficiency of life and avoid the
opposite, we demonstrated in Chapter IV the civil
association of men, inasmuch as through such
association they can attain this sufficiency, and
without it they cannot. Hence too Aristotle says in
the Politics, Book I, Chapter I: 'There is in all men
a natural impulse toward such a community'. . . .
If, therefore, the weightier multitude of men wish
the state to endure, as seems to have been well
said, they also wish that without which the state
cannot endure.   But this is the standard of the just
and the beneficial, handed down with a command,
and called the law. . . .

For most of the citizens are neither vicious nor undiscerning most of the time; all or most of them are of sound mind and reason and have a right desire for the polity and for the things necessary for it to endure, like laws and other statutes and customs. For although not every citizen nor the greatest number of the citizens be discoverers of the laws, yet every citizen can judge of what has been discovered and proposed to him by someone else, and can discern what must be added, subtracted, or changed. (50-51)

Individuals desire law, Marsilius writes, because it is the result of their natural desire to be united with each other. It is important to see law as originating within men rather than from an external authority even though the content of the law itself may end up being the same as that from the external authority. No one need invent the rules for everything he does, but everyone must evaluate the propriety of the law regulating his own social experience.

About the external authorities, Marsilius is emphatic. There are in the world three judges: Christ, the church (or priests), and the ruler of the state. All authority ought to base itself on the model of Christ:

But this judge's [Christ's] coercive power is not exercised over anyone in the world, to punish or reward transgressors or observers of the law made immediately by him. . . . For in his mercy Christ wished to give every person the opportunity to become deserving up to the very end of his life. . . . For Christ did not ordain that anyone should be forced to observe in this world the law made by him, and for this reason he did not appoint in this world a judge having coercive power over transgressors of this law. (164)

About the church, Marsilius goes on to say that "This other judge is the priest. . . . However, he has no coercive power in this world to compel anyone to observe these commands" (164). The power of the church, Marsilius writes, is analogus to that of a physician: "the priest with respect to his office should not be likened to a judge in the third sense, but rather to a judge in the first sense, that is, to one who has the authority to teach and practice, like the physician, but has no coercive power over anyone" (155). Coercive power is also denied to the pope as it is effectively denied to the ruler of the state when Marsilius asserts that the ruler must be chosen by free elections and subject always to the will of the majority of the people. Although the ruler must enforce the laws, the laws themselves, cannot be different from the will of the people. In effect, what Marsilius calls for is only the freedom of human beings to constantly modify their institutions but this means freedom from coercion on all levels. While his arguments do not precisely equate God's law to the repressive commands of the pope or the state, Marsilius is beginning to see that law taken as universal and immutable negates the ability of a civilization to endure as the behavioral programs of law change the experience of individuals (i.e., resolve the problems that gave rise to the institution) and create the necessity, thereby, for radical changes in the law and institution itself. I do not mean here the gradual change propelled by institutional inertia along a course implicit in its ultimate legitimations, but rather a modification in those first principles themselves.

Autonomy in faith offers a strategy for transcending the law and renews the unceasing quest for the sufficient life--justification as Luther called it--for it is a quest which begins within the human heart and creates as it develops the human being as well as the society. Palomides in following his Questing Beast seeks just this sort of sufficiency, faith, and fulfillment of potential, but his attempt to attain the social manifestation of these goals through the codes and behavioral paradigms of Knighthood and Love bring him to utter destruction. The codes necessitate hierarchies and competition among the knights which inevitably lead to the civil strife that tears the Round Table apart; the law eventually condemns those who support it because within the institution Palomides' identity can only be understood by himself or anyone else in relation to another knight's identity. Tristram and Palomides become enemies as they attempt both to fulfill the same and highest social role: "And in his harte, as the booke saythe, sir Palomydes wysshed that wyth his worshyp he myght have ado wyth sir Trystram before all men, bycause of La Beall Isode" (448).   For most of the romance, Palomides feels that his only chance of attaining the level of knighthood which will give him the socially validated sufficient life and identity he desires is in killing and shaming Tristram.   From the outside, we clearly understand that fighting Tristram is not a worthwhile effort, but it is the only behavioral program legitimated by the laws of the Round Table.   The social product of this law is Palomides' hatred for Tristram, and yet at certain moments he sees clearly that such hatred for a man who is essentially his brother is a sickness:

> `Sir, what is youre name?´ syede sir Trystram
> `Wyte you well,´ seyde that knyght, `my name is sir Palomydes.´
> `A, sir knyght, whyche knyght hate ye moste in the worlde?´ seyde sir Trystram.
> `For sothe,´ seyde he, `I hate sir Trystram most to the deth, for and I may mete wyth hym the tone of us shall dye.´
> `Ye say well,´ seyde sir Trystram, `And now wyte you well that my name is sir Trystram de Lyones, and now do your warste!´
> Whan sir Palomydes saw hym sey so he was astoned, and than he seyde thus:
> `I pray you, sir Trystram, forgyff me all my evyll wyll!   And yf I lyve I shall do you servyse afore all the knyghtes that bene lyvynge.   And thereas I have owed you evyll wyll me sore repentes.   I wote nat what eylyth me, for mesemyth that ye ar a good knyght; and that ony other knyght that namyth hymselff a good knyght sholde hate you, me sore mervaylyth.   And there I requyre you, sir Trystram, take none displaysure at myne unkynde wordis.´
> (426)

This remarkable scene should be compared with the confrontation between Bors and Lyonell discussed above. Although Palomides and Tristram are able to resolve their institutionally induced problems on this occasion, the hatred soon re-emerges as the competition of a tournament and the hierarchical ranking of prowess once again make them enemies. It takes them a long time to transcend the laws and behavioral imperatives of ideology, but they leave the romance loving each other, in spite of all the logic which seems to lie behind their hatred.   Upon the recognition that faith and love transcend the logical commands of law and that he can love both Tristram and Isode in ways that go beyond law, Palomides agrees to be baptized.

The scene leading up to Palomides' Baptism is important and deserves some close examination because in it Malory works out finally the terms on which Tristram is the redeemer who transcends the sickness of both the Round Table and Cornwall. Palomides embodies all the institutional sickness and he becomes the symbolic recipient of Tristram's transcending love. Briefly, Tristram and Palomides finally meet alone to fulfill their earlier pledge to fight to the death of one of them.   In the fight, however, they begin to analyze the causes of their hatred and discover that on a personal level no such causes apply. Palomides suddenly renounces all of the causes of their hatred and exposes their essential brotherhood even while the environmental conditions remain unchanged.   This is finally Malory's meaning of good faith, what the tone of his romance suggests a longing for:

> `As for to do thys batayle,´ seyde sir Palomydes, `I dare ryght well ende hyt.   But I have no grete lust to fyght no more, and for thys cause,´ seyde sir Palomydes: ´myne offence ys to you nat so grete but that we may be fryndys, for all that I have offended ys and was for the love of La Beall Isode.   And as for her, I dare say she ys pyerles of all othir ladyes, and also I profyrd her never no maner of dyshonoure, and by her I have getyn the moste parte of my worshyp.   And sytthyn I had offended never as to her owne persone, and as for the offence that I have done, hyt was ayenste youre owne persone, and for that offence ye have gyven me thys day many sad strokys and som I have gyffyn you agayne, and now I dare sey I felte never man of youre myght nothir so well-brethed but yf hit were sir Launcelot du Laake, wherefore I requyre you, my lorde, forgyff me all

that I have offended unto you!   And thys same day
have me to the nexte churche, and fyrste lat me be
clene conffessed, and aftir that se youreselff that I
be truly baptysed.   And than woll we all ryde
togydyrs unto the courte of knyghe Arthure, that we
may be there at the nexte hyghe feste folowynge.'
(510, emphasis mine)

The point is that Tristram and Palomides have been able
to resolve their mortal hatred for each other and are now able
to live "togydirs"--something that the Round Table knights are
increasingly less able to do.   The resolution has the form of
simply denying the dishonor in favor of the individuals involved.
One can only be dishonored if honor is defined and fixed and if
the individuals involved choose to view each other in terms of
the code of honor, as Bors consistently does.   What the code of
honor stipulates as dishonor, however, may in reality (or simply
from a different point of view) not injure the individual at all,
as Palomides claims: "I had offended never as to her owne
personne."   Palomides and Tristram look toward a changing and
growing relationship which is no longer based upon competition
for success in fulfilling the terms of Knighthood and Love.   They
have discovered, as pointed out at the beginning of Chapter
Three, that the will to truth--if Knighthood and Love are
truths--is in fact a will to death.   Bors, Lancelot, Gawain,
Lamerok and the Orkneys do not achieve this ability to resolve
the problems that they face, for they cannot make the shift in
orientation that would allow them to stop looking at
themselves, each other, and their personal problems from the
point of view of the laws and the institution.   It is, of course,
the laws which created the problems in the first place.   One can
simply decide that there is no dispute between you and me in
spite of what the institution tells us is real.
    To transcend this inherently tragic situation which
increasingly destroys the essential brotherhood of all men and
turns their instinctual aggressiveness against each other is
exactly what the Round Table needs Galahad for.   Tristram
undertakes the final fight with Palomides in order to lead him
to Baptism; to be Baptized is to be forgiven but forgiveness
must originate in the heart of Palomides.   Palomides will also be
Baptized for an autonomous expression of faith: "in my harte

and in my soule I have had many a day a good beleve in Jesu Cryste" (508). Tristram as redeemer leads men to this sort of self-forgiveness by accepting and confirming their expressions of brotherly love rather than expressions of hatred and competition demanded by the institution. He tells Palomides, "and as ye sey, so shall hyt be; and all my evyll wyll God forgyff hyt you, and I do" (510). To be forgiven is to be released, in this case, from the destructive inertia of the Round Table.

The Round Table needs Galahad to begin all over the self-creative quest which will transcend the growing tragedy. Malory emphasizes at the outset of the Grail Quest that Galahad is to be a second Arthur, and that he "shold passe hys fadir as much as the lyon passith the lybarde, both of strength and of hardiness" (542). When Galahad arrives at the Round Table, the knights as sons know only how to carry out the wishes of the father which keep them competing with each other and often killing each other. All the while tensions among the knights mount. At the origin of the Round Table, Arthur is given a sword, Excalibur, with which to carry out the development of himself and his civilization. Galahad's sword is, of course, the one which Balin carried and the one with which he became the murderer of his own brother. This is also the sword which wounded King Pelles and thus created the wasteland and the need for the redeemer: "Now I have the swerde that sometyme was the good knyghtes Balyns le Saveaige, and he was a passynge good kyght of hys hondys; and with thys swerde he slew hys brothir Balan, and that was grete pite, for he was a good knyght. And eythir slew othir thorow a dolerous stroke that Balyn gaff unto kynge Pelles, the whych ys nat yett hole, nor naught shall be tyll that I hele hym" (520). Galahad implies that he will undo the dolerous stroke which initiates the process of brother-knights killing each other; as it turns out, Galahad only makes the inevitable tragedy come sooner. As a redeemer, Galahad is an utter failure; his quest exhibits the retention of the orientations of sonhood carried to the extreme.

Galahad's adventure exhibits just what Malory believes is the tragedy inherent in institutional life: a will to truth and a renunciation of psychic energy. In translating the French Queste, Malory has consistently reduced the level of striving on Galahad's part, both by eliminating Galahad's secular adventures and by reducing his aggressiveness in the fights that he does take part in. As a knight, Galahad is big and strong, but he is almost inert from the standpoint of psychic energy and he becomes increasingly more so as the quest progresses. The quest is not moved along by Galahad's searching and energy but rather by God's will. For example, when the Grail is first revealed to Galahad, the French version demonstrates some energy expenditure:

> My knights, my servants and my faithful sons who have attained to the spiritual life whilst in the flesh, you who have sought me so diligently that I can hide myself from you no longer, it is right you should see some part of my secrets and my mysteries, for your labours have won a place for you at my table, where no knight has eaten since the days of Joseph of Arimathea. (276, trans., Matarasso)

The emphasis is upon attainment as a result of the individual's striving or labor, in short, eros. This is, of course, the "heavenly eros" which Anders Nygren equates to Platonic Love and a striving toward God. It underlies Wolfram von Eschenbach's portrayal of Parzival's quest for the Grail in which Parzival has "forced God by defiance to make His infinite Trinity grant your [Parzival's] will" (416). Or as on an earlier occasion, Wolfram tells even more clearly: "For whoever desires the Grail has to approach that prize with the sword. So should a prize be striven for" (269). In Agape and Eros, Nygren says that "Self-love is the force that drives men upward, and it reaches its culmination in love of God; this latter offers the highest and most perfect satisfaction of the desire of self-love for the eternal" (650-51). These are, however, entirely different kinds of relationships between man and God from what Malory presents in the figure of Galahad. His version of the passage in the French Queste cited above is:

> My knyghtes and my servauntes and my trew chyldren which bene come oute of dedly lyff into the spirituall lyff, I woll no lenger cover me frome you, but ye shall se now a parte of my secretes and of my hydde thynges. Now holdith and resseyvith the

> hyghe order and mete whych ye have so much
> desired. (603)

For a writer supposedly interested in the display of knight-errantry and secularism, it is remarkable how much less interested in human action Malory's passage is. He has removed all traces of human striving and given the content "hyghe order" to secrets and mysteries. Thus the high order, the institutional reality, is not the result of human striving but is rather laws given to men who submit their lives to God. Lancelot could never achieve the Grail because he could not renounce eros and striving; what the Grail Quest, as Malory presents it, requires is total and absolute renunciation of all human will. In terms of the conflict developed previously, the Oedipus Complex or the great sin of the world for which a redeemer is needed, Galahad's quest demonstrates a complete resolution of the father-son tension but on the terms of the father; Galahad retains the permanent condition of sonhood:

> And that same nyght, aboute mydnyght, cam a
> voyce amonge them whyche seyde,
> `My sunnes, and nat my chyeff sunnes, my frendis,
> and nat my werryours [enemies], go ye hens where
> ye hope best to do, and as I bade you do.´
> `A, thanked be Thou, Lorde, that Thou wolt
> whyghtsauff to calle us Thy sunnes! Now may we
> well preve that we have nat lost oure paynes.´
> (604)

Where Malory writes "go ye hens where ye hope beste to do, and as I bade you do," the French Queste has "go where you think you will be best employed and where adventure leads you" (278). Nothing could more concisely illustrate the shift from faith conceived as an undefined, unending, and autonomous adventure to faith as good works, law, and the repressive commands of an external authority. And yet the wording of the passage calls for a second Pentecost, the feast day, it will be recalled, of the Round Table and the day on which Arthur became king and began his quest for civilization. Galahad is the second Arthur, but he will produce no civilization, for the direction of his quest is not toward life and the development of selfhood in individuals, but rather it is away from life. As mentioned before, one of the most essential insights of Arthurian Romance and Courtly Love poetry is that civilizations exist in the service of eros, but Galahad's quest leads him increasingly to deny striving and thus leads him farther and farther away from the community of men with all of its unresolved tensions, hatreds, injustices, and, in short, all of its genuine need for a Galahad. The direction of Galahad's quest is not toward resolution as growth and adaptation but rather resolution as stasis and death. And these are, finally, the terms upon which the father will be reconciled with the son. Even in the life of Christ the pattern is apparent. The father demands the death of his own son in symbolic reparation for the sins or ego-expressions of all mankind. At the last moment, the son kneels down and prays to the father: "Father, if thou be willing, remove this cup from me; nevertheless not my will, but thine, be done" (Luke, 22: 42), but reconciliation with the father can take place only if the son submits to his fate and renounces his psychic energy to the father.

Galahad as redeemer clearly follows the paradigm established by Christ, and in doing so we should see that his actions are structurally identical to the knights of the Round Table who have exchanged the genuine quest for symbolic imitations, tournaments, and rituals. Rituals may repeat the original self-defining acts, but in present circumstances they have no power in themselves to create new social selves sufficient for responding satisfactorily to the present environment; or more precisely, the social selves that they do create are exactly the sickness or the problem for which the Round Table needs a savior. Rather than being a true redeemer who can go beyond the original Christ, Galahad like all other aspects of his culture is imitative and ritualistic and looks for new life in the deeds of the past. As the opening sections of Malory's romance demonstrate, however, it is only acts of the present which are aimed at resolving present conflicts that can move the civilization forward. This imitative concept of redemption was, of course, the only one which the medieval explanatory synthesis had to offer, and it was one which Malory saw as leading directly to death.

For Malory, Galahad's quest is clearly destructive. Along with other writers of Arthurian Romance, he discovered that although redemption means the resolution of tension with the father or creative source, it is not achieved by submitting to the father and remaining a son (i.e., death in life) but rather is achieved by re-creating the father, that is, by becoming a creator and a father oneself. We have already seen how Luther conceives of such a new life in creative faith, but the new redemption can also be seen in the works of Marsilio Ficino (1443-1499), a near contemporary of Malory. The substance of Ficino's Theologia Platonica: De Immortalitate Animarum is to devise a form of self-love or justified ego-expression as the basis for man's love of God and, therefore, of the immortality of his soul. Anders Nygren in Agape and Eros writes, "For in the fellow man we love, we recognize ourselves and love in him nothing other than ourselves." Ficino's starting point for human psychology is the contrary to St. Augustine's concept of a proper relation among things that are to be loved, and St. Augustine would see such self-love as the greatest sin since it inevitably results in, as Nygren puts it, "Ficino does not even shrink from reducing our love for God wholly to self-love. Love to God is the means, self-love the end--Ficino announces unequivocally." This is what Tristram shows Palomides how to do in the passage discussed a moment ago; in accepting Palomides's love for Isode and for himself, Tristram allows himself or Isode to be the means for Palomides' self-love and psychic recovery. Tristram accepts Palomides love when he understands the personal origin of it; he does not accept it when the love appears to be part of Palomides' effort to win worship, an external origin.

To follow the development of Ficino's argument a little further, we recognize in the relationship between man and God the Oedipus Complex: "It follows that his spirit is in essence almost identical with God's spirit. Indeed, man could make the heavens, Ficino thinks, if only he had the necessary tools and had access to the heavenly material. If one with all this before his eyes will not admit that the human soul is a rival of God, he is undoubtedly out of his mind, says Ficino." The final result of Ficino's ego-expressive redemption is man's assumption of the position of fatherhood himself: "It is [in Ficino's work] a question of the new emphasis which is laid on man in his temporal existence: empirical man is made, in such a way as never before, the centre of the universe. In a word, it is a question of the human god" (671-679).

Galahad refuses to acknowledge that the human soul is a rival of God. Ficino would call him out of his mind, but it is better perhaps to consider Galahad's adventure in terms of what Freud calls Thanatos or the Death Instinct. Malory's retelling of the Grail Quest is filled with instances of the renunciation of eros; we have just seen the cases of Percival, Bors, and Lancelot. The emphasis is upon virginity. Galahad's behavior on the quest becomes more and more what might be called regressive rather than aggressive, as marks the behavior of the Round Table knights. Near the end of his life, Galahad lives in perfect fulfillment, but as Malory shows at one point he finds this fulfillment in a deep hole: "[Estorause] toke hem and put hem in preson in a depe hole. But as sone as they were there oure Lorde sente them the Sankgreall thorow whos grace they were allwey fullfylled whyle they were in preson" (605-06). This fulfillment or redemption does not appear as a release from bonds and a flow of grace and energy into the body of the world, as Joseph Campbell notes is the traditional imagery for successful redemptive quests; rather it is a redemption that appears to be a return to a womb or a subsumption into the elements of the earth as in a grave. Of this kind of regressive fulfillment, Freud writes in Beyond the Pleasure Principle:

> At this point we cannot escape a suspicion that we may have come upon the track of a universal attribute of instincts and perhaps of organic life in general which has not hitherto been clearly recognized or at least not explicitly stressed. It seems, then, that an instinct is an urge inherent in organic life to restore an earlier state of things which the living entity has been obliged to abandon under pressure of external disturbing forces; that is, it is a kind of organic elasticity, or, to put it another way, the expression of the inertia inherent in organic life. (30)

Freud points out that instincts are normally considered as impulses toward change and adaptation--the increase of pleasure or dominance of the environment as we have seen in the case of the Round Table knights and as occurs as a result of external disturbing forces of birth or the soul's incarnation into a body.   All instincts have the aim of reducing environmental or internal tensions, and, if we think about it, death or a return to an inert state would present the ultimate resolution.   This theory of the Death Instinct helps distinguish ultimate motives or final solutions from immediate or partial motives.   On the level of the immediate, men struggle against obstacles and frustrations in order that they might live, but ultimately and in the most extreme sense "what we are left with is the fact that the organism wishes to die only in its own fashion" (33).   Galahad's quest raises the career of a knight to this ultimate level, the level of last or final things, the anagogical level.   He puts aside all immediate interests such as involve the other knights with the things of the world: Gawain's taste for food, Tristram's love for music and hunting, Dynadan's jokes, Lamerok's passion for Morgause, or Palomides' Questing Beast.   Galahad concentrates on the only anagogically important aspect of life: saving his soul and returning it to its original state.   Galahad's concern with only ultimate things is the final result of St. Augustine's total separation of bodily and spiritual concerns and separation of love of self and love of God.   What he desires is finally a separation from his body: "Thys othir day, when we sawe a parte of the adventures of the Sangreall, I was in such joy of herte that I trow never man was that was erthely.   And therefore I wote well, whan my body ys dede, my soule shall be in grete joy to se the Blyssed Trinite every day" (605).   What this means to Malory is a denial of the present life and a wish for death: "and sir Galahad felle on hys kneys and prayde longe tyme to oure Lorde, that at what tyme he asked, he myght passe oute of this worlde" (604-05).

The equation of redemption to death points to a very real crisis in Christian ideology, one which had by the late Middle Ages become a cultural problem so large that Christianity appeared to many individuals as a dead end and an institution that could no longer survive as it presently existed.   The pattern, as we should now be aware, exists in all institutions as the reality and ultimate legitimations upon which they are grounded pass into history and no longer correspond very well with the present conditions that individuals experience.   Christian doctrine through its agents in the church was demanding from individuals the sort of self-abnegation and longing for the past which amounted to death.   The church held absolute control of grace, the means to spiritual life, and it demanded as the price for grace the sonhood of all men.   In terms of the imagery of Galahad's quest and of much of the doctrine itself, the church as God's agent demanded just what Galahad gives: the death of the body for the life of the soul. This was, of course, an impossible situation, especially for men of the late Middle Ages awakening to the possibilities of the secular life.   Luther sees the paradox as originating with St. Paul:

> Sin still clings to the flesh, continually disturbing the conscience and hindering faith, so that we cannot joyfully see and desire the eternal wealth granted to us by God through Christ.   When he experiences this conflict of the flesh against the spirit, Paul himself exclaims (Rom. 7: 24): 'Wretched man that I am! Who will deliver me from this body of death?'   He accuses his 'body,' which he really should have loved, and gives it a very ugly name, calling it his 'death,' as though he were saying: 'my body afflicts and harasses me more than death itself.'   Even in his case this interrupted the joy of the spirit. (<u>Lectures on Galatians,</u> 26, 393)

In this manner, as Galahd says, "whan my body us dede, my soule shall be in grete joy"; death becomes a great release and a new life. Nothing could be more orthodox and more in line with Christian teachings than that one should orientate his whole life toward the final goal of unification with the father. But in Malory's portrayal, Christian doctrine simply and finally admits that it cannot solve the problems of life and turns its interests elsewhere toward death.   But humans must live; perhaps a race of Galahads might choose extinction, but in fact no such choice is needed.   The condemnation of life, beginning with St. Paul, is only the institutional interpretation, the constructed social reality to which individuals were coerced to adhere by increasingly specific canon laws. Palomides, Tristram, and Dynadan discover that they can, indeed, love life, love one another, and that sins and dishonor really do not matter much at all.   In the radical separation and animosity of the body and soul we see the conflict of the id and the super-ego.   The super-ego is, of course, the internalized commands of the father, and in both St. Paul and Galahad these commands are actually calling for the total submission and destruction of the psychic energic impulses of the id. This orientation is the institutional mal-adaptation which makes problem resolution impossible. To those who come to love life, however, the preoccupations of the father simply cease to matter except as the problems of life they will turn their energies toward resolving.

The direction of the Death Instinct should not be considered as leading to a real, physical death. Physical death, in this sense, is only the metaphor for the death-in-life that Galahad's quest offers to the knights of the Round Table. Galahad's death must be seen as a final renunciation of eros and of the source of his own life within himself; in other words, a final surrender to the notion that human problems cannot be solved and life itself, therefore, is to be hated. The Death Instinct is, finally, only a hatred of this life, and as such it is the command of the father and of historical redemptivism that the individual should repudiate all that is his own in order to be acceptable to the father or the past. As Anders Nygren sums up the medieval concept of mortification: "What is wrong with self-love is that man claims independence over against God. So long as any of this self-will remains in him, he cannot attain perfect union with God. He must do violence to his nature, empty himself of all that is his own, be stripped of all self-will. His life must take the form of `ein Entwerden.' His ego must be killed and annihilated; only so he can pass into God and become one with Him" (649).

The Death Instinct, therefore, means only the desire to remain perpetually a son, never to experience the trauma and suffering that the Oedipus Complex entails and never to achieve for oneself the autonomy of being that is the human potential. It is not surprising that in this Galahad finds even greater pleasure than eros could promise. The Death Instinct implies that the individual has ceased striving and ceased projecting himself out against his environment to become the master of it. In terms of the political and secular lives of the knights, this quest is no redemption at all; rather it represents the final triumph of the father over the sons and the final condemnation of their secular lives. The problem with the secular life is that it cannot avoid obstacles and stimulations from the environment; the knight riding on his quest through life cannot avoid the encounter with other knights, and through these confrontations, the actions and reactions they elicit and the resolutions achieved, he cannot avoid learning to know who he is and what he is in terms beyond the father's absolute control. The father denies redemption to such strivers and therefore disinherits them from the possibility of his salvation. As we see in the following passage, even this threatened withdrawal of love is only a strategy for preventing personal growth.

> Therefore thou [Galahad] must go hense [to Sarras, the spiritual city] and beare with the thys holy vessell, for this nyght hit shall departe frome the realme of Logrus, and hit shall nevermore be sene here. And knowyst thou wherefore? For he ys nat served nother worshipped to hys ryght by hem of thys londe, for they be turned to evyll lyvyng, and therefore I shall disherite them of the honoure whych I have done them. (603-04)

What the Round Table needs from its redeemer is not this condemnation, but rather a transcendence of the conditions that are now producing the tensions among the knights and a new direction for the energies of the individuals so that they can once again challenge genuine problems in their civilization and not one another in tournaments. The Round Table needs another Merlin who can direct the knights' energies or a redeemer the sort of which Luther conceives of Christ to be, a redeemer who offers freedom from the laws and codes of the present, not the restrictions of the laws:

> He was sent into the world by the Father to redeem those who were being held captive under the law. These words portray Christ truly and accurately. They do not ascribe to him the work of establishing a new law; they ascribe to him the work of redeeming those who were under the law. Christ Himself says in John 8: 15: `I judge no one´; and elsewhere (John 12: 47): `I did not come to judge the world but to save the world.´ That is: `I did not

come to promulgate a law and to judge men according to it, as Moses and other lawgivers did. I am performing a more sublime and better function. I judge and condemn the Law. The Law kills you, and I kill it in turn; and so through death I abolish death.' (Lectures on Galatians, 26, 368)

4.3 Synthetic
and Analytic Tragedy

St. Thomas Aquinas died in March of 1274, nearly one-hundred and fifty years before Malory's birth, but the events surrounding the death of Aquinas are important to our final understanding of Malory's attempt to write the whole book of King Arthur (see the headnote to this chapter). Malory's tale of the Round Table enlarges the personal issues exemplified in the last months of St. Thomas' life into the fall of a civilization, a tragic vision which suggests that the explanatory synthesis upon which the civilization was built has itself, finally, become destructive of human life. St. Thomas died psychically and spiritually to the medieval world before he died physically; it happened as he was working on the third part of the Summa Theologica. In the Summer of 1273, Thomas completed the long exposition of the Incarnation of Christ and progressed to the Sacraments, from Baptism to Holy Eucharist and then in the middle of the discussion of Penance the Summa stops. Bartholomew of Capua tells us "After the Mass, he never wrote nor dictated anything, in fact, he hung up his writing instruments."

The event that cost him his faith in his life's work of building the institution was the sudden perception of a higher level of reality and a world openness which made all of the

Summa seem too small and too limited to be of any significance. While celebrating Mass on December 6th at the chapel of St. Nicholas in Naples, Thomas for perhaps the first time in his life truly became aware of the infinite or the wholly other, and he realized that his attempt in the Summa to regard theology as the rational analogue of the religious experience was actually the destruction of the transcendental.

Reginald of Piperno, Thomas' secretary, confessor, and successor at the Chair of Philosophy at the University of Naples, in his Acta Bollandiana reports, "He was smitten with a wonderful change and after that Mass he neither wrote nor dictated anything more." In the weeks that followed, Reginald tells us that he questioned Thomas repeatedly about why he refused to write; finally and with much hesitation, Thomas told him: "I adjure you by the living God Almighty and by your duty to our Order and by the love you have for me, that so long as I am alive you will never tell anyone what I am going to tell you. And he went on: Everything that I have written seems to me worthless in comparison with the things I have seen and which have been revealed to me" (cited by Campbell, Masks of God, IV, 578-79). Shortly thereafter, in January of 1274, as Thomas rode from Naples to Lyons to the Council called by Pope Gregory X to consider the unification of Latin and Greek catholics, he struck his head on a low hanging branch and fell from his mule unconscious. He was taken to Maezna and later to the Cistercian monastery of Saint Mary at Fossanuova where, as Reginald tells, he lingered with great sickness until March. On the last day, Thomas asked to receive the Eucharist and prayed for forgiveness for anything he had written or taught against the will of God and then died on March 7, 1274.

What interests us in St. Thomas' death is the relationship between the explanations of the world he was writing and the transcendental, the wholly other, or the numinal aspect of human experience--the perception of which had the effect of destroying his belief in his own philosophy. In more general terms, this relationship is between the institutionalized structures by which the mind knows the world and the world itself as indeterminate and ultimately unknowable. St. Thomas in one tragic moment discovered that the totality of the world (or God) is different and radically beyond the socially constructed mind's conception of it, and that discovery exploded his faith in the great quest to demonstrate with the tools of logic and dialectic that the mind could know the world. Joseph Campbell writes, "to imagine a creation (causality) and a creator (First Cause) of the universe is only to project the categories of human experience and reason beyond their field; that is to say, to become in a rather refined way as guilty of anthropomorphism as any savage" (582-83).

Tragedy in its normal sense, what I call synthetic tragedy, asserts an isomorphism between the phenomenal world and the conceptions of the mind. The paradigm for this sort of tragedy is found among the Greeks whose tragedies have the expressed purpose of re-affirming the myths and gods by demonstrating that deviants, over-reachers, and in general those who trust too much in their own unique view of things will eventually be destroyed. Synthetic tragedy provides an example of the validity of the explanatory synthesis (whether called myths, philosophy, social reality, laws of science, doctrine, truths, or simply God) by showing how those who violate the precepts--even in such a magnificent way as Oedipus'--finally fail. Truth is substantiated in the fall of the hero who suffers symbolically for the impeity of all mankind, and mankind in general learns that he is not a god, is not entitled to remake the world in his own fashion, and that the propositions of the dominant explanatory synthesis which have placed him in the world lower than the gods but higher than animals are absolute. The hero's failure illustrates that the conceptions of the world he deviates from are isomorphic with the reality of the world. John Milton has written perhaps the most complete synthetic tragedy of the Christian era in his Paradise Lost. In the fall of Adam, the Christian explanation of the world is shown to be true; we know it is true because Adam did fall. The purpose of synthetic tragedy is Milton's great theme:

What in me is dark
Illumine; what is low, raise up and support;
That, to the height of this great argument,
I may assert Eternal Providence,
And justify the ways of God to Men.   (I, 22-26)

This mode of tragedy, however, does not explain very well what occurs in Arthurian Romance or what happened to St. Thomas, for in these cases we are not concerned with deviants and over-reachers such as Oedipus or Macbeth but with an individual's discovery that his explanatory synthesis is not isomorphic with the world, that the world is radically beyond his conceptions of it, and, in fact, that in itself the world or God is unknowable or transcendental. In short, analytic tragedy presents a narrative which demonstrates that what men believe is Eternal Providence and the ways of God are only social constructions or a symbolic universe which rose to dominance and the category of Truth as other knowledge was suppressed and destroyed and which, therefore, can never be isomorphic with the actual mind of God. God's ways as men presently know them cannot be justified.

The Thomistic scholar, Gerald B. Phelan, writes that "The philosophy of St. Thomas purports to provide the rational explanation (complete in principle and capable of indefinite development in demonstrative detail and application) of the universe as a whole and of its relation to God, as the Creator and Ruler of the world, insofar as such explanation can be afforded by the light of reason unaided by faith. The world of things and the world of thought, the world of freedom and the world of act are all embraced within that purview and each is envisioned in the light of the whole. Analogy permeates every realm and runs like a thread through the whole thought of St. Thomas" (St. Thomas and Analogy, 2-3). In analytic tragedy, the great rational quest of a St. Thomas is shown to be false; God returns to what mystic philosophers call the cloud of unknowing taking with Him all possibility of asserting as real logical extrapolations from a coherent set of first principles. Some time in his life--a time we shall probably never directly learn about--Thomas Malory must have undergone a similar collapse of faith in the order by which his own social world made sense.

C. S. Lewis in The Allegory of Love has called the appearance of Courtly Love in the late Middle Ages one of the three or four fundamental changes in human sentiment of all time, on a par with the evolutionary leaps associated with Socrates, Jesus, and post-modernism. These shifts cut across the complete spectrum of human activity so that eventually the human species comes to imagine the world in a fundamentally different way. In the sort of analytic tragedy recorded in Arthurian Romance, we see a profound collapse of confidence in the medieval explanations of the world and the beginning of a search for new first principles. For this loss of faith to occur, the individual must become aware of a transcendent or different level of reality from which he can, then, look back upon all of his nomic and social institutions and see them as arbitrary, incoherent, unworkable, and false. St. Thomas discovered the truly transcendental or extra-mental God, and that discovery destroyed for him the entire bulk of Christian doctrine. Fifty years after Thomas, William of Ockham, the nominalist, argued more generally that universals and concepts--the cognitive equivalent of the behavioral habituations of an institution--are only properties of the mind and language, not of the physical world. In the perceptual process of each individual, he locates a deeper level of reality from which to analyze existent conceptions about reality.

The late Middle Ages were a period of awakening interest in the present life and of self-assertion on the part of the individual. We see this awakening in Courtly Love literature and also in the various revolts among the peasants and, especially, in emerging Renaissance painting and sculpture which began to depict the human body as it had never been seen before in Christian times. Renaissance artists looked back to the Greek and Roman love for the physical and temporal aspects of human life, and, more importantly, they conducted for themselves research into human anatomy and physiology. Such an empirical approach to the objects of experience rooted in individual perceptual processes represents an inherent threat to the security of dominant explanations, for what if the researcher cannot find that the doctrine adequately explains the phenomena of his experience. The incoherence Malory discovers in medieval political and religious theory is the same kind of inadequacy Nicholas Copernicus (1473-1543) discovers in medieval science. In his preface to On the Revolutions of the Celestial Orbs, he indicates how revolutionary thinkers of the late Middle Ages finally regarded their inherited explanations and presents his own preference for resolving concrete problems in life, even if that means refuting a great many long standing truths. The preface is written as a letter to Pope Paul III:

I have accordingly no desire to conceal from Your Holiness that I was impelled to consider a different system of deducing the motion of the universe's spheres for no other reason than the realization that astronomers do not agree among themselves in their investigations of the subject. For, in the first place they are so uncertain about the motion of the sun and the moon that they cannot establish and observe a constant length even for the tropical year. Secondly, in determining the motion not only of these bodies but also of the other five planets, they do not use the same principles, assumptions, and explanations of apparent revolutions and motions.

The incoherence of present methods and explanations made scientists unable to resolve problems in daily life such as the calendar and therefore the old order had the result of making mortal life appear ugly and contemptible. It could not make the parts of the world fit together into the beautiful and tensionless whole that eros dreams of. Copernicus goes on,

Nor could they elicit or deduce from the eccentrics the principal consideration, that is, the structure of the universe and the true symmetry of its parts. On the contrary, their experience was just like someone taking from various places hands, feet, a head, and other pieces, very well depicted, it may be, but not for the representation of a single person; since these fragments would not belong to one another at all, a monster rather than a man would be put together. (4)

Eros aims itself at tensionlessness and beauty, but the experiences of Malory's knights in conducting their institutionally determined quests produce as a community exactly the sort of incoherent monster that Copernicus describes, precisely while in the romance we observe increasing levels of longing for harmony and beauty. Copernicus offers a greatly expanded image of the universe. Malory's Tristram loves Isode above and beyond his love of anything else. Such love bespeaks a powerful desire for beauty and it provides an ultimate vantage point from which a discreet and coherent body of doctrines might be deduced and legitimated and from which the lover might view all other explanatory systems. The lady becomes an object with which the lover can identify and thus look back upon his civilization and arrive at the judgment that it is far inferior to his new code of love. In the twelfth century, Andreas Capellanus announced that love is the origin of all good on earth. Just as St. Thomas' experience of the transcendental alienated him from his work and his doctrine, the lover becomes alienated from his social responsibilities as a citizen or knight.

Because he has the experience of Isode as a culturally transcendent being, Tristram cannot avoid concluding that something is terribly wrong with King Mark and Cornwall even though, as I have argued throughout, Cornwall and Mark represent the most highly developed polity according to what the Middle Ages knew about societies. With Tristram's death at the hands of Mark, we conclude that Cornwall and all it stands for is false and unjust. Mankind as a whole gradually begins to see, as Copernicus writes, "that I too would be readily permitted to ascertain whether explanations sounder than those of my predecessors could be found" (5) and the world itself comes to be seen in new images which, most importantly, will again allow for a new feeling of coherence in a new and seemingly infinite potential for expansion in behavioral and explanatory detail.

Arthurian Romance achieves its anti-explanatory and culturally vandalizing themes by building the narrative around the knights as individuals and around their experiences as members of an institution. It is truly remarkable that no important romance survives (and it is likely that none was written) which has Arthur as the principal actor; rather Arthur is always the institutional center against which or for which the knights carry out their individual lives. Self-assertion against the institution, as loving the king's wife suggests, becomes the individual's way of resolving essential tensions he feels in his relation to his institutions. Its frequently violent aspect injects into the highly ordered world of medieval political conceptions significant levels of explanatory disorder that would make modification of the ideology possible and desirable for later thinkers. The psychic health of human beings requires constant and radical modification of human institutions in response to incoherencies that cannot be resolved within the purview of the social reality. Martin Luther vandalizes orthodox theology by identifying with Christ the suffering son rather than God the Father or even Christ the Pantocrator. All of these movements culminate in the Renaissance conception of the Middle Ages as a dark and uncivilized time; Philip Sydney in his Defense of Poetry called it a "misty time"; Francis Bacon wrote in the Novum Organum that nothing of medieval philosophy, science, or knowledge was any longer of use for the men of his time.

Bacon's conclusion is essentially the same as St. Thomas': "Everything I have written seems worthless in comparison to the things that I have seen." Literary works which present the collapse of an institution, a civilization, or a regnant world view which destroys with it the world's heroes are tragedies just as much as normal tragedies, but they are not synthetic because in the fall of the civilization the explanatory synthesis is not left in tact nor is it substantiated. The fall proves that the principles upon which the civilization was built are inadequate, incomplete, and ultimately in opposition to the nature of the world itself. This sort of tragedy is analytic, for if synthetic tragedy adds to, supports, and further exemplifies the notion of a coherent world view, then analytic tragedy breaks down and resolves into parts that now incoherent entity. Synthesis looks for coherence, while analysis looks for incoherence as a strategy for deconstructing institutions and ultimately reconstructing new ones on different foundations. Synthesis springs from faith; analysis springs from the special kind of loss of faith that Morse Peckham has called "explanatory collapse." Analytic tragedy is the counterpart in art to what Thomas Kuhn has termed "revolutionary science." Revolutionary science, as opposed to normal science, is not concerned with sustaining the validity of present scientific laws but rather with discovering data that will refute them and lead to entirely new scientific paradigms or world-models from which wholly new sets of laws will follow. The transition from the Ptolemaic cosmological system to the Copernican model, Kuhn notes in The Copernican Revolution and The Structure of Scientific Revolutions, is a prime example.

In general, analytic tragedy and revolutionary science belong to periods in cultural evolution in which existing, maladaptive life-forms (i.e., institutions) are being rejected in favor of new adaptations which permit enhanced forms of life--at least while the behavioral strategies are being innovated. Morse Peckham's Explanation and Power argues largely that the mechanism by which humans evolve from one cultural stage to another is a process of exploiting the explanatory incoherence of the present dominant culture and this process is essential to cultural well-being:

> it does not seem to be accidental that Western culture, which exploited the incoherence of its ultimate explanatory systems by creating modern science, is also the geographical area in which there is to be found the greatest incidence or at least a modest exploitation of ideological incoherence and instability, nor that in the culture area of the West is to be found the greatest proportion of the population which experiences the life enhancement of the negative inversions of the ultimate sanctions: economic ease, the privileges of freedom, pleasures, and the enhancement of the individual's own value (i.e., human dignity). (243)

Charles Moorman in writing about Malory's tragic knights wonders how Malory could have started out to exemplify the beauties of knighthood and ended up by so effectively condemning it. The problem with so many of Malory's critics is that they expect Le Morte Darthur to be synthetic tragedy and without a theory of analytic tragedy end up calling the knights tragic. They are not tragic; their institutions are and the knights are simply destroyed in the fall of the institution. Usually analytic tragedy is associated with the nineteenth and twentieth centuries during which were written such works as Shelley's Prometheus Unbound, Wagner's Der Ring des Nibelung, Nietzsche's Twilight of the Idols, or Camus' Myth of Sisyphus, but it is more accurate to say that periods of synthetic and analytic activity alternate in a much larger pattern of what Mircea Eliade has called the "Cosmogonic Myth": stories of the creation of the world followed by its destruction and followed by its re-creation and followed again by its destruction.

The problem is, as St. Thomas or St. Augustine did not realize, that civilization is a human construct devised in order to resolve behavioral and experiential problems, and as new experiences, even the resolutions themselves carried out in behavior, create new sets of problems that call out for new explanatory resolutions, the old explanations lose cogency and are relegated by innovative thinkers to the domain of false knowledge. The late Middle Ages, as is not often well recognized, were a period of significant analysis and cultural innovation in all directions: from the logic of Ockham and the physiology of Leonardo da Vinci to the literature of the romance writers. These cultural innovations led up to, of course, the Renaissance and a new image of man and the world which began a new period of synthetic thinking--a new birth. Peckham explains why the arts are so central to cultural evolution:

> the arts are particularly adept in undermining ideologies by presenting signs which current ideologies cannot subsume, even an ideology which the work is otherwise exemplifying. This is borne out by the fact that the higher the cultural level at which the art is produced--that is, the nearer it is to the ultimate explanatory modes of a culture--the greater the categorial discontinuity the work is likely to offer. (Explanation and Power, 233)

The craving of orthodox culture for order, logic, and predictability creates a world that is a closed system. Significant portions of the lives of innovative individuals, however, cannot be included in this system. The essential sign which Arthurian Romance presents and which cannot be subsumed is the major knight's love for the king's wife, or in more general terms eros and the Oedipus Complex.

The character of the Round Table itself suggests this inclusiveness. Much is made of the fact that in seating the knights in a circular fashion the tensions that might be caused by a linear, hierarchical arrangement will be resolved. The Round Table is a tension resolving device, just as is on a more subtle level the whole ideology which lies behind it. The individuals in Malory's romance are ideologically bound to one

another; that means, the bond between them is the common
Weltanschauung they share, and because they share a world
view, they can expect each other to respond in a consistent
manner when in the same or similar situations.   The Middle
Ages always assumed that the bond or world view was derived
from the nature of God and His plan for creation, both of which,
of course, were held to be immutable.   At the beginning of the
final collapse of the Round Table, Malory keeps the character of
the bond clearly before the reader's eyes.   He refers frequently
to the oaths between Lancelot and Arthur or between Lancelot
and Gawain and he refers in general to the allegiance the
knights owe to the larger world view when he writes:

> For, lyke as wynter rasure dothe allway arace
> and deface grene summer, so faryth hit by unstable
> love in man and woman, for in many persones there
> ys no stabylite: for we may se all day, for a lytyll
> blaste of wynters rasure, anone we shall deface and
> lay aparte trew love, for lytyll or nowght, that
> coste muche thynge.   Thys ys no wysdome nother no
> stabylite, but hit ys fyblenes of nature and grete
> disworshyp, whomsoever usyth thys.
>
> Therefore, lyke as May moneth flowryth and
> florysyth in every mannes gardyne, so in lyke wyse
> lat every man of worshyp florysh hys herte in thys
> worlde: first unto God, and nexte unto the joy of
> them that he promysed hys feyth unto; for there was
> never worshypfull man nor worshypfull woman but
> they loved one bettir than anothir; and worshyp in
> armys may never by foyled.   But first reserve the
> honoure to God, and secundely thy quarell muste
> com of thy lady.   And suche love I calle vertuouse
> love.
>
> But nowadayes men can nat love sevennyght but
> they muste have all their desyres.   That love may
> nat endure by reson, for where they bethe sone
> accorded and hasty, heete sone keelyth.   And ryght
> so faryth the love nowadays, sone hote sone colde.
> Thys ys no stabylyte.   But the olde love was nat so.
> For men and women coude love togydirs seven yerys,
> and no lycoures lustis was betwyxte them, and than

> was love trouthe and faythefulnes. And so in lyke
> wyse was used such love in kynge Arthurs days.
> (649)

In these lines Malory affects the synthetic sentiments of his age by looking into nature and back into history for stable and virtuous conceptions of life, and he laments, therefore, the corruptions of the present. But these lines begin the tale of "The Knight of the Cart" in which Lancelot's love for Guinevere is demonstrated to be the hot and lustful love that Malory speciously condemns. What the tale itself demonstrates is the tragic disparity between the world of the ideal true lover and the world of real men and women. If, as Malory says a little later, Guinevere is a "trew lover," then the tale proves that the explanation of love is not operant in the world of even "kynge Arthurs dayes" and its highest lovers, Lancelot and Guinevere. This passage sets up the culmination of the theme of the irremediable tension between the individual and the mind's conceptions. One or the other, in the course of the romance, will be proven to be unreal. Following the hierarchical conceptions--supposedly derived from nature--that one must first love God and then his lady produces only the incoherent monster of war in which Lancelot, Gawain, Arthur, and Mordred simply watch the knights of the Round Table kill each other off.

The particular cognitive style of the romance writer is to imagine his culture at it appears from the point of view of the individual; in this way, the tragic outcome of the romance derives from the limitations created by explanations (such as the one in the passage above) and the writers frequently depict, therefore, the sort of behavior associated with close confinement and repression: adultery, feuding, intense competition for recognition, insanity or madness, periodic retreat to more open spaces, practical joking, over-ritualization, oath pledging, and gossip. All of these behaviors appear in the tales following "The Knight of the Cart," and the net result is a rapidly escalating disintegration of social bonds until one knight is faced-off with another in a life and death battle to preserve his own position of right. That two or more positions of right could develop demonstrates the incoherence of the world view the knights hold, even while it is exactly the problem that the Round Table in its roundness sought to prevent.

In the final chapters, Lancelot finds himself unable to act at all in a manner that would enhance life because of the cross-purposes of the faith he owes to the explanatory system. He believes that he must defend Guinevere from all of her accusers, but this act makes him King Arthur's enemy. He cannot fight Arthur, however, because Arthur is his king. In spite of Gawain's determined vengeance, Lancelot is paralyzed by explanatory imperatives which simultaneously direct him to fight with Gawain and not to fight with him. Lancelot continually attempts to enforce all the tenets of the synthesis as if those tenets were coherent, but rather they leave him unable to do anything to resolve the problem he faces. The codes, he believes, were instituted to resolve these conflicts and he places total faith in them by acting only according to them--which now means inaction. This fundamental incoherence, leaves the Round Table defenseless against the rebellion of Mordred. In this sense, Lancelot symbolizes all the fundamental inadequacy of late medieval ideology. His inability to act causes further problems since it prolongs the dispute and allows for the daily killing of lesser knights allied with Arthur, and it leaves Arthur vulnerable to the growing rebellion of Mordred. Lancelot had always been the force allied with Arthur's political leadership. What we see failing is the synthesis or bonds which held the society together by giving each man a role and identity. Lancelot does nothing to violate the explanatory bonds between himself and all others, and yet by adhering to those bonds he insures, in an even greater way, the destruction of all the knights. The laws become the destroyers of men. At the final battle, Arthur sees what has become of his social order: "'Jesu mercy!' seyde the kynge, 'where ar all my noble knyghtes becom? Alas that ever I shulde se thys doleful day! For now,' seyde kynge Arthur, 'I am come to myne ende'" (713).

This chapter began with a section titled "The Triumph of the Father" and its point is to suggest that the role of the father or the institutional inertia which precedes any individual's emergent and unique experience is the destructive and tragic force in culture. Malory and analytic tragedy in general assert that the triumph of the father means the destruction of the sons. This is the final portrait we are given of Arthur; his last act is to turn upon Mordred, his own natural son, and kill him in literal confirmation of the thematic: "`But wolde to God,´ seyde he, `that I wyste now where were that traytoure sir Mordred that hath caused all thys myschyff´" (713). Analytic tragedy shows, moreover, that this event means the death of the father and the civilization. Malory´s view is that Arthur has finally become this sort of life-denying force, for the son, in the symbolism of mythology, is the father´s future, a future, however, that transcends the father´s control and is not likely, therefore, to be exactly what the father would be if he were able to project himself into the future. The future is transcendent in the same way as are other numinal experiences--beyond the present social reality and often subversive of it. Sir Lucan argues for innovation and a return to the quest for civilization by abandoning the present battle and all that it signifies, but Arthur, at this point, is bent only upon destruction:

> Than kynge Arthur loked aboute and was ware where stood sir Mordred leanyng uppon hys swerde amonge a grete hepe of dede men.
> `Now, gyff me my speare,´ seyde kynge Arthure unto sir Lucan, `for yondir I have aspyed the traytoure that all thys woo hath wrought.´
> `Sir, latte hym be,´ seyde sir Lucan, `for he ys unhappy. And yf ye passe this unhappy day ye shall by ryght well revenged. And, good lord, remembre ye of your nyghtes dreme and what the spyryte of sir Gawayne tolde you tonyght, and yet God of Hys grete goodnes hath preserved you hyddirto. And for Goddes sake, my lorde, leve of thys, for, blyssed be God, ye have won the fylde: for yet we ben here three on lyve, and with sir Mordred ys nat one on lyve. And therefore if ye leve of now, thys wycked day of Desteny ys paste!´
> `Now tyde me deth, tyde me lyff,´ seyde the kyng, `now I se hym yondir alone, he shall never ascape myne hondes! For at a bettir avayle shall I never have hym.´ (713)

The basic motif of Arthurian Romance is the quest which implies that civilization and selfhood are unending processes through which individuals create themselves while groups of individuals on their quests create the social order. The quest itself necessitates a high level of responsiveness to environmental tensions for the questor can never be sure what danger or delight lies ahead. Ahead is the unknown, the other, the transcendental, the numinal, or, most simply, the world itself. And the successful questor is he who can adapt his behavior most appropriately to the situations he encounters. The quest metaphor makes the function of adaptation explicit, and yet in the process of the quest for civilization certain successful adaptational strategies are institutionalized and raised to the level of behavioral universals. This process in itself is a successful adaptational strategy for it enables the less experienced individuals to adapt more quickly by eliminating a great deal of trial and error. Such a strategy, it will be recalled, characterizes Arthur and Merlin at the outset of the Round Table. Arthur acts and Merlin interprets. The goal of the quest is the same in all cases and at all times: perfect adaptation to the world, complete mastery of environmental conditions, and stable behaviors and identities-- three ways of stating the same idea. The great temptation for any civilization which achieves a high level of stability, that is, a high level of successful adaptation, is to believe that it has achieved the goal of the quest, that its codes and explanations fully account for the phenomena of the world. The possession of any truth means that the concept in the mind is identical with the extra-mental condition or phenomenon of the world.

     In seeking finally to kill Mordred, Arthur confesses that he believes the quest to be at an end. He, as father and as truth, must repress the deviance of the son because his own being as king depends upon proving that the son's innovations are unsuccessful adaptations. This final battle is Arthur's final chance to substantiate the truth of his kingship, and he can do nothing else, therefore, than turn and attack Mordred. Galahad, too, believes that he has achieved the end of the quest; after all it is prophesied that he shall bring to an end the quest for the Holy Grail. But as Malory's romance shows, the end of the quest is death and destruction. Arthur's final proof of his own kingship is his own destruction just as Galahad's final vision becomes a longing for death. Malory's analytic tragedy calls out for an abandonment of the longing for ends and truth and freedom from the codes and explanations which claim the status of truth. In the deaths of Arthur and Galahad we see that their conceptions of the world are not identical with the world or, indeed, with life itself. Malory asserts, finally, in a negative and tragic way that life is a quest without end, an unceasing pursuit of a Questing Beast or an Isode who leads and guides the knight to be more tomorrow than he is today. One transcends the monstrous incoherence of the world the father presents to his sons by questing outward toward openness and the unknown.

References

Throughout this study I have consulted both the second three volume edition and the most recent single volume edition of Malory's <u>Works</u> as edited by Eugene Vinaver. Page references in my text are to the single volume edition (1971). I have omitted from the bibliography very well known primary works; that makes what follows mostly a list of secondary works and those primary works which would not generally be familiar to the literary student. All of the works listed below have in some way influenced the writing of this study, but of course a great many other influences that weave in and through the fabric of thought have not been possible to include.

Abelard, Peter. <u>Dialogue of a Philosopher with a Jew and a Christian</u>. Trans. Pierre J. Payer. Toronto: Pontifical Institute of Medieval Studies, 1979.

_____. <u>The Letters of Abelard and Heloise</u>. Trans. Betty Radice. Baltimore: Penguin Books, 1974.

Adler, Alfred. <u>The Neurotic Constitution</u>. Trans. Bernard Glueck. New York: Moffat, Yard, and Company, 1971.

_____. <u>Problems of Neurosis</u>. Ed. Philippe Mairet. New York: Cosmopolitan Book Corporation, 1930.

_____. <u>Social Interest: A Challenge to Mankind</u>. Trans. John Linton. London: Faber and Faber, 1938.

Aligheri, Dante. <u>On World Government</u> (<u>De Monarchia</u>). Trans. Herbert W. Schneider. Indianapolis: Bobbs-Merrill, 1949.

Althusser, Louis. <u>For Marx</u>. Trans. Ben Brewster. New York: Random House, 1970.

Arguelles, Hose and Miriam Arguelles. Mandala. Boulder, CO: Shambhala Publications, 1972.

Arieti, Silvano. The Intrapsychic Self: Feeling, Cognition, and Creativity. New York: Basic Books, 1967.

Atkinson, R. F. Knowledge and Explanation in History: An Introduction to the Philosophy of History. Ithaca, NY: Cornell University Press, 1978.

Auerbach, Eric. Mimesis: The Representation of Reality in Western Literature. Trans. Willard R. Trask. Princeton: Princeton University Press, 1953.

Augustine of Hippo. Confessions. Trans. R. S. Pine-Coffin. New York: Penguin Books, 1961.

_____. On Christian Doctrine. Trans. D. W. Robertson. Indianapolis: Bobbs-Merrill, 1958.

_____. The City of God. Trans. and abr. Vernon J. Bourke. New York: Doubleday & Company, 1958.

_____. On Free Choice of the Will. Trans. Anna S. Benjamin and L. H. Hackstaff. Indianapolis: Bobbs-Merrill, 1964.

Aurner, Nellie Slayton. "Sir Thomas Malory--Historian." PMLA 48 (1933): 362-91.

Bainton, Roland H. The Age of Reformation. New York: Van Nostrand Reinhold, 1956.

_____. Here I Stand: A Life of Martin Luther. New York: Abington-Cokesbury Press, 1950.

Barron, Frank. Creativity and Psychological Health. Princeton: D. Van Nostrand, 1963.

Bennet, J. W. A., ed. Essays on Malory. Oxford: The Clarendon Press, 1963.

Benson, Larry D. Malory's Morte Darthur. Cambridge, MA: Harvard University Press, 1976.

Benton, John F. "Clio and Venus: An Historical View of Medieval Love." The Meaning of Courtly Love. Ed. F. X. Newman. Albany: State University of New York Press, 1968.

Bettelheim, Bruno. Freud and Man's Soul. New York: Alfred A. Knopf, 1983.

Berger, Peter L. and Thomas Luckmann. The Social Construction of Reality: A Treatise in the Sociology of Knowledge. Garden City, NY: Doubleday and Company, 1966.

Bleich, David. Subjective Criticism. Baltimore: Johns Hopkins University Press, 1978.

Bloch, R. Howard.   "Tristan, the Myth of the State and the Language of the Self."   Yale French Studies 51 (1974): 61-81.

Bloom, Harold, Paul de Man, Jacques Derrida, and others. Deconstruction and Criticism.   New York: Seabury Press, 1979.

Bloomfield, Morton W.   "The Problem of the Hero in the Later Medieval Period."   Concepts of the Hero.   Ed. Norman T. Burns and Christopher J. Reagan.   Albany: State University of New York Press, 1975.

Bogdanow, Fani.   The Romance of the Grail: A Study of the Structure and Genesis of A Thirteenth-Century Arthurian Prose Romance.   New York: Barnes and Noble, 1966.

Bonaventura.   The Mind's Road to God.   Trans. George Boas. Indianapolis: Bobbs-Merrill Company, 1953.

Bonhoeffer, Dietrich.   Ethics.   Ed. Eberhard Bethge.   Trans. Neville H. Smith.   New York: Macmillan, 1955.

Brewer, Derek S.   "'the hoole booke.'"   Essays on Malory   Ed. J. W. A. Bennet.   Oxford: The Clarendon Press, 1963.

Brown, Norman O.   Life Against Death: The Psychoanalytical Meaning of History.   New York: Random House, 1959.

Bruner, Jerome.   Beyond the Information Given: Studies in the Psychology of Knowing.   New York: W. W. Norton, 1973.

_____, Jacqueline J. Goodnow, and George A. Austin.   A Study of Thinking.   New York: Science Editions, Inc., 1962.

_____ and Leo Postman.   "On the Perception of Incongruity: A Paradigm."   Journal of Psychology 18 (1949): 206-223.

Burlin, Robert B.   "'Dream of the Rood' and the Vita Contemplativa."   Studies in Philology 65 (1968): 23-50.

Burns, Norman T. and Christopher J. Reagan, eds. Concepts of the Hero in the Middle Ages and the Renaissance.   Albany: State University of New York Press, 1975.

Bush, Douglas.   Prefaces to Renaissance Literature.   New York: W. W. Norton & Company, 1965.

Calmette, Joseph.   "France, the Reign of Charles VIII and the End of the Hundred Years' War."   The Cambridge Medieval History.   Ed. J. B. Bury.   Cambridge: The University Press, 1957.   Vol. 8.

Campbell, Joseph.   The Flight of the Wild Gander: Explorations in the Mythological Dimension.   New York: Viking Press, 1969.

_____. The Hero with a Thousand Faces. Princeton: Princeton University Press, 1972.

_____. The Masks of God: Creative Mythology. New York: Penguin Books, 1968.

Camus, Albert. The Myth of Sisyphus and Other Essays. Trans. Justin O'Brien. New York: Random House, 1955.

Capellanus, Andreas. The Art of Courtly Love. Trans. John Jay Parry. New York: W. W. Norton, 1969.

Chadwick, H. M. The Heroic Age. Cambridge: The Univeristy Press, 1967.

Cheyney, Edward P. The Dawn of a New Era: 1250-1453. New York: Harper and Row, Publishers, 1936.

The Cloud of Unknowing. Ed. William Johnson. Garden City, NY: Doubleday, 1973.

Copernicus, Nicholas. On the Revolutions. Ed. Jerzy Dobrzycki. Trans. Edward Rosen. Baltimore: Johns Hopkins University Press, 1978.

Copleston, F. C. Medieval Philosophy. New York: Harper and Row, 1961.

Davies, R. T. "Malory's `Virtuouse Love,'" Studies in Philology 53 (1956): 459-69.

_____. "The Worshipful Way in Malory." Patterns of Love and Courtesy: Essays in Memory of C. S. Lewis. Ed. John Lawlor. Evanston: Northwestern University Press, 1960.

de Rougement, Denis. Love in the Western World. Trans. Montgomery Belgion. Princeton: Princeton University Press, 1956.

Dewey, John. The Quest for Certainty: A Study of the Relation of Knowledge to Action. New York: G. P. Putnam's Sons, 1929.

_____. Reconstruction in Philosophy. Boston: Beacon Press, 1948.

Dionysius the Areopagite. On the Divine Names and The Mystical Theology. Trans. C. E. Rolt. London: Macmillan, 1920.

Dixon, Theodore R. and David L. Horton, eds. Verbal Behavior and General Behavior Theory. Englewood Cliffs: Prentice-Hall, 1968.

Duby, Georges. The Knight The Lady and The Priest: The Making of Modern Marriage in Medieval France. Trans. Barbara Bray. New York: Pantheon, 1983.

Eckhart, Master. Parisian Questions and Prologues. Trans. Armand Maurer. Totonto: Pontifical Institute of Medieval Studies, 1974.

Eliade, Mircea. The Myth of the Eternal Return or Cosmos and History. Trans. Willard R. Trask. New York: Harper and Row Publishers, 1959.

_____. Myth and Reality. Trans. Willard R. Trask. New York: Harper and Row Publishers, 1963.

Erdelyi, Matthew Hugh. Psychoanalysis: Freud's Cognitive Psychology. New York: W. H. Freeman, 1985.

Erikson, Erik H. Identity: Youth and Crisis. New York: W. W. Norton & Company, 1968.

_____. Life History and the Historical Moment. New York: W. W. Norton & Company, 1975.

_____. Young Man Luther: A Study in Psychoanalysis and History. New York: W. W. Norton & Company, 1958.

Evans, Murry. "Ordinatio and Narrative Links: The Impact of Malory's Tales as a 'hoole book.'" Studies in Malory Ed. James W. Spisak. Kalamazoo: Medieval Institute of Western Michigan
University, 1985.

Felman, Shoshana, ed. Literature and Psychoanalysis: The Question of Reading Otherwise. Baltimore: Johns Hopkins University Press, 1982.

Ferguson, Arthur B. The Indian Summer of English Chivalry. Durham: Duke University Press, 1960.

Festinger, Leon. A Theory of Cognitive Dissonance. Stanford: Stanford University Press, 1962.

Field, P. J. C. "Description and Narration in Malory." Speculum 43 (1968): 476-86.

_____. "The Last Years of Malory." Bulletin of the John Rylands University of Manchester 64 (1982): 433-56.

_____. Romance and Chronicle: A Study of Malory's Prose Style. Bloomington: Indiana University Press, 1967.

Fine, Reuben. A History of Psychoanalysis. New York: Columbia University Press, 1979.

Fish, Stanley. "Normal Circumstances, Literal Language, Direct Speech Acts, the Ordinary, the Everyday, the Obvious, What Goes Without Saying, and Other Special Cases." Interpretive Social Science. Eds. Paul Rabinow and William M. Sullivan. Berkeley: University of California Press, 1979.

Fletcher, Joseph. Moral Responsibility: Situation Ethics at Work. Philadelphia: The Westminister Press, 1967.

La Folie Tristan. Trans. Gilbert Lely. Paris: Jean-Jacques Pauvert, 1964.

Foucault, Michel. Discipline and Punish: The Birth of the Prison. Trans. Alan Sheridan. New York: Random House, 1977.

_____. Madness and Civilization: A History of Insanity in the Age of Reason. Trans. Richard Howard. London: Tavistock Publications, 1967.

_____. The Order of Things: An Archaeology of the Human Sciences. New York: Random House, 1973.

Frankl, Victor. Man's Search for Meaning. Boston: Beacon Press, 1963.

Freire, Paulo. Pedagogy of the Oppressed. Trans. Myra Bergman Ramos. New York: Continuum, 1985.

Freud, Sigmund. Beyond the Pleasure Principle. Trans. James Strachey. London: The Hogarth Press, 1961.

_____. Civilization and Its Discontents. Trans. James Strachey. New York: W. W. Norton & Company, 1961.

_____. Dictionary of Psychoanalysis. Eds. Nandor Fodor and Frank Gaynor. Greenwich, Conn.: Fawcett Publications, 1958.

_____. The Ego and the Id. Trans. James Strachey. New York: W. W. Norton & Company, 1961.

_____. A General Introduction to Psychoanalysis. Trans. Joan Riviere. New York: Liveright Publishing, 1935.

_____. Group Psychology and the Analysis of the Ego. Trans. James Strachey. New York: W. W. Norton & Company, 1959.

_____. Moses and Monotheism. Trans. Katherine Jones. New York: Random House, 1939.

_____. An Outline of Psychoanalysis. Trans. James Strachey. New York: W. W. Norton & Company, 1949.

_____. The Psychopathology of Everyday Life. Trans. Alan Tyson. New York: W. W. Norton & Company, 1960.

_____. Totom and Taboo. Trans. James Strachey. New York: W. W. Norton & Company, 1950.

Friedrich, Carl Joachim. Inevitable Peace. Cambridge, MA: Harvard Univeristy Press, 1948.

_____. The Philosophy of Law in Historical Perspective. Chicago: University of Chicago Press, 1958.

Fries, Maureen. "Malory's Tristram as Counter-Hero to the Morte Darthur." Neuphilologische Mitteilungen 76 (1975): 605-13.

Froissart, Jean. Chronicles. Trans. Geoffrey Brereton. New York: Penguin Books, 1968.

Fromm, Erich. The Anatomy of Human Destructiveness. New York: Fawcett Crest, 1973.

_____. Escape from Freedom. New York: Holt, Rinehart, and Winston, 1941.

_____. You Shall Be As Gods: A Radical Interpretation of the Old Testament. Greenwich, Conn: Fawcett Publications, 1966.

Ganshof, F. L. Feudalism. New York: Harper & Row Publishers, 1961.

Gilson, Etienne. The History of Christian Philosophy in the Middle Ages. London: Sheed and Ward, 1955.

Gist, Margaret Adlum. Love and War in the Middle English Romance. Philadelphia: University of Pennsylvania Press, 1947.

Godfrey of St. Victor. The Fountain of Philosophy. Trans. Edward A. Synan. Toronto: Pontifical Institute of Medieval Studies, 1972.

Gottfried von Strassburg. Tristan. Trans. A. T. Hatto. Baltimore: Penguin Books, 1960.

Hanning, Robert W. The Individual in Twelfth Century Romance. New Haven: Yale University Press, 1977.

Heer, Friedrich. The Medieval World: Europe 1100-1350. Trans. Janet Sondheim. New York: New American Library, 1961.

Hegel, G. W. F. Reason in History: A General Introduction to the Philosophy of History. Trans. Robert S. Hartman. Indianapolis: Bobbs-Merrill Company, 1953.

_____. The Philosophy of Hegel. Edited by Carl J. Friedrich. New York: Modern Library, 1954.

Helterman, Jeffrey A. "The Antagonistic Voices of 'Summer Is Icumen In.'" Tennessee Studies in Literature 18 (1973): 13-17.

_____. "Beowulf: The Archetype Enters History." ELH 35 (1968): 1-20.

_____. "The Dehumanizing Metamorphoses of The Knight's Tale." ELH 38 (1971): 493-511.

_____. Symbolic Action in the Plays of the Wakefield Master. Athens: University of Georgia Press, 1981.

Hicks, Edward. Sir Thomas Malory: His Turbulent Career. New York: Octagon Books, 1928.

Hugh of St. Victor. On the Sacraments of the Christian Faith. Trans. Roy J. Deferrari. Cambridge, MA: Medieval Academy of America, 1951.

Huizinga, Johann. The Waning of the Middle Ages. New York: Doubleday & Company, 1954.

Huppe, Bernard. "The Concept of the Hero in the Early Middle Ages." Concepts of the Hero. Eds. Norman T. Burns and Christopher J. Reagan. Albany: State University of New York Press, 1975.

Hus, John. The Letters of John Hus Written During His Exile and Imprisonment with Martin Luther's Preface. Trans. Campbell Mackenzie. Edinburgh: William Whyte & Co., 1846.

Iser, Wolfgang. The Act of Reading: A Theory of Aesthetic Response. Baltimore: Johns Hopkins University Press, 1978.

Jackson, W. T. H. "Gottfried von Strassburg." Arthurian Literature in the Middle Ages. Ed. R. S. Loomis. London: Oxford University Press, 1959.

Jacobs, E. F. The Fifteenth Century, 1399-1485. The Oxford History of England. London: The Clarendon Press, 1961. Vol. 6.

_____. "Innocent III." The Cambridge Medieval History. Ed. J. B. Bury. Cambridge: The University Press, 1957. Vol. 6.

Jaffe, Aniela, ed. Carl Jung: Word and Image. Princeton: Princeton University Press, 1979.

James, William. Essays on Faith and Morals. Cleveland: The World Publishing Company, 1962.

_____. The Varieties of Religious Experience: A Study in Human Nature. New York: The New American Library. 1958.

_____. The Will to Believe. New York: Dover Publications, 1956.

John of Paris. On Royal and Papal Power. Trans. J. A. Watt. Toronto: Pontifical Institute of Medieval Studies, 1971.

John of Salisbury. The Statesman's Book of John of Salisbury.
    Ed. John Dickenson. New York: Russell & Russell, 1963.
Johnson, Roger A., ed. Psychohistory and Religion: The Case
    of Young Man Luther. Philadelphia: Fortress Press, 1977.
Jordan, William C., Bruce McNab, and Teofilo F. Ruiz, eds.
    Order and Innovation in the Middle Ages: Essays in Honor of
    Joseph R. Stayer. Princeton: Princeton University Press,
    1976.
Jung, Carl G. Memories, Dreams, Reflections.   Ed. Aniela
    Jaffe. Trans. Richard and Clara Winston.   New York:
    Random House, 1965.
_____. On Psychic Energy. Collected Works. Ed. R. F. C.
    Hull. New York: Pantheon, 1960. Vol. 8.
_____. Psychological Types. Trans. H. Goodwin Baynes.
    London: Pantheon, 1923.
_____. Psychology and Alchemy. Collected Works. Ed. R.
    F. C. Hull. New York: Pantheon, 1960. Vol. 12.
_____. Psychology and Religion. New Haven: Yale
    University Press, 1938.
_____, M-L. von Franz, and others. Man and His Symbols.
    New York: Doubleday & Company, 1964.
Kantorowicz, Ernest H. The King's Two Bodies: A Study in
    Medieval Political Theology. Princeton: Princeton
    University Press, 1957.
Kenndey, Beverly. Knighthood in the Morte Darthur. Dover,
    NH: Boydell and Brewer, 1985.
Kennedy, Edward. "Malory's King Mark and King Arthur."
    Medieval Studies 37 (1975): 190-234.
_____. "Two Notes on Malory: (1) Malory and the Spanish
    'Tristran' Further Parallels. (2) Tristram's Death in
    Malory's 'Morte Darthur.'" Notes and Queries, n.s. 19
    (1972): 7-10.
Ker, N. R., ed. The Winchester Malory: A Facimile of
    Winchester College MS 13. London: Oxford University Press
    for the Early English Texts Society, 1976.
Klapp, Orrin R. "Style Rebellion and Identity Crisis." Human
    Nature and Collective Behavior Ed. Tamotsu Shibutani.
    Englewood Cliffs: Prentice Hall, Inc., 1970.
Knight, Stephen Thomas. The Structure of Malory's Arthuriad.
    Sydney: Sydney University Press, 1969.

Knowles, David. The Evolution of Medieval Thought. New York: Alfred A. Knopf, Inc., 1962.

Kuhn, Thomas. The Structure of Scientific Revolutions. Chicago: University of Chicago Press, 1970.

Lambert, Mark. Malory: Style and Vision in `Le Morte Darthur.´ New Haven: Yale University Press, 1975.

Lea, Henry Charles. The History of the Inquisition. Abr. Margaret Nicholson. New York: Macmillan and Co., 1961.

Lewis, C. S. The Allegory of Love. London: Oxford University Press, 1938.

_____. The Discarded Image. London: Cambridge University Press, 1964.

_____. "The English Prose Morte." Essays on Malory. Ed. J. W. A. Bennet. Oxford: The Clarendon Press, 1963.

Leyerle, John. "The Game and Play of the Hero." Concepts of the Hero. Eds. Norman T. Burns and Christopher J. Reagan. Albany: State University of New York Press, 1975.

Life,`Page West, ed. Sir Thomas Malory and the Morte Darthur: A Survey of Scholarship and Annotated Bibiography. Charlottesville: University of Virginia Press, 1980.

Loomis, Roger Sherman. "Arthurian Influence on Sport and Spectacle." Arthurian Literature in the Middle Ages. Ed. R. S. Loomis. London: Oxford University Press, 1959.

_____. The Development of Arthurian Romance. New York: W. W. Norton & Company, 1963.

_____. The Grail: From Celtic Myth to Christian Symbol. New York: Columbia University Press, 1963.

Loseth, Eilert, ed. Le Roman en Prose de Tristan, Le Roman de Palomede, et la Compilation de Rusticien de Pise. New York: Burt Franklin, 1970.

Lukacs, John. The Passing of the Modern Age. New York: Harper and Row Publishers, 1970.

Lumiansky, Robert Meyer, ed. Malory´s Originality: A Critical Study of Le Morte Darthur. Baltimore: The Johns Hopkins University Press, 1964.

_____. "Malory´s Steadfast Bors." Tulane Studies in English 8 (1958): 5-20.

_____. "Tristram´s First Interview with Mark in Malory´s Morte Darthur. Modern Language Notes 70 (1955): 476-78.

Luther, Martin. The Christian in Society. Luther's Works.
Eds. Jaroslav Pelikan and Helmut T. Lehmann. Philadelphia:
Fortress Press, 1966. Vol. 44.
_____. A Compend of Luther's Theology. Ed. Hugh
Thomson Kerr. Philadelphia: Westminister Press, 1943.
_____. Lectures on Galatians. Luther's Works. Ed.
Jaroslav Pelikan and Walter Hanson. St. Louis: Concordia
Publishing House, 1955. Vols. 26-27.
_____. A Treatise on Christian Liberty. Trans. W. A.
Lambert. Philadelphia: The Muhlenberg Press, 1943.
_____. Three Treatises. Philadelphia: Fortress Press, 1970.
Mahoney, Dhira. "Malory's `Tale of Tristram': Sources and
Setting Reconsidered." Medievalia et Humanistica 9 (1979):
175-98.
Malinowski, Bronislav. The Father in Primitive Psychology.
New York: W. W. Norton, 1927.
Malory, Thomas. The Works of Sir Thomas Malory. 3 vols.
Ed. Eugene Vinaver. Oxford: Clarendon Press, 1967.
_____. Works. Ed. Eugene Vinaver. Oxford: Clarendon
Press, 1971.
Mannheim, Karl. Ideology and Utopia: An Introduction to the
Sociology of Knowledge. Trans. Louis Wirth and Edward
Shils. New York: Harcourt, Brace, & World, Inc., 1966.
Marcuse, Herbert. Eros and Civilizations: A Philosophical
Inquiry into Freud. New York: Vintage Books, 1955.
Maritan, Jacques. Creative Intuition in Art and Poetry.
Cleveland: The World Publishing Company, 1954.
Marsilius of Padua. The Defensor Pacis. 2 vols. Trans. Alan
Gewirth. New York: Columbia Univeristy Press, 1956.
Matthews, William. The Ill-Framed Knight: A Skeptical Inquiry
into the Identity of Sir Thomas Malory. Berkeley:
University of California Press, 1966.
Maurer, Armand, C.S.B. St. Thomas and Historicity.
Milwaukee: Marquette University Press, 1979.
Mead, George Herbert. Mind, Self, and Society: From the
Standpoint of a Social Behaviorist. Ed. Charles W. Morris.
Chicago: University of Chicago Press, 1962.
Miko, Stehen J. "Malory and the Chivalric Order." Medium
Aevum 35 (1966): 211-30.
Moody, Ernest A. "William of Ockham." The Encyclopedia of
Philosophy. Ed. Paul Edwards. New York: Macmillan, 1967.
Vol. 8.

Montaigne, Michel de. Complete Essays of Montaigne. Trans. Donald M. Frame. Stanford: Stanford University Press, 1948.

Moorman, Charles. "Courtly Love in Malory." ELH 27 (1960): 163-76.

_____. The Book of King Arthur: The Unity of Malory's Morte Darthur. Lexington: University of Kentucky Press, 1965.

_____. "Internal Chronology in Malory's Morte Darthur." JEGP 60 (1961): 240-49.

_____. A Knight There Was: The Evolution of the Knight in Literature. Lexington: University of Kentucky Press, 1967.

_____. "Malory's Tragic Knights." Medieval Studies 27 (1965): 117-27.

Morrall, John B. Political Thought in Medieval Times. Toronto: University of Toronto Press, 1980.

Mullahy, Patrick. Oedipus Myth and Complex: A Review of Psychoanalytic Theory. New York: Grove Press, 1948.

Munroe, Ruth L. Schools of Psychoanalytic Thought: Exposition, Critique, and Attempts at Integration. New York: Holt, Rinehart, and Winston, 1955.

Neisser, Ulrich. Cognition and Reality: Principles and Implications of Cognitive Psychology. San Francisco: W. H. Freeman, 1976.

Newman, F. X., ed. The Meaning of Courtly Love. Albany: State University of New York Press, 1968.

Newstead, Helaine. "The Origin and Growth of the Tristan Legend." Arthurian Literature in the Middle Ages. Ed. R. S. Loomis. London: Oxford University Press, 1969.

Niebuhr, H. Richard. Radical Monotheism and Western Culture. New York: Harper and Row Publishers, 1960.

Nietzsche, Friedrich. The Gay Science. Trans. Walter Kaufmann. New York: Vintage Books, 1974.

Nygren, Anders. Agape and Eros. Trans. Philip S. Watson. Philadelphia: The Westminister Press, 1953.

Otto, Rudolf. The Idea of the Holy. Trans. John W. Harvey. New York: Oxford University Press, 1958.

Osgood, Charles and Percy H. Tannenbaum. "The Principle of Congruity in the Prediction of Attitude Change." Psychological Review 62 (1955): 42-55.

Osgood, Charles and Robert W. Tucker. Force, Order, and Justice. Baltimore: Johns Hopkins University Press, 1967.

Owen, Douglas David Ray, ed. Arthurian Romance: Seven Essays. New York: Barnes and Noble, 1971.

Pachoda, Elizabeth. Arthurian Propaganda: Le Morte Darthur as an Historical Ideal of Life. Chapel Hill: University of North Carolina Press, 1971.

Painter, Sidney. French Chivalry. Baltimore: The Johns Hopkins University Press, 1940.

Panofsky, Irwin. Gothic Architecture and Scholasticism. New York: Meridian Books, 1957.

_____. Meaning in the Visual Arts: Papers in and on Art History. New York: Doubleday Anchor Books, 1955.

Parsons, Talcott. The Evolution of Societies. Ed. Jackson Toby. Englewood Cliffs: Prentice-Hall, 1977.

_____. On Institutions and Social Evolution. Ed. Leon H. Mayhew. Chicago: University fo Chicago Press, 1982.

Patin, W. A. The English Church in the Fourteenth Century. Toronto: University of Toronto Press, 1980.

Peckham, Morse. Beyond the Tragic Vision: The Quest for Identity in the Nineteenth Century. New York: George Braziller, 1962.

_____. Explanation and Power: The Control of Human Behavior. New York: Seabury Press, 1979.

_____. Man's Rage for Chaos: Biology, Behavior, and the Arts. New York: Schocken Books, 1967.

_____. Romanticism and Behavior: Collected Essays II. Columbia: University of South Carolina Press, 1976.

_____. Romanticism and Ideology: Collected Essays III. Greenwood, FL: Penkevill Publishing Co., 1985.

_____. The Triumph of Romanticism: Collected Essays. Columbia: University of South Carolina Press, 1970.

Perls, Frederick S. Ego, Hunger, and Aggression: The Beginning of Gestalt Therapy. New York: Random House, 1969.

Pelikan, Jaroslav. The Christian Tradition: A History of the Development of Doctrine. 5 vols. Chicago: University of Chicago Press, 1971-1984.

Peters, Edward, ed. Heresy and Authority in Medieval Europe: Documents in Translation. Philadelphia: University of Pennsylvania Press, 1980.

Phelan, Gerald B. St. Thomas and Analogy. Milwaukee: Marquette University Press, 1948.

Pickford, Cedric E., ed. Alixandre L'Orphelin: A Prose Tale of the Fifteenth Century. Manchester: Manchester University Press, 1951.

Plato. Symposium. Trans. Benjamin Jowett. Indianapolis: Bobbs-Merrill Educational Publishing, 1948.

Postan, M. M. The Medieval Economy and Society. New York: Penguin Books, 1972.

Prestage, Edgar. Chivalry. London: Kegan Paul, Trench, Trubner & Co., 1928.

The Quest of the Holy Grail. Trans. P. M. Matarasso. Baltimore: Penguin Books, 1969.

La Queste Del Saint Graal. Ed. Albert Pauphilet. Paris: Libraire Ancienne Honore Champion, 1923.

Rabinow, Paul and William M. Sullivan, eds. Interpretive Social Science. Berkeley: University of California Press, 1979.

Reiss, Edmund. Sir Thomas Malory. New York: Twayne Publishers, 1966.

Ricoeur, Paul. Freud and Philosophy: An Essay on Interpretation. Trans. Dennis Savage. New Haven: Yale University Press, 1970.

Robertson, Dwight W. "The Concept of Courtly Love as an Impediment to the Understanding of Medieval Texts." The Meaning of Courtly Love. Ed. F. X. Newman. Albany: State University of New York Press, 1968.

_____. A Preface to Chaucer: Studies in Medieval Perspectives. Princeton: Princeton University Press, 1962.

Le Roman de Tristan en Prose. 3 vols. Ed. Renee L. Curtis. Dover, NH: Boydell and Brewer, 1985.

The Romance of Tristan and Isolt. Trans. Norman B. Spector. Evanston: Northwestern University Press, 1973. (A translation of MS BN 103.)

Rumble, T. C. "Malory's Works and Vinaver's Comments: Some Inconsistencies Resolved." JEGP 59 (1960): 58-69.

_____. "The Tale of Tristram: Development by Analogy." Malory's Originality. Ed. R. M. Lumiansky. Baltimore: The Johns Hopkins University Press, 1964.

Sartre, Jean-Paul. Existentialism and Humanism. Trans. Philip Mairet. London: Eyre Methuen, Ltd., 1948.

Scattergood, V. J.   Politics and Poetry in the Fifteenth Century. London: Blandford Press, 1971.

Scheuler, Donald G.   "The Tristram Section of Malory's Morte Darthur." Studies in Philology 65 (1968): 51-66.

Scudder, Vida. Le Morte Darthur of Sir Thomas Malory and Its Sources. New York: E. P. Dutton & Co., 1921.

Sederberg, Peter C.   The Politics of Meaning: Power and Explanation in the Construction of Social Reality. Tucson: University of Arizona Press, 1984.

Selye, Hans. The Stress of Life. New York: McGraw-Hill, 1956.

Senior, Michael.   "The Phaedra Complex: Amour Courtois in Malory's Morte Darthur." Folklore 82 (1971): 36-59.

Seward, Desmond. The Hundred Years War: The English in France. New York: Atheneum, 1978.

Sherif, Muzafer. Social Interaction: Process and Products. Chicago: Aldine Publishing Company, 1967.

Shibutani, Tamotsu, ed. Human Behavior and Collective Behavior: Papers in Honor of Herbert Blumer. Englewood Cliffs: Prentice Hall, 1970.

Shubik, Martin.   "On Gaming and Game Theory: A Paper Delivered to a Rand Corporation Conference on Game Theory." Santa Monica: The Rand Corporation, 1971.

_____. . Readings in Game Theory and Political Behavior. Garden City: Doubleday & Company, 1954.

Shweder, Richard A. and Robert A. LeVine, eds. Culture Theory: Essays on Mind, Self, and Emotion. Cambridge: Cambridge University Press, 1984.

Sigmund, Paul E. "The Influence of Marsilius of Padua on XVth Century Conciliarism." Journal of the History of Ideas 23 (1962): 392-402.

Simpson, Otto von. The Gothic Cathedral. New York: The Bollingen Foundation, 1962.

Snyder, Robert Lance. "Malory and 'Historical' Adaptation." Essays in Literature 1 (1974): 135-48.

Southern, Robert William. The Making of the Middle Ages. London: Hutchenson's University Library, 1953.

Starr, Nathan Comfort. "The Moral Problem in Malory." Dalhousie Review 47 (1968): 467-74.

Stenton, Doris Mary. English Society in the Early Middle Ages, 1066-1307. The Pelican History of England. New York: Penguin Books, 1965. Vol. 3.

Sterns, Indrikis. "Crime and Punishment Among the Tuetonic Knights." Speculum 57 (1982): 84-111.

Stevens, S. S. "Psychology: The Propaedeutic Science." Philosophy of Science 3 (1936): 90-103.

Tanner, Tony. Adultery in the Novel. Baltimore: The Johns Hopkins University Press, 1979.

Taylor, Henry Osborne. The Medieval Mind. Cambridge, MA: Harvard University Press, 1951.

Thomas Aquinas. Basic Writings of Saint Thomas Aquinas. Ed. Anton Pegis. New York: Random House, 1944.

_____. Concerning Being and Essence. Trans. George G. Lecke. New York: Appleton-Century-Crofts, Inc., 1937.

_____. The Division and Methods of the Sciences. Trans. Armand Maurer. Toronto: Pontifical Institute of Medieval Studies, 1963. (Questions V and VI of "Commentary on the De Trinitate)

_____. On Kingship: To the King of Cyprus. Trans. Gerald B. Phelan. Toronto: Pontifical Institute of Medieval Studies, 1949.

_____. The Summa Theologica. 2 vols. Trans. Fathers of the English Dominican Province. Chicago: Encyclopedia Britannica, 1952.

Thompson, Alexander H. "Medieval Doctrine to the Lateran Council of 1215." The Cambridge Medieval History. Ed. J. B. Bury. Cambridge: The University Press, 1957. Vol 1.

Thomson, S. Harrison. "John Hus." The Encyclopedia of Philosophy. Ed. Paul Edwards. New York: Macmillan Company, 1967. Vol. 4.

Tompkins, Jane P., ed. Reader Response Criticism: From Formalism to Post-Structuralism. Baltimore: Johns Hopkins University Press, 1980.

Tuve, Rosemond. Allegorical Imagery: Some Medieval Books and Their Posterity. Princeton: Princeton University Press, 1966.

Vinaver, Eugène. "Epic and Tragic Patterns in Malory." Friendship's Garland: Essays to Mario Praz on His Seventieth Birthday. Ed. Vittorio Gabrielli. Rome: Edizoini di Storia e Letterature, 1966.

_____. "The Questing Knight." The Binding of Proteus: Perspectives on Myth and the Literary Process. Eds.

Marjorie W. McCune, Tucker Orbison, and Philip M. Within. Lewisburg: Bucknell University Press, 1980.

_____. The Rise of Romance. Oxford: The Clarendon Press, 1971.

Warriner, Charles K. "Groups are Real: A Reaffirmation." American Sociological Review 21 (1956): 549-54.

West, Charles K. The Social and Psychological Distortion of Information. Chicago: Nelson-Hall, 1981.

Watts, Alan. Myth and Ritual in Christianity. London: Thames and Hudson, 1954.

_____. The Wisdom of Insecurity: A Message for an Age of Anxiety. New York: Random House, 1951.

Wilhelmsen, Frederick. The Paradoxical Structure of Existence. Irving: The University of Dallas Press, 1970.

William of Ockham. Ockham's Theory of Propositions: Part II of the Summa Logicae. Trans. Alfred J. Freddoso and Henry Schuurman. Notre Dame: Notre Dame University Press, 1980.

_____. Philosophical Writings: A Selection. Trans. Philotheus Boehner, OFM. Indianapolis: Bobbs-Merrill, 1964.

William of Sherwood. Treatise on Syncategorematic Words. Trans. Norman Kretzmann. Minneapolis: University of Minnesota Press, 1968.

Wilson, Harold B. Love and Order in the Medieval German Courtly Epic. Leicester: Leicester University Press, 1973.

Wilson, R. H. Characterization in Malory: A Comparison with His Sources. Chicago: University of Chicago Press, 1934.

_____. "Malory's Naming of Minor Characters." JEGP 42 (1943): 364-85.

Wilson, R. M. "Three Middle English Mystics." Essays and Studies 9 (1956): 87-112.

Wollheim, Richard, ed. Freud: A Collection of Critical Essays. New York: Anchor Books, 1974.

Wright, Thomas. "The Tale of King Arthur: Beginnings and Foreshadowings." Malory's Originality. Ed. R. M. Lumiansky. Baltimore: Johns Hopkins University Press, 1964.

Wyclif, John. Select English Writings. Ed. Herbert E. Winn. London: Oxford University Press, 1929.

York, Ernest C. "Legal Punishment in Malory's Le Morte Darthur." English Language Notes 11 (1973): 14-21.

Index

Brent A. Pitts

THE FIFTEEN JOYS OF MARRIAGE

(Les .XV. Joies de Mariage)
Translated, with Introduction and Notes by Brent A. Pitts

American University Studies: Series II, (Romance Languages and Literature), Vol. 26
ISBN 0-8204-0216-8   180 pp.   hardback US $ 21.50*

*Recommended price - alterations reserved

The Fifteen Joys of Marriage is a new translation of the *.XV. Joies de Mariage,* the ironic, enigmatic, and ostensibly misogynistic tract written *ca.* 1400. Like many Old French fabliaux, the *Fifteen Joys* takes for its subject the reversals, the woes, and the deceptions of the married state. By contrast with the *fableors,* however, the anonymous author of the *Fifteen Joys* arranges his domestic scenes in series, thus parodying a well known devotional work while incanting his litany of despair. The present work revives in medieval context a classic long out of print in English translation. For the text the translator adopts the burgeoning, colloquial manner of the original French, providing commentary in his Notes. The Introduction discusses the structure and principal themes of the *Joys* while surveying recent studies of the text. The Bibliography marks a starting point for further study.

PETER LANG PUBLISHING, INC.
62 West 45th Street
USA - New York, NY 10036

Maureen Slattery

MYTH, MAN AND SOVEREIGN SAINT
King Louis IX in Jean de Joinville's Sources

American University Studies: Series II, (Romance Languages and Literature), Vol. 11
ISBN 0-8204-0111-0   229 pp.   hardback US $ 26.90*

*Recommended price - alterations reserved

This work demonstrates a methodology to extract the full cultural richness of a medieval text composed within a largely oral culture. Maureen Slattery re-examines the traditional literary manner of reading Joinville's classic medieval portrait of the famous thirteenth century king and saint: Louis IX of France. By distinguishing and analyzing the royal motifs of Joinville's oral, eye-witness and written sources, the study illustrates a plurality of social meanings surrounding King Louis.

Joinville's oral sources speak the collective popular myths and primitive mentalities surrounding the French monarchy. His visual witness, one of the first lay accounts of a Capelian king, individualizes Louis with the emerging modern vision of noble lineage. His written sources eulogize the king within clerical literary traditions of the public monarch and sovereign saint.

This textual analysis unearths distinct layers of tradition surrounding the king. Both Louis and Joinville emerge very different from what they were in earlier scholarship.

PETER LANG PUBLISHING, INC.
62 West 45th Street
USA – New York, NY 10036

Sigmund J. Barber

AMADIS DE GAULE AND THE GERMAN ENLIGHTENMENT

American University Studies: Series I, (Germanic Languages and Literature), Vol. 30
ISBN 0-8204-0075-0   186 pp.   paperback US $ 18.80

In 1805 Goethe revealed that he had read the *Amadis von Gallien,* but regretted having waited so long to get to know such an excellent work. However, what Goethe had read was not the popular and notoriously licentious work of the sixteenth century, but a revised edition of 1779. This study compares this version with the German *Amadis* of the sixteenth century with regard to the conception of love, the use of language in both versions, the role of nature, the presence of magic and sorcery, the conception of religion, and the portrayal of knighthood and chivalric society. These comparisons reveal that the eighteenth century work changed many essential components and concepts to suit the late eighteenth century perception of man and the world in which he lives.

PETER LANG PUBLISHING, INC.
62 West 45th Street
USA – New York, NY 10036